Sport in the Global Society

General Editor: J.A. Mangan

ETHNICITY, SPORT, IDENTITY

SPORT IN THE GLOBAL SOCIETY
General Editor: J.A. Mangan

The interest in sports studies around the world is growing and will continue to do so. This unique series combines aspects of the expanding study of *sport in the global society*, providing comprehensiveness and comparison under one editorial umbrella. It is particularly timely, with studies in the cultural, economic, ethnographic, geographical, political, social, anthropological, sociological and aesthetic elements of sport proliferating in institutions of higher education.

Eric Hobsbawm once called sport one of the most significant practices of the late nineteenth century. Its significance was even more marked in the late twentieth century and will continue to grow in importance into the new millennium as the world develops into a 'global village' sharing the English language, technology and sport.

Other Titles in the Series

Football, Europe and the Press
Liz Crolley and David Hand

The Future of Football
Challenges for the Twenty-First Century
Edited by Jon Garland, Dominic Malcolm and Michael Rowe

Football Culture
Local Contests, Global Visions
Edited by Gerry P.T. Finn and Richard Giulianotti

France and the 1998 World Cup
The National Impact of a World Sporting Event
Edited by Hugh Dauncey and Geoff Hare

The First Black Footballer
Arthur Wharton 1865–1930: An Absence of Memory
Phil Vasili

Scoring for Britain
International Football and International Politics, 1900–1939
Peter J. Beck

Women, Sport and Society in Modern China
Holding Up More than Half the Sky
Dong Jinxia

Sport in Latin American Society
Past and Present
Edited by J.A. Mangan and Lamartine P. DaCosta

Sport in Australasian Society
Past and Present
Edited by J.A. Mangan and John Nauright

Sporting Nationalisms
Identity, Ethnicity, Immigration and Assimilation
Edited by Mike Cronin and David Mayall

The Commercialization of Sport
Edited by Trevor Slack

Shaping the Superman
Fascist Body as Political Icon: Aryan Fascism
Edited by J.A. Mangan

Superman Supreme
Fascist Body as Political Icon: Global Fascism
Edited by J.A. Mangan

Making the Rugby World
Race, Gender, Commerce
Edited by Timothy J.L. Chandler and John Nauright

Rugby's Great Split
Class, Culture and the Origins of Rugby League Football
Tony Collins

The Race Game
Sport and Politics in South Africa
Douglas Booth

Cricket and England
A Cultural and Social History of the Inter-war Years
Jack Williams

The Games Ethic and Imperialism
Aspects of the Diffusion of an Ideal
J.A. Mangan

ETHNICITY, SPORT, IDENTITY

Struggles for Status

Editors

J. A. MANGAN

ANDREW RITCHIE

De Montfort University (Bedford)

FRANK CASS
LONDON • PORTLAND, OR

First published in 2004 in Great Britain by
FRANK CASS PUBLISHERS
Crown House, 47 Chase Side, Southgate, London N14 5BP

and in the United States of America by
FRANK CASS PUBLISHERS
c/o ISBS, 920 NE 58th Avenue, Suite 300
Portland, Oregon 97213-3786

Copyright © 2004 Frank Cass Publishers

Website: www.frankcass.com

British Library Cataloguing in Publication Data

A catalogue record of this book is
available from the British Library

ISBN 0-7146-5574-0 (cloth)
ISBN 0-7146-8458-9 (paper)
ISSN 1368-9789

Library of Congress Cataloging-in-Publication Data

A catalog record of this book is
available from the Library of Congress

Printed in Great Britain by Antony Rowe Ltd., Chippenham, Wilts

Contents

Illustrations

Notes on Contributors

Cecile Badenhorst is the Research Manager at the Graduate School of Public and Development Management at the University of the Witwatersrand, Johannesburg, South Africa. She can be contacted at.

Brendan Hokowhitu is at the School of Māori Studies, University of Otago, New Zealand.

Stuart E. Knee is Professor of History at the University of Charleston in Charleston, SC. He is the author of *The Concept of Zionist Dissent in the American Mind*, *Hervey Allen: A Literary Historian in America* and *Christian Science in the Age of Mary Baker Eddy*. He also loves baseball.

Michael E. Lomax is an associate professor and Program Director of the Physical Education and Sport Studies program at the University of Georgia. He is the author of *Black Baseball Entrepreneurs, 1860–1901: Operating by Any Means Necessary*.

Haruo Nogawa has been Professor in the Department of Sport Management at Juntendo University since 1998. He received his doctorate from Oregon State University in 1983. He taught sociology of sport on undergraduate and graduate courses in the National Institute of Fitness and Sport in Kanoya for ten years. He has published numerous articles in both domestic and international journals. The most recent contributions are articles in *Football Cultures and Identities* (Macmillan, 1999) and *Soccer Nations and Football Cultures in East Asia* (Rutridge Publishing, 2002). His major research interests are sport and ethnicity as well as sport tourism and the second careers of professional athletes.

Boria Majumdar is completing his doctorate at St John's College, Oxford. He is Deputy Executive Academic Editor of *The International Journal of the History of Sport*.

Douglas Midgett is Associate Professor of Anthropology at the University of Iowa. His research has focused on the Caribbean and has examined political economy, trade unionism, migration, tourism and expressive culture.

Gillian Poulter teaches Canadian history at York University, Toronto and Trent University, Peterborough, Ontario. Her dissertation is entitled, 'Becoming Native in a Foreign Land: Visual Culture, Sport, and Spectacle in the Construction of National Identity in Montreal, 1840–1885'. She is interested in the participation of visual culture in the construction of identities, and is currently researching the role of women's handicrafts in nation-building.

Charlene Regester is Adjunct Assistant Professor in the Department of African and Afro-American Studies, University of North Carolina, Chapel Hill, NC. She currently co-edits the *Oscar Micheaux Society Newsletter* published by Duke University, Durham, NC. She serves on the editorial board for the *Journal of Film and Video* and has published a number of essays on Black film history.

Andrew Ritchie had researched and written about the bicycle and sport of cycling for 25 years. He is currently on the editorial board of the *International Journal of the History of Sport* and is completing a book on the origins and growth of bicycle racing between 1865 and 1903. He is the author of *King of the Road* (London: Wildwood House, 1975) and *Major Taylor, The Extraordinary Career of a Champion Bicycle Racer* (Baltimore: Johns Hopkins University Press, 1996).

Goolam Vahed is Senior Lecturer in the School of Social Sciences, University of Durban-Westville. His research interests include the colonial encounter between Indians, Africans and whites, the making of Indian identities in South Africa, and the role of sport and culture in South African society. He has published in numerous refereed scholarly journals on these themes.

Series Editor's Foreword

This incandescent declamation says it all:

> How in the end does one acknowledge ... Muhammed Ali? Perhaps simply by remembering the men and women, living and dead, in remote global places who suffered the consequences of their refusal to let things stand, as for all too long, they so unjustly had been ... in particular, the men, women and children who died in the rain forests of the Congo laboring to produce a good portion of the wealth of modern Europe, of those of the Ohio and Mississippi valleys who suffered similarly in North America. Their descendents, whether black or white or other, are the global citizens who made Muhammed Ali the king of all the world. To tell the story of the Louisville boy Cassius who became Ali the king is to tell a story of the nameless people who admire the celebrity-hero because, in their names, he tricked two generations of colonizers out of a good many of their easy manners.[1]

The declamation inarms, surrounds and contains the purpose of *Ethnicity, Sport, Identity*.

J.A. MANGAN
IRCSSS
De Montfort University
(Bedford)
September 2003

NOTE

1. Charles Lemert, *Muhammed Ali: Trickster in the Culture of Irony* (Cambridge: Polity Press, 2003), p.208.

Prologue

J.A. MANGAN and ANDREW RITCHIE

Ethnicity, Sport, Identity illustrates the manner in which sport has served to project ethnicity in various, and frequently contradictory, ways. It depicts sport as an agent of conservatism and radicalism, superiority and subordination, confidence and lack of confidence. In modern times, sport has been a source of disenfranchisement and enfranchisement. It is appropriate to appreciate that at political, cultural, economic and psychological levels it has been a potent means of both ethnic restriction and release.

The common themes contained in the essays in *Ethnicity, Sport, Identity* are, firstly, discrimination directed at individuals or groups, resulting in their exclusion from full participation in sport and producing a consequent struggle for inclusion; secondly, ethnic and national identity as a source of social cohesion and political assertion within sport. In the cases explored here, injustices within sport are seen frequently as reflections of larger injustices in society as a whole: the struggle for status within sport is a microcosm of the struggle for rights, freedom and recognition in wider political and social contexts. Of course, sport is a means of building and asserting national or ethnic identity. This too receives attention, therefore, in *Ethnicity, Sport, Identity*. The struggle for status within sport may be, and in the case of South Africa for example has been, crucial in advancing the rights and liberty of oppressed groups. The geographical and chronological range of the essays in *Ethnicity, Sport, Identity* reveals the global role of sport in this advance.

The next essay concerns South Africa. Cecile Badenhorst covers the organization of sport for Africans until the imposition in South Africa of Apartheid structures in the 1950s. She describes how the first formal organizations of sport for Africans were not established until the 1920s, with the Helping Hand Club and the Bantu Men's Social Centre. A little later, the Bantu Sports Club (1931) and the Johannesburg African Football Association (1932) were founded. In time, these organizations became the two largest soccer associations in South Africa. Badenhorst explains how this expansion of African sport took place during a period of 'massive African urbanization, worsening township conditions and increasing African political militancy'. She records how white liberals and American missionaries first became the 'experts on controlled recreation', while later the Johannesburg City Council and the mining industry 'took the initiative in the organization of recreation for Africans'.

Badenhorst explores the 'unorganized' social and cultural life of Africans in Johannesburg, as well as 'the intense need of the whites to organize and control sport for Africans, to contain African culture'. In her initial inquiries, 'broader questions about culture, race and power continually surfaced. Were cultural activities, like sport, part of the non-coercive tools of domination? Could these non-coercive tools be resisted? How was organized sport linked to the racial discourse prevalent at the time? Why did some practices and invented traditions become incorporated into everyday life and others become the source of conflict? Why was sport seen as a successful "site" for the socialization and social control of subordinate groups? And, finally, what was the relationship between culture and power?' She answers these questions in the form of a broad conclusion, noting that 'liberals hoped that sport and recreation could divert African attention and provide a desired antidote to urban social ills', and that, 'sport was organized within a racial ideology as one non-coercive tool of domination to teach the values necessary for successful urbanization and to build bridges between the rural and the urban, the "tribal" and "detribalized" sections of society'. In short, sport was seen as a political safety valve which might divert attention away from radical political activism, specifically the growth of Communism. Thus, the informal activities of the missionaries were supplemented by those of a full-time sports organizer from Johannesburg's Non-European Affairs Department. Approved sport, of course, was sport sanctioned and approved by the white power structure: 'knobkerrie' or 'fighting stick' (a 'native' game) was not encouraged, whereas boxing was. European-oriented sport for the Africans, such as soccer, tennis and cricket, was also accompanied by an attempt to transmit the hegemonious ideals of 'sportsmanship' and 'fair play', which Badenhorst points out 'had their roots in the nineteenth-century "muscular Christianity" of the British public school system', ideals which for the Africans of Johannesburg 'must have sat uneasily beside the grinding poverty and crippling injustices they experienced daily'. Most interestingly, she describes a process whereby the utopian liberal plans of missionaries and government officials for sport for the Africans were ultimately turned into a means of political and social expression within black African culture. This is particularly well illustrated in the struggle for control of African soccer, led by the Johannesburg African Football Association. The history of organized sport in Johannesburg, Badenhorst concludes, 'suggests a pattern of resistance to attempts to mould African cultural life into patterns made elsewhere ... new traditions of "fair play" and "good sportsmanship" never entirely transferred into African sports ... There was clearly a huge gap between intentions and repercussions ... as foreign imperialists invented an Africa that would serve their purposes, so must Africans invent a West which serves African purposes.'

In the earliest of five explorations of the impact of institutional racism upon sport in the United States, Andrew Ritchie provides an account of the process whereby black cyclists were formally excluded from membership in the League of American Wheelmen (LAW), the largest sporting organization in the country, in the 1890s. The customary 'Jim Crow' segregation, which divided the races in many aspects of everyday life, was formalized and made into official institutional policy within a major, expanding sports organization. The addition of the word 'white' to membership rules ensured future black exclusion when, in Louisville, Kentucky, the 1894 LAW. Convention voted to amend membership regulations. Segregated black cycling clubs, formed during the bicycle 'boom' of the mid-1890s, were thus denied group membership in the LAW, with all of its recreational and social benefits, as were individual black cyclists. Nevertheless, black cyclists could still compete against white riders in many races, since not all competition was held under LAW jurisdiction and many races, particularly in the more liberal Eastern and mid-Western states, accepted black competitors. The most successful black rider, sprinter Marshall Taylor (known throughout his career as 'Major' Taylor), rose from a humble, suburban background in Indianapolis to become a world record holder over short distances, twice American sprint champion and world sprint champion in 1899. His professional career, from 1896 to 1910, carried him to Europe and Australia, and to competition at the very highest level of the sport. His early amateur and professional career in the United States was marked by intense and overt racism directed at him by white competitors and by the various governing bodies. On the track, he was jostled and even physically attacked. Even after his phenomenal success in America and Europe, Taylor was never free to compete without the debilitating effects of the racism that was directed at him. Taylor's career unfolded in the glare of the media publicity directed at the modern sport of bicycle racing and before African Americans were integrated into any sports other than boxing and horse racing.

In his piece, Rob Gregg charts the impact of the 'Jim Crow' (that is, *de facto* rather than *de jure*) segregation which spread from the South to the North following the end of slavery, and extended into the first half of the twentieth century. As Gregg states, 'black sporting institutions flourished as segregation intensified'. His essay shows how, in Philadelphia, basketball, football and baseball were social arenas in which the players 'confronted the segregated nature of the city'. The 'Personal Calvaries' of his title describes the understanding that African Americans gained of the nature of their inferior position in society though their participation in sport. They were athletic equals, but they were denied equal access and equal representation. Gregg's study focuses on the community organizations which helped channel black players into semi-professional teams, and notes that this organizational initiative (born of segregation) and the resulting sense of community identity, was 'virtually brought to an end by the process of integration in the 1950s'. Gregg contrasts the survival of older, character-forming sporting ideals within the black community with the later undermining of such beliefs by commercial sport. 'Sport', he writes, 'played a vital role in bringing together black communities' and 'many African Americans excelled in sport in spite of the barriers placed in their way'. Great sporting rivalries developed within the black communities, and in institutions such as the YMCA and YWCA, 'remnants of a "social gospel" ideology blended with concepts of "muscular Christianity"'.

Stuart Knee focuses on the life and career of the renowned baseball manager, Branch Rickey, whose contribution to the game of baseball, and thereby to improved race relations in American society, was to achieve the integration of Major League baseball by hiring Jackie Robinson to his team, the Brooklyn Dodgers. Knee sees this integration of Robinson in 1947 as having had a permanent impact on the future racial composition of American sports and on the Civil Rights movement. At the time, club owners and *The Sporting News* (the chief organ of baseball) 'took a position of unequivocal opposition to the mingling of black and white athletes', even though the black athletes in the Negro Leagues were recognized as of equal athletic ability. Rickey, both a moral and pragmatic businessman, was, argues Knee, 'the perfect man to introduce blacks into white baseball because he knew the hazards involved and was ready to meet the thrusts of racial purists with a most formidable weapon – silence'. Rickey moved slowly and carefully, negotiating with Dodgers' stockholders and New York politicians, and aided by anti-discrimination legislation which had been enacted during the War. Working with his scouts, Rickey knew that the man he chose had to be 'the right man', and gradually 'decided that Robinson was the man he would choose for his experiment'. Robinson's integration into professional baseball was controversial at the time, but quickly led to further signings (18 by 1952), and had a profound impact not only on sport but on daily life in general, for example, on integration in dining cars and restaurants.

Rickey 'feared no one and had no voters to placate. Hence, he was the ideal man for the pioneering step in integration'. The point that was proved was that 'on the ballfield, where men were compelled to work harmoniously, integration proceeded at a greater rate than off the diamond'. What was understood in this crucial symbolic statement was that 'Robinson the ballplayer and Robinson the citizen were inseparable'. Rickey wrote:

> I believe that a man's race, color and religion should never constitute a handicap. The denial to anyone, anywhere, anytime of equality of opportunity to work is incomprehensible to me. Moreover, I believe that the American public is not as concerned with a first baseman's pigmentation as it is with the power of his swing, the dexterity of his slide, the gracefulness of his fielding or the speed of his legs.

For Stuart Knee, Rickey's contribution in integrating Robinson into sport was 'a solution to a national problem found far away from traditional social and political arenas, indicative of the power of sport within society'.

Michael Lomax examines the struggle for racial equality within American baseball, but at a later date, within the context of the Civil Rights and 'Black Power' movements. Curt Flood, a leading player for the St Louis Cardinals, 'recognized as the best centerfielder in baseball', when he was traded to the Philadelphia Phillies in 1969, legally challenged the 'reserve clause', which essentially gave team owners the contractual right to buy and sell players, if necessary against their wishes. Lomax asserts that Flood's mood 'reflected the disillusionment with white society which set the tone for the Civil Rights movement as it entered its Black Power phase', and explains how the Major League Baseball Players' Association (the players' union) pleaded Flood's case as a question both of labour relations and of race relations. After an early career marked by 'Jim Crow' discrimination (separate changing rooms, eating and housing arrangements) and racial abuse from spectators, Flood was active in opposing the inferior position assigned to blacks. Although black players earned large salaries, they 'still experienced discrimination when they attempted to buy homes in the cities in which they performed'. Flood 'exemplified a new desire to speed up the dismantling of barriers to racial equality'; his outspokenness 'reflected the changing racial landscape of the post-World War II sports world'.

In 1963 Flood's athletic career unfolded against a background of civil rights demonstrations and bombings in the American South. Black and Latino players were already dominant in baseball and Flood himself won awards and was featured on the cover of *Sports Illustrated*. Labour disputes led to increased salaries for players, but August Busch, the owner of the St Louis Cardinals, publicly questioned his team's commitment, further straining relations. When he was traded in 1969, Flood chose to challenge legally the 'reserve clause'. Flood 'found out that his personal life, business connections, friends, family and the roots he had established in the community were of no importance to his employer … the reserve clause was a form of slavery'. In the context of the 'Black Power' movement, Flood wrote an angry autobiography, *The Way It Is*. His challenge of Major League baseball's 'reserve clause' was essentially 'a demand for the right to negotiate'. The 1970 ruling went against Flood, as did the appeal to the Supreme Court, but the 'reserve clause' was soon overturned. A passage from Malcolm X, quoted by Michael Lomax, summarizes the struggle waged by Curt Flood: 'It is not a case of dark mankind wanting integration or separation, it is a case of wanting freedom, justice and equality. It is not integration that Negroes want in America, it is human dignity.'

Boria Majumdar's contribution shifts the focus to cricket in India and explores elements of caste, class and privilege which have been instrumental in shaping access to the sport since its beginnings in India in the 1840s. Contrary to commonly held belief that cricket in India went through a gradual democratization process, Majumdar argues that there was in fact a good deal of opportunity for the under-privileged in the sport between about 1890 and 1947, concluding that 'there were more well-known, low-caste, economically under-privileged cricketers in colonial India than there were post-independence'. From 1947 to 1983, he asserts, Indian cricket was 'dominated by an affluent, educated upper-caste elite', and that after that date the game 'opened up among the middle-class and underprivileged sections of Indian society the possibility of cricket being a viable career option'. Even so, the game is 'still dominated by ... affluent, upper-caste echelons of society', reinforced by corporate sponsorship. Majumdar's account of the history of the sport shows, however, a deeper history of the participation of the under-privileged (indeed even of the participation of 'untouchables') between about 1890 and 1947, and charts the careers of players 'from diverse economic and cultural backgrounds' who rose to fame in cricket. Their prowess in the game 'had come to symbolize a ladder for social mobility', with the result that from the 1880s onwards, the game 'had been considerably democratized'. In fact, the leading aristocratic patrons and sponsors of cricket had ambitions to 'defeat the English at their own game', and saw it as 'a means for the assertion of indigenous strength'. The British, too, through their educational role, contributed towards the democraticization of cricket in the early twentieth century. Players such as Mani Das and Palwankar Baloo, from humble backgrounds, rose above the limitations of caste and class. In 1906, for example, the *Indian Social Reformer* commented of Baloo that 'so far as pollution from touch with a low caste went, the plucky Brahmins of Poona gave the slip to orthodoxy'. The newspaper argued that 'where national interest required, equal opportunity must be given to all of any caste, even though the offer of such opportunity involved the trampling of some old prejudices. Let the lesson learnt in sport be repeated in political, social and educational walks of life.'

Brendan Hokowhitu's chapter argues that sport and an emphasis upon the physicality of the 'Noble Savage' within the context of the State physical education system has 'contributed to the suppression of the indigenous New Zealand Māori'. Hokowhitu assert that the colonizers of New Zealand 'combined racial superiority and social Darwinism to construct Māori culture as encumbered within a primitive physical world'. The State education system 'employed the Māori physicality sterotype to channel Māori into physical, as opposed to academic, realms of life'. One individual in particular, Philip Smithells, at the University of Otago, Dunedin, 'further oppressed Māori by perpetuating their physical stereotype'. Hokowhitu concludes that 'Māori are successful only in areas of society that do not threaten their dominant representation as a physical people', and that 'colonization was justified through discourses on race and Europeans' right to rule' which 'constructed Māori as physical, unintelligent and savage'. Of the essays included here, Hokowhitu reaches back the furthest into history in charting relations between early New

Zealand colonizers and their reactions in their cultural encounters with the Māori, including early Māori sports and games. In this context, Hokowhitu explores the concept of the 'Noble Savage' and his physical attributes and concludes that this unjustifiable attitude towards the Māori has been unfairly perpetuated.

Cricket is also the subject of Douglas Midgett's essay. He explains how the British sport was appropriated by West Indians and became 'a cultural expression contributing to West Indian self-definition', a characteristic which it shared with another West Indian cultural institution – calypso, which in its turn commented upon cricket. Using examples from three periods of the history of West Indian cricket, Midgett explores the cultural role of the sport at the end of the colonial period, as the West Indies was in the process of gaining independence from the colonial master. In 1950, for example, black West Indian players (particularly the two spin-bowlers, Ramadhin and Valentine) contributed to the defeat of England in the Test Series, a victory which was celebrated in a calypso by 'Lord Beginner'. Midgett comments that 'the colony side came to the colonial centre and won with guile and trickery'.

Dissatisfaction among the West Indian public at the failure to appoint a black captain of the cricket team led in 1960 to a riot during a match against England in Trinidad, but the selection of black captains, first Frank Worrell in 1961, and then Garfield Sobers, was a turning point and ensured the victory over Australia in the 1965 Test Series, which once again resulted in a famous 'boasting' calypso, by The Mighty Sparrow. Midgett comments that 'at a time when the idea of West Indian nationhood was at a low ebb, when the future of many of the islands was uncertain, the cricket victories were rallying points for regional pride'. In the 1987 World Cup matches in India and Pakistan, the West Indian team who were the favourites to win the tournament, disappointed by not even making the semi-finals. But the resulting calypso, 'Rally Round the West Indies' by David Rudder, 'exhorts West Indians to get behind their declining side in its moment of need'. Midgett points out how this calypso 'engages themes of colonialism, neo-colonialism, identity and impotence in an era of global dominance … and unfettered capitalist exchange'. He concludes that 'cricket and calypso are two of the most compelling performer-audience activities for West Indians, and consequently provide sites for the examination of contestation, resistance, artistic expression and representation of those who participate'. Both cricket and calypso are identified as vehicles 'for contesting the relationship of colonial and post-colonial subordination'. In the absence of a West Indian nation, the 'collective selfhood' of the diverse West Indian countries was 'completely bound up in their devotion to their cricket teams'.

Complementing the later studies about the history of cricket in India and the West Indies, and others about South African sport, Goolam Vahed's 'Deconstructing "Indiannness": Cricket and the Articulation of Indian Identities in Durban, 1900–1932' turns its attention to cricket and the Indian community in South Africa, focusing particularly on Durban where most of Natal's Indians lived. Vahed 'questions the notion of a homogenous and self-contained community', and explores 'race, class, caste, ethnic, religious and linguistic differences among Indians, and how these were negotiated and articulated'. He considers 'the role of sport … in defining ethnic, racial and class identities', and asks: 'Did sport become the commonality between divergent groups … or did sport reinforce and cement differences?' The large, mostly poor, Indian population of Natal, viewed by the white elite with alarm, was nevertheless not a homogeneous community, being made up of workers, traders and a small, affluent, professional class. It was this latter, educated, Anglophone Indian elite which valued cricket and sport in general and saw it 'as a means to instil discipline, implant a healthy value system and teach social values such as teamwork, respect for rules and authority and fortitude in the face of adversity'.

Cricket in Durban dates back to 1886 and was formally organized in 1901. Yet the underprivileged Indian players suffered from inadequate facilities and inferior equipment and were met with resistance from the authorities when they attempted to press for improvements. The Indian cricket teams themselves were fragmented because of differences of language, region and class. In a heavily racialized climate, the Indians resisted the inclusion of 'Coloureds' in their cricket activities, although in 1913 they did briefly join the South African Coloured Cricket Board which did not recognize 'distinction of creed, nationality or otherwise', and promoted a tournament just before the First World War. South African cricket players did, however, send a team to play in India in 1922 and 'Indianness' within South Africa was fostered by bringing together Indian teams from various regions. Vahed draws attention to the complexities of Indian cricket in South Africa in the period under examination, and concludes that 'cricket created and cemented race identity at local and national levels', but 'was not a medium of cross-racial contact. It could not be in circumstances where the colonial census tagged Africans, Coloureds,

Indians and Whites as "races" and defined racial political identities through the force of law.'

The next essay further widens the international range of the explorations of national identity and patterns of discrimination expressed within sport. Haruo Nogawa's piece charts 'the pervasive discrimination' which has been directed at Korean athletes in Japan since the end of the Second World War which, he asserts, has been a neglected issue 'due to the minimal interest in the field of sport among social scientists in Japan'. Based historically in Japan's imperial past, this discrimination is all the more problematic and subtle since Korean and Japanese 'share a common Mongolian racial heritage and are physically indistinguishable from each other'. After the war 600,000 Korean immigrants became 'alien residents' stripped of their citizenship and voting rights; the discrimination was manifested in denial of educational opportunity in sports.

The discrimination directed at Japanese-Koreans has been blatant. Since they were not citizens and were not allowed to attend Japanese schools, they were denied access to 'official inter-high school and inter-collegiate competitions' in soccer, baseball, sumo, basketball, ice hockey and volleyball. They were also excluded by the application of 'a formal quota system on the basis of citizenship' for the composition of national teams, to prevent foreign domination of Japanese teams. Personal discrimination has also been directed at other non-Japanese individuals, for example, most prominently and controversially perhaps, the Samoan-American sumo wrestler, Konishiki, who was not promoted to 'Grand Champion' although he met the qualifications. From 1947 to 1981 alien residents were excluded from the National Sports Festival, the high-school and inter-collegiate championships, a situation which was remedied in 1981 for those attending Japanese schools. Nevertheless, Nogawa writes, in spite of the discrimination a 'significant number' of Japan-born Koreans succeeded in baseball, sumo and wrestling, and the Japanese Ministry of Education, Science, Sport and Culture and the Japanese Amateur Sports Association were forced into further reforms of their institutional discriminatory policies in 1994, when students of ethnic schools (including Korean schools) became eligible for formal national competitions. The integration of ethnic schools into Japanese sports associations proceeded through the 1990s, although the issue is still controversial and integration is still only partial, varying from region to region. Nogawa identifies the problem of discrimination in Japanese sport as a civil rights issue, at the same time as he concludes that 'slow but significant progress has been made to overcome inequalities directed at permanent alien residents'. Nogawa, incidentally, contends that little research in general has been directed at the relationship between minority ethnic groups (other than African Americans), their access to sport and the wider issue of their assimilation into the dominant society. This is a shortcoming which *Ethnicity, Sport, Identity* attempts in part to put right.

Gillian Poulter provides a provocative account of indigenous sport in nineteenth-century Canada. Questioning the idea of ice-hockey as the original 'Canadian national game', she explores the history of snowshoeing in winter and lacrosse in summer as distinctively Canadian indigenous sports. Promoted by a Canadian nationalist, the journalist W. George Beers, these activities became identified as specifically Canadian (as distinct from British or American) sports, expressing a sense of Canadian national identity: 'by taking over Native activities, colonists put themselves in the place of the *indigène*, thereby taking on the identity of native-Canadians … Immigrant and Canadian-born professionals, merchants and small businessmen adopted and adapted Native activities and clothing, and performed their new identity in the streets and playing fields of the city.' Poulter argues with justification that a similar process of sport creation as 'a national signifier' occurred in other colonies such as Australia, New Zealand and Africa. What was demonstrated in the creation of modern snowshoeing and lacrosse was that 'national identity is not purely a political construct or a mere reflection of political ideology, but is also actively produced in the cultural sphere … Identity is a multi-phased process in which the individual is both actor and performer.'

Snowshoeing 'dated back further than the recorded history of the continent', and enabled nineteenth-century settlers connected with the fur trade to function effectively in winter. Snowshoe clubs, founded from 1843 on, became popular by the 1880s, although for practical purposes showshoeing had 'become an anachronism in developing urban areas'. The clubs had distinctive uniforms drawn from a variety of cultural traditions and members 'were dressing up as composite native-Canadians'; in some respects, they resembled 'Canadians of old'. Through snowshoeing as sport, participants 'enacted a cultural fiction', taking on 'the rustic persona of sons of the soil'. Similarly, lacrosse was 'an appropriation and secularization of a significant aboriginal ritual … The transformation of *baggataway* into lacrosse was an act of power contested unsuccessfully by Native peoples who were gradually excluded from the game.' The first white lacrosse club was founded in Montreal in 1858 by members of the

Montreal SnowShoe Club and by 1884, 20,000 players were registered. Lacrosse and snowshoeing complemented each other. Lacrosse was 'a cultural activity through which colonists could construct, witness and perform a putative national identity'. Modern lacrosse formulated rules and regulations and 'imposed order' on the Native game, becoming a distinctively Canadian game. Although Native players continued in the sport, even touring England in 1876 with their 'primitiveness' used as an advertising gimmick, they were nevertheless gradually excluded from the modern, 'scientific' game, which also changed and redesigned lacrosse equipment. Thus, Canadian cultural identity in these sports was constructed from indigenous customs overlaid with allegedly modern qualities of 'order, discipline and fair play'.

Charlene Regester's essay offers an examination of the presence and significance of black athletes (mostly football players and boxers) whose athletic careers 'became marketable commodities' in the early film industry as Hollywood 'capitalized on the black athlete's strength and bodily beauty'. But on screen, 'they were transformed into objects of both danger and desire because of their blackness and their sexuality'. Regester pinpoints both the lures and the dangers of the success that confronted these African–American athletes whose lives were profoundly affected as they underwent the transformation from playing field and boxing ring to mass media. Before the days of television, this was a new route whereby successful black athletes (beginning with boxer Jack Johnson in 1910, and continuing later with Paul Robeson and Joe Louis) were thrust into the public eye. The danger was that 'the black athlete, in all of his violence, aggressiveness and threatening behaviour, became a spectacle to be exploited for financial purposes'. Success in sport was thus also full of contradictions, for although such media representation of black strength and prowess 'introduced a kind of black empowerment', nevertheless it also 'exacerbated white fear of blacks and blackness'. Thus, 'as the black athlete was transformed on screen, he represented both danger and desire … resulting in a problematized image'. Adding to the contradictions of this image in a racist society was the fact that the black athlete/actor was 'at the service or under the control of white institutional power and authority'. His transformation on screen, it is suggested, was therefore 'a duplicitous representation'. Ultimately, concludes Regester, the inclusion of black athletes with physical appeal in Hollywood films has had the unfortunate result of projecting 'all black males as objects of desire, danger and derision, thus perpetuating an untenable construction'.

1

The League of American Wheelmen, Major Taylor and the 'Color Question' in the United States in the 1890s

ANDREW RITCHIE

The League of American Wheelmen (LAW) is the oldest organization devoted to cycling in the United States. Originally founded in 1880, it survives today as the League of American Bicyclists and its longevity is evidence of the age and depth of the sport of cycling. This essay focuses specifically on the relationship between the League of American Wheelmen and African-American bicycle racer 'Major' Taylor (1878–1932), and in a more general sense on race relations within the sport of cycling in the 1890s.[1] But in order to set these events in a meaningful context, a brief account of the earliest history of cycling in the United States should first be given.

Cycling was a prominent new sport which engaged a rapidly growing middle-class participation in the United States in the 1880s and 1890s and created new social and economic relationships within sport, recreation and utility transportation. Following the introduction of the high-wheel bicycle from England in 1876–77, the earliest cycling clubs organized in North America were the Boston Bicycle Club (formed 11 February 1878), the Suffolk Bicycle Club (formed April 1878) and the Montreal Bicycle Club (formed December 1878).[2] Other clubs followed quickly in major urban areas, for example Buffalo (February 1879), Chicago (September 1879), Cleveland (September 1879), New York (February 1880), Philadelphia (May 1879) and San Francisco (November 1879). A list of American clubs published in 1880 showed 50 clubs in existence, and by 1882 a British publication listed 100 American clubs, all organized within the previous four years, a remarkable expansion of interest in a new sport.[3]

The League of American Wheelmen was constituted on 30 May 1880. Cyclists from 40 independent cycling clubs in Massachusetts,

Connecticut, Rhode Island, New York, New Jersey and Pennsylvania convened in Newport, Rhode Island and voted unanimously to found the first national cycling organization.[4] The League came into existence to answer a variety of social, sporting, recreational, practical and legal needs. It encouraged the formation of new cycling clubs and their affiliation with the League. The legal status of the cyclist as a new category of road user was still ambiguous in the early 1880s and legal solidarity was a strong motivation for the institutional protection of this minority group. The often threatened and occasionally implemented imposition of laws limiting the use of bicycles on public roads and in public parks occurred on a somewhat random state and city basis, and the League kept abreast of unfair restrictions and defended members who were occasionally the victims of assaults by other road users. Negotiating with the railways to carry bicycles was another issue. The condition of the roads quickly became a prominent concern, and the 'Good Roads' movement grew substantially into an effective lobbying force organized largely within national and state-run League of American Wheelman committees.[5] The publication of the *LAW Bulletin* was always a crucial informational and journalistic task, keeping members in touch with each other and with the bicycle industry which served their needs.[6] The League grew rapidly, providing an organizational, legislative and social focus for bicycle-related sporting, recreational and practical activities. By 1894, it had 37,000 members; by 1898 it had reached its peak, with 103,000 members, a number which declined to 50,000 in 1900 and to less than 3,000 in 1905.[7]

From its inception, the League also saw the organization and promotion of bicycle racing as one of its primary tasks, and a Racing Board was created which sanctioned race meetings and participated in the classification of amateur and professional riders.[8] The first official United States amateur cycling championships were held in 1881, and subsequently, throughout the 1880s and 1890s, annual LAW Conventions and championship meetings were attended by thousands of cyclists.[9] In addition, for many years, the League represented American cyclists in international competition.

Within such a large national organization, with its rotating national committee and decentralized state-run local Divisions, there was plenty of room for disagreement, and the annual League Conventions were hotbeds of wrangling and intrigue. Power, money and influence, as well as purely sporting rivalries, were at stake in this newly organized, expansive athletic world. The role of the powerful bicycle industry and its tendency to lure amateur riders towards professionalism within an organization which struggled to uphold amateur ideals was one constant source of tension. Who was and was not an amateur was a question which was constantly at issue in American bicycle racing, just as it was across the Atlantic in Great Britain. In America, the question of membership and race was another controversial issue, debated and voted on at the League conventions in the 1890s. As the League grew, in the Southern States as well as on the East Coast, in the Midwest and on the Pacific Coast, who should be accepted for League membership was contested. And during the years that the organization was most actively debating its 'white only' rule, that is between 1893 and 1897, a superb, young, black athlete, 'Major' Taylor, the 'ebony wonder', the 'black whirlwind', began to win important races on America's bicycle racing tracks, proving that a black athlete could dominate his white rivals in the new sport of cycling and issuing a challenge to the racism of a substantial proportion of the League membership, as well as to that of society in general.

Major Taylor began winning as an amateur and then, as a professional, he made a lot of money in the boom years of the sport, thus making a powerful personal statement about equal rights and equality of opportunity in competitive sport. He did not set out intentionally to make a racial and political statement with his life, but his career in cycling was, nevertheless, profoundly political and a milestone in the history of black integration into modern sport. Against the fierce opposition of many elements within the sport and business of cycling, the teenaged Marshall Taylor, a simple boy born into suburban poverty on the outskirts of Indianapolis, Indiana, climbed, in about seven years, from anonymity to win a world professional championship, break world records and become for one summer in 1901 perhaps the most prominent athlete in Europe. Major Taylor's struggle for the right to participate in bicycle racing in the United States in the 1890s was an extraordinary social and sporting drama. Although he reached the pinnacle of his sport in Europe, he was not, ultimately, successfully and permanently integrated into the sport in his own country.

Black boxers and black jockeys had become a presence in their sports, but no other contemporary black athlete impresses so forcefully, in his solitary and symbolic power, as Major Taylor. An almost naive figure away from the bicycle track and a competitor threatened by physical intimidation in many of his early, amateur races, Taylor became a superb athlete, an affluent, seasoned professional who could be relied on during his heyday to give outstanding performances before demanding American and European audiences. Throughout his career, Taylor was buffeted by business and economic pressures, and especially by racism; as a defiantly struggling teenager, attempts (both physical and bureaucratic) were made to exclude him totally from the sport. Standing alongside Major Taylor was a white mentor, trainer and father-figure, the ex-high-wheel champion and New England bicycle manufacturer, 'Birdie' Munger. Whereas racist pressures would have preferred that Taylor not be accepted into the sport, liberal promoters and business backers were willing to cash in on his growing notoriety as a crowd-puller and a box-office attraction. But in the latter part of his career, from about 1902 to his retirement in 1910, Taylor chose to compete mostly in Europe to avoid the inevitable hostility and difficulties which he encountered at home, and was thereby denied the American recognition which should have been accorded him as a mature athlete.

There is little evidence of black participation in cycling in the high-wheel bicycle days. Cycling in the 1880s was a mostly white, middle-class activity centred in club life in the middle-class urban centres, New York, Philadelphia, Boston, Chicago, San Francisco, and the Midwestern cities such as Indianapolis, Louisville, Toledo or St Louis. The high-wheel bicycle was expensive, out of the financial reach of the majority of blacks, and was the new recreation of energetic, middle-class white men. The safety bicycle, the pneumatic tyre and the growth of a large second-hand market in the early 1890s democratized the bicycle, bringing it within reach of the less well-off. As cycling clubs sprang into existence, in line with the prevailing social segregation of the period, all-black cycling clubs were also formed. On the more liberal East Coast, in Chicago and on the West Coast, black cyclists began to consider the benefits of joining the League of American Wheelmen, the only national cycling organization. In the world of work, church and community, relations between the races were in general assigned and predetermined, and segregation well-established, but within a new social grouping like the LAW, there was room for ambiguity and the possibility of black membership implied a challenge, a social familiarity and proximity which was unacceptable to many whites, especially in the south, where deeply ingrained tradition forbade social, especially recreational, contact between blacks and whites. There were two issues:

should 'colored wheelmen' and all-black cycling clubs be accepted into membership in the LAW and should black cyclists be integrated into races sponsored or sanctioned by the LAW?

At the 1892 League of American Wheelmen Convention in Columbus, Ohio, Colonel William Watts of Louisville, Kentucky, a lawyer, notary and President of the Commercial Law League of America, led a group of delegates in proposing to exclude 'the Negro' from membership in the League, although on that occasion he did not succeed in bringing the issue to a vote. An editor of Chicago's *Bicycling World*, pronouncing the League 'a great political party', expressed a pragmatic, liberal view in defending black membership in the large organization, although he supported maintaining the distinction between segregated local clubs and an integrated national organization:

> When a negro sends in his name and two dollars, and asks admission to the League, I claim that by that act he exhibits symptoms of patriotism and intelligence which puts the burden of proof on the pale faced dyspeptic who would keep him out ... We want every member and every dollar and every vote that is to be had. A black gentleman is infinitely superior to a white hoodlum. Let us size up the applicant by his behavior, not by his color. The League is too great and too comprehensive to be gauged by the same notions which are quite proper in a small club ... No rider in a race cares who is behind; he only worries about the men who are likely to take positions in front, from which location the odor of an over-heated 'nigger' would become intensely offensive in the aesthetic nostrils of our more fastidious Southern member. Let the Caucassian and the Ethiopian have each his own club. But for Heaven's sake, when it comes to the broad acreage of the League, let's draw the line only at respectability. If the colored man wants to come in, let us take him, not only willingly, but gladly ... And after we have taken in the man, his money, and his vote, let us behave ourselves well enough so that he won't be ashamed of us.[10]

In a follow-up comment a few weeks later, the same writer again supported the idea of black membership in the League which, he said, 'is not a club; it is a political party, and its members need not associate with each other if they don't want to any more than they need associate because each was a member of the Methodist church'. He denied, however, that his was a radical position – 'No one ever heard me say that people should attempt social equality.'[11]

In 1893, at the League Convention in Philadelphia, the exclusionist faction tried again, more forcefully, to gain support for their proposal to introduce the word 'white' into membership rules. The Southern delegates, according to *The Wheelmen's Gazette*, 'came all primed to make a strong fight against admitting the negro to the League'. The Watts faction, however, did not gain the two-thirds vote necessary for their motion to become League policy (the vote was 108 votes for, 101 against), and the issue threatened to disrupt brotherly relations between northern and southern delegates. *The Wheelmen's Gazette* thought that:

> the action of the Assembly on the color question voices the sentiments of every fair-minded LAW man. If you, or I, or some other man doesn't like the negro, that is no reason why he should be treated as if he had no rights or privileges. The Southerner has a natural antipathy to the colored man, and in view of the condition of the colored man in the South, they cannot be blamed for not wishing to mix with them socially. That's for them to settle. If they don't want negroes, they have their remedy. Let their local divisions settle the difficulty. Here in the North where prejudice is not so pronounced, or at least, where it is better concealed, we can handle the matter to our own satisfaction.[12]

Accounts of the numbers of black members already accepted into the League in this mid-1890s period varied from about 20 to several hundred – but it was clearly a small number.[13] A month later, the Associated Cycling Clubs of Chicago (which was affiliated to the LAW) demonstrated that prejudice was not confined to the South when it barred black riders from entering the famous Pullman Road Race, one of the most prestigious national road races. By doing so, commented Roland Hennessy in *The Wheelmen's Gazette*, the Associated Cycling Clubs 'has placed itself in the position of antagonism to colored League members. It is evident that this body of Chicago wheelmen is not impressed with those stirring words of the great abolitionist, James Russell Lowell, that caused such a wave of enthusiasm to roll over the country during the Civil war: "Before man made us citizens, great Nature made us me."' It was, thought Hennessy:

> not a question of sentiment, but of justice. If we allow the colored

man to come into our house, surely we should not turn our backs on him as soon as he enters ... It is quite evident from the actions of clubs and individuals all over America that the colored rider is only tolerated in cycle circles. But it does seem strange for a body of sportsmen to hold forth the hand of good fellowship one day and pull it back with great vehemence the next.[14]

Later, the same writer expanded further on his perceptions of the complex situation:

We of the North have been very denunciatory of the South and its treatment of the colored rider, and yet on occasions have we not been just as inconsiderate, and far more hypocritical? Have we not praised him with our tongues and turned our eyes away from him when he has presented himself for participation in our affairs? In other words, have we not treated him unjustly according to the rules we have wished to lay down for others?[15]

When the delegates assembled for the 1894 Convention in Louisville, Kentucky, 'Negro exclusion' was a burning issue. Colonel Watts and his supporters in both the North and South had 'worked like beavers' in preparation for the meeting, and Kentuckians had previously succeeded in introducing the 'color line' as a clause in the constitution of the Kentucky League's constitution.[16] In the press, the exclusion of black members was generally referred to as 'the drawing of the color line'. George Barrett, the visiting editor of *Bearings*, told a Louisville newspaper that he favoured the 'white only' amendment for the good of the League, because 'the negro can never get into the League in numbers large enough to do the organization any good', and because 'a very few of them can do much harm, especially in the South. The League should be built on lines that will give the greatest good to the greatest number ... The North cannot be benefited by the admission of the negro, while the South can and will be benefited by his exclusion.' W.C. Harris, the Chief Consul of the Alabama division of the League (which had also approved the 'white only' rule in its Constitution), told the same reporter that 'we don't want any negroes ... and neither would the Northern men if they were in our place. We have about one hundred riders of color in Birmingham (Alabama) and you should see them! The people in the North only see the colored men who have sense enough to leave this country of ease and plenty, and work their way up in the world, instead of living off of some one else.'[17]

Watts made an energetic speech to the whole assembly, attended by about 180 delegates (representing about 37,000 League members)[18] and many editors from the large national cycling press, including *Cycling Life* (Chicago), *Bearings* (Chicago), *The Referee* (Chicago), *Bicycling World* (Boston), *The Wheel* (New York), *The Cyclist* (Hartford, CT) and *Sporting Life* (Philadelphia).[19] The American cyclists present on that occasion were described as 'a fine body of young men, athletic and healthy in appearance, from their outdoor exercise. They were a good argument in favor of this rapidly spreading sport.'[20] In 'an eloquent speech', Watts presented what was in fact a profoundly moral issue pragmatically – he did not 'oppose the negro for personal reasons',[21] but the failure in 1893 to bar Negroes from membership, he said, had caused some members to resign and persuaded others not to join; he claimed that the League would get 5,000 new members in the South if his motion were carried. Watts then took the extraordinary step of reading aloud a letter which he claimed had been sent to him unsolicited by Frederick Scott, president of Louisville's Union Cycle Club, the largest black cycling club in the South, the text of which read:

> Dear Sir – The undersigned club, composed of twenty-five members, is fully acquainted with the amendment offered by you whereby a color line is proposed to be established in the constitution of the League of American Wheelmen. And being so acquainted are of the belief that it is offered for the good of the organization, in that its membership will be largely increased in the southern states. And as this club of twenty-five gentlemen desires to see carried out the great objects of the league, of which highway improvement is one, and believes that those objects can be best carried out by increasing the membership, and believes that the adoption of that amendment will materially increase the membership in the southern states, we take this method of assuring you that you have our best wishes for ultimate success. If we can be of any service to you, command us. Fraternally – The Union Cycle Club, Frederick J. Scott, President.

Scott, Watts reported to his listeners, had told him, 'We understand that no good in an organization of this kind can be done by mixing the races … We do not want to belong to an organization where we are not wanted, because we are gentlemen and men of sense, and understand these things. There are many men who would not join an organization in which colored men are allowed to become members.'[22]

Watts' speech was 'warmly applauded' by his audience. 'We need to strengthen our membership, gentlemen', he told the assembly, before reminding them to take the bottles of whiskey which had been donated by a Colonel Johnson, of Kentucky. *Outing* reported that 'very little argument was made on the floor of the Assembly at Louisville, for all the talking had been done previously. It was voted to proceed to the ballot without further discussion.'[23] No defence of the rights of the already enrolled and future black League members was advocated, even from the liberal delegates from Massachusetts, New York or Pennsylvania, and a secret vote was proposed and taken, 'as had been agreed upon at the request of the Eastern delegation, who seemed desirous of drawing the color line without putting themselves on record to that effect'.[24] Another account confirmed the perceived delicacy of the issue and the reluctance of anti-racists to speak out publicly against the measure, explaining that 'the Easterners who have opposed the measure are willing to vote for it provided they are not compelled to go on record'.[25] The constitutional amendment to bar blacks from membership, by the introduction of the word 'white' into membership rules, was thus carried by 127 votes to 54 (a 70 per cent majority), the Massachusetts delegation voting unanimously against it.[26]

The ruling elicited a front page headline in the *Louisville Evening Times*: 'Drew The Color Line – Delegate Watts Carries the Day with Ease', although it did not generate further public discussion.[27] But strong reaction to the decision was expressed from other quarters. Letters of resignation from the League were sent in from New England and New York.[28] The *New York Tribune* wrote that: 'Wheelmen must look with disfavor upon the outcome of the convention of the LAW at Louisville ... Fair-minded men will condemn the exclusion of colored men.'[29] Boston's all-black Riverside Cycling Club was outraged and explored the possibility of legal action, and Bob Teamoh, the only black member of the Massachusetts House of Representatives, introduced into the House a resolution of condemnation which 'deprecates the action of the organization ... and regards the enforcement of discrimination of this character as a revival of baseless and obsolete prejudice'.[30] In Boston, a meeting of black LAW members was held which 'expressed great indignation at the LAW, and endorsed the action of the Massachusetts delegation in casting a solid vote for the coloured man, and expressing doubt as to the authenticity of that letter which Mr. Watts read in the Convention from the Union Club of Louisville'. These cyclists were 'trying to create a public opinion on the subject, and have not yet succeeded except with their own race'.[31] The Riverside Cycle Club sent an incredulous letter to the Louisville's Union Cycle Club: 'Believing you gentlemen incapable of forgetting yourselves so far as to stand in your own light, and knowing that among our white oppressors there is no limit too low, mean and inhuman acts, we are in doubt as to whether or not said actions be true. As a brother cycle club, we feel justified in seeking for an explanation.'[32] *Bearings* sent a reporter to interview the Union Cycling Club's Frederick Scott, who:

> found him to be a pleasant and intelligent man and very willing to talk about the matter ... Mr. Scott is one of the few who do not care to force themselves where they are not wanted and persuaded his club to the same opinion. For having the courage to express his opinion, he has been very strongly condemned by negroes all over the country and is receiving many letters asking about his support of the amendment.[33]

But the sharpest kind of racist reaction came from the Chicago paper, *The Referee*, whose writer 'Phoebus' made a vituperative attack on the alleged inferiority of the negro as a race, a remarkable, openly-stated expression of prejudice. 'Phoebus' was:

> heart and soul with Mr. Watts in his manly and impersonal crusade against an evil which would sooner or later have ruined the LAW in the great southland. If the men who have championed and are still championing the negro in this matter were only broad enough to see and recognize that the south understands the ways of her own people better than they, and that the negro has very little interest in the LAW anyway, there would be less coil over that which had to be done for the good of the body. Were these enthusiastic lovers of the blacks to question those who know, they would learn that the negro has little interest in anything beyond his daily needs, his personal vanity and a cake walk or barbers' hall now and then.
>
> The darkey is essentially a creature of today. His interest (unless it be in the advent of a circus next month) is taken up entirely with the matters just at hand. He is a lazy, happy-go-lucky animal

wherever he is, but much more so on his native heath than in our northern clime, where our cold hospitality of the negro-loving white population would let him starve like a common white man if he didn't rise up and hump himself. In the south, where he is better understood, the people who do not want him in the league or any other white man's organization, put up with his indolence, his lack-brain carelessness and his thievish and other uncomfortable proclivities (unless he commits a great crime), and when he is hungry feed him and let him go the even tenor of his care-free way. The negro, outside of a few lemon-hued and saddle-colored specimens with enough white blood to make them cheeky, have no wish to belong to the LAW, and mighty few of them have the necessary $2 to spare...

I have no desire to deprecate either these men or their race. Both are useful and perhaps necessary in their place, but it really wearies me to read labored essays from Tom, Dick and Harry, whose only acquaintance with the black man is in the matter of 'a shine, boss?' or as a waiter in a second-class restaurant ... who feel that we ought to champion the much abused Sambo, even though they would not eat, sleep, marry or tolerate as a companion the creature with the flat nose and black skin. The League does not need him. Why should it admit one with whom not one of its members would dance at a public or private ball?[34]

A separate black League was talked about: 'The colored brother retaliates on the white man that he is going to form a National League of his own, and he states that the constitution will be so worded as to exclude every one who has not colored blood in his veins.'[35] Contrary to Watts' optimistic predictions, membership in the League in fact *declined* by about 10,000 from 1894 to 1895, rather than increasing, a fact which undermined the self-expressed logic of his position.

This evidence shows that the deeply prejudiced activities of one racist spokesman, supported by others in a secret vote, and working within a formally democratic process, succeeded in enabling the racist feelings of more than 70 per cent of the League delegates to be expressed, and in defining the League as a racist organization. What the LAW did, however, was no different from what other organizations were also doing formally and informally at a time of intensifying segregation. During the 1880s and 1890s, many of the rights won by ex-slaves during

Reconstruction were attacked and reversed by 'Jim Crow' laws. Blacks were denied the vote in many areas of the South by the introduction of educational or other requirements designed to exclude them. Segregation in trains, streetcars and, restaurants became general. The new legal codification of white supremacy, of which Colonel Watts' legislation within the LAW was but one small example, was intended to prevent blacks from rising in society. Discrimination went unchecked by the failure of the Supreme Court to rule in favor of the civil rights of blacks in a series of test cases, culminating in the notorious 1896 case of Plessy v. Ferguson, which held that 'separate but equal' facilities did not violate the Fourteenth Amendment of the Constitution.[36]

Where new segregation laws did not succeed in keeping African American males in their place, white Southerners took the law into their own hands. More lynchings took place in the 1890s than in any other decade: between 1890 and 1900 (the decade of the bicycle 'boom'), 1,217 lynchings by hanging, burning, shooting and beating were recorded; the vast majority of the victims were blacks. Between January and October 1900, newspapers reported 114 lynchings, all but two of them in the South. 'It is evident that the white people of the South have no further use for the Negro', wrote an Arkansas minister to the *Christian Recorder*: 'He is being treated worse now than at any other time since the surrender.' Only in 1900 was the first bill introduced into the House of Representatives designed to make lynching a federal offence.[37]

It was within this wider social context – frequently described as the darkest period in race relations in United States history – that the League of American Wheelmen's rejection of black membership was carried out, and a black teenager named Marshall Taylor was working in a bicycle shop in Indianapolis and beginning to win races against white cyclists. The number of black racing cyclists actually affected by the LAW ruling was comparatively small, but the 'white only' rule was significant as a sign of the times. As Major Taylor's career developed and he became more prominent, his presence in amateur, and subsequently, professional racing circles became a test of the attitudes of the white riders and officials with whom he came into contact. Because he was so obviously an outstanding athlete, Taylor's presence was provocative and controversial from the beginning. Contrary to the suppressed condition of, and limited possibilities open to, the average African American, Major Taylor's dramatic assertion of athletic superiority as he swept across the finishing line ahead of his white rivals was impossible to deny or ignore.

There was, however, continued and energetic resistance to the League's racist policy from the Massachusetts, New York and Pennsylvania divisions of the League. Before the 1895 Convention in New York, the Riverside Cycle Club took the initiative in pressing for 'a set of resolutions instructing the delegates from Massachusetts to take steps towards the reinstatement of the colored man'. The Club resolved that:

> The members of the Riverside Cycle Club of Boston do enter our objections and protests against the rules depriving the negro of the right to become a member of the LAW, feeling that discrimination is an injustice and inhuman and unworthy the act of a body whose principles are based upon equality.[38]

The resolution was withdrawn, however, and did not come to a vote at the actual Convention.[39] At the race meeting associated with the Convention held at Asbury Park, New Jersey, Kittie Knox, 'a comely colored girl from Boston, who recently won the 1st prize in the Malden Cycle Parade for wearing the most tasteful and artistic women's wheeling garb', was refused privileges normally accorded to League members, in spite of the fact that she had become a League member long before the 'white only' ruling had come into effect in 1894:

> When Miss Knox, whose appearance and dress had been objects of admiration all day, walked into the committee room at the local clubhouse, and presented her League card for a credential badge, the gentleman in charge refused to recognize the card, and the young woman withdrew very quietly and went her way. 99 out of every 100 members express the heartiest sympathy for Miss Knox and condemnation for the hasty action of the committee.[40]

According to the *Southern Cycler*, 'This murky goddess of Beanville, this tar-colored constituent', was 'several checks shy of the complexion requirement, and is not eligible and, therefore, not a member, despite the fact that she holds a membership card'.[41] In 1896, the black Hannibal Athletic Club, of Washington DC, proposed a complete boycott of the League and the formation of a parallel black League at a convention in their city. As a demonstration of their determination, they proposed a 'grand parade of colored wheelmen' as well as a race meet, an idea which

FIGURE 1.1
Officers of the All-Black Oakland Cycling Club Depicted in 1896
(*San Francisco Call*, 12 July 1896)

J. C. Moore, First Lieutenant.   HARRY F. WILLIAMS, Captain.   WILLIAM S. MORREY, Second Lieutenant.
MRS. IDELLA JOHNSON (née Allen), Captain Ladies' Annex.
OFFICERS OF THE OAKLAND CYCLING CLUB.

encountered difficulties, 'managers of the several local tracks being opposed to the idea of having colored race meets on their tracks'.[42]

The pressure to extend membership in the League was also felt in California. In July 1896, when the all-black Oakland Cycling Club held its picnic and race meet, it was described as 'the leading colored cycling club on the coast', but had been unable to join the League (see Figure 1.1). It had an active women's section led by Mrs Idella Johnson, who 'has been looking for a race with white lady cyclers for championship honors'. She told the *San Francisco Call*: 'I now hold the world's ladies' racing record and I intend to retain it. I do not wish to do so unless it belongs to me, and the only way to definitely decide the matter is for these ladies to ... show what they can do. We hope to bring the white and colored cyclers together soon.' Captain Harry Williams told the newspaper:

FIGURE 1.2

'Kemble Illustrates the Piccaninny Club Awheel; a Brush with Brack [*sic*] Trash'. Published without comment
in a major San Francisco newspaper, this caricature defines the overt racism which excluded African-American
cyclists from membership in the League of American Wheelmen in the mid-1890s
(*San Francisco Examiner*, 8 August 1897)

We have a flourishing club; every member is a reputable citizen, and there are some remarkably good riders. Our races are open to all comers, and there does not appear to be any valid reason why we should not join the LAW I do not think the reason we have not been recognized is due to race prejudice, but there is a desire to avoid the issue.[43]

Williams was, of course, constrained not to be openly critical of racist public attitudes. That there could have been no doubt in his own mind of the true reason that the members of the Oakland CC were not accepted into the LAW was demonstrated by the publication in a major San Francisco newspaper at the same period of a typically insulting racist caricature, showing the 'Black Trash' of the 'Piccaninny Club Awheel' (see Figure 1.2).[44] By April of the following year, Captain Williams said that he had been trying for three years to have his club accepted by the LAW 'We have had great difficulty in trying to obtain recognition', Williams told the *San Francisco Call*:

> There are several colored cyclist clubs on the coast ... At the present time we have no recognition whatever. We do not want to obtrude ourselves where we are not wanted, and, on the other hand, we do not want to be slighted. It seems to be the prevailing impression that if we are admitted to the Coast League we shall demand the right to enter in all their races ... This is not our motive nor our desire.[45]

At the 1897 Philadelphia Convention, strong resistance to the 'white only' membership clause was once again mounted by Pennsylvania cyclists. *Bearings* reported that 'a movement looking to the recognition of colored riders has been forming and has reached such proportions that the support of many prominent League members and delegates to the assembly has been secured and they have declared their intention of making a strong fight'. Dr Howard, president of the Meteor Wheelmen, 'one of the foremost colored organizations in the country', told the paper that 'it has been proven that the several hundred colored riders who have been members of the League for several years have always conducted themselves as well as their white brethren and have never asked for anything more than the League affords to all its members'.[46] This movement to remove the racist membership ruling confirms that within the League there was vigorous liberal and democratic opposition to the strong discriminatory forces. The 'white only' ruling proved on a nationwide basis to be only partially effective since local chapters of the LAW could overrule membership regulations by accepting black participation in their local activities. Further detailed study of the source material may well reveal a consistent history of resistance to discriminatory practices within the sport of cycling. Exactly how long the exclusion ruling remained effectively and practically in force is not clear. It may have fallen into disuse in many states, but to date the evidence shows that it was apparently not formally repealed until 1999, when then-President of the League, Earl Jones, at an anniversary rally in Louisville, spoke of the 'color ban' as a 'past wrong', expressed his organization's 'commitment to diversity', and bestowed a posthumous League membership on Major Taylor.[47]

The League of American Wheelmen's attempt to create an 'Apartheid' within the governing body of the American sport was most

significant in excluding black members and giving voice to segregationist convictions and emotions in society at large, rather than in specifically
limiting Major Taylor's young career, and it certainly did not succeed in
preventing him (as an exceptional case) from coming to the fore. The
League was a national club and social association, with jurisdiction over
a wide range of cycling activities, but was not exclusively an athletic
organization. Its jurisdiction was limited, and a great deal of organized
racing took place under the banner of local municipal committees,
cycling clubs and other athletic organizations. Taylor won segregated
races as a teenager in Indianapolis and Chicago and was soon acknowledged as 'colored champion of America'. Soon after the 1894 Louisville
convention, Chairman Raymond of the Racing Board of the LAW made
a ruling that 'the action of the League in barring colored men from
membership in the organization did not make them ineligible to race in
LAW meets'.[48] Although the League banned black membership, Taylor
was nevertheless licensed as a professional cyclist by the Racing Board in
1896 and had powerful East Coast commercial and sporting interests
backing him. Such support, however, did not protect him from danger
and hostility on the race track during actual competition, and could not
offer any remedy when Taylor's chances of winning a high place in the
national championship circuit races in 1897 and 1898 were dashed
through having his entries rejected by Southern promoters.[49]

   During his first few years as a professional in the United States (1896
to 1900), Major Taylor aroused an intense hatred among some white
riders as he began to challenge them for the best prizes – hefty purses of
gold coins. A first place in an important regional race could easily be
worth $100, equivalent to perhaps ten times that amount in today's
values. Some riders, especially on the East Coast, accepted him with
good grace and even openly praised his exceptional natural abilities. In
Boston, in July 1897, he was accepted by four white riders as a member
of a five-man team which defeated a Philadelphia team in a five-mile
pursuit race (see Figure 1.3).[50] But other competitors, from Kentucky,
Ohio or California, found his presence on the starting line intolerable
and were personally outraged when he won, which he sometimes did
with what seemed to them to be an almost insulting ease. Short-distance
bicycle racing on the track was then, as now, a fast and dangerous sport.
Jostling and elbowing were part of the excitement the crowd paid to see.
A conspiracy grew among the white riders to exclude Major Taylor from
victory. They ganged up against him and tried to block him, forcing him

FIGURE 1.3

In 1897, Major Taylor participated in an integrated five-man Boston Team in a pursuit race against
Philadelphia. This was probably the first such integrated team in
American Bicycle Racing (*Bearings*, 29 July 1897)

BEARINGS   2681

At 9.40 the men lined up in front
of the grand stand and were introduced to the crowd. Boston won the
toss for position and wisely selected
the backstretch, as they had the wind
on their backs on the start. Before
going farther the conditions of the

THE BOSTON TEAM.

FRANK BUTLER.   ''MAJOR'' TAYLOR.

BURNS PIERCE.   NAT BUTLER.   E. A. M'DUFFIE.

to ride from the front (the hardest way to win) and pull victory out of
seemingly impossible situations. They were verbally abusive and physically hostile both on and off the track.

'Taylor rides in all his big races in deadly fear of his racing companions', said the *New York Sun* in September 1897, 'Taylor was recently thrown at Worcester and badly bruised in a race ... The situation calls for prompt action on the part of the Racing Board. Taylor now ranks among the fastest men in the country, but the racing men, envious of his success and prejudiced against his color, aim to injure his chances whenever he competes.'[51] Taylor himself confirmed this fear: 'I have a dread of injury every time I start in a race with the men who have been on the circuit this year. They have threatened to injure me and I expect that before the season is finished they will do so', he told the *Worcester Telegram*, his home town newspaper.[52] At Taunton, Massachusetts, Taylor was physically attacked and choked into unconsciousness by a white rider, William Becker, after Taylor had beaten him into second place in a one mile sprint race (Figure 1.4). The crowd, agitated and angry at Becker's attack, threatened him, and only the police presence prevented an already ugly incident from becoming uglier. Becker was not arrested, and the incident was a sharp reminder of the aggressive feelings aroused by Taylor's challenge within a sport dominated by whites. *Bicycling World* called the incident 'one of the deplorable features of the racing season of 1897 ... It is such incidents as these that bring discredit on a sport whose promoters have strenuously endeavoured to keep it clean and honest.'[53] When Taylor went south to Savannah, Georgia at the beginning of the season of 1898, to put in some early-season training in the warm climate, he was threatened, following a training encounter on nearby public roads, by local white riders who sent him a letter with a crude drawing of a skull and crossbones: 'Mister Taylor', it read, 'if you don't leave here before 24 hours, you will be sorry. We mean business. Clear out if you value your life. Signed – White Riders.' An intelligent black person did not argue with such a threat in the racial climate of the day, and Taylor left.[54] That season, 1898, he told the reporter from the *Worcester Telegram*: 'I am riding faster this year than I was last, and that has saved me a good many times. I simply ride away from the rest of the bunch and do not give them a chance to pocket me ... It always falls to my lot to set the pace and it is not always pleasant to have to push out in the lead ... That is the way I have won all my races this season.'[55]

At a moment of spectacular expansion, the sport of cycling profited from an unconventional, upstart personality like Major Taylor, even though some white riders and Mid-Western and Southern promoters, for reasons of pride and racial animosity, did their very best to exclude

FIGURE 1.4
In his struggle for acceptance into American Bicycle Racing in the late 1890s,
Major Taylor was subjected to physical attacks from certain white riders in public, and opposition from racist
forces within the bureaucracy of the sport
(*Boston Globe*, 24 September 1897)

CHOKED TAYLOR

Police Had to Interfere at Taunton.

Becker Pulled the Major From His Bicycle.

Colored Man Was Second in the Race.

Crowd Came Near Going For His Assailant.

Event Was Run Over, with Taylor Out of It.

TAUNTON, Sept 23—The bicycle races held here today in connection with the Bristol county fair were well attended, but the spectators were not well pleased with the action of some of the riders in the one-mile open race.

In getting away there was a bad mix-up. Tom Butler crossed the tape first with Maj Taylor second and W. E. Becker third.

After the riders had crossed the tape Becker wheeled up behind Taylor and grabbed him by the shoulder. The colored man was pulled off his wheel and thrown to the ground. Becker choked him into a state of insensibility and the police were obliged to interfere.

It was fully 15 minutes before Taylor recovered consciousness and the crowd was on the point of assaulting Becker when the police put an end to the trouble.

Becker maintains that Taylor crowded him into the fence during the race. Becker was disqualified and the race was run over again, Tom Butler winning.

Dennis Daley of Taunton, won the amateur championship of Bristol county for one mile, receiving a gold lined loving cup. His time was 2m 26 1-5s. The summary:

One-mile open, second race—Won by Tom Butler, Frank Butler second, Watson Coleman, Springfield, third. Time 2m 27 2-5s.

Two-mile handicap, professional—Won by A. T. Caldwell, Manchester, N H; Watson, Springfield, second; L. B. Arnold, Woonsocket, third. Time 5m 6 1-5s.

him. Bicycle racing was a modern sport, within which new alliances were relatively easily made, and where new opportunities certainly existed. Major Taylor was good for box office receipts, the hostility he provoked in America at the beginning of his successes made for tense, dramatic sport, and his victories over white riders created discussion in the press and publicity for his employers. His decision not to race on Sundays, for religious reasons, was greeted with derision, and racist caricatures were published in the cycling press (Figure 1.5). He had friends within the LAW, even as he had enemies out in the racing world. Between 1898 and

FIGURE 1.5
Racist caricatures were published in the cycling press
(*Bearings*, 1898, Exact date unknown)

1900, professional cyclists formed a new organization, the National Cycling Association (NCA), and after Taylor had been persuaded to join the NCA, this body tried to exclude him from the sport, making it necessary for Taylor to re-apply to the LAW for a professional licence. For a few months he was effectively without a professional affiliation. As Taylor's struggles with the American cycle racing bureaucracy continued through the period from 1897 to 1900, his case became increasingly identified in the public eye and in the press as a question of rights and fairness to a star athlete. Taylor's most influential supporters were the writers working for cycling magazines and daily newspapers, who watched the development of his career with admiration and sympathy. They appreciated that Taylor stood at the center of an ongoing social debate and that his fight with the white cyclists was symbolic of a wider social conflict. An article in the *Worcester Spy* underlined the strength of public support for him:

> Major Taylor, colored whirlwind, world's record holder, world professional 1-mile champion, and for two years bone of contention in cash prize racing circles ... is floundering wildly about and gasping for help ... The riders have drawn the color line. It is unconstitutional, un-American, unsportsmanlike. It is wrong in the abstract, unrighteous in the concrete. It is indefensible, particularly at a time when you are dealing with something other than theory, and all the more so since the color line will not be accepted by the American public as a valid excuse for the ruling off of a champion. Major Taylor is a stern reality. He is here in flesh and blood, and he must be dealt with as a human being, entitled to every human right.[56]

The saga of Taylor's dealings with the governing bodies of the sport in the late 1890s is told in my biography and cannot be explored in detail here.[57] In spite of the racist opposition, Major Taylor broke world records, became world sprint champion in 1899, took the League of American Wheelmen professional sprint championship in 1899 and the National Cycling Association championship in 1900 (Figure 1.6). In 1901, he undertook a triumphant tour of Europe, proudly representing the United States (Figure 1.7) and subsequently competed mostly abroad, climbing to the pinnacle of the international sport. In Europe, between 1901 and 1909, he succeeded in maintaining a position as one of the best sprinters in the world, although his American career was effectively extinguished by the racism he continued to encounter at home. Returning in 1902 from his second successful European season, Taylor was greeted with the renewed and organized hostility of the white riders. 'Major Taylor has been harassed to a point of desperation by these cheap fellows who seem determined that he shall not win the championship of America again', reported a New York newspaper.[58] A hero in France, in the United States Taylor was harassed and insulted by his fellow white competitors and had constant problems finding hotels and restaurants willing to serve him when he was on the road. It is not surprising that he refused to compete in any American championship after 1902, and made contracts only with his trusted French promoter, Robert Coquelle, to race in Europe and Australia.

FIGURE 1.6
As a professional, Major Taylor established world records riding the technologically advanced chainless
transmission manufactured by the Sager Gear Company
(Author's collection)

In spite of the League's racist 'white only' policy voted into existence in Louisville in 1894, the liberal factions within the organization appear to have struggled to treat Major Taylor fairly and respectfully. Between 1896 and 1899, the League licensed him and allowed him to compete in its races. After a long struggle, the League gave up its control of professional racing in 1900, and Taylor was no longer affiliated with it. The almost total exclusion of Major Taylor from American bicycle racing occurred after 1901, when the League's rival, the National Cycling Association, had taken over control of the professional sport. In April 1901, while Taylor was in Paris, he was reported by the *Worcester*

FIGURE 1.7
At the peak of his international athletic career, Major Taylor posed in Paris with
his French manager, promoter and journalist Victor Breyer
(Author's collection)

Telegram as 'the best advertized sporting man in Europe at the present time ... Notices taking up columns are the general rule ... The races in which he competes will mark an epoch in the history of cycle racing in France, judging by the intense interest taken in him now.'[59] A month later, the same newspaper called him the 'King of Paris'.[60] A French journalist wrote to a friend in Chicago that he was 'literally amazed to find Taylor better educated than the average foreigner who comes over and possessed of far better manners than our own riders'.[61] Although he was phenomenally successful in Europe and Australia, Taylor was no longer prepared to endure the constant abuse he had to encounter in the United States. The superb Frank Kramer reigned as American professional sprint champion from 1902, and the sport itself suffered as the young Kramer went unchallenged by a Major Taylor absolutely in his prime. Major Taylor versus Kramer in a regular contest for the championship of America in the years from 1902 to 1910 would certainly have created a highly profitable box-office for promoters.[62]

Major Taylor's career in sport was thus, for its entire duration from 1893 to 1910, a litmus test of racist attitudes within American society at large.[63] These attitudes were expressed on a formal, institutional level by the legislation fought over within the League of American Wheelmen. In spite of concerted attempts to exclude him totally from cycling, Taylor insisted on his right to compete and battled his way to the very top of his profession, winning championships and setting world records, and proving that he was capable of satisfying the publicity needs of his sponsors. Open and honest recognition of his world class was, however, only possible in Europe, where racism did not dominate the fair evaluation of his athletic status. Even though his highly successful career was deeply scarred by the racism which he encountered and against which he had to fight constantly in America, Major Taylor – a devout Christian who refused to race on Sundays – struggled heroically to avoid a vindictive attitude.

In his autobiography, *The Fastest Bicycle Rider in the World*, written towards the end of his life and self-published in 1928, a book in which for personal reasons he was under pressure not to give an emotionally committed, fully detailed account of his extraordinary life experiences, Major Taylor explained why he had retired from bicycle racing, and wrote of:

> the great mental strain that beset me in those races, and the utter
> exhaustion which I felt on the many occasions after I had battled

under bitter odds against the monster prejudice, both on and off the track. In most of my races I not only struggled for victory, but also for my very life and limb. Only my dauntless courage and the indomitable fighting spirit I possessed allowed me to carry on in the face of tremendous odds.[64]

He went on to speak of his struggle to accept and forgive the hostility which had been directed against him:

Notwithstanding the bitterness and cruel practices of the white bicycle riders, their friends and sympathizers, against me, I hold no animosity toward any man. This includes those who so bitterly opposed me and did everything possible to injure me and prevent my success ... Life is too short for a man to hold bitterness in his heart ... In fact I have never hated any rider I ever competed against. As the late Booker T. Washington, the great Negro educator, so beautifully expressed it, 'I shall allow no man to narrow my soul and drag me down, by making me hate him'.[65]

A BRIEF CHRONOLOGY OF MAJOR TAYLOR'S LIFE AND CYCLING CAREER

26 Nov. 1878   Born in Indianapolis, Indiana.

1891–95   Worked in Indianapolis bicycle shops; amateur cycling career resulting in his status as 'colored' champion of America.

1896   Became a professional; Six Day race, Madison Square Garden, NY.

1897   Member of Boston pursuit team which beat a Philadelphia team in a five mile race, probably the first formally integrated team in professional cycling; Taylor was fiercely resisted and excluded from LAW national professional sprint championship circuit.

1898   Taylor's presence on the LAW circuit again resisted while he climbed to second place in the standings; championship could not be decided because of rift between the LAW and the rival, breakaway professional organization, the National Cycling Association.

August, set 1 mile world record (1m 41 2/5s, standing

start, paced), in match against Jimmy Michael.

Nov., riding a chainless bicycle, Taylor broke 1 mile world record (paced, 1m 31 4/5s); ended season holding 7 world records between ¼ and 2 miles.

1899 July, 1 mile world record in Chicago (1m 22 2/5s, paced).

Aug., 1 mile World Championship, Montreal.

Nov., 1 mile world record in Chicago (1m 19s – 46.56 mph, paced).

Two American sprint championships run in parallel, by LAW and NCA; Taylor won the LAW contest, while Tom Cooper won the NCA contest.

1900 First place, US National Cycling Association professional sprint championship, Frank Kramer – second.

1901 March–June, First European tour; won matches against all European sprint champions, Willi Arend (Germany), Thorwald Ellegaard (Denmark), Louis Grogna (Belgium), Gascoyne (England) and Edmond Jacquelin (France).

US professional championship won by Frank Kramer, Major Taylor second; Taylor continued to meet racist opposition in the United States.

1902 Second European tour based in Paris.

Fierce racist opposition from Kramer, Lawson and McFarland on the professional championship circuit effectively excluded Taylor, who subsequently hardly competed in the United States.

1902–3 First Australian tour.

1903 Third European tour based in Paris.

1903–4 Second Australian tour; birth in Sydney, Australia, 11 May 1904, of Taylor's only child.

1904–6 Temporary retirement.

1907–9 Came out of retirement for three further European seasons based in Paris.

1910 Retirement from racing; lived in Worcester, MA from then on.

1932 Died 21 June in Chicago, and was buried there.

1948 Reburial, with memorial.

NOTES

1. An account of the League of American Wheelmen and race relations in the 1890s can be found in A. Ritchie, *Major Taylor: The Extraordinary Career of a Champion Bicycle Racer* (Baltimore: Johns Hopkins University Press, 1996), Ch. 3, 'Bicycle Boom and Jim Crow', pp. 29–42, upon which this article is partially based. See also A. Ritchie, 'Major Taylor and the League of American Wheelmen's "Color Barrier"', *Bicycle USA* (Magazine of the League of American Bicyclists), Sept./Oct. 1999, 9–11.

2. See C.E. Pratt, 'Our First Bicycle Club', *The Wheelmen*, March 1883, 401–12.

3. C.E. Pratt, *The American Bicycler: A Manual for the Observer, the Learner, and the Expert* (Boston: Private Printing, 2nd edn, 1880), pp.245–7; C.W. Nairn and H. Sturmey, *The Cyclist and Wheel World Annual* (Coventry and London: Iliffe, 1882), pp.281–7.

4. Various accounts document the creation of this national organization: K. Kron, *Ten Thousand Miles on a Bicycle* (New York: Karl Kron, 1887), Ch. XXXVI, 'The League of American Wheelmen', pp. 615–33; C.E. Pratt, 'The LAW and Legal Rights', *Outing, an Illustrated Monthly Magazine of Sport, Travel and Recreation* (Jan. 1886), 454–6; Editorial, 'The League in 1886', *LAW Bulletin*, 31 Dec. 1886; 'The Founding of the LAW', *LAW Bulletin* (Aug. 1887), 83; C.E. Pratt, 'A Sketch of American Bicycling and its Founder', *Outing*, (July 1891), pp.342–9; A. Bassett, 'The League of American Wheelmen – Items from Its History', in L. H. Porter, *Wheels and Wheeling* (Boston, Wheelman Company, 1892), pp. 10–26; A. Bassett (Secretary of the LAW), 'League of American Wheelmen, A Concise History of the Great Bicycle Organization', *Louisville Courier-Journal*, 9 Aug. 1896.

5. It is not often remarked that cyclists were the first users to make modern demands on the neglected and inadequate roads of the United States. Cycling in its broadest sense, that is both as a recreation and a utility, was seen as something to be encouraged and which could give great benefit. Racers, too, could go faster on better roads. The Good Roads movement drew cyclists into local activism. The whole question of the LAW and the Good Roads Movement is very ably covered in P.P. Mason, 'The League of American Wheelmen and the Good Roads Movement, 1880–1905' (unpublished Ph.D. thesis, University of Michigan, 1957).

6. *Bicycling World*, which ran continuously through the 1880s and 1890s, contained ongoing accounts of LAW activity and racing, and at various times was published in Boston as the official organ of the League, which also contracted briefly with *Amateur Athlete* to do the same thing before struggling to make an economic success of publishing its own house journal, *League of American Wheelmen Bulletin*, first published in July 1885.

7. Figures quoted in P.P. Mason, 'League of American Wheelmen'. The wider reasons for the decline of the bicycle 'boom' still remain to be thoroughly researched. Contrary to often-stated speculation, the automobile cannot be credited with the decline in sales of bicycles and membership in the LAW, as popular ownership of the automobile did not come until much later. More likely, cheaper urban street-car transportation absorbed some of the heavy bicycle traffic of the 1890s, sales declined because many people already owned a used bicycle, and recreational use declined after an initial surge of popularity.

8. The 1880 (second) edition of Pratt, *The American Bicycler* (see Note 2 above) documented activity since 1878 to exclude professionals from amateur cycling, and gave evidence that the new sport of cycling was defined in the context of other already existing sports:

> Since the first edition of this book was issued many more of the clubs have adopted rules defining and excluding professionals. These rules are nearly uniform in substance, though not in phrase, and some of them are already accessible in print. The National Association of Amateur Athletes of America is at present the highest and most widely recognized authority on such matters in this country, and has within a year adopted and promulgated a definition which might well be taken verbatim as a standard and universal rule on the subject. It is as follows: 'An amateur is any person who has never competed in an open competition, or for a stake, or for public money, or for gate-money, or under a false name, or with a professional for a prize, or where gate-money is charged; nor has ever, at any period of his life, taught or pursued athletic exercises as a means of livelihood' (p.244).

This definition was essentially identical to the definition of amateurism already established by the English Bicycle Union.

9. The annual League Conventions and League race meetings (which were not always the races where National Championships were decided those later were contested on a points basis over a series of events) were held at the following locations: 1880 – Newport, 1881 – Boston, 1882 – Chicago, 1883 – New York, 1884 – Washington, DC, 1885 – Buffalo, 1886 – Boston, 1887 – St Louis, 1888 – Baltimore, 1889 – Hagerstown, PA, 1890 – Niagara Falls, NY, 1891 – Detroit, 1892 – Washington, DC, 1893 – Chicago, 1894 – Denver, 1895 – New York, 1896 – Baltimore, 1897 – Philadelphia.

10. 'Sterling' Elliott, 'Our Colored Brother', *Bicycling World and LAW Bulletin*, 3 June 1892.

11. 'Sterling' Elliott, 'Our Colored Brother Again', *Bicycling World and LAW Bulletin*, 1 July 1892.

12. 'Are They Any Better Off?', *The Wheelmen's Gazette*, (Indianapolis) (March 1893), 43.

13. See *Boston Globe*, 25 Feb. 1894 – 'Last year there were less than 20 colored members in the entire organization, as reported by Secretary Bassett at Philadelphia, and there cannot be more than 50 now at the greatest number', and *Bearings*, 7 Jan. 1897, 'It has been proven that the several hundred colored riders who have been members of the League for several years have always conducted themselves as well as their white brethren'.

14. R. Hennessy, 'It looks bad for the colored cycler', *The Wheelmen's Gazette*, (May 1893), 71.

15. R. Hennessy, 'The North, the South and the Color Line', *The Wheelmen's Gazette*, (Nov. 1893), 169.

16. 'The Exclusion of Negro Wheelmen', *Outing*, (April 1894), 14.

17. Both reactions quoted from *Louisville Courier-Journal*, 18 Feb. 1894.

18. *Louisville Courier-Journal*, 20 Feb. 1894 gave the following League membership information: total membership, 36,950, a gain of 1,989 over the 1893 total; new members, 13,411; Atlantic Coast membership – 22,487, Middle States – 11,597, Mississippi Valley – 5,691, west of Rocky Mountains – 1,639, Pacific Coast – 1,183, New England – 10,139, South of Mason-Dixon line – 3,345.

19. Accounts of the 1894 Louisville convention can be found in: *Bearings*, 23 Feb., 2 March, 9 March, 30 March 1894; *Outing*, April, May, June 1894; *Cycling Life*, 29 March 1894; *The Referee*, 30 March 1894 and 8 Feb. 1895. There is news coverage in *Louisville Courier-Journal*, 17–21 Feb. 1894, *Louisville Evening Times*, 17–21 Feb. 1894, and *Louisville Commercial*, 17–21 Feb. 1894.

20. 'Cyclists in Session', *Louisville Courier-Journal*, 20 Feb. 1894.

21. 'Cycling Celebrities', *Louisville Courier-Journal*, 18 Feb. 1894.

22. *Bearings*, 23 Feb. 1894. Another account, in the *Louisville Evening Times*, 20 Feb. 1894, reported in similar terms, Scott having said that 'the colored wheelmen do not care to go into a body in which they are not wholly welcome, and recognizing the situation, and being desirous of seeing the bone of contention removed from an organization which benefits every man with a wheel, whether a member or not, they favor the drawing of the color line'.

23. 'The Exclusion of Negro Wheelmen', *Outing*, (April 1894).

24. 'All Questions Settled', *Louisville Courier-Journal*, 21 Feb. 1894.

25. *Louisville Commercial*, 19 Feb. 1894.

26. *Louisville Evening Times*, 20 Feb. 1894; *Bearings*, 23 Feb. 1894; according to *LAW Bulletin* (July 1885), 37, membership regulations already included the word 'white', leading to the assumption that at some stage in the later 1880s, 'white' was removed from regulations. I have not been able to document exactly when this occurred.

27. 'Drew the Color Line', *Louisville Evening Times*, 20 Feb. 1894.

28. *Bearings*, 2 March 1894.

29. *New York Tribune*, undated, quoted in Robert Smith, *A Social History of the Bicycle* (1972), p.163

30. *Bearings*, 2 March 1894. Teamoh was described (*Bearings*, 9 March 1894) as 'a young colored politician with more push and nerve than brilliance and more of the quality which sometimes places him in social gatherings where he might better be conspicuous by his absence'.

31. 'Negroes are Indignant – Massachusetts Colored Men Trying to Arouse Public Sympathy', *Bearings*, 9 March 1894.

32. 'Mr Scott, colored, Replies', *Bearings*, 30 March 1894.

33. *Bearings*, 30 March 1894. The whiskey given out to the delegates was evidently also given to the black members of the Union Cycle Club.
34. *The Referee*, 30 March 1894.
35. *Outing*, (May 1894), p.43.
36. The Fourteenth Amendment states – 'No State shall make or enforce any law which shall abridge the privileges of citizens of the United States, nor shall any State ... deny to any person ... the equal protection of the laws.'
37. Information cited in L. Hughes and M. Meltzer, *A Pictorial History of the Negro in America* (New York: Crown Publishers, 1956), p. 232.
38. 'A Precarious Position', *The Referee*, (Feb. 1895).
39. 'The National Assembly – The Colored Brother Again Side-tracked', *Southern Cycler* (Louisville, Kentucky) (March 1895).
40. *(Worcester?) Telegram*, 10 July 1895.
41. 'The Knox Incident', *Southern Cycler*, (Aug. 1895).
42. 'Organizing a colored League', *Bearings*, 30 July 1896.
43. 'Colored Riders Arrange a Meet', *San Francisco Call*, 12 July 1896.
44. '"Kemble Illustrates the Picaninny Club Awheel; a Brush with Brack (*sic*) Trash"', *San Francisco Examiner*, 8 Aug. 1897.
45. 'Colored Cyclists Want Recognition', *San Francisco Call*, 20 April 1897.
46. 'Will Demand Admission', *Bearings*, 7 Jan. 1897.
47. See E. Jones, 'Diversity: A New Look at an Old Challenge', Editorial in *Bicycle USA*, (Sept./Oct. 1999).
48. *Outing*, (June 1894).
49. The League of American Wheelmen professional championships were decided out on a 'circuit', which carried the riders all over the country in a series of identified championship contests, to take the racing to as wide an audience as possible. Major Taylor's entries to races in the South were rejected by promoters, which meant that it was impossible for him to win points in those events.
50. The white riders were Nat and Frank Butler, Burns Pierce and Eddie McDuffie. This may have been the earliest integrated team in American bicycle racing. See Ritchie, *Major Taylor*, pp.69–70.
51. *New York Sun*, 18 Sept. 1897.
52. *Worcester Telegram*, 20 Sept. 1897.
53. *Bicycling World*, 1 Oct. 1897; also 'Choked Taylor – Police Had to Interfere at Taunton – Becker Pulled the Major From His Bicycle', *Boston Globe*, 24 Sept. 1897.
54. Unidentified newspaper clipping in Taylor scrapbook, Indianapolis Historical Museum.
55. *Worcester Telegram*, report from late July 1898, newspaper clipping in Taylor scrapbook, Indianapolis Historical Museum. It should be emphasized here the extent to which bicycle racing on the track is a tactical sport, in which advantage is gained from riding in the slipstream of another rider. Having to ride from the front is therefore a severe tactical disadvantage.
56. *Worcester Spy*, 29 April 1900, also published in *Cycling Gazette*.
57. Ritchie, *Major Taylor*.
58. Unidentified New York newspaper clipping in Taylor scrapbook, Indianapolis Historical Museum.
59. *Worcester Telegram*, 8 April 1901.
60. *Worcester Telegram*, 8 May 1901.
61. *Cycle Age*, 18 April 1901.
62. Kramer was second to Major Taylor in the 1900 National Cycling Association sprint championship, contested on a points basis. From 1901 onwards, Major Taylor did not contest the American championships and Kramer held the sprint title in an extraordinary unbroken run until 1916, with 16 consecutive titles. He won twice more, in 1918 and 1921, before retiring.
63. In terms of chronological priority, Taylor's career as a pioneer black athlete was very early. When Taylor won the world championship in Montreal in 1899, he became the second black world champion in any sport. The first was George Dixon, known as 'Little Chocolate', who won the bantam-weight world title by beating his British and American rivals in a series of fights through 1890 and 1891 and defended it until 1900. According to N. Fleischer, *Black*

Dynamite, the Story of the Negro in the Prize Ring from 1782–1938 (New York: C.J. O'Brien, 1938), 'He lived a life of dissipation. After winning the title, wine, women and song were sweet music to his ears. He made a fortune and he squandered it'. Boxer Jack Johnson's world heavyweight championship did not occur until 1908, Joe Louis' defeat of Max Schmeling for the world championship did not occur until 1938 and Jackie Robinson was not integrated into professional baseball as a member of the Brooklyn Dodgers until 1946.

64. Major Taylor, *The Fastest Bicycle Rider in the World* (Worcester, MA: Wormley Publishing Company, 1928), p.420.

65. Ibid., p.422.

2

'Curt Flood Stood Up for Us': The Quest to Break Down Racial Barriers and Structural Inequality in Major League Baseball

MICHAEL E. LOMAX

On 8 October 1969, the St Louis Cardinals and Philadelphia Phillies completed a seven-player trade. The Cardinals traded Tim McCarver, Joe Hoerner, Byron Browne and Curt Flood to the Phillies for Richie Allen, Cookie Rojas and Jerry Johnson. When he heard that he would be traded to the Phillies, Curt Flood said that he would retire from baseball. He felt that after 12 years in the big leagues, he deserved something more dignified than an impersonal phone call and a little card in the mail telling him that he was traded. But instead of retiring, Flood stayed on to challenge Organized Baseball's perpetual reserve clause, which gave the owners a virtual hegemony over their players for 90 years.[1]

Previous research into this issue has focused on the Flood case within the broader context of the fight of the Major League Baseball Players Association (MLBPA) against the reserve system. It shows how the Flood case was a court test of the reserve clause, analyses the tactics utilized by lawyers on both sides, and traces the events leading to its defeat in the Supreme Court. While the Supreme Court refused to overturn Major League Baseball's anti-trust exemption, the Court termed baseball's exemption an 'anomaly' and an 'aberration' in the light of other professional sports anti-trust liabilities.[2]

Critical evaluation of it has enhanced our understanding of the Flood trial in the context of Organized Baseball's post-Second World War labour relations. By 1968, Curt Flood had reached his peak as a ball player and was recognized as the best centerfielder in baseball. At the same time, he had developed a reputation as a businessman. However, the research does not adequately explain why Flood would have risked sullying all of his achievements by challenging the baseball establishment. Previous scholars give little insight into how Flood's experiences as a ballplayer in the Major and Minor Leagues led him to challenge baseball's reserve system. The studies overlook the impact which several influential people, such as his business partner John Jorgenson, had on shaping his aspiration to dismantle the barriers to racial and structural equality. This paper, therefore, attempts to analyze the forces that led to Flood's challenge of Organized Baseball's reserve system. Four themes will serve to guide the narrative: first, the impact several mentors had on shaping his perspective on race relations and influencing his career aspirations; second, how his minor league experience fuelled his desire to succeed and to combat discrimination; third, his quest for racial harmony among the Cardinal players; and finally, the factors leading to his decision to challenge the baseball establishment.

Curt Flood sought an 'equal opportunity' to compete within professional baseball and American society, without the debilitating restriction of race. Both his exploits on the diamond and his entrepreneurial endeavours highlighted Flood's dream of 'freedom' – social acceptance and upward mobility within the very centres of corporate power. Once he established himself as a ballplayer and businessman, Flood agitated for change with the ambition of achieving racial and structural equality. Like other African American ballplayers of his era, he was influenced by the dramatic changes in the economy, in demography and in American racial attitudes. Flood expected to live in a new America, in a new sports world. By 1969, however, the shock of the tongue-lashing which Cardinals owner August A. Busch gave to the club during spring training, the Cardinal's dismal fourth place finish, and Flood's trade to Philadelphia, all served to dash Flood's pursuit of the American dream. His mood reflected the disillusionment with white society which set the tone for the Civil Rights Movement as it entered its Black Power phase. Instead of seeking out various civil rights organizations to challenge the baseball establishment, Curt Flood turned to the MLBPA to combat the game's long-standing reserve clause. By turning to the MLBPA for support, Curt Flood's case became the players' case, although he fought the battle alone. He served to raise the consciousness of everyone involved in baseball by questioning why the national pastime should be granted a license to operate as a monopoly. While Flood's place in baseball history was not as important as Jackie Robinson's, his decision to challenge the reserve system took at least as much courage.

Curtis Charles Flood was born in Houston, Texas, on 18 January 1938. His family moved to Oakland, California when Curt was ten, at a time when the East Bay Region was undergoing a dramatic transformation. Oakland was located in the middle of an extensive zone of shipyards and other defense industries that attracted thousands of migrants, both black and white. Flood's parents were employed in the health care industry as menials, his father, Herman Flood Sr., working two jobs at the same occupation. Curt's mother, Barbara, mended parachutes on a piecework basis, to make extra income.[3] Curt's father sparked his son's interest in drawing. He constantly bought sketchpads so all the children could draw, and from the outset Curt and his older brother, Carl, exhibited the potential to become artists. Flood stated that it was a reward to their parents to see their children 'sprawled on the living room floor, engrossed in a pastime so remote from the meanness of the streets'. Flood's parents harboured a vision of middle-class respectability for their children. Like many African-American parents of low socio-economic status, the Floods sought to raise upright children, achieve a degree of economic prosperity and become model citizens in American society.[4]

Flood began playing baseball at the age of nine as a catcher for Junior's Sweet Shop, a club sponsored by the police in the midget league. Simultaneously, he met George Powles, who became one of the best baseball coaches on the West Coast. At McClymonds High School, Powles helped to develop many big league stars, like Frank Robinson, Vada Pinson, Billy Martin and Joe Morgan. He also helped Boston Celtic star centre Bill Russell. Powles was a thorough and patient teacher, stressing the importance of mastering the fundamentals of baseball. He was not only instrumental in helping Flood reach his potential as a ballplayer, but Powles also influenced Flood's views on race relations.[5] As a mentor, Powles pointed out that Flood had the ability to become a professional ball player, while at the same time citing some obstacles the young Californian would confront, primarily being both small in stature and a Negro. He also indicated that no matter what Flood did, some people would try to marginalize his accomplishments. Much of this advice proved alien to Flood. He was not yet mature enough to recognize discrimination on the basis of size or race. In fact, the very expression of racism and structural inequality, the ghetto, served to isolate him from discrimination. It was only after he left the Oakland ghetto that Flood began to understand the message Powles had attempted to convey to him.[6]

In 1956, the Cincinnati Reds signed Curt Flood to a one-year contract for $4,000, with no signing bonus. Reds scout Bobby Mattituck promised Flood that he would get a real shot with a superior minor league club, just as Frank Robinson had the year before. He would train with the Reds at their spring training base in Tampa, Florida before being assigned to a minor league club. Flood was about to experience his first lesson in race relations, outside of Oakland's segregated walls. Upon arriving in Tampa, Florida, Curt Flood experienced the initial phase of being indoctrinated into 'Jim Crow' segregation. It began with a chilly reception at the Reds' hotel. At the front desk, Flood was instructed to follow a bellhop who led him through the lobby to a side door, and the bellhop told a black cab driver to take Flood to 'Ma Felder's'. 'Until it happens you literally cannot believe it', Flood explained. 'After it happens, you need time to absorb it.' The cab driver drove Flood five miles outside of town to Ma Felder's boardinghouse. There, he met Frank Robinson, George Crowe, Chuck Harmon, Joe Black and Brooks Lawrence. While many of the older players did not mind living in the boarding houses, the initial experience of Jim Crow left a lasting impression on Flood.[7]

At the conclusion of spring training, the Reds assigned Flood to the High Point-Thomasville club in the Class B Carolina League. Both High Point and Thomasville were small industrial centres located 20 miles southwest of Greensboro, North Carolina. Hailed as the leading furniture manufacturing centre in the South, High Point rivaled Chicago and Grand Rapids, Michigan, in furniture production at the end of the Second World War. Seeking to capitalize on this opportunity presented by the Reds, Flood sought to make a good impression on the High Point-Thomasville fans, find a nice apartment, and establish himself as a 'respectable' citizen within the community. He would then proceed from Class B to the fame and fortune that awaited him and within one year be promoted to the major leagues.[8]

However, the naive, young Californian was about to receive his second serving of Jim Crow segregation. His bus ride to this industrial village was marred by racial slurs directed at him. When the bus reached Fayetteville, North Carolina, Flood overheard an individual say, 'There's a goddamned nigger son-of-bitch playing ball with them white boys! I'm leaving.' Most of the players were offended by Flood's presence and would not socialize with him even off the field. White players who did not share those sentiments were intimidated by those who did. Team manager Bert Haas made it clear that his life was sufficiently difficult without any added pressure brought on by Flood. According to baseball legend Henry Aaron, the hatred in the Carolina League sent Flood back to his room in tears.[9] Nothing illustrated this alienation better than the 'Meet the Hi-Toms Day' at various businesses in the High Point and Thomasville communities. Various players would spend the day at a local business, such as the Hudson-Belk Co. in Thomasville, to stimulate fan interest and promote the team's sponsors. Of the businesses which participated in this event, not one invited either Flood or the club's other minority players, Orlando Pena or Johnny Ivory Smith.[10]

This alienation sparked the same kind of emotion in Flood that would ignite the riots in Harlem, Detroit, and Newark – black rage. Instead of engaging in destructive behaviour, however, Flood vented his anger on Carolina League pitching with his bat. He broke the Hi-Toms' records in home runs, runs batted in, and stolen bases. He was a unanimous choice for several all-star teams. Flood was voted the 'Most Popular Hi-Tom of 1956' by the fans; he was also voted the Carolina League's Player of the Year. Bert Haas wrote: 'Curt Flood has certainly come through wonderfully. He's been worth his weight in gold … and he's proved to be invaluable on the base paths and there isn't a better defensive outfielder in Class B ball.' This was an ironic statement from a man who at first told the Californian not to make waves.[11]

Flood's accomplishments with the Hi-Toms established him as a star player and also served to free him from the Carolina League. Enduring the League's version of Jim Crow served only to spur him to perform at a level that ensured he would never return there. During a pre-game practice toward midseason, a little black child jumped onto the field, grabbed a loose ball, and climbed back into the stands. A Hi-Toms pitcher screamed: 'Hey you black nigger, come back with that ball!' He proceeded to jump into the stands, took the ball from the child, and returned to the field. Flood was waiting when the pitcher returned to the field. 'Don't use that word around me', Flood growled, 'You owe more respect than that. White kids steal baseballs all the time without interference.' Flood added, 'I was hoping that he would swing at me, but he skulked off and gave me a wide berth for the rest of the season. His peers became more civil now that they sensed my rage.' In essence, the incident typified Flood's willingness to stand up for those who could not or would not stand up for themselves.[12]

By the end of the year, Flood had adjusted to the abuse from the stands. He developed rationalizations for the fans' behaviour. Because they were little men, the opportunity to insult a baseball player served to increase their stature; they were beneath his contempt. Besides, his .340 batting average was his response to the insults and abuse from both players and fans. Striving to perform at a high level became his goal to insure his '[emancipation] from North Carolina for keeps'. Flood added: 'I believe that I would have quit baseball [rather] than return there.'[13]

In 1957, the Reds assigned Flood to the Savannah Redlegs of the Class A South Atlantic League. He arrived in Savannah while Georgia Governor Marvin Griffin was leading a massive resistance movement against federally-mandated school desegregation. At the same time, extreme segregationists attempted to pass a state law prohibiting all interracial sporting events. Although the bill was defeated, Georgia law still prohibited blacks and whites from sharing the same locker room. Thus a separate cubicle was constructed for Flood, Johnny Ivory Smith and Leo Cardenas, a Cuban shortstop who would later play for the Cincinnati Reds and the Minnesota Twins.[14] Some of the white players detested the dressing arrangement and other various Jim Crow customs imposed upon these minority players. Buddy Gilbert, the Redlegs's star centrefielder, brought food to Flood, Smith and Cardenas in the bus, so that they would not have to wait at the back door of a restaurant. But of all the indignities, none angered Flood more than the 'routine on the bus'. Nothing humiliated black players more than waiting on a bus while their teammates ate in a restaurant. After playing a doubleheader, it was 'absolutely maddening to sit all sweaty and sticky and funky in the rotten bus instead of walking like a human being into a restaurant'. Benevolence from players like Gilbert, though well intentioned, only served to exacerbate the system of caste.[15]

These indignities did not affect Flood's fiery competitiveness on the field. On 10 July 1957, the Macon Dodgers beat the Redlegs 4–2 in a game played under protest by Savannah manager Jim Brown. According to the *Savannah Morning News*, Flood 'kicked so strenuously on a close play in the fifth [inning], that he was thumbed out [of] the game'. He had moved from the outfield to third base, with the intention of replacing Cincinnati's third baseman, Don Hoak. He batted over .300 and made the South Atlantic League All-Star team at third base. Savannah manager Jim Brown stated that Flood had the potential to play third base in the majors, and after a couple of years at the position the Californian would make the transition. He already had the ability to hit 'big-league' pitching. Flood had accomplished all this in spite of the racial indignities he had endured, and a sore spot on his right arm that would, according to Savannah sportswriter Archie Whitfield, have '[sent] me to bed with medical counsel on hand around the clock'.[16]

However, Flood's 41 errors at third base were more than the Cincinnati organization could bear. At the end of the 1957 season, the Reds traded Flood to the St Louis Cardinals. The Reds were more impressed with Vada Pinson's work in the minors during the same season, and because he was bigger and faster, Flood became expendable. Although he was only 19, the trade would have a significant impact on the young and sensitive Flood. In his view, the Reds had given up on him, choosing the bigger and faster Goliath over the smaller and more determined David. But the trade had also touched off a fierce determination in Flood.

'WITH ALL DELIBERATE SPEED': THE FIGHT AGAINST DISCRIMINATION AND THE QUEST FOR RACIAL HARMONY

From 1958 to 1960, Curt Flood's baseball career was mediocre at best. He started the 1958 season at the St Louis Triple-A farm club in Omaha, Nebraska, but after 15 games and a .340 batting average, Flood returned to the Cardinals. The black rage that ignited his desire to succeed resulted in him attempting to become a power hitter. Because of this tendency to swing for the fences, the ball club used Flood primarily as a defensive replacement. By 1961, three events occurred in Curt Flood's life that turned his career around.

The first was Cardinal teammate George Crowe's help. Flood said that Crowe knew 'more batting theory and was more articulate about [hitting] than anyone else on the Cardinals', and Crowe helped Flood improve his hitting style during the 1959 season.[17] Flood's tendency to swing for the fences led him to over swing and he developed a hitch in his swing. It resulted in him having trouble hitting above .250. Crowe taught Flood to shorten his stride and swing, eliminate the hitch, keep his head still and his stroke level. Crowe worked with Flood for hours, and his teaching paid dividends.

The black players' protest against segregated living conditions during spring training was the second event that transformed Flood's career. Objections to these living conditions from black stars like Henry Aaron and Bill White, and the stand taken by the National Association for the Advancement of Colored People (NAACP) official Ralph

Wimbish, had an impact upon Flood's life. A prominent member of the black community in St Petersburg, Florida, and a medical doctor, Wimbish was the president of the local chapter of the NAACP. He played an important role in the struggle to end segregation in the 'capital' of spring training. He had also spearheaded a successful drive to desegregate several variety and department store lunch counters. Wimbish owned rental property and for years reaped the financial rewards that came with housing black players in St Petersburg for the New York Yankees and St Louis Cardinals. But in an era that historians August Meier and John Bracey referred to as a 'revolution in expectations among American blacks', Wimbish came to terms with the paradox of the practice. He came to the conclusion that in lodging black players, he was contributing to forced segregation and was, therefore, in conflict with the very cause he was fighting for – racial equality.[18]

At a press conference on 31 January 1961, Wimbish told reporters he would no longer act as the Yankees's unofficial housing representative. He had located accommodation for black players for years and had even housed Elston Howard in his own home. To demonstrate his commitment, Wimbish announced that he would not offer Howard accommodation that season and urged other black landlords to follow suit. He also called on Yankees and Cardinals officials to push for an end to segregated practices at their respective headquarters, the Vinoy Park and Soreno hotels.[19] The following day, the *New York Times* reported that New York Yankees co-owner Dan Topping had taken what appeared to be the first steps towards ending segregation at the American League champion's spring training camp. Topping said that he would like to have the whole team – including the club's minority players Elston Howard, Hector Lopez and Jesse Gonder – 'under one roof'. He added that it was time for the Yankees and the St Louis Cardinals to take the initial steps to end segregation. On the other hand, Cardinal's General Manager Bing Devine was cautious, stating that the Cardinals did not 'make the rules and regulations for the various localities'. Despite Topping's reported desire to end segregation, a spokesman for the Soreno said that the hotel remained firm on its policy of excluding blacks. The spokesman added that the Soreno would be happy to continue to house the Yankees 'on the same basis'. This 'same basis' meant, of course, that black players would have to seek separate accommodation.[20]

Concurrently, several black players voiced their opposition to the segregated living arrangements. This was in response to statements made by Milwaukee Braves' Executive Vice-President, George 'Birdie' Tebbetts, who declared that racial segregation had never presented a problem for the Braves in spring training in Bradenton, Florida. When asked if the Braves planned to follow the lead of the Yankees in attempting to house black and white players at the same hotels, Tebbetts replied that such a problem did not exist among the Braves' black players. However, he added, if any of their black players requested hotel accommodation, the organization would attempt to accommodate them.[21]

Braves' outfielders Henry Aaron and Wes Covington were outspoken in their dissatisfaction with the living arrangements. The Braves' black players, said Aaron, 'resented having to live away from the rest of the club'. Their feelings were never made known because no one had asked them. When it was pointed out that Tebbetts had 'carefully selected' the black players' accommodation, Aaron responded: 'Carefully selected? From what? There's not but one place down here for us to stay in.' Covington, on the other hand, pointed out that the situation did not affect him directly, because he owned a home in Bradenton. He was, however, quick to point out how problematic it was when a black player brought his family to spring training: 'They [hotel and boarding house owners] see you coming and they want to make a fortune off you', he said. Black players received less than whites for the same money. Both Aaron and Covington claimed that there was no decent housing in Bradenton, and that most restaurants and entertainment outlets denied them service.[22]

In Florida, several black players spoke out against the indignities of Jim Crow segregation. New York Yankees catcher Elston Howard pointed out that 'all players' should be accorded the same treatment off the field as on it. Detroit Tigers outfielder Bill Bruton pondered who or what gave anyone 'the idea that we [black players] shouldn't have wanted the same accommodations as were accorded the rest of the guys'. Perceptively he added: 'I realize the ball clubs are small compared to states, but they take a lot of money into the cities and they're important enough to be listened to.' Bruton continued: 'After all, take the Braves out of Bradenton and what have you got?' Cincinnati Reds outfielder Vada Pinson declared: 'Nobody enjoys being regarded as something inferior – not good enough to live with his brothers.' Pittsburgh Pirates outfielder Roberto Clemente indicated that he was 'against segregation in any form …', and that he 'didn't like it in Fort Myers and never will so long as we are treated on a segregated basis'.[23]

Curt Flood had also grown weary of deplorable living conditions. Before the start of spring training in 1961, Cardinals' General Manager Bing Devine called Flood into his office to discuss the living arrangements in Florida. According to Devine, Flood expressed his displeasure with the Florida situation. When he was told there was nothing the Cardinals could do about the situation, Flood retorted, 'train some place else'. When he was told moving would be expensive, Flood replied that baseball 'had a hundred years and money you haven't even counted'. What bothered Flood most was that white rookies got better treatment in Florida than black veterans. According to the *Pittsburgh Courier,* Flood complained: 'The rookie who is trying to win my job can bring his wife to camp and live in the most lavish surroundings. Me, I'm forced to leave my wife at home because we can't find a decent place to stay.'[24]

In March, another episode occurred that outraged the St Louis Cardinals' black members. The St Petersburg chamber of commerce sponsored an annual 'Salute to Baseball' breakfast in honour of the Yankees and Cardinals. Bill White and the other black players discovered they had been excluded from the invitation list. City and team officials declared that they had not intended for the breakfast to be a whites–only affair. Invitations were meant to include all team members, but White and the others had not found the invitations to be so explicit. They were fully aware that racial protocol called for the exclusion of blacks from such affairs.[25]

Following the lead of Ralph Wimbish and acting as the unofficial spokesman for the Cardinals's black players, Bill White used the incident to condemn publicly the discriminatory practices at spring training locations in Florida. The black players called for team officials to pressure their respective headquarters, the Vinoy Park and Soreno Hotels, to end their segregated practices. At first, the Cardinals management maintained a low profile, though Bing Devine admitted that the policies in spring training presented a problem. According to Bob Gibson, White mentioned the invitation list to Joe Reichler, an Associated Press sportswriter from St Louis. Reichler wrote a story which was published in a black newspaper in St Louis, calling for a boycott of Anheuser-Busch, the brewery which owned the Cardinals.[26] This unwanted publicity resulted in Cardinals owner August A. Busch, Jr., taking up the cause. Busch threatened to move the Cardinals if conditions did not change. Team officials in St Petersburg began working behind the scenes to arrange integrated living arrangements at hotels other than the Soreno and Vinoy Park. In 1962, the Colonial Inn housed the newly arriving New York Mets, while the Cardinals bought their own hotel in the St Petersburg area.[27]

The efforts to desegregate spring training facilities marked the start of Curt Flood's efforts, to eliminate racial barriers. Flood, among others, exemplified a new desire to speed up the dismantling of barriers to racial equality. Aaron maintained that blacks were among the best players in the National League and had earned the right to stay in big league hotels during spring training. Despite their exploits on the field, black players endured the same racial indignities that their parents' generation had experienced. Although it was not a coordinated effort, this generation of black players refused to accept the status quo. According to Vada Pinson, black players no longer wanted to be regarded as 'inferior', particularly when their performances on the field proved otherwise. Curt Flood, and others like him, expected to mature in a different America. Their youth had been marked by sweeping changes in the economy, in demography and in American racial attitudes. Their outspokenness reflected the changing racial landscape of the post-Second World War sports world.[28]

The final factor that transformed Flood's baseball career was the hiring of Cardinals manager Johnny Keane. Midway through the 1961 season, the Cardinals fired Solly Hemus and called Keane up from its Omaha farm club. Keane thought very highly of Flood and praised his performance at Omaha. According to Flood, the new Cardinals manager had been responsible for his escape from the minors in 1958. The day he took over the club, Keane had told Flood, 'You're my centerfielder.' Under Keane, Flood was allowed to 'do his thing'. He finished the 1961 season with a .322 batting average. Two years later, he led the National League in both at bats and runs scored, and batted .302. In 1964, Flood led the league in at bats and runs scored, batted .311, and was instrumental in the Cardinals winning the pennant and World Series.[29]

After establishing himself as a major league baseball player, Curt Flood sought other worlds to conquer. Following the lead of Bob Gibson, he strove for racial harmony among the Cardinal players. This had more to do with winning games, pennants and World Series, than with establishing social relationships off the field. Curt Flood's emergence as a major league star coincided with the movement of black athletes, freed from the insecurity of the early years of integration, and becoming increasingly outspoken against inequitable conditions. By the late 1950s, the last three major league clubs – the Philadelphia Phillies, the Detroit Tigers and the Boston Red Sox – integrated their all-white cast. For the first time several black athletes voiced a variety of complaints that included mistreatment in the minor leagues, the hated spring training ritual and the recurring problems in hotels. Although they earned relatively large salaries, black players still experienced discrimination when they attempted to buy homes in the cities in which they performed. Their hard-won success on the field did not bring rewards off it. Integrating the player force resulted in major league clubs having to deal with a more culturally diverse group, due to the influx of black and Latino players. This transition was often a rocky one.[30]

The efforts to break down racial barriers in spring training established a mood in the Cardinals, particularly among blacks, to eliminate similar obstacles within the club. Led by Bob Gibson, Curt Flood and Bill White, the objective was purely an economic one. It began with both Gibson and Flood 'deliberately kicking over traditional barriers to establish communication with [whites]'. Essentially, at the end of a game, blacks had gone to their own social world and whites to theirs. In order to break this pattern, Gibson and Flood began asking white players – many of whom had never socialized with blacks before – to have a drink after a game. They were rejected more than once, but Gibson and Flood persevered and before long the spirit became contagious. After all, black players had proven their worth on the field and the social experiment was merely an effort to establish comfort zones between the races. This socialization process, which took approximately five to six years, led to the development of an overused cliché in team sports – 'chemistry'.[31]

To sustain this 'chemistry', a network emerged between a core of black and white players. According to Gibson, if a player was indicted for a racial offence, either White or the Cardinals pitcher would confront the offender and tell them that such behaviour would not be tolerated. In addition to White, Gibson and Flood, white players Ken Boyer, Tim McCarver and Mike Shannon assisted in helping to maintain racial harmony. Even if these players disagreed on a particular issue, like interracial marriage, they maintained a climate of tolerance so that they could express their respective positions. Flood and Gibson were proud of the legacy. As Flood pointed out, 'The men of that team were as close to being free of racist poison as a diverse group of twentieth century Americans could possibly be'.[32]

The legacy of racial harmony was negotiated among the players themselves, without the assistance of management or any other external group. This relationship was forged out of the fact that black players demonstrated their ability to win ball games, and their presence on the field did not repel white fan support. Racial harmony among the Cardinals represented the ideal of integration. Black and white ball-players worked together in reaching their ultimate objectives – National League (NL) pennants and World Series championships. In this way, the St Louis Cardinals exemplified an ideal image of blacks and whites cooperating for the good of the race and the nation. African-American ballplayers were, however, well aware of what was happening to their people outside the sports world. By 1963, Sheriff Bull Connor commanded Birmingham firemen to turn their hoses on civil rights demonstrators. In late August, Martin Luther King led a quarter of a million people on the March to Washington and delivered his often quoted 'I Have a Dream' speech. A little over two weeks later, a bomb exploded at the Sixteenth Street Baptist Church in Birmingham, killing four little girls who had arrived for Sunday school. As Henry Aaron explained: 'The national climate called attention to our [ballplayers] color, and we knew we were being watched.' He added: 'We had targets on our backs and two things on our side: each other to lean on and our Louisville Sluggers to swing.'[33]

The efforts of Curt Flood and Bob Gibson to create a harmonious relationship with their white teammates coincided with the rise of the sit-in movement, resulting in a wave of non-violent direct action protests. Unlike student activists, black players were limited in the ways in which they could challenge the status quo. But black players, like whites, were well aware of the power of the owners. Instead of sit-ins and boycotts, black players, according to Aaron, 'leaned hard and swung from the heels, and there was hell to pay if you hung a curve ball'. Their performances on the diamond were remarkable. All the ten National League homerun leaders of the 1960s were either black or Latino. In an analysis of batting averages and homeruns, 37 of 50 batting leaders and 41 of 50 homerun leaders were either black or Latino. A white player did not even finish second in homeruns during the decade. Concurrently, African-American and Latin players won the National League Most Valuable Player award on seven occasions. Considering the constraints on African-American players, their performance on the field repre-sented their challenge of the status quo. Their success had conspired to raise their aspirations, to fuel their hopes.[34]

FORMING NEW RELATIONSHIPS

While Curt Flood made his mark as a ballplayer, several individuals influenced his interests outside the baseball world. John Jorgenson owned an industrial engraving plant, and Flood described him as a direct, open-minded individual who faced the world without fear. His wife Marian grinned exuberantly, listened intently and was supportive of her husband. Husband and wife were kindred spirits, humanistic in their philosophy of life, and believed in the powers of love and honour. Jim Chambers, Flood's art teacher at Herbert Hoover Junior High School in Oakland, introduced Flood to the Jorgensons at a dinner party at the end of the 1962 season. Chambers had kept alive Flood's passion for art. After the dinner party, the Jorgensons and Flood engaged in a conversation that was unique in his experience until then:

> That night we discussed the politics of Oakland, of California, of the nation, of peace, of war. We discussed people, love and family. I had never experienced conversation before! Not like this. The more we talked, the more my world enlarged and the more elated I became at my incredible luck. I knew so little of life! There was so much to learn! How could these dear, generous people stand my prattle? I *knew* how! They liked me – without caring a damn whether I played center field or pushed a broom. They did not pretend that I was white. They did not pretend that they were black. They were not at all uptight. I felt as if I had been transported into the twentieth century.[35]

John Jorgenson offered Flood an opportunity to work in his tool and die firm. From the minute he started, Flood felt he had 'been born to the craft'. Utilizing a power-driven pantograph to engrave tiny letters on metal dies required absolute perfection, one mistake could be costly and irreparable. Jorgenson was a perfectionist, and in time he instilled the same quality in Flood. As he progressed, Flood began taking dies through the whole process, from preliminary drawings to finished products. Flood's attention to detail so impressed Jorgenson that he made him his business partner. He saw Flood as his successor in the shop. Yet Jorgenson did not pressure him to quit baseball. As Flood explained, 'Johnny did not believe that *any* business deserved full attention except in the satisfying exertions of craft.' This might have been the life Flood pursued after his playing career, but unfortunately it was not to be as Jorgenson was brutally murdered in 1966.[36] Despite the tragedy, Flood's friendship with the Jorgensons left a lasting impression that would dramatically impact on his baseball career. They aroused an intellectual hunger in Flood that led him to 'rush to books' to feed his quest for knowledge. He sought to emulate the way they cherished life, and most important of all, stand on principle. Flood even credited the Jorgensons for his role in pursuing racial harmony among the Cardinals, saying that, 'Whatever I contributed to the unique morale of the Cardinals was part of this growth, and so, of course, was my decision to have it out in public with the owners of organized baseball.'[37]

By the end of the 1968 season, Curt Flood had established himself in business and as a major league star. As early as 1960, he had been a member of the St Louis Cardinals' Speakers Bureau, making approximately one hundred public appearances before civic, service and children's groups. Two years later, he worked in the public relations firm of Anheuser-Busch Inc. By 1967, he had established Curt Flood & Associates, Inc., a commercial photography and portrait painting business. The following year Flood was putting in eight-hour days in the studio during the off-season, and painted a portrait of Cardinals owner, August A. Busch, Jr. He got the inspiration to paint Busch's portrait 'because Gussie [has] such a classic face – wrinkles, good features, intelligent eyes', and the Cardinals owner steered a lot of business in Flood's direction. In the following years, Flood gained notoriety when he painted the portraits of Dr Martin Luther King, Jr., and Archbishop of St Louis, Cardinal Carberry.[38]

On 19 August 1968, Flood was featured on the cover of *Sports Illustrated*. He had won his sixth Golden Glove Award, given to the best defensive player at their position, and was regarded as the best centerfielder in professional baseball. In 1966, Flood had tied a major league record by going through an entire season without committing an error. This was a significant accomplishment because he handled more chances than any other major leaguer. Midway through the 1967 season, Flood extended his errorless streak to 226 games, the longest by a National League outfielder at that time. In the same year, he finished third in the National League in batting average and was instrumental in the Cardinals winning the pennant and World Series. The Cardinals repeated as National League champions in 1968, only to lose to the Detroit Tigers in the World Series. As determined by traditional standards of American society, Curt Flood was living the 'American

Dream', but by the end of the 1969 season, the dream had turned into a nightmare.[39]

THROWN OUT AT HOME PLATE

Once he achieved the status of a star player, Curt Flood considered himself an agitator. He continued to champion breaking down racial barriers and maintaining racial harmony among the Cardinals. He was also outspoken against working conditions, like the doubleheader and the 162 game schedule, and, of course, the reserve clause, which bound a player to the team which initially signed him until he was traded, sold or released. By 1969, he began protesting more vigorously than usual and some of his outspokenness was leaked to the press.

In 1968, while the Cardinals marched to their second straight National League pennant, Organized Baseball's management faced its most difficult labour crisis of the post-war era. Baseball's labour–management relations changed dramatically, moving from peaceful coexistence to confrontation. Ever since Commissioner Albert Chandler's 1949 decision to make baseball's national television income the source for pension funds, the pension plan remained a source of conflict. Twenty years later, the size of the major league pension had increased more than five times its original amount. The major league television and radio revenues, however, were 45 times larger.[40]

Under the aggressive leadership of former steelworker representative Marvin Miller, the MLBPA demanded that baseball owners raise the minimum salary of players. Before the start of the 1968 season, rumours of a strike swirled throughout the baseball world, but a strike was averted when the minimum salary was increased from $7,000 to $10,000. Professional baseball's first 'Basic Agreement' also improved working conditions, set the size of the owners' contribution to the pension fund, and established an arbitration procedure under the commissioner; but the reserve clause was left on the negotiating table for further study.[41]

Simultaneously, Miller was involved in another marathon negotiation with the owners over the renewal of the pension plan. The MLBPA attempted to increase the size of the owners' payment and link the pension plan firmly to baseball's national television income by having management pay a set percentage of its television rights into the pension fund. This was in response to the new television contract that the owners negotiated with the National Broadcasting Company for $49.5 million.

Annoyed by the owners' stalling tactics, Miller threatened a player boycott of spring training if the pension issue was not settled.[42] In a show of solidarity, the players rallied behind Miller. On 3 February 1969, Miller and several player representatives held a press conference to announce that about 450 players would not sign their contracts until the pension issue was resolved. It was an impressive list of stars which included Willie Mays, Henry Aaron, Brooks Robinson, Tom Seaver, Bob Gibson, Rusty Staub, and Roberto Clemente. Curt Flood was also listed among the marquee players. The player solidarity resulted in the owners capitulating and resolving the dispute.[43] The proposed boycott also contributed to several Cardinal veterans holding out for higher salaries. After all, they had won three pennants and two World Series in five years. Although they lost the 1968 World Series to the Detroit Tigers in seven games, the Cardinals were still the best team in baseball. While he wanted a contract with a salary of $100,000, Flood settled for $90,000. Combined with the salary increases given to veterans like Bob Gibson, Lou Brock, Nelson Briles and Mike Shannon, the Cardinals's 1969 payroll was a reported $950,000.[44]

The combination of the labour disputes and the salary demands was a bitter pill for Cardinals owner August Busch. In an unprecedented move, Busch berated his players at a spring training meeting and he also invited members of the press to witness this dressing down of the best team in baseball. Busch linked the MLBPA rebellion with the civil unrest in American society in the 1960s. He questioned the players' commitment to the game: the players' pension fund, he said, 'would make most Americans envious'. The Cardinal's president added, 'It takes hundreds of people, working every day, to make it possible for eighteen men to play a game of baseball that lasts about two hours.' According to Flood, Busch was talking to the players in code: they were being 'put in their place' and told to behave themselves. Despite their success on the field, the players were still chattels to be purchased, traded, sold or released. Flood no longer felt like a $90,000 ball player, he felt like a green recruit. The speech, he thought, demoralized the 1969 team.[45]

To further complicate matters, the Cardinals got off to a slow start in the regular season, playing near or below .500 ball until July. By late August and early September they began to catch fire and appeared to be making a late season run to catch the division-leading Chicago Cubs. But much to the dissatisfaction of Flood and other Cardinal veterans,

management decided to play rookies at certain positions for the remainder of the season. The moves angered Flood so much that he expressed
his opposition to them in the press. 'They've already sold a million-and-
half tickets this season', Flood argued, 'so they can well afford to prevent
us from having good years. Wait and see how they rub it in at contract
time next winter.' Flood confided to Jack Herman, a sportswriter for the
St Louis Globe-Democrat, that he thought that management had given up
on the 1969 team. His views were published in the press and attri-buted
to an unnamed veteran.[46] The die was cast. Much of the chemistry the
players tried to maintain was lost. The Cardinals were an irritable and
touchy team. They limped through the remainder of September, finishing a dismal fourth. Because they had not lived up to their $950,000
price tag, changes were inevitable.

For Curtis Flood the belief in the American Dream had 'lapsed', but
the dream died hard. It still remained dormant within him, but not
destroyed. Upon hearing the news of his being traded, Flood swore that
he would retire instead of reporting to Philadelphia. His reaction to the
trade illustrated his disdain: 'If I had been a foot-shuffling porter, they
might have at least given me a pocket watch', Flood argued, 'But all I got
was a call from a middle-echelon coffee drinker in the front office.'
Despite the Cardinals' dismal performance, Flood had had a decent year
at the plate, hitting .285. He had been a pivotal figure in the team's
success for five years. But after playing in the Cardinals organization for
12 years, he thought that general manager Bing Devine could have at least
informed him of the trade. Instead of retiring, Curt Flood chose to sue.[47]

Three factors emerged that appeared to influence Flood's decision.
The first was black rage. First directed at the segregation and discrimination he had endured as a ball player, it fueled his desire to excel on the
field. Now the rage was directed at the reserve clause. As Marvin Miller
accurately pointed out, Curt Flood found out that his personal life,
business connections, friends, family and the roots he had established in
the community were of no importance to his employer. However, the
Cardinals organization had made a public display of demanding
devotion and loyalty from him and his teammates.[48]

To Flood, the reserve clause was a form of slavery. Sportswriter Bob
Broeg of the *St Louis Post-Dispatch* criticized Flood for making such a
comparison: did he not make $90,000 from a club that had finished
fourth out of a six-team division – nobody was forcing him to play
professional baseball. Flood countered by quoting the sentiments of

Judge Jerome N. Frank of the US Circuit Court of Appeals in the 1949 case involving Danny Gardella. Gardella had been an outfielder for the New York Giants in 1945, and in 1946 had signed a contract to play in the outlawed Mexican League. When the League collapsed, Gardella applied for reinstatement and was refused. After losing his case in the lower courts, Gardella won a victory of sorts in the Court of Appeals. Instead of waiting for the case to be returned to the District Court, Gardella had settled out of court. Judge Frank had written, 'If the players be regarded as quasi-peons, it is of no moment that they are well paid ... Excusing virtual slavery because of high pay is only an excuse for the totalitarian minded.'[49]

Cardinals' owner August Busch intensified the rage by dressing down the world champions in front of the media. Previously, Busch had compared the labour unrest in baseball with the civil disobedience in American society, and Flood's position reinforced this notion. Flood's challenge of the baseball establishment coincided with the Civil Rights movement as it entered its 'Black Power' phase. From the outset, 'Black Power' was not a coherent ideology and never developed an agreed programme supported by a majority of its proponents. 'Black Power' first exemplified a mood, a disillusionment and alienation from white America, race pride, and self-respect or 'black consciousness'. The slogan's meaning was contingent upon who defined it. 'Black Power' could be an effort to develop a black political party or control the political machinery inside the ghetto without the guidance and support of white politicians. It could also be the attempt to create independent, self-sufficient black business enterprises, or foster a new sense of racial pride and self-confidence.[50]

By the late 1960s, professional black athletes reflected this disillusionment with the baseball world and were speaking out louder than ever before against racism and structural inequality. Frank Robinson was fiercely critical of major league baseball for not having a black manager. Detroit Tigers pitcher Earl Wilson argued that the baseball establishment assumed blacks were 'too dumb' to work in the front office. Wilson won 22 games for Detroit in 1967 and was instrumental in the Tigers winning the pennant and World Series in 1968. According to the Tigers' pitcher, upper-management told blacks to wait five or ten years for the doors to open. However, Wilson pointed out that he could not wait that long and that if those 22 wins were taken away from him he would be 'just another black man'. Roberto Clemente pointed out that while baseball officials asked 'can a colored player do this or do that ... They never ask the white player. They just give him a job.' Henry Aaron was one of the most outspoken players during the 'Black Power' phase, asserting that blacks had made virtually no progress in either middle- or upper-management positions. Although former Giants outfielder Monte Irving held a position in the commissioner's office, Aaron stated that such a hiring was mere 'tokenism'. White stars such as Stan Musial and Ted Williams, he added, were assured jobs after their playing days were over, but black players received a pat on the back and a 'See you later'. Aaron warned that black players were no longer satisfied with getting menial jobs, such as scouts, when they retired; they wanted to become managers and have front office positions. These black players indicted major league baseball for not doing enough to open avenues for blacks in management positions. This same angry mood permeated Curt Flood's autobiography.[51]

When Curt Flood chose to sue Major League baseball, he sought the help of the MLBPA. The player representatives quizzed him extensively. Philadelphia Phillies player representative Jim Bunning asked whether Flood would drop his suit if the owners offered him a deal, as they had in the case of Gardella. Flood replied that if the MLBPA made a commitment to help him in the lawsuit, he would not withdraw the suit under any circumstances. Tom Haller, player representative for the Los Angeles Dodgers, raised the question that was on the minds of a lot of players, who were hesitant to raise the issue. He first highlighted the turbulence of the 1960s, the struggle over civil rights and black power, a new consciousness about race relations, past injustices and efforts to correct them. He asked, 'Are you doing this simply because you're black and you feel baseball has been discriminatory?'[52]

Flood clarified his motives in challenging the baseball establishment. 'All the things you say are true', he replied, 'and I'd be lying if I told you that as a black man in baseball I hadn't gone through worse times than my white teammates.' The changes in black consciousness, he said, had made him more sensitive to injustice in every area of his life. He emphasized that he was challenging the baseball establishment as a ball player, a Major League ball player. It was reprehensible that ball players had stood by and watched this situation go on for so long and had never cooperated to do anything about it. In essence, Curt Flood's individual case had just become the players' common cause.[53]

The second factor centred on the opportunity to negotiate reasonable conditions of employment. The MLBPA did not seek to totally dismantle the reserve system, but they looked for ways to modify it. Before the Flood case, the MLBPA had offered suggestions to modify the reserve clause. Proposals had included the possibility of allowing a player to be free to negotiate after a certain number of years of service; a contract specifically covering a period of years, with freedom to negotiate after that; or that a player be consulted and compensation considered before a trade was concluded. These opportunities were not afforded by the existing reserve system.[54]

Some of the owners and League officials also recognized the need to modify the reserve system. Kansas City Royals owner Ewing Kaufman did not want the anti-trust exemption lifted because of his six million dollar investment in his club, but he indicated that he would have been willing to pay Flood $100,000 to $125,000 for his services, had Flood been free to sell his services to the highest bidder. It should also be noted that the reserve clause prevented owners from tampering with players under contract. Baseball Commissioner Bowie Kuhn recognized the need for modification, but pointed out that it should occur within the collective bargaining process and not in the courts. Former baseball owner Bill Veeck argued that the reserve system should be replaced gradually to give the players more freedom. This gradual elimination would not only do no harm but might benefit management as well as the players.[55]

No one put Curt Flood's case in better perspective than Brooklyn Dodger legend Jackie Robinson. Upon entering the court room Robinson came directly to Flood, shook his hand and congratulated him on his stand. Robinson pointed out that all Flood was asking for was the right to negotiate and that Flood was a 'sensitive man', concerned about everybody's rights. 'We need men of integrity like Curt Flood and Bill Russell who are involved in the area of civil rights and who are not willing to sit back and let Mr. Charlie dictate their needs for them', Robinson added.[56]

Curt Flood's willingness to stand on principle was most crucial in influencing his decision to challenge the baseball establishment. Throughout his minor and major league career, Flood agitated for change once he established himself as a star player. Although his individual case was the players' common cause, he stood alone. The players who would have benefited from a victory in his case were conspicuous in their silence and their absence from the courtroom. The players' silence was indicative of the power that the owners wielded over them. Despite some concessions won in management–labour negotiations, the owners still had autonomy in determining the fate of the players, whether they were stars or merely team members. This paternalism created a psychological mindset which kept the players in line and ensured they made only small demands. Marvin Miller pointed out that his biggest challenge in attempting to gain player solidarity was to eradicate this paternalistic psychology from the players' minds. The major league players were similar to the black child in High Point, North Carolina who had not been able to stand up for himself against the Hi-Toms' white pitcher. Because he was an established Major League star, Curt Flood saw himself as the man who would stand up for the players against the baseball establishment.[57]

CONCLUSION

On 12 August 1970, Curt Flood lost the first round of his challenge of baseball's reserve system. In a 47–page opinion, Judge Irving Ben Cooper ruled in favour of the owners, noting that 'decisions of the Supreme Court are not lightly overturned, particularly those which have a history as long as this one'. After the testimony Cooper declared, 'We find no general or widespread disregard of the extremely important position the player occupies … Clearly the preponderance of credible proof does not favor elimination of the reserve clause.' He added that 'negotiation' and 'arbitration' were advised to modify the controversial feature. Flood's lawyer, former Supreme Court justice Arthur Goldberg, appealed the verdict to the circuit, hoping for the same vindication Danny Gardella had won in his case before the same courts. However, Flood and Goldberg realized that it would take the Supreme Court to determine the outcome of his case.[58]

While his lawyers prepared his case for appeal, Washington Senators owner Bob Short contacted Flood and offered him a job for 1971. Goldberg gave Flood assurances that his litigation would not be impaired because he had suffered damages from missing the 1970 season. Not only had he suffered physically and legally, but his business ventures had collapsed and he needed money. Unfortunately, Flood lasted less than a month of the 1971 season; his skills had been eroded by his unwanted layoff. In October 1971, the second circuit in New York refused Flood's appeal, and eight months later, the Supreme Court ruled in favour of the owners.

Curt Flood's challenge of baseball's reserve system does not adequately contextualize his place in baseball history. He exemplified

the African-American athlete who sought to hasten the dismantling of
barriers to racial and structural equality in the professional sports world.
Their uncoordinated verbal protests, their spectacular performances on
the field, combined with the efforts of grassroots civil rights officials like
Ralph Wimbish and the black press, represented a frontal assault against
existing racial barriers to political, economic and social equality in the
professional sports world. Flood's desire for black and white cooperation
was practical and ideological. After he established himself as a professional ballplayer and entrepreneur, Curt Flood was also a 'race man' who
fought against racial and structural inequality whenever it confronted
him.[59]

In his autobiography, Flood cited a famous quote attributed to
Frederick Douglass. 'If there is no struggle', Douglass reportedly said,
'there is no progress. Those who profess to favor freedom, and yet
depreciate agitation, are men who want crops without plowing up the
ground ... Power concedes nothing without a demand. It never did and
never will.'[60] Curt Flood had become convinced that he was not a
commodity and that he had earned the right to decide where he would
finish his baseball career. The Constitution and the laws of the United
States applied to him as a ballplayer and as an African American. Flood's
challenge of the baseball establishment illustrated Malcolm X's distinction between desegregation and integration that civil rights leaders such
as James Farmer, A. Philip Randolph, Roy Wilkins and Thurgood
Marshall could never grasp. 'It is not a case of [dark mankind] wanting
integration or separation, it is a case of wanting freedom, justice and
equality. It is not integration that Negroes want in America, it is human
dignity.' Flood sought this human dignity when he confronted 90 years
of baseball injustice.[61] Clearly it took the same courage to stand up to
baseball's barons that it took for Jackie Robinson to cross the colour line.
Oakland Athletics, and later New York Yankees, outfielder Reggie
Jackson acknowledged that Flood had suffered in his efforts to institute
change. 'Everybody wants change', Jackson said, 'but nobody wants to
pay the dues.' Once the reserve clause had been overturned and the free
agency era began, St Louis Cardinals catcher Ted Simmons recognized
that 'Curt Flood stood up for us'. Nothing typified Curt Flood more
than his willingness to pay the price and stand up for those who could
not, and would not, stand up for themselves.[62]

NOTES

1. 'Organized Baseball' is the name given to the professional baseball industry. It had its roots in the late nineteenth century, when professional leagues came together and devised rules to protect those players who were under contract (see Seymour, *Baseball: The Early Years*). The creation of the National Agreement, arguably the constitution of professional baseball, resulted in the development of a hierarchical structure that became known as Organized Baseball. The classification included the Major Leagues – the American and National Leagues – and the Minor Leagues. The Minor Leagues were further subdivided into three classifications – AAA, AA and A.

2. Scholarly sources which examine the Curt Flood case include: L. Lowenfish, *The Imperfect Diamond: A History of Baseball's Labor Wars*, rev. edn (New York: Da Capo Press, 1991); D.Q. Voigt, *American Baseball Volume III: From Postwar Expansion to the Electronic Age* (University Park, PA: Pennsylvania State University Press, 1983); J.B. Dworkin, *Owners versus Players: Baseball and Collective Bargaining* (Boston: Auburn House Pub. Co., 1981); G.W. Scully, *The Business Of Major League Baseball* (Chicago: University of Chicago Press, 1989); J.E. Miller, *The Baseball Business: Pursuing Pennants and Profits in Baltimore* (Chapel Hill: University of North Carolina Press, 1990); C.C. Alexander, *Our Game: An American Baseball History* (New York: Henry Holt and Co., 1991); Paul D. Staudohar, *The Sports Industry and Collective Bargaining* (New York: ILR Press, 1989); R.C. Berry, W.B. Gould and P. Staudohar, *Labor Relations in Professional Sports* (Dover, MA: Auburn House Publishing, 1986). Contemporary and player accounts include: C. Aikens, 'The Struggle Of Curt Flood', *Black Scholar*, 3 (Nov. 1971), 10–15; B. Kuhn, *Hardball: The Education of a Baseball Commissioner* (New York: Times Books, 1987); J. Durso, *The All-American Dollar: The Business of Sports* (Boston: Houghton Mifflin Co., 1971); M. Miller, *A Whole Different Ball Game: The Sport and Business of Baseball* (New York: Birch Lane Press, 1991); B. Gibson and L. Wheeler, *Stranger To The Game* (New York: Penguin Books, 1994). Another insightful account which addresses the Curt Flood case is J. Helyar's *Lords Of The Realms: The Real History of Baseball* (New York: Ballantine Books, 1994). The definitive account of Curt Flood's life is his autobiography, *The Way It Is* (New York: Trident Press, 1970).

3. Flood, *The Way It Is*, pp.19–20. For an account of Oakland, California, during the period Curt Flood lived there, see M. S. Johnson, *The Second Gold Rush: Oakland and the East Bay in World War II* (Berkeley: University of California Press, 1993).

4. Flood, *The Way It Is*, p.21.

5. For accounts regarding the influence of George Powles, see B. Russell and T. Branch, *Second Wind: The Memoirs of an Opinionated Man* (New York: Random House, 1979), pp.60–62; F. Robinson and B. Stainback, *Extra Innings* (New York: McGraw-Hill, 1988), pp.24–5.

6. Flood, *The Way It Is*, pp.31–2. Frank Robinson reinforces this notion of the ghetto as isolating him from any form of discrimination. It was not until his rookie year in Ogden, Utah, that Robinson became conscious of discrimination on the basis of race. See Robinson and Stainback, *Extra Innings*, pp.26–7.

7. Jules Tygiel deals with black players' early experience in spring training in the 1950s in *Baseball's Great Experiment: Jackie Robinson and his Legacy*, rev. edn (New York: Oxford University Press, 1997), pp.311–19. In 1954, Chuck Harmon was the first black player to integrate the Reds. See L. Wheeler and J. Baskin, 'In the Shadows: Cincinnati's Black Baseball Players', *Queen City Heritage*, 2 (Summer 1988), 17.

8. For an account on the High Point-Thomasville area, see R. Marks and J. Fox, *High Point: Reflections of the Past* (High Point Historical Society, Inc., 1996).

9. Flood, *The Way It Is*, pp.37–40. H. Aaron and L. Wheeler, *I Had A Hammer: The Hank Aaron Story* (New York: Harper Paperbacks, 1991), p.210.

10. The *High Point Enterprise* carried a two-page advertisement with the players representing the respective business in High Point and Thomasville on 27 April 1956.

11. For an account on black rage, see W.H. Grier and P.M. Cobb, *Black Rage* (New York: Basic Books, 1968). For Flood making several all-star teams, see *High Point Enterprise*, 6 July 1956; 6 Sept. 1956. For Flood voted as most popular Hi-Tom of 1956, see *High Point Enterprise*, 5 Sept. 1956. Bert Haas's comments in *High Point Enterprise*, 31 Aug. 1956.

12. Flood, *The Way It Is*, p.40.
13. Ibid.
14. For an account on the proposed segregation banning interracial sporting contest, see C.H. Martin, 'Racial Change and "Big-Time" College Football in Georgia: The Age of Segregation, 1892–1957', *Georgia Historical Quarterly* 80, (Fall 1996), 532–62.
15. For the accounts of other black players' experience regarding the 'routine on the bus', see Tygiel, *Baseball's Great Experiment*, p.315.
16. *Savannah Morning News*, 11 July 1957. For Flood making the all-star team, see *Savannah Morning News*, 14 July 1957. For Archie Whitfield and Jim Brown comments, and Flood's injury, see *Savannah Morning News*, 25 Aug. 1957.
17. Flood, *The Way It Is*, p.63. R. Hines, 'George Crowe – an original two-sport athlete', *Sports Collectors Digest* (27 May 1994), pp.100–101. Known as 'Big Daddy', Crowe played for the New York Black Yankees of the Negro Leagues. When the Black Yankees had folded, Crowe was recommended to, and signed by, the Boston Braves, and in 1951, he had made his debut in the major leagues. Crowe was traded to the Cincinnati Reds in 1956, and the following year he had his best year in the majors, hitting .271 with 31 homeruns and 92 runs batted in. In Oct. 1958, Crowe was traded to the St Louis Cardinals and had an excellent season as a pinch-hitter. He led the National League in pinch hits at bats (62) and pinch hits (17).
18. For an account on the efforts to desegregate spring training facilities, see J.E. Davis, 'Baseball's Reluctant Challenge: Desegregating Major League Spring Training Sites, 1961–1964', *Journal of Sport History*, 19 (Summer 1992), 144–62; *New York Times*, 1 Feb. 1961. For an account regarding the 'revolution in expectations among American blacks', see A. Meier and J. Bracey, Jr., 'The NAACP as a Reform Movement, 1909–1965', *Journal of Southern History*, 59 (Feb. 1993), 26–7.
19. *New York Times*, 1 Feb. 1961.
20. *New York Times*, 2–4 Feb. 1961; *St Louis Post-Dispatch*, 2 Feb. 1961.
21. *Milwaukee Journal*, 2 and 4 Feb. 1961. See also Chicago *Defender*, 11 Feb. 1961.
22. Aaron and Covington's comments in *Milwaukee Journal*, 3 Feb. 1961; *New Jersey Afro-American*, 11 Feb. 1961; see also Chicago *Defender*, 11 Feb. 1961. Black sportswriter Wendell Smith reported that the *Pittsburgh Courier* was mounting a campaign to end segregation in spring training on 11 Feb. 1961. Secondary accounts include: Aaron, *I Had A Hammer*, pp.210–13; J. Robinson, *Baseball Has Done It* (Philadelphia: J.B. Lippincott Co., 1964), pp.134–44.
23. *New York Times*, 3 Feb. 1961; *Milwaukee Journal*, 3 Feb. 1961; *New Jersey Afro-American*, 11 Feb. 1961 and 11 March 1961; *Pittsburgh Courier*, 4 March 1961. Branch Rickey and Roy Campanella also spoke out against segregated spring training facilities in *Pittsburgh Courier*, 4 Feb. 1961, 25 Feb. 1961.
24. Flood, *The Way It Is*, pp.78–9. *Pittsburgh Courier*, 11 Feb. 1961, 18 March 1961. It should be noted that Flood was competing for the centrefield spot with a white outfielder Don Landrum. See *St Louis Post-Dispatch*, 23 March 1961.
25. Davis, 'Baseball's Reluctant Challenge', 145.
26. Ibid., 159; *Pittsburgh Courier*, 18 March 1961; Gibson and Wheeler, *Stranger to the Game*, pp.57–8; Aaron and Wheeler, *I Had A Hammer*, p.212.
27. Ibid. For an account of the Mets moving into the Colonial Inn, see *Pittsburgh Courier*, 10 March 1962.
28. Aaron and Wheeler, *I Had A Hammer*, p.210.
29. Flood, *The Way It Is*, p.72. W. Leggett, 'Not Just A Flood, But A Deluge', *Sports Illustrated*, 29 (19 Aug. 1968), 20. Flood's statistics in D.S. Neft and R.M. Cohen, *The Sports Encyclopedia: Baseball*, 16th edn (New York: St Martin's Griffin, 1996).
30. For an account on baseball integration, see Tygiel, *Baseball's Great Experiment*; R. Ruck, *Sandlot Seasons: Sport in Black Pittsburgh* (Urbana: University of Illinois Press, 1987). For an account on black players voicing their complaints, see Robinson, *Baseball Has Done It*. For an account on the influx of Latino players into Major League Baseball, see R.G. Echvarria, *The Pride of Havana: A History of Cuban Baseball* (New York: Oxford University Press, 1999).
31. Flood, *The Way It Is*, pp.78–87; Gibson and Wheeler, *Stranger to the Game*, pp.131–2, 148–52. While the following articles do not deal with the notion of racial harmony, they do reinforce

Flood and Gibson's notion of 'chemistry' among the Cardinals. See M. Mulvoy, 'Cha Cha Goes Boom, Boom, Boom!', *Sports Illustrated*, 27 (24 July 1967), 18–21; W. Leggett, 'Out In Front In Fun and Games', *Sports Illustrated*, 27 (4 Sept. 1967), 22–4; 'Birds Fly High', *Newsweek*, 76 (5 Aug. 1968), 64–5.

32. Flood, *The Way It Is*, p.86.
33. Aaron's quote in *I Had A Hammer*, pp.231–2.
34. Ibid. For accounts on the sit-movement, see, for example, M. Marable, *Race, Reform And Rebellion: The Second Reconstruction In Black America, 1945–1982* (Jackson: University Press of Mississippi, 1984); W.H. Chaffe, *The Unfinished Journey: America since World War II* (New York: Oxford University Press, 1991); H. Sitkoff, *The Struggle For Black Equality 1954–1992*, rev. edn (New York: Hill and Wang, 1993). For the statistical analysis of black and Latino players in the 1960s, see Neft and Cohen, *The Sports Encyclopedia: Baseball*.
35. Flood, *The Way It Is*, p.116.
36. Ibid., pp.121–2.
37. Ibid.
38. For Flood as a member of the St Louis Cardinals's Speakers Bureau, see *St Louis Cardinals Sketchbook* (St Louis National Baseball Club Inc., 1960). For Flood working in public relations for Anheuser-Busch, see *New Jersey Afro-American*, 10 Feb. 1962. For Flood's business pursuits, see N. Gross, 'Curt Flood: His teammates call him "Rembrandt"', *Ebony*, 23 (July 1968), 70–72. See also *Cardinals 1969 Media Guide* (St Louis National Baseball Club, Inc., 1969). The *New Jersey Afro-American* carried Cardinal Carberry's portrait on page 8 on 6 Sept. 1969. The *St Louis Globe-Democrat* also carried Cardinal Carberry's portrait on page 3B on 22 Aug. 1969.
39. Flood appeared on the cover of the 19 Aug. 1968 issue of *Sports Illustrated*.
40. For an account on Chandler's 1949 negotiations, see Lowenfish, *Imperfect Diamond*, pp.183–4. For the disparity between owner revenue generated from television and their contributions to the pension fund, see Miller, *The Baseball Business*, p.141.
41. Lowenfish, *Imperfect Diamond*, pp.202–203; Miller, *A Whole Different Ball Game*, pp.95–8.
42. *New York Times*, 3 Jan. 1969; *St Louis Post-Dispatch*, 5 Feb. 1969.
43. *New York Times*, 4 Feb. 1969. Miller provides a complete list of star players who favoured the boycott. See *A Whole Different Ball Game*, p.101.
44. *St Louis Post-Dispatch*, 4 March 1969.
45. Flood provides the whole speech in Appendix B of his autobiography. For newspaper accounts, see *St Louis Post-Dispatch*, 23 March 1969; *St Louis Globe-Democrat*, 23 March 1969; *New York Times*, 23 March 1969. Flood, *The Way It Is*, pp.171–4.
46. W. Leggett, 'The Cardinals Are Coming Tra La Tra La', *Sports Illustrated*, 31 (1 Sept. 1969), 15–16; *St Louis Globe-Democrat*, 30 Aug. 1969, 5 Sept. 1969, 9 Sept. 1969. A similar account was also printed in the *St Louis Post-Dispatch*. According to sportswriter Neal Russo, Cardinals manager Red Schoendienst was responding to his players' complaints.
47. Flood, *The Way It Is*, p.187.
48. Miller, *A Whole Different Ball Game*, p.172.
49. For a comprehensive account of the Gardella case, see W. Marshall, *Baseball's Pivotal Era, 1945–1951* (Lexington: University Press of Kentucky, 1999), pp.233–49. Broeg's comment in *St Louis Post-Dispatch*, 14 Aug. 1970. Durso raises the same issue in *The All-American Dollar*, pp.160–1. There was a precedent of quasi-peonage regarding player contracts. During the Federal League war of 1914–15, organized baseball attempted to use the courts as a means of curbing player defections. They received a major setback when Hal Chase jumped to the Federal League in the middle of the 1914 season violating his contract, not just his reserve. Since clubs could release a player at any time giving them ten days notice, Chase reversed the tables on Comiskey and gave the White Sox owner ten days warning before he left. A New York state judge then refused Chicago's request for an order requiring Chase to return. The court ruled that major league contracts had an 'absolute lack of mutuality' and limited players' freedom to the extent that they were left in a state of 'quasi-peonage'. For a detailed account on the Chase case, see K. Krause, 'Regulating the Baseball Cartel: A Reassessment of the National Commission, Judge Landis and the Anti-Trust Exemption', *International Journal of the History of Sport*, 14 (April 1997), 55–77. Frank quote in Flood, *The Way It Is*, p.139.

50. For an account on the Black Power Movement, see W.L. Van Deburg, *New Day in Babylon: The Black Power Movement and American Culture, 1965–1975* (Chicago: University of Chicago Press, 1992). For the revolt of the black athlete, see H. Edwards, *The Revolt of the Black Athlete* (New York: The Free Press, 1970); D. Spivey, 'Black Consciousness and Olympic Protest Movement, 1964–1980', in idem (ed.), *Sport In America* (Westport, CT: Greenwood Press, 1985), pp.239–62; D.K. Wiggins, 'The Year of Awakening: Black Athletes' Racial Unrest and the Civil Rights Movement of 1968', *International Journal of the History of Sport*, 9 (1992), 188–208. Ron Briley examines racial unrest among black players in organized baseball in 'It Was 20 Years Ago Today: Baseball Responds to the Unrest of 1968', in P. Levine (ed.), *Baseball History: An Annual of Original Baseball Research* (Westport, CT: Meckler, 1989), pp.81–94.

51. Wilson and Clemente's comments in J. Olsen, 'The Black Athlete', *Sports Illustrated*, 28 (22 July 1968), 39. Aaron's comments in *Pittsburgh Courier*, 23 Aug. 1969; *New Jersey Afro-American*, 27 Dec. 1969. It should be noted that Stan Musial was the St Louis Cardinals's general manager in the mid-1960s, while Ted Williams managed the Washington Senators in the late 1960s and early 1970s.

52. Miller, *A Whole Different Ball Game*, p.185.

53. Ibid., pp.185–6.

54. *New York Times*, 18 Jan. 1970.

55. Kaufman's assessment in *New York Times*, 5 June 1970. Kuhn's call for collective bargaining in *Hardball*, pp.86–7. Veeck called for gradual elimination in *New York Times*, 11 June 1970.

56. Robinson's quote in Flood, *The Way It Is*, p.196.

57. Miller, *A Whole Different Ball Game*, pp.33–62.

58. Judge Cooper's comments in 'Curt Flood Strikes Out', *Newsweek*, 76 (24 Aug. 1970), 62.

59. 'Race man' is a term commonly used in African American historical literature. It refers to blacks who advocated the economic philosophy attributed to Booker T. Washington, although it pre-dates him. Through acquiring wealth, developing thrifty habits and advocating middle-class values, blacks would theoretically be assimilated into the mainstream of American society and prejudice would be eliminated.

60. Flood, *The Way It Is*, p.206.

61. Miller, *A Whole Different Ball Game*, p.172. Malcolm X's comments in Marable, *Race, Reform and Rebellion*, p.62.

62. Ted Simmons's comment in Helyar, *Lords Of The Realms*, p.180. Reggie Jackson's comments in 'A Loss for Curt Flood', *Newsweek*, 80 (3 July 1972), 67.

3

Jim Crow Strikes Out:
Branch Rickey and the Struggle for
Integration in American Baseball

STUART KNEE

Speaking candidly before the National Association for the Advancement of Colored People (NAACP) in 1947, President Harry Truman remarked: 'It is my deep conviction that we have reached a turning point in the long history of our country's efforts to guarantee freedom and equality to all our citizens.'[1] The President was alluding to the profound impact of the Second World War and its aftermath upon black people. 'First-class' and 'second-class' citizens were comrades in arms against the enemy. Ironically, it was thousands of miles from United States' shores where blacks gained a modicum of equality. Bullets do not discriminate and sometimes neither did soldiers, even Southern ones, during times of crisis. Only under the most extreme and perilous circumstances did the democratic spirit occasionally prevail; when the Nazis were defeated and the Japanese succumbed, black Americans returned home to perceive that another war had yet to be fought.[2] Truman's optimism, however, was not unfounded. The single step had been taken in the thousand mile journey, a journey which was to go through Little Rock, Selma, Washington, Watts and Newark. It was taken before the nation witnessed the insurgency of Martin Luther King, Malcolm X, Stokely Carmichael and 'Rap' Brown; it was taken by a white man with a love of sport and a hatred of bigotry.

By 1942, Branch Rickey had already reached the zenith of his fame and, for the man who was called 'David Harum' and 'The Brain',[3] there seemed to be few worlds left to conquer. He was an exceptional individual who chose baseball for his life's endeavour and succeeded in democratizing and revolutionizing the game in much the same way that a politician would pledge to 'clean up' a city. This analogy must be kept in mind if one wishes to give proper weight and recognition to Rickey's nationalizing the national pastime, an achievement which is not relegated to the sports pages. It is significant that 55 years after Rickey's experiment, racism has declined in American life; people who have no contact or are still uncomfortable with blacks have their illiberal preconceptions challenged on a daily basis. In the summer, for example, hardly anyone can avoid watching a ball game, watching black and white, Southerner and Northerner, playing the way Branch Rickey and all Americans desire the game should be played.

The rise of Branch Rickey to national prominence is the typical, American, Horatio Alger tale. Rickey's childhood and upbringing has been compared to that of William Jennings Bryan.[4] Rickey was born in Stockdale, Ohio, the grandson of an itinerant Baptist minister and the son of a farmer.[5] He was pious, a moralist and a Republican after the fashion of Abraham Lincoln, adhering to the classic values of mid-nineteenth-century Westerners and Northerners: free soil, free speech, free labour and free men. And, like many moral American men of Protestant background, he was able to channel his rectitude so it would never interfere with practical matters of business. Having rarely encountered a black in his early years, he had two experiences which tested his Christian convictions. The first occurred in 1904 when Rickey, who worked his way through Ohio Wesleyan University, was managing the University of Michigan baseball team. The team, including one black, arrived in South Bend, Indiana, and was lodged in the hotel. Only the black player was refused accommodation. The hurt felt by this athlete was also felt by his manager. 'Rickey was to say that he decided after the ... [incident] ... that he would contribute something to better racial understanding if ever the opportunity were presented to him.'[6]

A suitable opening did not come along for many years. In the interim, Rickey received a BA from Ohio Wesleyan and graduated from the University of Michigan Law School. While successfully pursuing an intellectual life, Rickey never lost his love for baseball. For many years, he managed the Ohio Wesleyan and University of Michigan baseball teams and was himself sufficiently talented to play minor and major league ball. While in attendance at the Law School, he played in the Major Leagues, first with the St Louis Browns and then with the New York Highlanders. His real talents were not exhibited on the ballfield, however, and, after a bout with tuberculosis and a sore arm, Rickey's playing days ended. He practised law in Boise, Idaho, but he was restless. The owner of the Browns offered the young lawyer a front-office position and he accepted it eagerly.

The post of vice-president and general manager of the Browns marked the inauguration of Rickey's 40-year career in baseball. He moved from the Browns to the Cardinals and then to Brooklyn. He never left a city without leaving his calling card. Until 1942, his most important achievement was the building of the farm system, which remained an institution in baseball until the 1960s. As a stockholder and president of the Cardinals, Rickey witnessed discrimination for the second time. The owners of the St Louis club would not allow blacks to sit in the grandstand at Sportsman's Park.[7] Rickey quashed his feelings on race and settled, temporarily, for 'an academic expression of a passive abhorrence of an inexcusable situation'.[8]

Rickey hardly endeared himself to either the Cardinals or the Dodgers but, as one of his loyal adherents would later claim, 'he isn't afraid of anyone or anything'.[9] In the days when college-educated ball players could be counted on the fingers of two hands, Rickey was an anomaly. His strict abstinence and his absence from Sunday baseball games made him particularly vulnerable to attack. Besides originating and perfecting the farm system, he invented the sliding pit and turned baseball into a 'family' game by instituting ladies' day. Yet, his ideas were too original and, as field manager of the Cardinals, his lectures on baseball theory sailed over the heads of the players.

Rickey's reputation for penury followed him from St Louis to Brooklyn where, in 1942, he replaced the Dodgers' colourful and dynamic president, Larry MacPhail. By this time, the United States had entered the Second World War and young men from all walks of life were being summoned to duty. The drain on baseball talent was immediately apparent. For a variety of social and political reasons, among them the genocidal and racist nature of German aggression in Europe, the stirring of black militancy during the years of the New Deal, and an Executive order establishing the Fair Employment Practices Commission (FEPC), whose charge it was to end discrimination in hiring among industries competing for war contracts, the time had come for a new era in baseball. Some were aware of it even before 'the Mahatma', as Rickey was now called. The *Sporting News*, the organ of baseball, subsidized by the club owners, took a position of unequivocal opposition to the mingling of white and black athletes.[10] For years, the capabilities of athletes in the Negro Leagues were recognized as equal to those of white players in the American and National Leagues. However, fear of riots and the racial attitudes of club owners precluded the possibility of integrating baseball.[11]

Rickey, who was more a businessman than a moralist, remained unhampered in his racial views: 'He is nothing like the Chautauqua character the baseball press has made him. He is neither sonorous nor aggressively pious. He does not make double talk. His English is intricate but clear.'[12] He was the perfect man to introduce blacks into white baseball because he knew the hazards involved and was ready to meet the thrusts of racial purists with a most formidable weapon – silence. Before talking with anyone, Rickey examined the rules of baseball: 'I had heard there was a rule in the National League forbidding the signing of colored players. I investigated; I could not find such a rule in any league record or book.'[13] It is important to remember that Rickey's primary concern, at this early date, was to secure his position as president of the Dodgers and 'revitalize' the team. When Rickey scouted Caribbean, South American and Mexican players he was not committed to ethnic reform – 'He was conscious of it, naturally, but getting good players was his motivation.'[14]

'For two intensely secretive years, Rickey studied what was to be his most important innovation in a historical sense.'[15] By the end of 1944, he was not yet prepared to present a practical alternative to segregation. He had not found the right man, although his scouts had been canvassing the country, ostensibly searching for black talent to play in the new Negro United States League. Meanwhile, the 'Brain' openly espoused the black cause in a speech he delivered to the Rotary Club in 1944. He made it clear that, although he disdained violence, he disliked the exploitation in the Negro leagues wherein Major League club owners (for example, the Washington Senators' Clark Griffith), renting their parks to black teams, took as much as 15 per cent of receipts from games played between all-coloured clubs.[16]

The War ended in 1945. Before the end of the year, baseball had taken tremendous strides in integration, outdistancing business and industry. Liberals and intellectuals theorized, wrote pamphlets, visited depressed areas and wrote articles. As early as 1942, the erudite leader of the Dodgers was considering blacks for the Major Leagues, but his field of action did not narrow to the United States until 1944. Rickey was well-situated to deal with the problem. In New York City, the foundations for integration were already being laid. Branch Rickey was able to work effectively with both Governor Thomas E. Dewey and Mayor Fiorello LaGuardia. Before Rickey arrived at an understanding with the two political heads of New York, he had to put his own house in order. No objection was raised by Dodger stockholders when Branch Rickey said that his Brooklyn rebuilding programme might include a few black players. Rickey's scouts were not informed that any black talent they found might eventually break the colour line:[17]

> Rickey remembered several of his scouts were Southerners with ingrained prejudices. If he told them they were looking for an all Negro team, they would bring him accurate and honest reports on the various players, but some would be handicapped if told that they were looking for a Negro who eventually would play with white boys. This was particularly true of Wid Mathews, a Mississippian whom Rickey considered very prejudiced against Negroes, but was one of the best scouts in the country.[18]

Rickey was aided in the post-war struggle by LaGuardia and Dewey. On 12 March 1945, New York State passed a law against discrimination in employment. Following the appointment of a Fair Employment Practices Committee, which dealt with discrimination in war industries, the Ives-Quinn law extended anti-discrimination laws to all businesses and provided for punishment of those who violated the edict.[19] LaGuardia quickly established a committee of four which was super-seded by a committee of ten. The committees were charged with examining employment practices and making recommendations. A prominent member of the committee of ten was Branch Rickey,[20] for the Mayor knew that Rickey was eager to sign a black. Rickey's idea was received favourably by the Mayor, although when the former presented his proposal at a joint meeting of the Major Leagues, 15 clubs adopted a resolution opposing blacks in Big League baseball. After this, he never discussed the matter again at any baseball conference.[21] The baseball season of 1945 began and ended with controversy. Before Branch Rickey consented to give blacks Major League tryouts, Boston was confronted with a knotty problem. Congressman Isadore Muchnick attempted to blackmail the Red Sox into giving blacks a fair chance. If the Boston club refused to give the black athletes an opportunity, Muchnick promised that he would personally see to it that Sunday baseball was outlawed in that city. To pacify the irate Congressman, the Red Sox gave three blacks a tryout but signed no one, not even a player as talented as Jackie Robinson.[22] Rickey, at the urging of Joe Bostic, editor of the black newspaper *People's Voice*, gave two blacks tryouts but, unfortunately, Robinson was not one of them. Rickey did not think the athletes he saw were of Major League calibre and said so. This sort of honesty casts doubt upon the arguments of those who contended that Rickey's signing of Robinson was an example of sheer opportunism. Rickey criticized the American Communist Party, particularly active in New York, which was agitating for the right of blacks to play baseball. Communist Councilman Benjamin Davis published a rather lurid pamphlet depicting a dead black soldier and a black baseball player on the cover. The caption read: 'Good enough to die for his country but not good enough to play baseball.'[23] Dodger President Rickey had an answer even to this: 'I am for your cause [that is, the black cause] more than anybody else I know ... but you are making a mistake using force ... dictating in this matter ... It will fail because it is a matter of evolution, not revolution.'[24] The baseball season opened on an ominous note as blacks in New York, who had established an 'End Jim Crow' Committee, were prepared to demonstrate at the Polo Grounds.[25] They were prevented from doing so at the last moment by LaGuardia, who convinced them that he was working on a less militant solution. When the committee of ten was established, it was immediately censured by Larry MacPhail of the Yankees and Horace Stoneham of the Giants.[26] All through the season, LaGuardia was trying to prevail upon the three New York franchises to sign a special Fair Employment Practices Law relating only to baseball. Of course, the Yankee and Giant representatives declined.

Rickey, meanwhile, was calmly receiving reports from his scouts on Jackie Robinson. By July, he had decided that Robinson, then of the Kansas City Monarchs, was the man he would choose for his experiment. Time and time again, Rickey spoke of the six criteria that a black ballplayer would have to meet in order to play Major League baseball: the man chosen had to be right off the field; the man chosen must be right on the field; black people had to like the man chosen; the press reaction had to be favourable; a place must be opened on the roster for the proper player; and the reaction of his fellow players had to be right.[27]

Mentally tough, tenacious, talented, touchy and well-educated, former Army officer and Negro League baseball star, Jack Roosevelt Robinson, remembered his rough and tumble roots as the son of a Georgia sharecropper. His memories were painful. Nevertheless, it was for his consummate athletic ability and 'indomitable spirit' that he became Branch Rickey's integration choice following their secret meeting on 28 August 1945 in Brooklyn. The meeting itself was a test and Robinson passed.

Later, Rickey claimed that Robinson 'showed the necessary intelligence and strength of personality, but had a deeper racial resentment than was hoped for or expected'.[28] Rickey posed as a bigoted hotel clerk and a Southern ballplayer, shot insults at Robinson and dared him to retaliate. When Robinson did not, Rickey assumed a gentler attitude. He 'spent several minutes reading a chapter from *The Life of Christ* by the ... Italian priest Giovanni Papini'. He made his athlete realize 'that integration required ... some Booker T. Washington compromises with surface inequality for the sake of expediency. It would require constant ... silent reaction to abuse.'[29] At the end of the three hour session, Robinson was signed with the Montreal Royals and 'the admonition, you can't fight back! had been established as the only foundation on which Robinson's move into organized baseball could be built'.[30] Finally, Rickey extolled the virtue of baseball as a uniquely unbiased instrument: 'A box score is a democratic thing. It doesn't tell ... what church you attend, what color you are or how your father voted in the last election. It just tells what kind of a baseball player you were on a particular day.'[31] With those words, and the warning to remain silent until the signing could be safely announced, Rickey ushered Robinson out of his office.

Surprisingly, Rickey was able to keep silent for two months. Although some have labelled him a moral crusader,[32] albeit a conservative one in all but integration, his ethics were always tempered with pragmatism. For precisely this reason, both the sociological and athletic experiments were successful. In October 1945, Rickey resigned from the Mayor's committee because he felt that 'with the signing of a Negro player, his position among the group was no longer a sincere one'.[33]

It was just at this time, when LaGuardia was having little success in pressing the other New York teams to sign an anti-discrimination pledge, that the Mayor decided to reveal Rickey's signing of Robinson.[34] 'The Mahatma' prevailed upon him not to do this, for Rickey wanted to make the statement himself. The reaction to Rickey's announcement of 23 October was favourable in all walks of life except where it counted, in baseball. On the credit side, most people outside the sport were willing to give Robinson a fair trial.[35] A number of writers were pessimistic about his chances;[36] some thought Robinson's signing was merely a publicity stunt 'to make turnstiles click'.[37] The black community held its breath and spoke in guarded terms of the experiment: 'No one knew but the twenty-six year old Jackie Robinson how high a barrier he had to scale', wrote Ludlow Werner in *The New York Age*, 'I'm happy ... but sorry for Jackie ... Unlike white players, he can never afford an off-day ... and Lord help him with his fellow Negroes if he should fail them.'[38] On the debit side was the reaction of prominent baseball players and officials. Judge William Bramham, the Minor League baseball commissioner said, at Durham, North Carolina, that his office would approve Robinson's contract because there was no legal basis for disapproval, but he lashed out at Rickey's action, predicting that it would 'inevitably prove harmful to organized baseball'. He called Rickey 'a carpetbagger' whose sole desire was to have the grateful Negroes of Harlem build temples in his honour. Batting champions Rogers Hornsby and Dixie Walker, as well as strikeout king Bob Feller, all predicted a short career for Mr Robinson.[39] Clark Griffith, hereditary ruler of the Washington Senator empire, deplored the fact that the signing of blacks to Major League contracts would 'kill' the Negro Leagues.[40] Rickey answered Griffith personally, branding Negro baseball a 'racket'.[41]

The year 1946 was the interim between steps one and two of the experiment. If Robinson did well at Montreal, a contract would be waiting with the Brooklyn Dodgers. Entering into Rickey's decision to place Robinson at Montreal was the fact that race prejudice was slight in that Canadian city. However, there were many peaks which Robinson was forced to scale. The manager of the Montreal team was a native Mississippian, Clay Hopper, who doubted Robinson's humanity.[42] By the end of the season, however, after Montreal played in the Little World Series, Hopper was calling his dark-skinned athlete 'a real ballplayer and a gentleman'.[43] Early in the season, the president of the International League, Frank Shaughnessy, assured Rickey that if Robinson played in Baltimore, violence would erupt. Rickey demanded that Robinson play and there were no incidents.[44] To fulfill step six of his integration criteria, Rickey did not bring Robinson up from the Minors at the end of 1946. He believed that to bring him into the Majors in the midst of a pennant fight between the Dodgers and the Cardinals would not be advisable. Rickey preferred to elevate Robinson to the parent club in 1947, 'under conditions where he was more likely to have the support of the Brooklyn players'.[45] The lesson of Clay Hopper proved invaluable to Rickey's old contention: 'Prejudice runs away from truth [and] is a coward in the face of fact. Proximity is the solution to the race problem if only we could get enough of it.'[46] By the end of 1946, Robinson was no longer the only black in the Dodger organization. The hiring of John Wright, Roy Campanella and Don Newcombe proved to America that Rickey was very serious in his attempt to develop a black star.

In the face of malignant criticism, Rickey remained silent. The Dodger President 'could easily ignore the charge of ulterior motives in hiring blacks by his single premise often stated: "I want players to help me win a pennant in Brooklyn."' No one could question his desire to win or to make victory paramount, or his right to win with any eligible player. Rickey never spoke of social consequences; he had firm beliefs about the equality of man, but these were never a factor in his decision. The sole issue was 'a player's ability to play organized baseball'.[47] This was to be Rickey's philosophy throughout the trying year of 1947.

During the year that Robinson was at Montreal, Rickey became a 'devoted Abraham Lincoln fan'.[48] He studied the social dilemma of blacks; his constant reading companion was Professor Frank Tannenbaum's *Slave and Citizen*. The book was published in 1947, the year Jackie Robinson made it to Brooklyn. In private, Rickey talked at length on the manumission principle. He named four prime factors in integration: proximity, professional opportunity, the flexibility of the social strata and religion. The Dodger President hoped that with Robinson's first at bat in the Majors, integration history would be made.[49]

To the public in general and also to the black people of New York City, Rickey remained aloof from the social implications resulting from baseball integration. Avoiding any utterances which might be miscon- strued, he said nothing about Robinson[50] until the Brooklyn players forced him to. Thirty prominent black leaders were invited to a dinner given by Rickey on 5 February 1947. The purpose of the gathering was to make 'the Negro aware of the terrible responsibility faced, not just by Jackie Robinson but by every Negro who went to the ballpark to cheer him'. Rickey made it clear that he wanted no display of pride by Negro fans once they arrived at Ebbets Field and absolutely no incidents which would turn Robinson into a social symbol. The audience, warmly responding to Rickey's entreaty, by April organized the 'Don't Hurt Jackie's Chances' committee to mobilize public opinion behind Robinson the athlete rather than Robinson the black.[51]

Years hence, Rickey said, with much justification, that integration in baseball started public integration in Pullmans, dining cars and restau- rants in the South long before the issue of public accommodations became daily news.[52] In the spring of 1947, however, Rickey deliberately eschewed newspaper headlines. To remove some pressure from Robinson and to accustom the Dodger team to playing 'mixed' baseball, 'the Mahatma' took his club to Havana. It was not long before the Dodgers began circulating an exclusion petition, protesting against the presence of 'Negroes' on the team. It is interesting to note that the Dodgers most opposed to Robinson were Southerners: Bobby Bragan and Kirby Higbe of North Carolina, Hugh Casey from Georgia and Dixie Walker from Alabama.[53] Rickey, forced into a position which to him was absolutely intolerable, made it plain that the Dodger players would neither decide team policy nor usurp the presidential preroga-tive.[54] Rickey caustically remarked that a black on the team 'may cost Brooklyn ... a number of ballplayers ... particularly if they come from certain sections of the South ... Some may even quit. But they will be back after they work a year or two in a cotton mill.'[55]

Unlike integrationists outside baseball, Rickey feared no one and had no voters to placate. Hence, he was the ideal man for the pioneering step in integration. He dealt effectively with his players and, within a few weeks, the Dodger exclusion petition was only a memory. On 9 April 1947, Rickey officially announced the signing of Jackie Robinson.[56] However, as Arthur Daley noted, the move was skillfully camouflaged, for the suspension of Dodger Manager Leo Durocher received most of the headlines during the month of April.[57] The season itself, which commenced on a grim note, ended in triumph for Robinson and the man who fought for him. Two factors hampering the Rickey cause in 1947 were a St Louis Cardinals ultimatum and the manager of the Philadelphia Phillies. While magazine articles applauded Rickey's bold stand,[58] a fierce battle was being waged throughout the National League. First the Phillies and then the Cardinals threatened to strike if the Dodgers took the field with their Negro first baseman. The Phillies' plot never materialized, but the Cardinals protest got far enough for Ford Frick, President of the National League, to counter-threaten any Cardinal who participated in such a strike with suspension.[59] Stanley Woodward, sports editor of the *New York Herald Tribune*, implicated Marty Marion and Terry Moore as the ringleaders.[60] Not as easily quieted were the men who operated deliberately to break Robinson's spirit. One of the most caustic of baseball's race baiters was the Phillies' manager Ben Chapman, 'a fierce, intelligent hatchet man'.[61] Chapman's pitchers threw at the black man regularly and, in the field, Robinson was subjected to unsportsmanlike spiking. The result of Chapman's aggression was the converse of what was expected. 'Even today, Rickey can lecture for an hour about how Chapman, a prejudiced man from Alabama, unwittingly helped consolidate the position of the Negro in organized baseball: "Chapman did more than anybody to make Dixie Walker, Eddie Stanky and other Dodgers speak out in Robinson's behalf ... he created a thing called sympathy, the most unifying force in the world".'[62]

Rickey urged Robinson to reject any offers to make endorsements after the 1947 season, lest it lead to more prejudice on the part of those people who would attack blacks as venal.[63] Robinson's performance during his rookie season was electrifying. He batted nearly .300 and ran the bases like the 1920s Detroit Tigers superstar Ty Cobb. Rickey was aided by Robinson's achievement in his discussions about integration with Bill Veeck, dynamic owner of the Cleveland Indians. In July 1947, baseball's greatest showman signed Larry Doby to a contract with the Indians. Thus, Doby became the first Negro to play in the American League.[64] Since April, Rickey had been circulating reports on Doby to other magnates, hoping that someone would sign him. In Rickey's estimation, Veeck was not motivated by ethnic considerations: 'He [Veeck] would be the first one in baseball to embrace this innovation ... not because he was grappling with a social problem. That was completely foreign to him. He would not let any tradition interfere with his policy of winning a pennant for his Indians.'[65] Once again the point was proved; on the ballfield, where men were compelled to work harmoniously, integration proceeded at a greater rate than off the baseball diamond.

Before 1947 ended, the Dodgers won the pennant and Jackie Robinson participated in his first World Series. The *Sporting News*, still noticeably lukewarm toward integration, could not deny Robinson as an athlete and voted him rookie of the year.[66] Only then did Rickey begin to talk publicly like the moralist he had always been. Robinson the ballplayer and Robinson the citizen were inseparable; Rickey did not crusade any more for blacks than he did for all humanity:

> I believe that a man's race, color and religion should never constitute a handicap. The denial to anyone, anywhere, anytime of equality of opportunity to work is incomprehensible to me. Moreover, I believe that the American public is not as concerned

with a first baseman's pigmentation as it is with the power of his swing, the dexterity of his slide, the gracefulness of his fielding or the speed of his legs.[67]

Part of Branch Rickey's success in integrating baseball stems from the fact that he knew when to permit blacks to shoulder the burden. By 1951, Rickey was no longer with the Dodgers but, as usual, he left something of his genius behind. Rickey had 'put the Negro problem in the right perspective'.[68] He removed the political, social and racial bitterness from the struggle and replaced it with Robinson's big bat. With the pressure easing, Robinson was able to let the more explosive side of his personality emerge. Rickey, who had once stifled Robinson's competitiveness for the good of baseball and blacks, now encouraged the star to be himself. 'The chains that set him apart from all other Big Leaguers were off.'[69] Robinson, with Rickey's encouragement and assistance, prepared a speech which he delivered before the House Un-American Activities Committee in July, 1949. Robinson denied actor/singer Paul Robeson's assertion that blacks were becoming increasingly active in Communist organizations and that they would not fight if the United States became embroiled in a war with Russia.[70] 'Branch Rickey has said that the making of the speech that day in Washington was an event even more significant and more reaching than the acceptance of Negroes in baseball.'[71]

Before Rickey left the Dodgers, he advanced the cause of integration by selling one of his budding black stars, Sam Jethroe, to the Braves. His purpose, as he stated it, was to bring 'another club into the Negro field'.[72] By 1952, 18 black players were dispersed among six Major League teams.[73] Articles detailed Jackie Robinson's accomplishments, no longer self-consciously avoiding the mention of his heritage. Even as late as 1955, when Rickey could safely have claimed some credit for breaking the colour line, he did not.[74] Until his death in 1965, Rickey, a lifelong political conservative, remained active in the cause of civil rights and possibly became a shade more militant. In 1957, President Eisenhower (Rickey had always been a staunch Republican) appointed him vice-chairman of the seven-man President's Committee on Government Employment Policy.[75] Rickey stated, unequivocally, that all-Negro professional baseball was dead and that there was no longer room for all-Negro owned and operated leagues within the framework of organized baseball.[76] Rickey was most gratified to learn that Robinson had been admitted to the Hall of Fame in 1962: 'The Baseball Writers of America elected him to the Hall of Fame on merit. It is unfair to them and without due honor to Robinson to say that the vote was determined by colour.'[77] Although Rickey had to curb Robinson's natural aggressiveness in 1947, he later came to question those moderates who did not take a militant stand once the initial breakthrough had been accomplished.[78] The statement made by Branch Rickey concerning Jackie Robinson is a fitting tribute to both men: 'Jackie needs no hero worship by his people ... He asks nothing from anyone other than an equal chance for a place to live, to go, to come, to speak as one pleases with decency and the law.'[79]

CONCLUSIONS

Apparently, there is more to baseball than batting averages and, at least in this instance, a solution to a national problem was found far away from traditional social and political arenas. Two other American team sports, basketball and football, were integrated at about the same time as baseball, but the latter symbolized white supremacy in American sports. Therefore, baseball received the most intense scrutiny from both blacks and whites. Desegregation of the armed forces and the 1954 Brown vs. Board of Education Supreme Court decision are said to be landmarks in the progress of blacks toward equality and they are, but no more so than Branch Rickey's contribution. Many writers and a number of sociologists claim that, apart from the Supreme Court's ruling on school integration, Rickey's crossing the colour line in baseball produced more beneficial results than any other single act.[80] Some have claimed that 'it paved the way for the school integration decision'.[81]

Rickey was suited to his self-appointed task in a unique way. He appreciated the race problem as only a rock–ribbed, fundamentalist son of the prairie could, and was able to calculate the merits of integration. He was educated, had an intellectual professional orientation and was able to anticipate trouble before it started. He clearly recognized the sociological and historical plight of blacks, but subordinated morality to pragmatism. He read Tannenbaum but did not preach him. He talked with black leaders and white sociologists but refused to parade the 'cause' on the athletic fields of the nation. It was only this sort of a person, intelligent enough to grasp the pathos of the blacks but restrained in action, who could have accomplished integration with so little damage to national sensitivities. The fact that such a man was found in baseball is a credit to the game. In two years, he accomplished on the field what it has taken 55 for others to accomplish off it. That blacks should be accepted gradually as the equal of whites in several fields of athletics attests to the democratizing influence of sports in the United States. It is significant that the first progressive step toward equality in the post-Second World War era should have been taken in sport, particularly by a major segregated sport claiming to be the 'national pastime'. The battlefield and the ballfield proved that when men work together towards a common goal, an accord can be reached. The Republican Rickey appreciated the tribute paid to baseball by Herbert Hoover, a man who lived by and was eventually defeated by his scrupulous morality: 'The rigid voluntary rules of right and wrong, as applied in American sports are second only to religion in strengthening the morals of the American people ... and baseball is the greatest of all team sports.'[82]

The day Rickey defined the right was 15 April 1947. Before the shadows covered the field on that afternoon, he shattered the weakest link in the chain of black misfortune, tolled the bell marking the end of an era and erected a lasting memorial to himself and his achievement.

NOTES

1. H.S. Truman, *Public Papers of the Presidents of the United States* (Washington: US Government Printing Office, 1963), p.311. This citation is from the 1947 collection.
2. A. Carter, 'Sports', in F. Murray (ed.), *The Negro Handbook* (New York: The Macmillan Co., 1949), p.293.
3. 'Sport', *Time*, 39 (13 April 1942), 65.
4. L. Allen, *The National League Story* (New York: Hill and Wang, 1965), p.178.
5. Unless otherwise stated, all background material on Branch Rickey may be found in the following: A. Mann, *Branch Rickey: American in Action* (Boston: Houghton Mifflin, 1957), pp.5–6; J. Tygiel, *Baseball's Great Experiment: Jackie Robinson and His Legacy* (New York: Oxford University Press, 1983), pp.48–52; J.C. Chalberg, *Rickey and Robinson* (Wheeling, IL: Harlan Davidson, Inc., 2000), pp.15–42.
6. A.S. Young, *Great Negro Baseball Stars* (New York: A.S. Barnes & Co., 1953), p.8; A. Rampersad, *Jackie Robinson: A Biography* (New York: Knopf, 1997), pp.121–2; Tygiel, *Baseball's Great Experiment*, pp.51–2, 75, 116–17; Chalberg, *Rickey*, pp.24–5. Baseball simulated a 'civil religion' to Branch Rickey, and thus he was consistent in transferring much of his piety into the game which was, essentially, his life's work. See Chalberg, *Rickey*, p.149.
7. Mann, *Branch Rickey*, p.4; M. Robinson, 'Branch Rickey's Three Gifts', *Baseball Digest*, 25 (Feb. 1966), 13–14.
8. R. Cousins, 'All Star Second Baseman', *Saturday Review of Literature*, 33 (15 July 1950), 10.
9. J. Robinson, *My Own Story*, as told by Jackie Robinson to W. Smith (New York: Greenberg, 1948), p.23.
10. C.T. Rowan, *Wait Till Next Year: The Life Story of Jackie Robinson* (New York: Random House, 1960), p.101. For the sake of profit, promoters sometimes turned a blind eye to the participation of selected blacks in individual sports. World champion (1899) cyclist, Marshall W. 'Major'

Taylor, attracted large crowds, but other black competitors in this sport could race only in 'all-Negro' events (see A. Ritchie in this volume). Heavyweight boxing champion (1908–15) Jack Johnson achieved notoriety in a sport that thrived on racial antagonism and Olympic Gold Medalist (1936) Jesse Owens was hailed by whites for his symbolic rather than substantive achievements on behalf of blacks. Team competition, on the other hand, presented a more threatening dynamic for the majoritarian psyche, that of equality and fraternity for the common good. Such a cooperative mode was unacceptable during the era of 'Jim Crow'. See B.G. Rader, *American Sports: From the Age of Folk Games to the Age of Televised Sports*, 4th edn (Upper Saddle River, NJ: Prentice Hall, 1999), pp.130, 205–206.

11. E.B. Henderson, *The Negro in Sports* (Washington: Associated Publishers Inc., 1939), pp.158–60. Rader, *American Sports*, offers a brief overview of black baseball from 1920–45 and Tygiel, in *Baseball's Great Experiment*, is comprehensive.

12. S. Woodward, 'In the Rickey Manner', *Baseball Digest*, 9 (July 1950), 20.

13. J. Robinson, *Baseball Has Done It*, Charles Dexter (ed.) (Philadelphia: L.S.B. Lippincott Co., 1964), p.41.

14. A. Mann, 'The Truth About the Jackie Robinson Case', *Saturday Evening Post*, 222 (13 May 1950), 19–21, 122–3; *Saturday Evening Post*, 223 (20 May 1950), 149–54. Rickey, however, did have a sense of his own destiny. This 'self-made man' was desirous of intervening 'in the moral history of the nation'. D. Falkner, *Great Time Coming: The Life of Jackie Robinson from Baseball to Birmingham* (New York: Simon and Schuster, 1995), pp.104–105; A. Rampersad, *Jackie Robinson: A Biography* (New York: Alfred A. Knopf, 1997), p.122.

15. 'Man of Empire', *Newsweek*, 34 (8 Aug. 1949), 63.

16. Mann, *Branch Rickey*, p.217.

17. Ibid., pp.212–14

18. Rowan, *Wait Till Next Year*, p.108.

19. J.H. Franklin and I. Starr (eds), *The Negro in Twentieth-Century America: A Reader on the Struggle for Civil Rights* (New York: Vintage, 1967), pp.415–16; Tygiel, *Baseball's Great Experiment*, p.38; Chalberg, *Rickey*, p.96.

20. Mann, *Branch Rickey*, p.223; Rampersad, *Jackie Robinson*, p.123.

21. Robinson, *Baseball Has Done It*, p.42; Chalberg, *Rickey*, p.113.

22. Mann, 'The Truth About the Jackie Robinson Case', 21; Tygiel, *Baseball's Great Experiment*, pp.43–5; Chalberg, *Rickey*, pp.90–91.

23. Mann, *Branch Rickey*, p.20.

24. Allen, *National League Story*, p.238

25. Bill Roeder, *Jackie Robinson* (New York: A.S. Barnes, 1950), p.77.

26. Mann, 'The Truth About the Jackie Robinson Case', 122; Chalberg, *Rickey*, p.122; Tygiel, *Baseball's Great Experiment*, pp.69, 80.

27. G. Holland, 'Mr. Rickey and the Game', in Charles Einstein (ed.), *The Fireside Book of Baseball* (New York: Simon and Schuster, 1956), p.192.

28. B. Rickey (with R. Riger), *The American Diamond* (New York: Simon and Schuster, 1965), p.46; H. Goren, 'Are They Giving Jackie Robinson the Works?', *Baseball Digest*, 14 (Sept. 1955), 79.

29. Rampersad, *Jackie Robinson*, p.127; Falkner, *Great Time Coming*, p.107; Tygiel, *Baseball's Great Experiment*, p.66; Chalberg, *Rickey*, p.9.

30. Mann, *Branch Rickey*, p.223. The Montreal Royals were the Triple-A minor league affiliate of the Brooklyn Dodgers.

31. Rowan, *Wait Till Next Year*, p.116.

32. T. Meany, *Baseball's Greatest Players* (New York: Dell Publishing Co., 1955), p.194.

33. Mann, *Branch Rickey*, pp.223–4.

34. Rowan, *Wait Till Next Year*, p.119. Rickey displayed a general preference for ethnics once he became president of the Dodgers. A quick glance at the personnel comprising his 1947–49 teams demonstrates this rather forcefully. Apart from Jackie Robinson, Roy Campanella and Don Newcombe, his three black players, the rosters included two Scandinavian Americans (Phil Haugstad and John 'Spider' Jorgensen), an Irish American (Kevin 'Chuck' Connors, who became a TV star in the 1950s), a German American (Harold 'Pee Wee' Reese), a Puerto Rican (Luis Olmo), three Italian Americans (Ralph Branca, also part Hungarian, Harry 'Cookie' Lavagetto and Carl Furillo), a Slovakian American (George 'Shotgun' Shuba), a Jewish

American (Cal Abrams) and the usual American stocks of Scottish-Irish and English. In the 1930s and 1940s, ethnics were most eager to prove their proficiency in sport since that was a primary entry point for them into the American mainstream. Rickey drew deeply from this pool since working-class ethnicity was a Brooklyn trait and fans from that borough found it empowering to make a symbolic connection with their local heroes. See P. Levine, *Ellis Island to Ebbets Field: Sport and the American Jewish Experience* (New York: Oxford University Press, 1992), pp.120, 131, 281.

35. 'Brooklyn Dodgers Sign First Negro to Play in Organized Baseball', *Life*, 19 (26 Nov. 1945), 133–4.
36. 'Playing Ball', Editorial in *Saturday Review of Literature*, 38 (26 Nov. 1945), 12.
37. Cousins, 'All Star Second Baseman', 11.
38. 'Sport', *Time*, 46 (5 Nov. 1945), 77. Other black journalists who believed Rickey's initiative was of vital concern to American blacks were Wendell Smith of the *Pittsburgh Courier*, Sam Lacy of the *Baltimore Afro-American*, Frank Young of the Chicago Defender and Joe Bostic of Harlem's *People's Voice*. See Falkner, *Great Time Coming*, p.95; Rampersad, *Jackie Robinson*, p.120.
39. Rowan, *Wait Till Next Year*, pp.121–2.
40. Young, *Great Negro Baseball Stars*, p.21. The Negro Leagues 'died' after integration, between 1948 and 1960. Rader, *American Sports*, p.298.
41. Roeder, *Jackie Robinson*, p.69. Rickey was aided in his campaign by Communist newspapers such as the *Daily Worker*, urban, black newspapers, among them those mentioned in Note 38 and liberal white newspapers such as the *New York Daily News*, whose sports columnist Jimmy Powers had agitated against baseball's colour ban since 1931. He was aided by other white journalists, including Westbrook Pegler, Ed Sullivan, Damon Runyan, Shirley Povich and Dave Egan. See Rampersad, *Jackie Robinson*, p.120; Falkner, *Great Time Coming*, p.95.
42. Rowan, *Wait Till Next Year*, p.11.
43. Ibid.
44. Ibid., p.156.
45. Ibid., p.164.
46. Ibid., p.166; Falkner, *Great Time Coming*, Ch.15; Rampersad, *Jackie Robinson*, Ch.7.
47. Mann, *Branch Rickey*, p.216.
48. E. Fitzgerald, 'Branch Rickey – Dodger Deacon', *Sport*, 3 (Nov. 1947), 61.
49. J. Lardner, 'The Old Emancipator', *Newsweek*, 48 (2 April 1956), 85; M. Polner, *Branch Rickey: A Biography* (New York: Atheneum, 1982), pp.169–70.
50. A. Murray, 'Rickey Sees His '47 Dodgers as Best Ever',*The Sporting News*, (26 Feb. 1947), 10.
51. Rowan, *Wait Till Next Year*, p.168; H. Frommer, *Rickey and Robinson: The Men Who Broke Baseball's Color Barrier* (New York: Macmillan Publishing Co., Inc. 1982), pp.123–4.
52. Robinson, *Baseball Has Done It*, p.45.
53. Rowan, *Wait Till Next Year*, p.168.
54. H.C. Burr, 'Rickey Won't Poll Dodgers About Jackie', *Sporting News* (9 April 1947), 7.
55. Young, *Great Negro Baseball Stars*, p.19.
56. Mann, *Branch Rickey*, p.259.
57. A. Daley, 'Play Ball', *New York Times*, 15 April 1947, 31.
58. 'Baseball's Color Bar Broken', *Christian Century*, 66 (23 April 1947), 517.
59. Rowan, *Wait Till Next Year*, p.185; Chalberg, *Rickey*, pp.126–7; Polner, *Branch Rickey*, p.199; Frommer, *Rickey*, pp.138–9.
60. Young, *Great Negro Baseball Stars*, p.45.
61. Lardner, 'The Old Emancipator', 85.
62. Rowan, *Wait Till Next Year*, p.183; Falkner, *Great Time Coming*, pp.163–5; Chalberg, *Rickey*, pp.123–5; Rampersad, *Jackie Robinson*, pp.172–6.
63. Rowan, *Wait Till Next Year*, p.190; Tygiel, *Baseball's Great Experiment*, pp.213–19.
64. Carter, 'Sports', p.293. The best scholarly work on Cobb is C.C. Alexander's outstanding monograph, *Ty Cobb* (New York: Oxford University Press, 1984).
65. Robinson, *Baseball Has Done It*, p.58.
66. Rowan, *Wait Till Next Year*, p.193. Most of the press was fair and Jackie Robinson even appeared on the cover of *Time* magazine. See Tygiel, *Baseball's Great Experiment*, Ch.10 and especially his comprehensive citations on pp.362–3. Also helpful is Chalberg, *Rickey*, p.131.

67. Robinson, *My Own Story*, foreword.
68. J. Chamberlain, 'Brains, Baseball and Branch Rickey', *Harper's Magazine* 196 (April 1948), 355.
69. H. Goren, 'Jackie Robinson's Himself Now', *Baseball Digest*, 7 (Oct. 1948), 65–7.
70. Rowan, *Wait Till Next Year*, pp.202–11.
71. Roeder, *Jackie Robinson*, p.151. Branch Rickey notwithstanding, Robinson's involvement in the Robeson episode is problematic, as was his entire post-baseball civil-rights career. His anti-Communist, and therefore anti-Robeson, speech was very popular in 1949, but was less so two decades later, when guilt by association or innuendo was no longer motivating for the American mind. Shortly before his death, Robinson backed away from the most accusatory elements of that speech, although not from its general tenor. See Tygiel, *Baseball's Great Experiment*, p.334 and Rampersad, *Jackie Robinson*, p.216. As a concerned citizen in the arena of civil rights during the 1950s and 1960s, Robinson was tireless and generous but did not always strike a responsive chord with blacks or whites. At times, he was uncomfortable or disillusioned with the NAACP, Malcom X, Martin Luther King, John F. Kennedy, Nelson Rockefeller, Richard Nixon and Lyndon Johnson. Therefore, he was neither a consistent Republican nor Democrat. See Chalberg, *Rickey*, pp.191–228. One possible explanation for his indecision might be that the public expected too much of him. In fact, he was no ideologue and the sole consistencies of his life were commitments to black civil 'equality', a hate of race prejudice and a high regard for the Protestant work ethic. Above all, he was pragmatic rather than intellectual and that is why those with theories found him disappointing, even anachronistic.
72. Woodward, 'In the Rickey Manner', 21.
73. 'Sports', in J. P. Guzman (ed.), *1952 Negro Year Book* (New York: William H. Wise and Co., Inc., 1952), p.18.
74. Holland, 'Mr. Rickey and the Game', p.188.
75. Mann, *Branch Rickey*, p.303.
76. 'Branch Rickey Discusses the Negro in Baseball Today', *Baseball Digest*, 16 (July 1957), 63.
77. Rickey, *The American Diamond*, p.47.
78. F. Graham Jr., 'Branch Rickey Rides Again', *Saturday Evening Post*, 236 (9 March 1963), 66.
79. Rickey, *The American Diamond*, p.46.
80. E. Fitzgerald, 'Branch Rickey, Baseball Innovator', *Sport*, 33 (May 1962), 63.
81. Lardner, 'The Old Emancipator', 85.
82. Rickey, *The American Diamond*, p.2. Rickey supported Hoover in his quest for the presidency. See Polner, *Branch Rickey*, p.116.

4

Personal Calvaries: Sports in Philadelphia's African-American Communities, 1920–60

ROBERT GREGG

At the beginning of the twentieth century, segregation, or 'Jim Crow', as it was called by contemporaries, began to spread out of the American South to many cities around the northern United States.[1] Although signs would not be posted in cities such as Philadelphia designating 'colored' washrooms or 'white-only' fountains, and segregation would remain *de facto* rather than *de jure*, there was one arena in particular where segregation was both visible and, in a sense, also legal. In the second half of the nineteenth century, black athletes had been able to play both alongside and against white athletes. But gradually, Jim Crow gained acceptance in American sports, the most important division occurring in baseball's National League, which established a 'Gentleman's Agreement' in the 1890s to bar black players from its teams.[2] Some sports, like football and boxing, remained integrated to a certain extent, but segregation was almost complete in most others.

Rather than diminishing sport participation among African Americans, however, it appears that black sporting institutions flourished as segregation intensified. As was the situation in Trinidad described by C.L.R. James in *Beyond a Boundary*, 'caste and class did not retard but stimulated' sport among African Americans. This realization was for James a 'personal calvary', and African Americans in Philadelphia would also have recognized that for them the sporting arena was 'a stage on which selected individuals played representative roles which were charged with social significance'.[3] Indeed, when African Americans played basketball, football and baseball in Philadelphia during the first half of the twentieth century, they immediately confronted the segregated nature of the city. Further, engaging in sports necessitated that they come to understand their class, gender and racial positions in society.

This essay attempts to outline some of the major themes of this largely unwritten history. Although many of Philadelphia's leading black sportsmen and women (for example, Roy Campanella, Zachary Clayton, Charles 'Tarzan' Cooper, Inez Patterson and Ora Washington) are quite well known, as are the city's leading black sports teams from the period (Hilldale, the Stars and the Warriors), the relationship of sports to community formation (especially the impact of segregation and integration) is less well understood.[4] While we have a relatively clear understanding of the sporting contributions of African Americans and the many problems and dimensions of race in sport, we have still not advanced far beyond the situation outlined by Melvin L. Adelman 20 years ago, when he complained that there was 'no historical scholarship on sport in the black community'.[5] It is this relationship between sport and community that I wish to explore here, using the words of many of the participants themselves.[6]

Rather than focusing on well-known sports heroes, such as boxers Jack Johnson and Joe Louis, track-and-field star Jesse Owens, or baseball star Jackie Robinson, this paper looks at the communities from which such figures emerged. Moving beyond the semi-professional sporting teams that developed within the communities, it describes the institutions that were established to help channel players into these teams. In the process, it reveals a history of organizational initiative in Philadelphia's African-American communities that was virtually brought to an end by the process of integration in the 1950s.

The need to describe this history is emphasized by the fact that over the last 40 years sports have taken on a different role from that which they had between the world wars. For many of today's African Americans, sport is seen (perhaps mistakenly) as a last chance for the lowest-class members of society, something for which total preparation is required to the exclusion of academic studies and other pastimes. In the inter-war period, on the contrary, sports clubs and institutions were dominated largely by the better-off members of the community, and these people tended to see sports as a means to keep children in school and to guide them to a better career in adulthood. In short, the old Victorian ideals associated with sports, that they would be character forming and lead to good associations, survived within the black community, when commercial sports had already started to undermine such beliefs in other communities.[7]

Sport played a vital role in bringing together black communities. Although the sporting institutions were dominated by leading members of the community, the participants and many of the most successful sportsmen and women came from poor backgrounds, and sport became their avenue to acceptance and prestige within (certainly not outside) the community. This occurred just at the time when the community seemed to be fragmenting, when northward migration brought to the city thousands of southern African Americans who had had very different religious and social backgrounds from most of the longtime urban black residents. Since the churches were beginning to lose their exclusive hold over the black community, many people who might have turned to the church for a chance to become prominent within the community now turned to sports organizations. Churches, in some ways, became less significant in terms of uniting the community than the quasi-religious organizations like the Young Men's and Women's Christian Associations, the Boys Clubs and the Fraternities. Clearly, none of these institutions rejected the churches and their important role in the community, but until the churches themselves began to realize the importance of sport, they were to lose some of the prominence they once had.[8]

Many African Americans excelled at sport in spite of the barriers placed in their way. These men and women used sport to help them deal with life in neighbourhoods, schools, colleges and at the work place. So successful were African Americans' attempts to build community around sporting activities, that the decline of many black sporting institutions after the return of integration had a major impact on black community development in the city.

BLACK SPORTS AND PASTIMES IN NINETEENTH-CENTURY PHILADELPHIA

Organized sport, with teams, venues and leagues, began to emerge in Philadelphia during the second half of the nineteenth century. African Americans participated in this process right from the start, forming their own teams and competing alongside white athletes. African Americans became especially identified with boxing and horse racing, two of the oldest professional sports. Black Philadelphians also played baseball and football, and participated in the 1890s cycling craze.[9] Boxing was particularly popular among Philadelphia's African Americans because it was a relatively democratic sport. Any young man who wanted to do so could participate and no expensive equipment or training was needed. Other team games required expensive gymnasia or playgrounds before they could be performed, and these were not readily available for poorer people in Philadelphia during the nineteenth century. Boxing, however, could be practiced on the streets.

Philadelphia produced a number of good African-American boxers prior to 1900, the most successful of whom was Walter Edgerton. He challenged George Dixon, a black man from Boston, to meet him for the world lightweight title during the mid-1890s. Before he could meet Dixon, however, Edgerton was involved in a shooting incident on Lombard Street, ending his dream of becoming the titleholder. Ironically, given the later stereotypes that would emerge, the style of boxing associated with African Americans was that of grace and intelligence. While Irish and Italian boxers were noted for their aggressive style, attempting to knock down their opponents with thunderous punches, black boxers at this time attempted to use skill to outsmart their opponents. But boxing was not racially egalitarian; some white boxers were willing to fight against African Americans, others were not. Moreover, the elite clubs would never treat blacks as equals. In 1892, for example, the Ariel Club staged a tournament for black boxers in which the top prize was a janitorial job at the club itself.[10]

During the 1880s, thoroughbred racing was open to black jockeys. The two most successful were former Southerners, Isaac Murphy and George Simms. Murphy, an ex-slave, had earned over $200,000 by 1890. During the 1890s, however, a campaign to make racing 'respectable' intensified, the main aim of which was to exclude blacks. From about 1895 onwards, therefore, African Americans were kept out of the sport altogether.[11]

In spite of the expense of baseball, the need for equipment and playing fields, and the fact that the game was initially associated with the white elite, black Philadelphians did participate in this sport. The most important black team, the *Pythians*, was organized by 'Jake' White, Jr. in the early 1860s. The *Pythians* challenged the Philadelphia *Athletics* in 1867, after the white team had won the inter-city title. The *Athletics* declined the offer, perhaps because they feared the *Pythians'* reputation. Had the match been played the black team might have become the equivalent of national champions. In 1869, not only did white teams refuse to play them, they barred the *Pythians* from the state league. Instead, the black team entertained other black teams from places as far away as Chicago and Washington, DC. The *Pythians* faded as a club during the 1870s, perhaps because of the difficulty of finding teams to play against.

During the 1880s, however, the *Cuban Giants* emerged as a very popular team. The Philadelphia connections of the *Giants*, who played in Trenton, New Jersey, were strong. A number of the best players on the team, including pitcher Shepard Trusty, came from Philadelphia. The *Giants* had an excellent record playing against National League teams, but were never able to join the league itself. In the 1890s, National League officials like Albert Goodwill Spalding and Cap Anson, the leading white player of the day, set about excluding from professional baseball not just black teams but black ballplayers as well. The last African American to play in the major league before Jackie Robinson desegregated baseball once again in the 1940s, was Moses Fleetwood Walker, who was a successful player for Toledo in the American Association.[12]

African Americans also played American football in nineteenth-century Philadelphia. Lincoln University was famous for an undefeated record in 1898. However, no black football clubs existed in the city until the formation of clubs at the YMCA and the Settlement Houses in the 1920s. Instead, individual African Americans were accepted onto and recruited for mostly white school and college teams.[13]

The sudden development of bicycling around the country during the 1890s placed in the hands of poorer members of society a relatively inexpensive form of transportation. Those who bought bicycles to get to work and to move around the city cheaply began to see that their two-wheelers had other possibilities and found fun in racing. Philadelphia's African Americans, in particular, turned bicycling into a team sport. Although they were barred from the white cycling organizations and were often excluded from the cycling parks or rinks that sprang up around the city, blacks formed their own clubs and held their races along many of the city's streets. By 1892 there were three black clubs in the city, one of which, the *Ebon*, was founded by bicycling policemen. So popular was the sport among the region's African Americans, that it was often associated with them in Philadelphia. It was also a sport in which black women could participate, in spite of prevailing Victorian values that tended to restrict women's participation in sport. Indeed, in 1894, African-American women established a racing club of their own, with the suggestive name of *Stars of Hope*.[14]

Black women's participation in sport, however, was limited on the one hand by the working positions of many poorer women and the gender-divided customs of those fortunate enough to have leisure time on the other. Throughout much of the nineteenth century, sport tended to be a middle-class preoccupation. Leisure denoted status, and wealthier people liked to show that they could relax and play while poorer people were working. Since most African Americans were in the poorer section of society, access to sport was limited for them. If this was true for the black community generally, it was even more so for black women.[15] Most black women worked as domestics, and such people were often not even given time off to attend church, let alone to play sport.[16]

There was a fairly sizeable black middle-class in Philadelphia, but as with white middle-class women, Victorian values dictated against sports participation for women. Sport was intended to prove masculinity. So, while men could compete against each other at club and college levels, women were often excluded from such events. These values began to lose sway, however, around the turn of the century. With the increase in women's education and the establishment of institutions like the YWCA, attitudes towards women's sport began to change. The ideology associated with sport became more nuanced, adding to its focus on masculinity, competitiveness and violence, a concern for character building, team spirit and racial uplift. In this context, educators and public health officials began to promote sport among women as the best way to respond to the ailing health of urban women.[17] However, the black community did not support women's sport to the same extent that men's sport was patronized.

Black participation in sport during the nineteenth century, then, had some similarities with the situation today. In certain sports, boxing and football in particular, the skills of black sportsmen were beginning to be celebrated and colleges and promoters attempted to benefit by including them on their teams. Not surprisingly, these two sports (with basketball, and track and field) either remained integrated or desegregated more quickly than baseball. In other sports in which African Americans participated during the nineteenth century, such as baseball and horse racing, the talents of black players were also recognized. However, in these sports they were seen as unwanted competition. Such sports became segregated and throughout the first half of the twentieth century, white participants put up stiff resistance to any attempts to re-integrate. While baseball finally succumbed to the notion of competition for all after the Second World War, horse racing has never recovered a significant black presence and remains an almost exclusively white sport.

THE SEGREGATED YEARS, 1890–1947

Before the Second World War, black Philadelphians established or participated in many great teams. At all levels, except the major leagues from which they were excluded, African Americans made important contributions to Philadelphia's sporting tradition. Neighbourhood clubs, business associations and church teams thrived in black communities at this time. These organizations were developed within the local neighbourhoods. Black Philadelphians' lives revolved around their communities and increasingly in Philadelphia this meant the local neighbourhoods within South, North and West Philadelphia, as well as Germantown and the other surrounding suburban communities which had a large enough black population to support institutional formation beyond the churches. As Grace Lindsay, an active participant in sport during her youth, later recalled: 'We were all neighborhood people. Everyone stayed within the neighborhood. You didn't venture too far away ... You might have done something with your church, but basically everyone stayed within their neighborhood.'[18] Each of the city's neighbourhoods had its own teams located at the Y's, the settlement houses, boys clubs, boxing gyms and playgrounds. Many black Philadelphians also participated in the African–American amateur and semi-professional teams which competed not just against other teams in the neighbourhood but also against teams from other black communities in the city and even against teams from other ethnic communities. Out of these games great neighbourhood rivalries developed.

These rivalries were often intense. Even today there is some resentment among longtime residents of one part of Philadelphia toward those living in another section. Interviewed in 1992, John Seawright still claimed that South Philadelphia teams had always fielded the same players and that they were afraid to play against the teams from his neighbourhood in North Philadelphia. The '"Toastie boys" wouldn't play us', Seawright claims, 'their fraternity world was another world'. Moreover, when a player left the neighbourhood fold, there was often ill feeling towards him. One such player, according to Seawright, had been trained to play center for a basketball team in North Philadelphia, and had gone off to Jefferson City, Missouri, where he parlayed his talents into a reputation as a great basketball player and membership in a fraternity. When he returned to Philadelphia, Seawright remembered with some resentment, he turned his back on his former companions and 'started playing with the fraternity boys'.[19]

South Philadelphia included the city's wealthiest African Americans, in part because this section housed the city's oldest black community. As such, it was able to support more sporting facilities for African Americans than any other Philadelphia neighbourhood. According to Anne Garrott, a former coach and director of the Young Women's Christian Association, people came from all over Philadelphia to compete in the games played in the black Ys, and at the section's many playgrounds: 'Streetcar number 40 came down South Street. I remember people getting out of it in droves at 16th Street and coming down to the Y. There were a lot of people coming from other sections [of the city].'[20]

The two most important institutions for sport in South Philadelphia were the Christian Street YMCA and the Southwest-Belmont YWCA. In these two institutions we can see the remnants of a 'social gospel' ideology blending with concepts of 'muscular Christianity'.[21] Consequently, both institutions could maintain an uneasy balance between reaching out to the poorest members of the black community and simultaneously protecting the prestige of black middle-class members. Sport was an important vehicle for achieving this balance, as those who showed prowess in particular games could enter a world that would otherwise have excluded them.

Established in 1889 at 1724 Christian Street, the black Young Men's Christian Association had a great influence on the development of sport in Philadelphia. The Y had its own gym and a small swimming pool, and many teams used it as their home base. Among the sports organized by, or played at, the Y, were basketball, football, swimming, badminton, table tennis and tennis. More important, though, the Y promoted a social philosophy with sport as its cornerstone. By helping young men to improve their physiques, members of the Y believed, they were also helping to improve their minds; by promoting leadership on the court or field, they believed they were also teaching young men leadership in other, more important arenas.

Elmer Griffin, the Y's physical director, taught swimming, boxing, basketball, and tennis and became an inspiration and mentor for many youngsters like Albert Bishop and 'Shing' Willis. He took children to nearby tennis courts to give them lessons. He also led groups on hikes along the Delaware River north of the city. Griffin himself had been one of the best basketball players in Temple University's history, as well as the first black athlete at that institution, from 1920–22 exhibiting unusual ability as a guard.[22]

Along with many others, Zachary Clayton learned his basketball at the YMCA. Clayton had been a member of Wissahickon Boys Club, but his coach, Abe Ballard, told him that the only place that he could get the practice and coaching he needed was at the Christian Street Y. So Clayton went down from Nicetown on the streetcar to join in the games at the Y. The first time he went there he did not even have the money for the streetcar fare and walked the several miles across the city. When he arrived he also did not have the 25 cents non-members needed to play, but Cal Graves, another YMCA coach, saw him 'hanging around the gym' and let him in to play. Once inside the gym, he was observed by Otto Briggs, the ex-Hilldale baseball player who was part owner of the *Philadelphia Tribune* (the city's leading black newspaper). Briggs liked Clayton's style and invited him to play for the Tribune Men, who practiced at the Y. Zach received $2.50 for each game to start with, but Briggs soon raised this to $3.00.

The Southwest-Belmont YWCA was another focal point for the black community. Built in 1923, it had the newest facilities in the area, so many organizations held their meetings there – sororities, the Urban League and the NAACP, for example.[23] Anne Garrott, later the YWCA's director, learned many of her sports at Southwest-Belmont. Other sports were taught in conjunction with the YMCA, but swimming was Anne Garrott's great love. Cal Graves, who had been nicknamed 'Toad', helped organize and coach the swim teams. The Y teams held yearly meets against the Colonial Club of New York, the Banneker Club in Washington, DC, and a Pittsburgh team. When this event was held in Philadelphia the venue was the McCoach playground pool, where the Y and YW held all their meets, because the Y pool was far too small for competitive swimming.[24]

The YWCA also ran badminton teams. In the Spring of 1941, one of their teams attended tournaments in Chicago and St Louis, for which they needed to raise money from the local community. On the road, the YMCA and YWCA teams had the same problems finding places to stay as other black teams playing outside Philadelphia. Players needed contacts in other cities because they were not allowed to stay in hotels. Often such contacts were made through churches. On one occasion when the YWCA badminton team visited Chicago for the tournament there, a church arranged for them to stay in the nearby armory.[25]

Support was hard to come by for the women's teams, however. A few notable benefactors, like Charlie Chew, Sr. and James Howard could be found, but generally people were less willing to support the girls' teams than the boys.' One man told Anne Garrott: 'The ladies ought to support the men. We have to bring up the boys.' She replied, 'You've got to remember that they're going to marry these young girls, so we need help to nurture young girls.' But support for women in sport remained limited at least until the 1950s.[26]

The O.V. Catto Elks Lodge at 16th and Fitzwater Streets was a center for fraternity basketball. On Sunday afternoons games were held between different black fraternities. In the morning, people dressed up in their best outfits, women wearing their hats, go to Sunday school and church, and then head over to the lodge in the afternoon to watch the basketball. At least 50 people could watch the games sitting on folded chairs at courtside.

The black communities of North Philadelphia formed after those in the southern section of the city. Between the two world wars, African Americans lived in small pockets north of Market Street, surrounded by European immigrant communities. According to John Seawright:

> From 25th and Oxford to the Park was Polish and Irish people. And if you got caught out there you were in trouble. Across Broad Street you were in the 'jungle' … 1700 North to Lehigh Avenue was supposed to be a better grade of Negro. Then after the war, everything was a jungle. Broad Street was a boundary line. If you got caught on the other side of Broad Street, you had to fight. I could go on both sides.

The area was fast changing, however, as Seawright noted:

> All around 24th and Jefferson, when I first moved into this neigh-bourhood, in 1936, everything here was white, and by '40, by the time the war came, it was all black. Most of the people in South Philly stayed in South Philly. If you came [from the Southern states] to North Philly you stayed in North Philly.[27]

The relatively small size of the black community meant that for much of the 1920s and 1930s, African Americans had trouble gaining access to playgrounds and facilities that were associated with white ethnic communities. With some bitterness, Seawright remembered:

> We [lived] at 24th and Jefferson. The playground was at 26th and Jefferson, but it was for white people. It had everything in there. It

had a recreation yard. But the Negro didn't know that place until after the war. It had music, dancing, everything that white boys needed, that's what they had in that building.[28]

Prospects for blacks began to change with the opening of the Wharton Settlement House, located at 22nd and Columbia Avenue, which quickly became one of North Philadelphia's most important athletic centers open to African Americans. Established in 1930, the center followed in the tradition of the old settlement houses in attempting to 'uplift' the urban poor. Like other settlement houses and the Ys, the Wharton Center placed great emphasis on sport in helping the spread of what it considered 'American' values of thrift, sobriety and self-reliance.

Wharton Center's significance to North Philadelphia can be seen in the story of the Vagabonds, the premier club organized at the Settlement House. The Vagabonds had emerged in 1927 out of a bitter North Philadelphia neighbourhood rivalry. According to the club's own description of its formation, the Sharswood Streeters and the Garnet Streeters had 'tongue lashed' each other to such a point that physical combat seemed likely. Rather than street brawling, however, the leaders of both groups decided to settle the question of 'supremacy' on the football gridiron. When the game occurred at the park at 25th and Diamond Streets, it ended, after what participants maintain was a 'titanic struggle', tied at 6–6. But, instead of arranging to replay the game, the Sharswood and Garnet Streeters decided to unite, and took the name *Vagabonds*, a name clearly chosen to symbolize and even celebrate the class position of the new club's members.[29]

The club was not just a loose gathering of neighbourhood athletes; it became a well-run organization, holding meetings, paying dues to buy uniforms and pay for game officials, establishing qualifications for admittance, electing officers and writing a constitution. The club also incorporated itself: the members turned to the most prominent African-American lawyer in the city, Raymond Pace Alexander, to file the incorporation papers. Interestingly, the club was incorporated under the name 'Valabonds', because Alexander objected to the name Vagabonds, believing it brought the race into disrepute.[30] But the North Philadelphians cared less about such issues and continued to use their original name. After the Wharton Center opened, the Vagabonds used it as their base.[31] Rapidly the club established football and basketball teams which could compete with all-comers: 'You name them, we played them', Seawright remembered, 'Wissahickon, Black *Meteors, Pioneers, Panthers, Randy Dixon* [the club formed by the prominent black journalist], the *Buccaneers.*' And the Vagabonds generally defeated them all. 'When black teams got tired of losing to us', Seawright added, 'we went around beating the white boys – teams like *Cardoza*, the Jewish 'Y', *Passions*, and *Pearsons.*'[32] In 140 football games played in its first ten years, the club lost only 20, and recorded six undefeated seasons between 1928 and 1933.

In 1936, Philadelphia's Settlement Houses formed the Allied (basketball) League, which included, among others, Wissahickon Boys Club, Nicetown Boys Club and the Wharton Settlement House (represented by the Vagabonds). Of the seven teams, only Wissahickon and Wharton were black. Wharton beat all the other teams twice and split their two games with Wissahickon. As a result of this, Seawright maintained, the white teams broke up the league and started a new one the following year without the Vagabonds.

The Vagabonds also attempted, according to Seawright, to 'break up the turf', both by inviting players to join their team who came from neighbourhoods other than those in North Philadelphia, and by playing teams from all the other neighbourhoods. The more class-conscious South Philly teams, however, often would not play them. Many of the Vagabonds resented the 'O-P's' (Old Philadelphians) for their air of superiority, and believed that the South Philadelphia teams always fielded the same players in a desperate attempt to defeat them. Others, like Milton Bailey, made friends with members of the Y (people such as Frank 'Tick' Coleman, Zack Clayton and 'Shing' Willis, who themselves had lower-class migrant origins); and some Vagabonds even moonlighted, playing for the 'Vags' while also representing South Philadelphia fraternity teams.[33]

Composed mainly of the servants of upper-middle-class whites, Germantown's African-American community had been small throughout most of the nineteenth century. Like the communities in other sections of the city, however, the black community in Germantown grew rapidly during and after the 'Great Migration' of African Americans from the Southern states, which began during the First World War. With this growth, the community began to establish its own teams and soon earned a reputation for its sportsmen and women. Jack Saunders, a journalist for the *Philadelphia Tribune* remembered that – 'Up in

Germantown, everybody was [an athlete] up there. The Ballards, the Shields – Lonnie and his brother, the Smiths, everybody. They played something. They either played tennis, or basketball, or football, or they were good swimmers. They played golf.'[34] The most significant black sports club was the Wissahickon Boys Club, affiliated with the Boys' Council of Philadelphia. The Germantown Y was also open to young black boys and girls who wished to participate in sport. It was here that Ora Washington, the national black tennis champion, first learned her strokes.

The object of the Wissahickon Boys' Club was, in the words of its Superintendent, W.T. Coleman, 'to give the young men and boys "something to do" and to provide them with the right sort of thrill'. 'Character building' was considered the fundamental job of this institution. In 1926, the Boys' Club had a membership of 1,100 boys and men, more than 150 neighbourhood constituencies, and a summer camp at Camp Emlen catering for over 400 boys. Many hobbies were taught, cooking, candy making, cane seating, fancy work and hammock making, shoe repairing, show-card lettering, basketry and poster work. Great emphasis was placed on athletics, however, and in order to compete 'clean living' was essential – 'each boy must be above reproach in this respect'. Teams were fielded in baseball, football and track. The assistant director at the club for many years was Abe Ballard, who had a great influence on many black youngsters who made it to the highest levels of black sport. It was he who first recognized Zach Clayton's talent and sent him to play at the Christian Street Y. The Speed Marvels, the Vagabonds' great rivals, also used the Boys' Club for their home games.

Like the northern section of the city, West Philadelphia had clearly demarcated boundaries between different ethnic and racial communities. According to Eugene Benson, who grew up in the area:

> Parrish street was the border line between black and white. If we were caught on the wrong side of Parrish Street we'd have to run; and if they got caught on the other side they'd have to run. And that went on for years. They had a big dairy there that was the border line, called Scott Powells.[35]

Added to this, the black communities were also divided between 'top' and 'bottom'. North of Lancaster Avenue, towards Fairmount Park and from 57th to Cobbs Creek, was generally considered the 'top', an area with more prestige, while the area closer to the University of Pennsylvania was looked down upon. Bitter rivalries often developed across these boundary lines, sometimes witnessed in the schools and on the sandlots or streets.

As in the case of North Philadelphia, there were few facilities open to African Americans living west of the Schuylkill River. Bob Black and other children living in his mixed neighbourhood around 39th and Parrish played games like baseball, handball, football, tireball, halfball, boxball, wallball in the streets.[36] Grace Lindsay remembered only one playground in the area:

> At one point we lived at 57th and Haverford, it was an apartment building, and that's right around the corner from 57th and Summer. We went to the playground there (it might have been called Haddington playground at the time), nothing but a huge lot, like they all were, with one big building laboratory and, of course, arts and crafts. But everything else was just the swings, the maypole and a baseball diamond. That's all that was really there.[37]

Even so, while the facilities were limited, the playground was still important to black children in the area.

The athletes from all of Philadelphia's African-American communities were often brought together at Lincoln University, a black university founded in 1854 when three black men who wanted to go to a seminary were turned down by Princeton University. During Lincoln's first 100 years (before the Brown vs. Board of Education Supreme Court case, which ended segregation in 1954), 40 per cent of all African-American doctors and lawyers in the country graduated from Lincoln. Consequently, many of the most prominent black Philadelphians in the first half of the century hoped that their sons would share the 'Lincoln experience'. Not surprisingly, Lincoln appealed to Philadelphia's youngsters such as Frank 'Tick' Coleman when they were finishing up at high school and were looking for a college to attend. Coleman maintained that he had no choice but to go to Lincoln: 'I came up through the Y, and the Y had the volleyball team with all the doctors and lawyers and all the business people. And the different doctors and lawyers who I was very close to, they were from Lincoln.'[38] Athletics and academics complemented each other at Lincoln. Great emphasis was placed on sport, but, according to Coleman, a student was not able to represent the college unless he was performing well academically.[39]

The Philadelphia connection with Lincoln was very strong, and people who came from Philadelphia looked out for their peers. According to 'Tick' Coleman, there was a pride to uphold: 'If you were from Philadelphia and you were a freshman and your grades began to slip off, a senior from Philadelphia would tell you to come to his room to study with him. If you failed they would take you in the woods and [tan your hide].'[40] For black Philadelphians, the Lincoln–Howard game, which was held every year on Thanksgiving day, was an important community celebration. Beginning in 1919, the two schools would play every year in Philadelphia, usually at Shibe Park, the city's major league baseball park. It was the apex of sport for Philadelphia's African Americans. As many as 27,000 people attended the game, newspapers covered it, and other social events were organized around it.[41] After the football game, a big dance was organized. Anne Garrott remembered this annual ritual:

> When you're talking about basketball games you're talking about local community. When you're talking about the Lincoln–Howard classic, you're talking about alumni. A whole lot of people came from a whole lot of places … Conventions of groups … were planned to link either in Washington or Philadelphia at the same time. That was a much bigger thing even than the Sunday basketball games.[42]

The annual game lasted until 1960, when the tradition weakened owing to the effects of desegregation. White colleges started to recruit black students and Lincoln and Howard lost their standing as the two premier universities attended by African Americans.

Like the Lincoln–Howard classic, the Penn Relays were an important social occasion within the black community. Anne Garrott used to spend days preparing her clothes for this event. She and her friends were close to the men from Lincoln, so they never missed the Relays. But the Penn Relays were not entirely free of discrimination against African Americans. During the 1930s, according to Bert Lancaster, the black colleges were kept apart from the main events, placed in the Colored Intercollegiate Athletic Association grouping. There were a couple of occasions, he felt, 'when Lincoln would have won the straight championship, but they didn't get a chance to run against the white teams'.[43]

Churches did not become heavily involved in sport until the 1940s and 1950s. Occasionally a church might field its own team, but this would depend on the interest and religious beliefs of a particular minister. The more fundamentalist ministers, according to Al Bishop, tended to reject sport, while others used it as a way of attracting members into the fold. This sometimes led to the alteration of a particular church's involvement in sport with a change of pastor. At Union Baptist, 'Tick' Coleman's church, for example, Reverend Kirkland was open to sport, but he was followed by a more conservative minister who felt very differently and acted accordingly.[44] Instead, 'Tick' Coleman went over to St Simon's Church at 22nd and Reed, so that he could participate in the scouting troop there under a Mr Morgan. Reverend John Logan, Sr., minister of St Simon's, also established a small basketball court in the church basement where Coleman could play.[45] Three other churches which provided some sports facilities were Zoar Methodist Episcopal Church, St Peter Claver's Roman Catholic Church and Camphor Memorial Baptist Church. The last of these developed a very successful basketball team, winning the YMCA basketball league from 1946 to 1948. Camphor Memorial had its own basketball court and this helped attract young men and women to join the church.

Another way in which ministers became involved was in getting scholarships for youngsters in the community. According to Bert Lancaster, the Rev. Luther Cunningham sent people all over the country:

> See, they traveled. The ministers knew what colleges needed. 'I've got a kid in Philadelphia and he can do this.' 'Well, we've got a scholarship for him.' In those days you could go to a school for $250 a year. So you just had to give him a hair cut and enough money to get there.[46]

Nevertheless, in the heyday of sports in black communities, ministers and their congregations played a relatively minor role supporting sporting initiatives. This changed after the Second World War.

Before turning to further discussion of the impact of desegregation, it is worth focusing briefly on the three sports – boxing, baseball and basketball – in which African Americans were to contribute to a major transformation following the Second World War. Continuing from the nineteenth century, boxing had a strong following among African Americans in the city. Philadelphia was very much the headquarters for black boxers. Although they claimed residence in other cities, the leading

black boxers were very much in evidence in Philadelphia's black community between bouts. Before the Pennsylvania state legislature created a
boxing commission to supervise the sport in Pennsylvania, the Director
of Public Safety controlled boxing in the city. One director, Cortelyou,
was unfavourably disposed towards 'mixed bouts', and black fighters
were not given an equal opportunity to compete during his administration. However, with the advent of the State Athletic Commission, the
situation changed.[47] Governor Gifford Pinchot appointed an African-
American lawyer and former college athlete called Charles Fred White
to serve as one of the members of his first commission. He served from
October 1925 until September 1926, and this precedent was maintained
until 1939.

One of the reasons for Philadelphia's strength in boxing was the
presence of so many amateur boxing clubs in the city. During the 1930s,
there were four all-black athletic clubs whose major interest was boxing:
the John N. Marquess Athletic Club, the Crispus Attucks, the Benezet
Boys and the Wharton Community Center. The Eastside and Seymour
Clubs were white organizations, but a large number of black boxers was
also included in their membership. At one time, Sigma Theta team (later
renamed John M. Marquess) ruled the amateur boxing ranks, for many
years producing team and individual champions who defeated practically all competition. While blacks were strongly represented among
boxers' ranks, no club in the city held bouts promoted by an African
American.

Boxing captivated the minds of many young black children growing
up in Philadelphia. Throughout his years growing up, in spite of his own
uncle's death in the ring, Bob Black used to do almost anything to find a
way to watch a bout:

> When I was a kid I started going to the fights when I was in
> elementary school. Then when I was in junior high school, Lucien
> Blackwell's brother and I were in class [together], and he started
> me selling papers to get into the fights. And we used to go to the
> Arena, Municipal Stadium, Shibe Park, and we sold papers to get
> into all the fights. And after we sold our papers, or the fight started,
> I don't care how many papers I had left, I'd throw them away.
> Because you'd get your money back. You'd pay 40 cents for 40
> papers.[48]

Philadelphia has been the home of great fighters, trainers and referees.

Prominent among the first black professional fighters were Jack Blackburn, who later trained Joe Louis, Hank Griffin, Joe Butler and Joe Walcott. Joe Frazier, heavyweight champion of the world during the early 1970s, was another product of Philadelphia. The city also witnessed the emergence of great black trainers like 'Shing' Willis, George Gibbs (who was blind), and Sam Solomon, as well as World Championship referees like Zach Clayton, who became one of the most sought after referees in the world.

Members of Philadelphia's black communities were very prominent in the development of the Negro baseball leagues. In 1902, Barry Smith, a baseball writer for the *Tribune*, envisioned a professional team to represent Philadelphia. With the aid of H. Walter Schlichter, a white sportswriter for the Philadelphia *Item*, and shortstop Sol White, he formed the Philadelphia Giants. The team played under the shadow of the Cuban X-Giants until Rube Foster joined them and gave the team much-needed pitching strength.[49]

In 1904, the *Giants* waged their second fight for the title 'Colored Champions of the World', on that occasion succeeding by winning two of a three-game series in Atlantic City. By 1906, the *Giants* were established as the strongest black team in the country, holding the Negro League championship from 1905 to 1907. Other black baseball greats played alongside Foster: shortstop Grant 'Home Run' Johnson, outfielder Pete Hill, second baseman Charlie Grant and pitcher Dan McClellan. And, between 1903 and 1904, the team also featured the boxer Jack Johnson, playing at first base. Johnson left to pursue his boxing career (becoming the first African-American world heavyweight champion in 1908), but he would return occasionally to umpire a game and help fill the bleachers.

Foster complained that the players were not making enough money, and so at the end of the 1906 season eight of the team decided to join a team in the West. From that point on the *Giants* began a gradual decline, and they were replaced by Hilldale as Philadelphia's number one team. Hilldale Baseball Club was established in 1910 by Edward Bolden, a former Texan who worked for the Post Office, and by Charlie Drew, who ran buses out in Darby. Bolden began by bringing together a group of young black Philadelphians ranging in age from 15 to 17. Soon the team was incorporated and the first ball club ever to be owned outright by black capital became established. Bolden began hiring players from all over the country and gradually one of the best teams in America emerged. When Hilldale reached its peak, in 1925, none of the original players remained on the team.[50] Bolden was an extremely effective manager and president of Hilldale. Not only did he pick and train a squad of players which could compete with both local and national teams, but he also raised the money to pay the salaries and kept the club financially solvent.

The breakthrough year for Hilldale was 1923. In that year, Bolden signed several stars from western teams. He also helped to establish the Mutual Negro League, formed around the six best clubs in the East. In the following year, the Negro World Series was established in which the champions of the East, Hilldale, were matched against the champions of the West, the Kansas City Monarchs. The Monarchs won the series in ten games, but in 1925 Hilldale won the second Negro World Series, defeating the Monarchs 5–1.[51] Throughout these years Hilldale played barnstorming Major League teams in the off-season. Hilldale usually won, leading several commentators to proclaim them the best team in all of baseball. In the autumn of 1923, for example, Hilldale played seven games against white Major League teams winning six of them. Commissioner of Major League Baseball, Kenesaw Mountain Landis, embarrassed by his teams' performances, decreed that no Major League team under its own name could play a Negro League team. Henceforth, barnstorming teams were to be called 'All-Stars' and games were generally to be held outside the country (accounting for the growth of baseball leagues in places like Cuba and the Dominican Republic).

In 1931, however, Hilldale collapsed – yet another victim of the Great Depression. But two years later, Bolden organized a second baseball team in Philadelphia, the Stars. Webster McDonald was instrumental in the formation of this team. The Stars played first at 48th and Spruce Street before moving to 44th and Parkside. In its second year, the club won the Negro National League Championship, defeating Cole's American Giants in the playoff. The Stars lost some of their best players, however, and could not sustain their position at the top of the Negro League. According to Webster McDonald, the Stars developed a formidable line-up, and for two years 'did everything', but never quite reached the level of Hilldale.[52] The Stars lasted until 1950, when the integration of baseball led to the collapse of the Negro Leagues.

Black Philadelphia's many basketball clubs were responsible for producing a great many exceptional players, who went on to transform the way the sport was played in the United States. Responsibility for this transformation lay with the clubs rather than with Philadelphia's high schools, because many of the players were either excluded from their high school teams, or played fewer minutes than the often inferior white players. It was in the neighbourhoods away from school that their skills were honed, and where the traditions of black basketball emerged. By the end of the 1930s, basketball had become the most popular sport among Philadelphia's African Americans. More than 100 teams of all sizes, ages and classes played in more than a dozen halls nightly during the basketball season. Courts were maintained at the Ys and all the boys' clubs and settlement houses, while the semi-professional teams played at the Olympia, at Broad and Bainbridge Streets. During the 1940s, a double-header was staged by various fraternities on alternate Sundays at the O.V. Catto Hall, to which churchgoers would flock after their church services ended.[53]

The team that dominated the city's courts was the Philadelphia Giants, made up with one exception of South Philadelphians, players who had developed their skills at the Christian Street YMCA and playing for the Tribune Men. The team included Charles 'Tarzan' Cooper, Jackie Bethards and Bill Yancey. Before this team could make its full mark on national basketball, however, these three players were lured to the New York Renaissance, a team owned by a West Indian named Robert L. Douglas, previously dominated by West Indians.[54] The Rens, as they were known, had many accomplishments. In 1929, they defeated the New York Celtics and every team in the American Pro Court League in a number of series. In 1932, in Cleveland, Ohio, a two-game series between the Rens and the Celtics (starring Joe Lapchick and Nat Holman) drew 11,000 people on Saturday and 15,000 on Sunday. In 1933–34, they doubled the Celtics' 1925 professional record of 44 straight games by achieving an 88-game winning streak. In the same season, they defeated the Celtics in seven out of eight games. And, in 1939, the year Zach Clayton joined the team, the Rens won the first World's Championship in Professional Basketball, beating the New York Gothams. During their 27–year existence, their record was 2,588 wins to 539 losses.[55]

Among black women, three women – Inez Patterson, Ora Washington and Lula Ballard – shaped the development of basketball in Philadelphia. Inez Patterson had been brought up in West Philadelphia. She attended Temple University, and, before graduating in 1929, she made all-collegiate teams in hockey, tennis, basketball, track, volleyball, swimming and dancing – breaking many records in the process. The year she graduated from Temple University, Inez Patterson organized, managed, coached and captained the Quicksteppers, a basketball team that played at the YWCA and McCoach playground.[56] In its first season, this team won 15 out of 16 games. In the next season, the Quicksteppers competed against many white and black teams and won the Eastern United States championship, but the Germantown Hornets, captained by Ora Washington and coached by Joseph Rainey, defeated them. At the end of that season, in 1930, Patterson turned over her Quicksteppers to Otto Briggs, of the *Philadelphia Tribune*. And, after a very successful year defeating all comers, the Quicksteppers engaged in a five-game series with the Hornets and won.

When Ora Washington and Lula Ballard, the two tennis stars, defected from the Hornets to join Patterson's team, the Tribune Girls came into being. The team also featured Jessie Turner and Aretha Harris, and was now coached by the one-armed star from Peerless, Earl 'Shorty' Chappelle. From 1933 to the end of the decade, the Tribune Girls were outstanding; they were the champion women's basketball team in Pennsylvania (the only black team to play in the competition), and during the 1937–38 season the players engaged in a 3,000–mile tour of the South. In nine years of existence the team lost only six games to African-American teams around the country.[57] The Tribune Girls played according to 'boys' rules'. Educators had established 'girls' rules' earlier in the century in the earnest (if mistaken) desire to ensure that young women did not over-exert themselves, thereby risking their health, their femininity and their reputations.[58] The Tribune Girls, however, confronted many of the restrictions against women's participation in sports directly. Moreover, they played pick-up games with the men at McCoach playground and learned many of their skills from the Tribune Men, the other team owned by Otto Briggs.

The coming of the war in 1941 seems to have forestalled the transformation that was on the verge of taking place in women's basketball. The beginning of the war led to the disbanding of many leagues, which were never re-established.[59] After the war, many white women who might have participated in such leagues moved into the suburbs (following both renewed black migration and the passage of the veteran soldiers' 'Bill of Rights', which gave returning servicemen the ability to purchase their own houses). In addition, the sustained support for women's participation in sports was not available within the black community. Otto Briggs had been the exception. Anne Garrott's arguments that women needed financial support were powerless to halt the decline in support for semi-professional women's basketball, when the level of resources available at the semi-professional level generally declined so precipitously after the war.[60]

This is not to suggest that women's sport ended altogether. The leagues established by churches for young people after the war may actually have continued to increase participation among young women. What was different, however, was that these church initiatives were merely designed to keep 'youth' out of trouble – off the streets and out of the gangs – and as such were neither self-sustaining nor capable of redefining the nature of women's sports. In baseball and softball, in particular, these church initiatives maintained a clear division between boys and girls by establishing hardball leagues for the boys, and softball leagues for the girls.

THE GREAT TRANSFORMATION

Barriers to black participation in American sport began to collapse during the 1930s with the contests between the Rens and Celtics, and with the white and black barnstorming teams playing in the off-season and throughout Latin America. But 1946 brought the great step forward in the struggle for integration. In this year the Brooklyn Dodgers under the direction of Branch Rickey signed Jackie Robinson, formerly of the Kansas City Monarchs.

Ironically, the combination of the signing of Jackie Robinson by the Dodgers followed by the Brown vs. Board of Education Supreme Court decision in 1954, left many black communities in a weakened position. The integration of baseball represented the beginning of the end for viable, moneymaking, black sports organizations in the city. Soon after Jackie Robinson became a Dodger, the appeal of black semi-professional and club games waned, and the whole infrastructure that had developed around associated sporting activities seemed to crumble. Within a few years the Negro Leagues collapsed, and many players who had been making a living from baseball, but who were not picked up by major league teams, found themselves looking for new work.[61] Spectators who had turned out in their hundreds to watch local games and in their thousands to watch the semi-professionals play, now began to follow Philadelphia's major league teams. The ideological imperatives of local, ethnic sport, that it should uplift people and allow for an enjoyable diversion from working lives of considerable toil, gave way to the ideological imperative of professional sport, that it should entertain the many and profit the few.[62]

Once Jackie Robinson had broken the colour line, very few people, white or black, wanted to pay to watch games in the Negro Leagues, believing that the best talent had been taken up by the major leagues. Consequently, these teams were unable to pay their players the same salaries and soon they had to disband altogether. In the words of Gene Benson:

> Integration made us go out of business. Black leagues folded up because everybody was going to the major leagues and nobody supported black baseball anymore, so they started talking about cutting salaries and all that sort of stuff, and we weren't making anything to start with. And I quit. I quit before the league folded because I was too old to go into the majors, and I wasn't going to go into any minor league clubs, because if I wasn't going to play in the majors I wasn't going to bother with baseball anymore.[63]

The Brown decision meanwhile led to an exodus from the black colleges, with particularly devastating results to their sports programmes. Lincoln, for example, having been a powerhouse in football prior to the 1950s, and having in its Howard-Lincoln game provided African Americans in Philadelphia with their Thanksgiving festival, disbanded its football programme in 1961. The recruiting of students for teams, while not a totally new phenomenon (Lincoln University had given support to many student athletes), now became endemic as universities attempted to lure the best athletes to their institutions. In the process, many individuals who might have maintained strong ties to their communities now went to colleges distant from Philadelphia. In the short term, benefits could be reaped from integration, particularly in sports. Those individuals nurtured by black sporting clubs would become the superstars of professional and national collegiate sports. But the sporting institutions that helped produce these players would not survive to bring along more players. Moreover, the individualistic ethic of professional sport would result in the accumulation of wealth for individuals with minimal diffusion of wealth into the communities from which those athletes came.

Philadelphia's Department of Recreation was an extremely important site in which integration had its greatest impact, both positive and negative. Before the establishment of the Department of Recreation, city bureaus had had very few dealings with the city's black communities. This changed, however, with the election of Joe Clark, the city's first Democratic mayor. The establishment of the Department of Recreation coincided with large shifts in the city's population. Thousands of African Americans arrived in the city from the South, and the white population moved into the expanding northeast section of the city, or into the suburbs. As a result of these demographic shifts, many playgrounds which had previously been used by white ethnic communities now opened up to blacks. The Strawberry Mansion area of the city, for example, had been in a predominantly Jewish area, but it soon became dominated by African Americans. Consequently, while the recreation arm of the city government had never before had much impact on the lives of blacks in the city, the new Department was now in charge of parks located in African–American neighbourhoods. Since the political coalition which had brought the Democrats to power was built around African–American votes, city officials realized that they had to cater to the recreational needs of this population.

The first Commissioner of Recreation, Frederick R. Mann, responded to African–American communities by including a large number of black appointees in the expanding department. Very few African Americans had been appointed by the city to administrative positions before the 1950s and almost none before 1930.[64] In addition, the Department began undertaking numerous construction projects (most of them in the new Northeast – white – tracts of the city), and acquiring new properties that could be converted into recreation centers. Finally, the Department used its national, state and local funding to start leagues, and to hold athletic events and training clinics which would open the recreation centers to all Philadelphians. This massive expansion of the Department of Recreation's work helped to accelerate the process of integration which was occurring at this time in schools and universities as well as in professional sports.

This process of integration was also part of a transformation occurring in the social organization of the city, as residents' attention gradually shifted from the neighbourhood to the municipal level. African Americans and other city dwellers were being drawn out of their neighbourhood organizations – the boys' and girls' clubs, the city's Ys, fraternities and settlement houses – into the new recreation centres. At first, the recreation centres built on these local organizations, establishing competitions between the different clubs and organizations, but increasing municipal activism, the Department's relatively lavish funds, and the lure of state-of-the-art equipment, led to a decrease in the number of these neighbourhood organizations.[65]

The 1950s and 1960s were the successful decades of integration, when, in spite of the beginning of the relocation of industry outside the city limits, the city was growing sufficiently and receiving federal funding to enable such integration to occur, and for all neighbourhoods to receive improved services. After 1970, however, with increased de-industrialization and prolonged economic recession, this process slowed to a halt. The transformation from neighbourhood to municipal organization, the replacement of local organizations by city-run centres, had been so great that the declining fiscal health of the city had a far greater impact on inner-city residents than even the Great Depression of the 1930s had had.

After the Second World War, the involvement of the churches in sport grew significantly. Many ministers who had felt threatened by sport (as they had also felt threatened by the movies) now realized that rather than keeping children away from church, sports could be used to bring youth into the congregations. The need for such approaches then also seemed more pressing as gang violence was on the rise and concerns about the rise of juvenile delinquency were widespread. A few churches had provided space for basketball courts and other sporting activities, but now it became widely accepted among ministers and leading members of the churches that this was essential and that teams could be sponsored as well. In a declining community, however, these were rearguard actions. Whereas sport had been linked into all aspects of the communities' economic and social life during the 1920s and 1930s, it was now sprouting roots in the midst of urban blight.

CONCLUSION

The role of sport in African-American communities has undergone considerable change during the twentieth century. Before the 1940s, sport helped to bind communities together, which although threatened by outside pressures (discrimination and the limited availability of jobs), nevertheless remained strong. After the Second World War, both the sporting institutions, and the communities which relied upon them, began to disintegrate. In Philadelphia as a whole, greater emphasis was then placed on sport as spectatorship and diversion, with the focus being on the city's major league teams, rather than on participation and community formation. With the exception of basketball, which only required a basket of any shape and dimension, and the church leagues, Philadelphia's African Americans participated less in *organized* sport than they had before the war. Gone were the days when these sports could bring together a community. With the decline of sporting institutions, churches, which now began to use sport to bring new members into their congregations, were able once again to re-establish themselves as the *sine qua non* of institutional life in Philadelphia's ghettos, a position that they had not held since before the First World War.

NOTES

1. R. Gregg, *Sparks from the Anvil of Oppression: Philadelphia's African Methodists and Southern Migrants, 1890–1940* (Philadelphia: Temple University Press, 1993), Ch. 2; K. Kusmer, *A Ghetto Takes Shape: Black Cleveland, 1870–1930* (Urbana: University of Illinois, 1976).

2. P. Levine, *The Promise of American Sport: A.G. Spalding and the Rise of Baseball* (New York: Oxford University Press, 1985).

3. C.L.R. James, *Beyond a Boundary* (New York: Pantheon, 1983), p.72.

4. In the last 20 years, African Americans' participation in sports has begun to receive increased attention from journalists, sociologists, historians and social anthropologists. Numerous book-length studies have appeared concerning major sporting individuals, such as R. Roberts, *Papa Jack: Jack Johnson and the Era of White Hopes* (New York: Free Press, 1983); J. Tygiel, *Baseball's Great Experiment: Jackie Robinson and His Legacy* (New York: Oxford University Press, 1983) and A. Edmonds, *Joe Louis* (Grand Rapids, MI: Eerdmans, 1973). Many of the great black sports stars and personalities, both men and women, have written their autobiographies (for example, Wilt Chamberlain, Kareem Abdul-Jabbar). Several volumes have appeared, based upon extensive oral interviews, focusing on the old Negro Baseball players, for example, R. Peterson, *Only the Ball Was White: A History of Legendary Black players and All-Black Professional Teams* (New York: Oxford University Press, 1992) and J.B. Holway, *Voices from the Great Black Baseball Leagues* (New York: Da Capo Press, 1992) and *Blackball Stars* (Westport: Meckler Books, 1988). Much less is known, however, about past achievements and involvement of African Americans in games other than the major commercial sports. Arthur Ashe's *A Hard Road to Glory Glory: A History of the African-American Athlete, I: 1619–1918; II: 1919–1945* (New York: Warner Books, 1988), an encyclopedia of African-American sportsmen and sportswomen, has contributed a great deal in this respect, as has Edna and Art Rust Jr.'s *Illustrated History of the Black Athlete* (Garden City, NY: Doubleday, 1985).

5. M.L. Adelman, 'Academicians and American Athletics', *Journal of Sport History*, 10 (Spring 1983), 80–106; see also, S.A. Riess, 'The New Sport History', *Reviews in American History*, 18 (Sept. 1990), 311–25.

6. The words of these participants are drawn from interviews undertaken by Donna De Vore, tapes and transcripts housed at the African-American Historical and Cultural Museum (AAHCM), Philadelphia. The following individuals were interviewed: Milton Bailey (1992); Edward B. Bell (9 April 1993); Eugene Benson (9 Feb. 1992); Lucy Mae Berry (15 Feb. 1992); Albert Bentley Bishop (5 Jan. 1992); Bob Black (21 Dec. 1991); Booker Brown (24 and 31 Aug. 1992); Benjamin Cain (11 July 1992); William Cash (9 Jan. 1992); John Chaney (12 Oct. 1992);

Zachery Clayton (29 Feb. 1992); Harold Coles (17 Aug. 1992); Frank Coleman (20 Sept. 1992); Ira S. Davis; Peterson F. DeVore (29 Aug. 1992); Mahlon Duckett (13 Aug. 1992); Anne Garrott; Katherine Jones (31 Jan. 1992); Columbus Knox (12 June 1993); Bert Lancaster (5 Oct. 1992); Albert Larke (12 Aug. 1992); Grace Lindsay (2 Feb. 1992); Jimmy Meyers (4 Jan. and 6 July 1992); Eric I. Mitchell (9 March 1992); Connie Morgan; Sam Solomon; Alice Swann (1 March 1993); John Seawright (8 Jan. 1992); John H. Thompson (26 Jan. and 16 Feb. 1992); Andy Warthen (11 July 1992); Sue Watson (12 July 1992) Nathaniel Washington (24 Jan. 1992) Walter Willis (9 Jan. and 18 Jan. 1992). Notes throughout the paper refer to these interviews thus, for example: AAHCM: Seawright. The Museum also has a transcript of an interview by Allen B. Ballard of John Saunders (AAHCM: Saunders). In addition, the author participated in meetings held at AAHCM (tapes held at the museum). The meetings included Benson, Clayton, Coleman, Garrott, Lancaster, Seawright, and Willis. Notes to these meetings are designated thus: AAHCM meeting: Garrott, for example.

7. This explains some of the recent appeal of the Negro Leagues. The ball players seemed more autonomous, less dictated to by management, and some of the love of the game remained, etcetera. This theme has been taken up by sports historians who have employed modernization theory (for example, A. Guttman, *From Ritual to Record: The Nature of Modern Sports* [New York: Columbia University Press, 1983]). For a description of the Victorian ethos in sports, see V. Ranjitsinhji, *The Jubilee Book of Cricket* (London: Thomas Nelson and Sons, 1897); James, *Beyond a Boundary*; Levine, *Promise of American Sport*; H. Green, *Fit for America* (Baltimore: Johns Hopkins Press, 1986).

8. Gregg, *Sparks from the Anvil*, Ch. 2.

9. R. Lane, *William Dorsey's Philadelphia and Ours: On the Past and Future of the Black City in America* (New York: Oxford University Press, 1992), pp.324–5

10. Ibid., p.322.

11. Ibid., p.321–2.

12. Ibid.; Peterson, *Only the Ball was White*; Tygiel, *Baseball's Great Experiment*.

13. Works Progress Administration (WPA). Records of the WPA Pennsylvania Historical Survey, 1933–42 – 'The Negro in Philadelphia: Recreation and Athletic Development – Sports' (unpublished typescript, copy held at AAHCM, 1942).

14. Lane, *William Dorsey's Philadelphia*, p.324.

15. In *Righteous Discontent* (Cambridge: Harvard University Press, 1993), Evelyn Brooks Higginbotham notes that college women from Spelman used to break up ball games among women in rural Georgia, suggesting that such games were quite common in that area.

16. Gregg, *Sparks from the Anvil*.

17. R. J. Park, 'Sport, Gender and Society in a Transatlantic Victorian Perspective', in R.J. Park and J.A. Mangan (eds.), *From 'Fair Sex' to Feminism* (London: Frank Cass, 1987), pp. 58–87; C.L. Himes, 'The Female Athlete in American Society, 1860–1940' (unpublished PhD dissertation, University of Pennsylvania, 1986); S.A. Riess, *Major Problems in American Sports History: Documents and Essays* (Boston: Houghton Mifflin, 1997), pp. 85–7, 94–103, 247–58.

18. AAHCM: Lindsay.

19. AAHCM: Seawright.

20. AAHCM meeting: Garrott.

21. E. Lasch-Quinn, *Black Neighbours: Race and the Limits of Reform in the American Settlement House Movement, 1890–1945* (Chapel Hill: University of North Carolina Press, 1993); Green, *Fit for America*.

22. AAHCM Meeting: Willis.

23. K. Mittelman, *A Spirit that Touches the Problems of Today: Women and Social Reform in the Philadelphia Young Women's Christian Association, 1920–1945* (unpublished PhD dissertation, University of Pennsylvania, 1987).

24. AAHCM: Garrott.

25. Ibid.

26. Ibid.

27. AAHCM: Seawright.

28. Ibid.

29. 'The Vagabonds, 25th Anniversary Commemorative Pamphlet', and other materials donated

by John Seawright to AAHCM.
30. Records of Raymond Pace and Sadie T. Alexander: Wissahickon Boys Club Ledger, University of Pennsylvania Archive; Wharton Settlement House records, Temple University Urban Archives.
31. For information on Wharton (though significance of sport is omitted from the analysis), see Lasch-Quinn, *Black Neighbours*.
32. AAHCM: Seawright.
33. AAHCM: Bailey, Willis, Coleman and Clayton.
34. AAHCM: Saunders.
35. AAHCM: Benson.
36. Boxball was a popular game, according to Bob Black. A box with four bases was drawn in the street and a game of baseball was played, but without bats. Each player used his hands. Boxball taught the children timing and how to catch; AAHCM: Black.
37. AAHCM: Lindsay.
38. AAHCM: Coleman.
39. Ibid.
40. Ibid.
41. AAHCM: Garrott.
42. Ibid.
43. AAHCM: Lancaster.
44. AAHCM: Bishop.
45. AAHCM: Coleman.
46. AAHCM: Lancaster.
47. WPA, 'The Negro in Philadelphia'.
48. AAHCM: Black.
49. WPA, 'The Negro in Philadelphia'; Peterson, *Only the Ball was White*.
50. AAHCM, Records of Hilldale Baseball Club.
51. Ibid.
52. Holway, *Voices from the Great Black Baseball Leagues*.
53. WPA, 'The Negro in Philadelphia'; 'Basketball', *Philadelphia Tribune*, 1 Jan. 1963.
54. *Philadelphia Tribune*, 1 Jan. 1963.
55. Ibid.
56. WPA, 'The Negro in Philadelphia', p. 15.
57. 'Basketball', *Philadelphia Tribune*, 1 Jan. 1963.
58. Riess, *Major Problems in American Sports History*.
59. One explanation for this might be found in the attempts of baseball owners to lure white women athletes into baseball and softball leagues, as a way of maintaining the 'American game' throughout the duration of the war.
60. AAHCM: Garrott.
61. AAHCM: Benson.
62. P. Hoch, *Rip off the Big Game: The Exploitation of Sports by the Power Elite* (Garden City, NY: Anchor Books, 1972); L. Lowenfish, *The Imperfect Diamond* (New York: Da Capo Press, 1991).
63. AAHCM: Benson.
64. AAHCM: Corbitt.
65. Ibid.

5

New Traditions, Old Struggles: Organized Sport for Johannesburg's Africans, 1920–50

CECILE BADENHORST

In the second half of the nineteenth century, following the pattern of British colonial control, sport became increasingly institutionalized among the African petty bourgeoisie and the 'coloured' community. In the Cape Province, cricket and rugby were by far the most popular sports. Sporting organizations for Africans were organized much later in Johannesburg than in the rest of the country. As workers flooded to Johannesburg and the surrounding Witwatersrand after the turn of the century, informal sports events began to take place. Soccer particularly appealed to working-class Africans. A fairly unorganized soccer league called the Witwatersrand District Native Football Association was set up in 1917 by the recruiting corporations of the gold mines. But it was disbanded in 1920 because there were too few grounds to play on and not enough organizational support.[1]

The period between 1920 and 1950 was one of tremendous change for South Africans living in and around Johannesburg. Rapid urbanization, the economic depression of the 1930s, acute housing shortages, high unemployment, rising crime rates and increased political activity provided the social context for Africans moving from the rural areas to Johannesburg. Yet the period was also characterized by the development of a rich social and cultural life among Africans in the city. Even though informal sports activities took place from Johannesburg's earliest days, it is significant that the first formal organization of sport for Africans was not founded until the 1920s. In 1919, the Helping Hand Club (HHC) for women was established, followed by the Bantu Men's Social Centre (BMSC) in 1924. Both of these clubs served as the umbrella bodies for organized African leisure-time. Recreation for women, though, was never organized to the same extent or with the same intensity as men's leisure. The Bantu Men's Social Centre, by far the most important cultural institution launched during this period, was constituted as a 'gentlemen's club' and offered reading rooms, debating forums and indoor games. At the indoor gym, African men played volleyball, basketball, other ball games and athletics. In 1929, the Johannesburg Bantu Football Association was formed. In 1931, the Bantu Sports Club (BSC) was set up to host a variety of sports such as cricket, tennis, athletics, boxing and basketball. Leagues were run from this club with affiliated clubs participating. Finally, from the BSC, the Johannesburg African Football Association was organized in 1932. The two soccer associations were the largest in Johannesburg, indeed in the whole of South Africa, during this period. During the 1930s, the formal organization of sports expanded rapidly.[2]

This expansion of organized recreation coincided with economic and political upheaval during the same period. The BMSC was established during a period of instability after the First World War. The Bantu Sports Club and soccer associations emerged during the uncertain Depression years of the early 1930s. The expansion of organized sport during the latter half of the 1940s coincided with massive African urbanization, worsening township conditions, and increasing African political militancy. On the gold mines, efforts to organize recreation kept pace with African mineworkers' collective activities. When these culminated in the 1946 mineworkers strike, the mining industry's interest in recreation intensified considerably.[3]

The organization of African sport and recreation in Johannesburg can be divided into two periods. During the 1920s and 1930s, white liberals and American missionaries became the 'experts' on controlled recreation. They decided which activities were 'beneficial' for Africans. In the second period after 1940, the Johannesburg City Council and the mining industry took the initiative. Throughout both periods, however, all of these actors – the liberals, missionaries, municipality and mining industry – were involved to a greater or lesser extent in the organization of recreation for Africans.

This essay examines the people who were involved in organizing African sport and tries to understand their intentions from the 1920s until the imposition of Apartheid structures in the 1950s. The primary source material for this research is archival. Besides the Bantu Men's Social Centre and the Helping Hand Club records on women's recreation, which still exist, documentation for most of the other clubs and associations has either been destroyed or dispersed. In addition, between 1920–50, there were no separate records for African sport in official sections of the archives. Consequently, the structure, management and development of the clubs and associations discussed in this essay have been pieced together from a variety of archival sources that range from personal records to official health and police files. Throughout the detailed process of constructing this story of the organization of British and American sports among Africans in Johannesburg, some issues were much clearer than others and some people's positions more evident. When this project was first started, I was fascinated by the rich 'unorganized' social and cultural life of Africans in Johannesburg during the 1920s, 1930s and 1940s. I was equally interested in the intense need of the whites to organize and control sport for Africans, to contain African culture, which was so evident from the surviving documentation. The archival sources indicated that the story of organized sport in Johannesburg was particularly complex. In the face of such complexity, broader questions about culture, race and power continually surfaced. Were cultural activities, like sport, part of the non-coercive tools of domination? Could these non-coercive tools be resisted? How was organized sport linked to the racial discourse prevalent at the time? Why did some practices and invented traditions become incorporated into everyday life and others become the source of conflict? Why was sport seen as a successful 'site' for the socialization and social control of subordinate groups? And, finally, what was the relationship between culture and power?

It is no coincidence that the unsettled period following the First World War, when the Industrial Commercial Union and Communist Party were formed, and trade unions and industrial action increased, also produced the liberal inter-racial Joint Councils organization and clubs like the Bantu Mens Social Centre in Johannesburg.[4] The liberals hoped that sport and recreation could divert African attention and provide a desired antidote to urban social ills.[5] The liberals, missionaries and the municipality were aware that it was the appalling conditions of urban life that produced the 'social ills' they railed against. As one commentator noted:

> African crime is not an isolated factor. It is linked with the subordinate position of the Bantu in the Union. It is to be found in their grinding poverty, their illiteracy, their treatment by Europeans. It

is to be sought in the slums they live in, their lack of recreational facilities and it may in part be attributed to the fact that they are a people in transition, ill-equiped to deal with the problems of urbanization and readjustment.[6]

Aware of the restricted and subordinate position of Africans in Johannesburg, was it just that the liberals, missionaries and the municipal officials were unable to see beyond the paternalistic racial hegemony which blamed Africans for their inability to adapt to 'civilization'? Although they realized that poverty was one of the main reasons for crime, gambling and juvenile delinquency, they saw the answer in teaching Africans more 'civilized' ways of coping with urban life. For many of the liberals and missionaries, state efforts at policing the city and the townships had few reformative results. By contrast, many believed that organized sport could and did effectively address these urban problems. Ray Phillips, an American Board Missionary, remarked that the number of African law 'offenders' was reduced at weekends in Johannesburg because of organized soccer. In addition, the number of assaults in casualty wards 'decreased noticeably' after the Bantu Sports Club was established.[7] Sport, then, was organized within a racial ideology as one non-coercive tool of domination to teach the values necessary for successful urbanization and to build bridges between the rural and urban, the 'tribal' and 'detribalised' sections of society.

CULTURE , 'RACE' AND 'INVENTING TRADITIONS'

Two types of societies confront one another in the colonial experience, each with its own memory. The colonial system seems monolithic, and is supported by its expansionist practices. It faces a multitude of African social formations with different, often particularist memories competing with each other ... Offering and imposing the desirability of its own memory, colonization promises a vision of progressive enrichment to the colonized. How does the transformation of diverse African memories take place?[8]

Mudimbe expands on this analysis by outlining how an education system, an administration and a language discourse contribute to this transformation. In the process of European empire building, discourses were constructed in Africa around strategies of power and subjection, of inclusion and exclusion, of renaming the already named. As a rationalization for the domination of 'inferior' people, a racist discourse was indispensable. Indeed, it was not essential or central to exploitation but existed as a justification for inequality, injustice and the use of force. Moreover, it played a greater role in the absence of force. Nineteenth-century British colonial racial ideology acknowledged only one 'civilization', one path of 'progress', and one 'true religion'.[9] The theory that people evolved through distinct social stages – from savagery to civilization – led to self-congratulatory domination that actively encouraged the popular belief in the inferiority of the African. The depiction of the 'civilizing mission' as an aesthetic project was an old and familiar strategy in European imperialism. It was a way of interpreting the Other as not only available for, but actually in need of, outside intervention.[10] The flexibility of racial ideology is unequivocally evident in the creation of racial stereotypes. The abstracted images, with their accompanying baggage of pre-given traits, often contradict one another, but are used nonetheless to smooth the path of conquest and justify the course of domination. The greater the situation of unequal power, the stronger the stereotypes.

Racial typologies were so pervasive that these racial caricatures penetrated all levels of colonial African society. In nineteenth-century Southern Africa, whites distinguished between the different African 'races' or 'tribes' on the basis of cultural attributes. These 'racial' distinctions, as Ranger has shown, had no meaning for nineteenth-century Africans, who did not think of themselves in racial terms. They did not recognize themselves as 'tribes', but felt allegiance to hierarchies within dispersed clans. Nevertheless, the colonial project treated existing divisions and cultural groupings as either non-existent or alike. Ranger also shows that domination was not unilinear and that the less powerful could and did manipulate racial ideologies for their own interests.[11]

Part of colonial racial discourse in Africa revolved around the 'invention of tradition', or as Mudimbe has suggested, 'converting memories'. The manipulation of tradition by dominant groups historically – in Europe as well as abroad – was a common strategy for control because it was within the sphere of these activities that ritual, symbols, custom and meaning were defined. And as Comaroff and Comaroff have noted, 'the silent power of the sign, the unspoken authority of habit, may be as effective as the most violent coercion in shaping, directing and even dominating social thought and action'.[12] In Africa, the 'invention of tradition' gave symbolic form to developing types of authority and submission. For Europeans, traditions were invented to justify dominant roles and to provide models of subservience for Africans. Africans, by contrast, sought to draw on and manipulate European invented traditions for themselves. Indeed, most 'new' traditions offered them points of entry into the colonial world. The flexibility of the racial discourse attached to changing African traditions is never more evident than on the gold mines surrounding Johannesburg. The mining industry, in an effort to avert the consequences of urbanization, preferred Africans to remain part of 'traditional' rural communities, communities whose image they had themselves invented. Sports and recreation for miners were organized around the idea of a 'tribalized' African who did not want to participate in urban (white) sports.[13] This idea was promoted despite the popularity of soccer among African mineworkers. The mining industry created its own version of 'tribalism' complete with a re-invented version of 'tribal dancing' as a competitive sport.

THE PROBLEM OF URBANIZATION

One of the principle 'common sense' beliefs about race among whites in Johannesburg in the 1920s and 1930s was that Africans were culturally unable to cope with industrialization and urbanization. This premise informed much of their desire to control Africans socially in the urban areas. The racial discourse asserted that Africans experienced a physical and moral degeneration when they were in the unnatural environment of the cities. This degeneration, especially the assumed moral decay, occurred because Africans were lower down on the evolutionary scale of civilization and, by implication, more in touch with the land. While the rural areas brought out the best in 'the African', the cities were alien environments which brought out the worst. Once in the city, Africans were perceived to be confronted by vice and immorality to which they inevitably succumbed, and it was a process over which they appeared to have little control. As a result, they had to be encouraged to live where they were most comfortable, that is, in the rural areas.[14]

It is perhaps not surprising that this racial discourse should have intensified during a period of rapid African urbanization and white fears about this process, and the underlying truth of a labour system based on migrants. Nor is it surprising that, from the 1920s, urban social welfare became an area of concern for whites in the urban centres. In Johannesburg, white missionaries and liberals first took up the torch of social welfare in an attempt to arrest the physical and moral 'decay' of 'the African' and to defuse the potential for social conflict.[15] The flame of social welfare also extended to instil a Protestant work ethic and encourage industrial harmony.

Underlying the desire to 'save' the urban African was a very real conviction of a moral duty and a paternalism on the part of white missionaries and liberals. The justification for this 'right' to intervene in the private social lives of Africans was bolstered by the assumption that Africans belonged to an evolving but dependent 'child race'. Dubow shows how this metaphor of the colonial family gave rise to ideas of separate development and trusteeship.[16] Many of the educated black middle class in Johannesburg also believed in the 'child race' metaphor and felt that the responsibility of their race weighed heavily on their shoulders. They were, after all, examples of the evolution of African 'civilization'. These 'common sense' beliefs about the inability of Africans to cope with industrialization and urbanization were supported by intellectuals, in particular the anthropological community. South African anthropologists refined nineteenth-century European racial ideology in the South African context. Monica Hunter, for example, in her book *Reaction to Conquest* (1936), argued that Africans began 'by adopting Western ways eagerly and wholeheartedly', but with increasing cultural contact, Native societies experienced a series of 'rapid and forcible transformations' which were 'patently disadvantageous to the Natives'.[17] This process of 'detribalisation' included an erosion of rural loyalties, kinship bonds and networks, a rejection of traditional rituals, customs and practices, and a weakening of rules, taboos and conduct.[18] The missionaries sought to replace these eroded 'tribal' customs with new, urban ones.[19]

THE AMERICAN BOARD MISSIONARIES

The urban mission was a new departure for missionary groups in South Africa, especially for the American Board of Missions (ABM), whose earlier work had been in the rural areas of Natal.[20] J. Dexter Taylor and Frederick Bridgman, for example, took the mission to the urban areas where they sought to improve religious, health, education and recreation facilities.[21] From the turn of the century, these American missionaries became increasingly occupied with urban social welfare for Africans, and the main emphasis of their city mission was rescue work. Dexter Taylor argued that city missionaries were necessary because 'the lack of moral consciousness and the want of self-control lead them (the Africans) away from all that is wholesome and good, to fall an easy prey to the demoralising influences of town life'.[22]

In 1918, Ray Phillips joined Frederick Bridgman in the Johannesburg urban mission and later his wife, Dora Phillips, also came to help in the new social welfare programme. Phillips arrived in South Africa confident that he had knowledge of 'race relations' and 'racial tensions', which he had experienced from growing up in the rapidly growing industrial city, Duluth, Minnesota, which had a large black population.[23] By 1928, Ray Phillips was in charge of the Social Service Department of the American Board Mission and was described by the liberal, white community as 'the leading authority in the country' on urban social welfare and missionary services.[24] Like Rheinallt Jones, Phillips radiated an 'intellectual' authority which was respected among whites and the African middle-class. Under the supervision of Frederick Bridgman, Clara Bridgman, J. Dexter Taylor, Ray Phillips and Dora Phillips, most of the structures for African sport and recreation were established for both men and women in Johannesburg.

MISSION-ORGANIZED RECREATION

The organization of African sport and recreation was a pressing goal for the American missionaries, who believed in the intrinsic qualities of controlled play. If properly organized, sport and recreation would combat the social problems arising from urbanization, smooth the transition between rural and urban cultures and teach 'civilizing' values. Recreational activities for urban Africans were part of a holistic 'redemptive programme', as Dexter Taylor commented:

> A great part if not the whole of the 'Native problem' is the problem of enabling the Native to make the transition from the pastoral stage of civilisation to the industrial stage. It is a huge problem of adaptation to a new environment. Recreation is a natural point of adaptation. Because its experiences are pleasant its lessons and benefits are retained. The Native who is enabled to participate in the forms of recreation peculiar to our forms of civilization is thereby protected from falling into criminal habits.[25]

Ray Phillips drew on the contemporary academic discourse, that Africans experienced severe maladjustments in the transition from traditional to urban life, to explain the need for controlled recreation.[26] American missionaries directed their activities at Africans who were in the process of becoming 'detribalized'.[27] To assist Africans in completing the transition to urban life successfully, the urban missionaries established a programme combining Christianity and social welfare. Phillips argued that religion had to be 'supplemented' by controlled recreation: 'It has been recognised that the preaching of the Gospel and the purely spiritual ministry of the Church must be supplemented by the addition of the playground, Boy Scouts and athletics, as well as by school and Sunday School.'[28] 'Proper' play, therefore, could help avert some of the 'maladjustments to the social order' and allow Africans to become 'better workers, keener mentally and physically, better citizens less likely to be criminals, better neighbours, less likely to be anti-white, more likely to possess a true sense of community values'.[29]

In 1938, Phillips completed a book on the 'cultural adjustment' of Africans on the Witwatersrand. The book is fascinating, not only for its detailed account of African life in the 1930s through missionary eyes, but for its explicit outline of the missionary agenda. In the book, Phillips examined the practical side of African urban life, the poverty, the lack of housing, the lack of health facilities, the lack of education. All of these he attributed to uncontrolled, rapid urbanization and the change from the simple way of traditional African life to the material desires of urban life. Phillips discussed the social problems that arose from this material existence: the breakdown of the family, decreasing traditional discipline, growing immorality, gambling, drinking and crime. While he did suggest practical solutions to all these problems, the overarching solutions, he argued, lay in religion and organized recreation.

Religion, of course, would help the transition from rural to urban, from 'primitive' to 'civilized' to occur more smoothly. Possibly, once the spiritual transition had occurred, the material benefits of 'civilized' life would also be realized. Recreation, as an extension of religion, would satisfy Africans mentally because of the thrill of the game and, at the same time, teach the morals and social conduct of 'civilized' life.[30] To this end, organized recreation took two related forms: first, by inventing traditions and second, by teaching lessons from these new traditions. It is to both of these forms that the discussion now turns.

THE FIRST NEW TRADITION – THE EXAMPLE OF THE 'ADULT RACE'

For the missionaries, organized sport and recreation was a vehicle for civilizing Africans. Phillips argued that 'the provision of wholesome, leisure-time activities in the place of heathen ones makes it possible for our Native people to develop healthily a threefold life, physical, mental and spiritual, instead of one or two'.[31] Phillips' mission was to divorce Africans successfully from what he perceived to be 'the fearsome side of tribal, heathen life'.[32] The missionaries argued that 'tribalized' Africans used their leisure time in pursuits like hunting and combat, but that these traditional forms of 'play' did not transfer successfully to the city. On the contrary, the missionaries argued, they led to the wrong kinds of self-expression in the urban areas. These unacceptable activities included drinking, fighting and promiscuity, 'the demon of sensuality'.[33] White society, Phillips argued, presented Africans with an example of 'civilized' society. By imitating whites, by learning white traditions, and by playing white games, Africans could learn to become 'civilized'. Phillips suggested, for example, that 'to take the place of the heathen dance, associated as it is with the whole heathen system, and yet to provide for the strong craving for rhythmic expression, white musical games and folk-dances are encouraged among the children'.[34]

THE SECOND TRADITION – THE SPIRIT OF POLITICAL MODERATION

The American missionaries, like other whites in Johannesburg, felt the increasing labour militancy and growing political tensions during the 1920s and 1930s. R.V. Selope Thema expressed much of the prevailing anxiety when he wrote that 'there can be no doubt that South Africa is regarded as a fertile field for Bolshevism because the country contains six millions of people who are seething with discontentment and dissatisfaction because of the oppressive and repressive laws that are imposed on them'.[35] The missionaries paid special attention to their duty to improve 'race relations' and defuse 'race tensions'.[36] They urged the municipality to provide recreational facilities for Africans in Johannesburg to divert their attention from political pursuits. They worried that on Sundays – the only day off work for most Africans – many spent the day 'listening attentively while the white agitator and his

Native assistants seek to arouse in him a spirit of revolt against the capitalist, the government, the missionary, and the white labour leader'.[37]

Ray Phillips also warned whites in Johannesburg that Africans were 'seething with discontent' and that if their interests were not directed elsewhere, Africans would turn to 'hot-mouthed agitators' and the Communist Party for answers.[38] If, however, Africans spent their Sundays playing soccer or other sports they would be occupied in a satisfying activity and not have the time or feel the need to become involved in politics. Social centres like the Bantu Men's Social Centre, Phillips argued, were essential to counteract communism.[39]

Other American missionaries, less enthusiastic than Phillips, did have reservations about the potential of sport to be apolitical. When a Pan-African Olympic Games was suggested during the late 1920s, Dexter Taylor argued that although he applauded the attempts to develop 'first-rate athletic ability' among Africans, he worried about the danger of developing an African race consciousness and the unification of African feeling through sport. It was necessary, he argued, to moderate sport – it must be tempered with religion and education. Consequently, he thought, recreation had to be carefully selected, organized and supervised.[40]

THE THIRD TRADITION - THE 'SOBER' CITIZEN

Only 'clean, wholesome and character building' traditions were to be taught to Africans.[41] The leisure activities that Africans participated in, independent of white help, proved to Phillips that white control was necessary. Urban African leisure without white interference consisted of men and boys gambling on the streets during the day with coins, dice or cards. The nights were spent at shebeens and Marabi dances. With leisure time spent like this, Phillips argued, it was but a short step to a life of crime and violence.[42]

In 1938, a full-time sports organizer from the Johannesburg municipality's Non-European Affairs Department (NEAD) was hired to arrange activities for unemployed youths. The programme for boys included 'physical culture', indoor competitive games, talks on hygiene, nutrition and music. Activities for girls were similar, with additional attention to handicrafts and cooking. Furthermore, said Phillips, authorities in South Africa and overseas had proved the 'salutary effect on delinquency and disorderly conduct of the provision of playing fields'.[43]

Organized recreation and sport could create 'sober' citizens – sober from alcohol, sober in morality and sober in character.

The unspoken qualification was that only recreation organized by whites was worthwhile. Phillips, like his liberal contemporaries, did not support African-organized recreation of any sort. For example, during the 1940s, male domestic workers from Johannesburg's suburbs formed themselves into traditional 'stick-fighting' gangs. Yet they were denied access to the Bantu Sports Club until they had agreed to try out boxing instead. It was to be a simple exchange: 'whereas the energy which now finds outlet through a knife or knobkerrie (fighting stick), would just as easily, and far more safely, be expended on footballs or boxing gloves'.[44] Yet many of the activities organized by Africans themselves were innocent of the vices the missionaries attributed to them. When the Johannesburg African Football Association decided to become independent of white help, Phillips and other white organizers reacted furiously and refused to sanction the move. Instead, they did everything they could to hamper the activities of the club.[45]

There were other 'traditions' that Phillips did not want Africans to adopt. For example, he deplored the cheap sale of pulp magazines like *True Confessions* and *Modern Romances* which advertised the bad side of European behaviour. He also objected to the kinds of films which showed white women 'half-naked' in 'compromising positions'. Even though films were censored, the non-European cinemas in Johannesburg showed uncensored films regardless. Phillips was horrified to find out that films, like *Sin Ship*, *Why Change Your Husband*, *The Gay Divorcee* and *Bad Girl*, supposedly banned to Africans, were being shown to anyone who would pay the entrance fee. He was adamant that organizing sport and recreation meant a whole programme of carefully selected activities and not just a recreational hall or, as he described it, 'four walls and a roof'. He illustrated the difference between organized recreation and merely providing the facilities by arguing that an unsupervised facility, like a hall, could be used for any 'questionable' activity.[46]

THE FOURTH TRADITION – 'FAIR PLAY'

Organized sport was a particularly useful way of teaching the lessons of civilization because each game, like soccer or cricket, contained rules and codes of play. For the missionaries, sports taught essential ideals of conformity like 'fair play', 'good sportsmanship', 'rivalry without hatred', and most important of all, 'learning to be a good loser'.[47] By participating in sport, Africans would learn 'sportsmanship'. It was more than a word, it was 'an attitude towards the other fellow, a philosophy of living'.[48] Good sportsmanship was a reflection of citizenship, of fairness and of basic human decency; it meant manliness, selflessness, fair-mindedness, generosity and sincerity. In addition, 'sportsmen' could play fair on the field because 'sport was the great leveller' and 'all men were equal on the playing fields'.[49] These ideals of sportsmanship had their roots in the nineteenth-century 'muscular Christianity' of the British public school system. As members of these schools later moved to the far corners of the empire, their ideals were transferred first to whites and then to indigenous populations.[50] For Africans in Johannesburg, these ideals must have sat uneasily beside the grinding poverty and crippling injustices they experienced daily. That this lesson of competing fairly and losing with grace did not successfully transfer into organized African sport is evident from the amount of violence that continually surfaced at soccer and boxing matches.

During the late 1930s, the American missionary efforts to organize sport and recreation for Africans reached its peak. They were its prime motivators and instructors. Their influence was strongly felt in all Joint Council activities, Johannesburg City Council policies and Chamber of Mines programmes regarding recreation. Ray Phillips was sought out for advice and practical know-how by anyone one who wanted information on organizing African sport and recreation across the country. By the 1940s, however, the American missionary influence gradually weakened and African sport lost much of its religious 'character-building' undertones. After this, many of the clubs and activities initiated by the missionaries were taken over by the Johannesburg's NEAD.

THE JOHANNESBURG CITY COUNCIL'S INTEREST IN ORGANIZED SPORT

It was some time before the City Council assumed responsibility for 'Native affairs' in Johannesburg. Until 1927, no committee was solely responsible for Native affairs. Administration of African townships fell under the Parks and Estates Committee. In May 1927, the Town Council appointed a Manager of Native Affairs, Graham Ballenden, and in 1928 the first Non-European Affairs Committee was appointed. The Native Affairs Department, however, was a relatively low status department for the first ten years of its existence. By the late 1930s, this had changed and increasingly the Department gained more civil service muscle and more power over the lives of urban African residents.

The history of the NEAD is intricately linked to the organization of sport and recreation for Africans. Combined with a more coercive system of legal restrictions and police enforcement, the NEAD assumed the role of controlling African social life through recreation as an additional measure. Indeed, initially, recreation was one of NEAD's main responsibilities. The more coercive measures were left to the South African Police, the Native Commissioner's office and the Director of Native Labour. The personalities of the managers, the sports organizers and later the recreation officers, were important. Their attitudes dictated much of the conflict and shaped the organization of many sports. While the missionaries performed the 'pioneering' work in social welfare and recreation, it was only in the late 1930s that the municipality became involved in sustained welfare work.[51] Two fairly distinct periods characterize the City Council's involvement in sport. During the early period (1927–36), the City Council focused on social welfare and 'uplifting the African' and, in the later period (1937–50), the discourse of control shifted subtly. When the Native Affairs Department was formed and the Native Affairs Committee constituted, their aim was to foster a 'better understanding' between the Town Council and Africans.[52] One of the first additions to the Department was a Sports Organizer in 1929.

By 1934, in the aftermath of the Depression, however, issues other than organized recreation became pressing. The Department was preoccupied with enforcing the 1923 Urban Areas Act, countering unemployment and providing housing, hostels and health facilities. Despite the enormous problems facing the Department, recreation still formed a considerable portion of the activities. The primary reason for the extensive attention paid to organizing African sport by Ballenden and his Department was that, following the example of Ray Phillips, recreation became synonymous with social welfare. During this period, in addition to controlling African social time, the Department was convinced that the morals and values attached to well-organized sport could help Africans to be stronger people and in doing so, the urban social ills would be addressed and ultimately overcome.[53]

> It is very evident, from experience gained so far, that by properly organising and directing Native sport and the provision of

adequate playing fields and facilities, a great deal more can be done
to improve the moral tone of the Native population, and save many
of them from trouble, got into through sheer lack of congenial and
healthy occupation during their leisure hours. Unlike the
European population, they have neither the means nor the organizing ability to help themselves in this direction.[54]

Sport continued to be regarded as a means to avoid trouble and the
Department devoted a considerable amount of effort to soccer, rather
than tennis and cricket, because those two sports did not draw enough
spectators.[55] They aimed to reach as many urban Africans as possible
with organized sports.

During the second period, 1937–50, the City Council's involvement
in sport changed its focus. In 1937, the City Council's Native Affairs
Department underwent some restructuring to include Indian and
'coloured' affairs and became the NEAD. Social Welfare became a
section separate from recreation, indicating a shift in ideology and
policy.[56] With the rapid growth in population by the end of the war and
the massive demand for housing, available resources were totally inadequate and the City Council was swamped with an increase in the 'social
ills' of the 1930s.[57] During this period of massive squatting, overcrowd-
ing in African townships and the exhaustion of services, the idea of sport
as an effective means of social welfare and social control faded. This shift
reflected the realization by the NEAD that social welfare encompassed
more than organized sport and recreation. Indeed, in the late 1930s, the
recreation section became a subsection of the Social Welfare branch.[58] It
was also a recognition of the failure of sport to perform as Ballenden
desired, despite his commendations: 'I am highly satisfied with the good
being done in providing healthy leisure time occupation for Natives and
in fostering sportsmanship and self and mass discipline.' He wrote,
'When I look back to the time of my arrival in Johannesburg and
contemplate the state of affairs existing then as compared with to-day, I
marvel how Johannesburg escaped serious trouble among its Native
population.'[59]

This change in status did not mean the end of interest in sport by the
NEAD. In fact, the organization of African sport expanded dramatically
during the 1940s.[60] What it did mean was that the language of sport as a
solution to social problems was discarded. Ballenden, and other later
managers, realized that regardless of the number of fields, facilities and

organizations they produced, they were not going to solve the drastic housing shortage, the poverty and the rise in political militancy of Africans in Johannesburg. Instead, sport had become a way of keeping Africans 'happy' without addressing the real problems. They could advertise that they were coping by showing pictures of 'happy' Africans to other Africans and the broader public of South Africa, and indeed, throughout the 1940s and early 1950s, NEAD published pamphlets advertising its progress with housing, health and sport. One pamphlet, entitled 'Health, happiness and education', gave an account of 'the broad picture of where the Native lives once he has left his traditional hut and his lazy agricultural life' and promised that, 'Natives take eagerly to sport both as performers and spectators, and it seems a natural development from their strenuous and dramatic tribal dancing.'[61]

This new turn in NEAD's attitude to African sport is reflected by fears expressed in the English-speaking newspapers as postwar urbanization continued.[62] African sport became an attempt to allay white panic, to occupy Africans during their after-work hours, and to make them invisible to whites. NEAD dropped the accompanying package of lessons which marked the missionary involvement in sport, and concentrated their efforts, almost desperately, on leisure-time control.[63] Towards the end of the 1940s, NEAD facilities for recreation expanded tremendously.[64] A white recreation officer, Graham Young, was hired to research, plan and implement activities.[65] By 1948, the recreation section consisted of eight white and nine African sports organizers.[66] In 1949, it was further divided into a Physical Education section (sports, athletics, games), a cultural section (music, bands and choirs) and a cinema section.[67]

This expansion period of the 1940s can also be related to two external developments. One was the birth of 'Physical Education' as a means of worker efficiency which was developed overseas. The other was the legislation allowing the NEAD to brew beer, which in turn provided the recreation section with the funds for expansion.

PHYSICAL EDUCATION: 'TO REMAKE MEN'[68]

Research on 'Physical Education' for Africans in South Africa was pioneered by Ernst Jokl, who became yet another intellectual and authority in the field of African sport.[69] Jokl undertook research to examine the physical and athletic ability of South African Blacks. After

conducting athletic performance tests, he concluded that African performance was poor. Tests were conducted on 'raw' (tribal) Africans as well
as educated (detribalized) Africans. The reason for this division was to
'consider whether the poor standard of Native performances might
perhaps somehow be related to the rather primitive state in which large
numbers of South African Bantus at present exist'. Jokl concluded that
'mentally primitive Natives are as a rule defeated on the sports field by
their more intelligent or educated brothers and sisters'; Jokl thought that
the more 'detribalised' an African was, 'the more likely he/she is to be
physically efficient'.[70] A programme of physical education among urban
Africans would lead to 'superior standards of social behaviour'. In
addition, physical education, he said, also developed the motor skills
necessary for manual labour.[71]

In 1938, a national scheme of physical education was launched in
South Africa, when the government decided to follow other 'civilized'
countries, such as the United States, in developing physical education
programmes. These programmes were boosted by the threat of war.
From 1938–42, the South African parliament voted a sum of £50,000
annually to develop physical education across the country.[72] Although
only a little of this filtered down to African sport or recreation, the trend
was important in terms of attitude towards the necessity for a scientific
physical education programme. During the war, members of the
National Advisory Council for Physical Education met with the
Manager of the NEAD to discuss the implementation of physical education classes among Africans. Two instructors were hired initially, one for
the Wemmer Hostel and another at Orlando, with the objective of five
instructors running a programme which would embrace all the
locations. This was specifically to improve African labour efficiency, and
to avoid 'repercussions on the industries and defences of the country'. In
addition, it was hoped that these physical education courses would
combat juvenile delinquency and crime.[73] With this 'scientific' justification for organizing sport, NEAD embarked on an enhanced recreational
programme for Johannesburg's Africans. The funding for this expansion
was provided by Africans from money generated by the beerhalls.

FUNDING FOR ORGANIZED SPORT – BEER PROFITS

Before 1938, NEAD obtained its revenue from rents from houses and
hostel beds. In 1938, legislation enabled municipalities to brew African

beer, and the NEAD opened a brewery.[74] Beerhalls were established, ostensibly to counteract the illicit liquor trade, but the profits were also welcomed by the NEAD. The Department had always argued that they never had enough money for African services and facilities. Under the 1923 Natives (Urban Areas) Act, a separate Native Revenue Account was required to be established. All revenue derived from Africans – rents, fines, licences and profits from the sale of municipal beer – had to be paid into this account, and payments out of it could only be made for African benefit.[75] Before 1938, deficits on the Native Revenue Account were met by the City Council (ranging from £3,000 to £20,600), and, in addition, the Council contributed £3,000 every year to African charitable and social welfare work.

In 1938 this policy was abruptly changed and the Native Revenue Account became self-balancing. The cost of housing and social services was, therefore, laid on the shoulders of the people already too poor to pay for the minimum conditions of healthy living. Despite this change in policy, the Native Revenue Account showed a marked growth in revenue and expenditure in 1938 because of the establishment of municipal beer canteens. In 1938, the profits were £7,092, in 1939, £32,768 and in 1940, £63,752. In 1939–40, the profits from municipal beer amounted to approximately one-third of the income of the Account, while rents provided most of the other two-thirds.[76] An amendment of the 1923 Act in 1944 required that the Beer Account be kept as a separate sub-account of the Native Revenue Account. The Beer Account paid for the manufacture, sale and supply of beer, and for African social or recreational facilities approved by the Minister of Native Affairs.[77] During 1944, the beer profits amounted to £121,477. Of this, £25,414 went to medical services, £11,239 to Grants-in-Aid (sports, clubs, associations), £15,858 to social welfare and £380 to cinema performances.[78] These profits came from the four beerhalls in Johannesburg at the time: Western Native Township, Denver, Salisbury-Jubilee and Mai Mai.

The establishment of beerhalls highlights the contradictory nature of a racial discourse which sought to control alcohol consumption by providing low alcohol beer at these regulated halls, while at the same time making profits from the consumption of alcohol. The beerhall system was unpopular amongst Africans, missionaries and liberals.[79] For the liberals and missionaries, the whole structure of beerhalls contradicted the idea of 'healthy' leisure; the 'teeming crowds' that once roamed the streets and mine dumps now congregated around beerhalls.[80]

They hoped that expanded recreational facilities would 'act as counter-attractions to excessive drinking'.[81] Ironically, this is what most of the funds from the beer profits were directed at – providing organized sport and recreation, and facilities were expanded during the 1940s. Yet, despite the profits from the sale of beer, the facilities provided continued to be inadequate and poorly maintained.

AFRICAN SPORTS MANAGERS

The African middle class, consisting of rural elites and the urban petty bourgeoisie, was heavily involved in organizing and participating in sport during this period. Bonner has identified the nature of this class by referring to three distinct characteristics. The first was that the African middle class straddled the gulf between whites on the one hand and working-class Africans on the other. Thus, in the context of South African society, they stood between capital and labour and were pulled in both directions. Second, the African middle class was 'shunted and repressed' by the forces of colonialism and racism. Finally, it was a group united as a class primarily on an ideological level.[82] Many middle-class Africans were intricately tied to the liberal ideology of the 1920s and 1930s and participated in contemporary liberal institutions, such as the Joint Councils Movement and the South African Institute of Race Relations. Many also became the organizers and managers of the sports clubs and associations started by whites in Johannesburg.

As an urban social category this African middle class lacked a strong sense of its own class identity and was often prone to political fraction-alization.[83] Its identity and cohesion was related to rural and family networks, mission school ties and professional links. Thus, the African middle class in Johannesburg based its identity on exclusivity, particu-larly in relation to the African working class. It reinforced is cohesion by maintaining a social network of clubs and cultural associations, such as drama groups, literary clubs, debating societies and musical groups. It also involved itself in organizing sports.[84]

The close relationship between the African middle class and the white liberals and missionaries in Johannesburg is one which deserves further study. Cobley suggests that the relationship was more significant than the commonly held view that white liberals effectively controlled radical black opposition during the 1920s and 1930s. He argues that African leaders cooperated so closely with whites, not because they were duped into supporting a strategy of white domination and black subordination, but because it was in their interests. First, a close relationship with whites was an advantage when negotiating with white administrators to maintain social privileges. In addition, the network of white liberals and missionaries organized and funded the clubs and social activities which contributed to their exclusivity. Second, contact with whites at a social level emphasized their status and distinctiveness. Thirdly, they were able to extract concessions by challenging liberal whites to live up to their self-professed non-racial ideology. It was from this group of middle-class Africans that the African National Congress (ANC) drew its leadership, and people such as John Dube, D.D.T. Jabavu, R.V. Selope Thema, Selby Msimang and A.B. Xuma became leading members of both the Joint Councils and the ANC.[85]

In the period before the Second World War, most of the African middle class was earnestly involved in the liberal project of combating urban social ills with some form of organized recreation in Johannesburg. Many people were on the numerous social welfare committees set up by the Joint Councils. Many also gave evidence as the African voice at conferences, commissions and hearings. From the late 1930s, however, the African middle class found it increasingly difficult to maintain its economic exclusivity. Socially, it began to realize that it would not be able to obtain sustained advantages from whites. Politically, especially after the passage of the Hertzog Bills, African middle-class tensions coincided with working-class ones. The ANC started to radicalize after 1939 under the leadership of Xuma, a process that continued through the 1940s, and intensified after the 1946 Miner's Strike.[86] For many of the African middle class involved in the BMSC, the Bantu Sports Club and the football associations, the growing disenchantment with white liberals and missionaries first became clear during the 1940s.

While many of the African middle class were closely associated with white liberals and missionaries, their resentment of white control of African sports was evident. Dan Twala, for example, became a key figure at the BSC and president of the Johannesburg African Football Association. He defended the 'civilizing' values of sport. 'Sport', he argued, 'would raise our barbarous brothers from idle, criminal and uncontrollable savage habits to that of a steady industrous, humble and moral endeavour.'[87] Yet, Twala was forced to engage in a long drawn out struggle with the NEAD over resources because the organization he represented chose to develop independently of white control. Twala's conflicts with the NEAD paralleled the gradual radicalization of the African middle class.

When the BSC was established, Africans managed to insist on African-only managers, but they still had to report to a white Board of Trustees. But this minor level of independence from the NEAD allowed Johannesburg's Africans a cultural space where they could hold political meetings. The Club had the added bonus of an open sports field situated centrally and conspicuously in Johannesburg. Numerous protesters and demonstrators made use of the location. From the early 1940s, May Day demonstrations were held annually on the soccer fields.[88] The Bantu Sports Club's monthly bulletin also advertized African newspapers, ran a commentary on current political events, promoted legal aid bureaus and dispensed information about meetings of various political associations and trade unions.[89] Trade unions and other progressive organizations held their meetings at the Club. At some stage during the 1940s, the BSC began to provide secretarial services for the new trade union movement.[90]

THE SPORTING PARTICIPANTS AND SPECTATORS

The early story of organized soccer in Johannesburg perhaps illustrates more clearly than other sports at this time how the attempts to organize African sports were fraught with struggles. On the one hand, the municipality and the missionaries found that their efforts were not always gratefully accepted and the 'new traditions' were more often than not subverted. On the other hand, the people who managed and participated in these sports found that organization also meant control. They had to fight for access to fields, equipment and gate-takings. Through the 1940s, the municipality attempted to control the leagues, the schedules and to decide who could play and who could not. Consequently, this period is one which is characterized by struggles between the Johannesburg NEAD and Africans for the control of organized African sport, and the struggle is most evident in the case of soccer.

In 1929, the Johannesburg Bantu Football Association (JBFA) was formed by Ray Phillips and the municipality as an umbrella organization for associated clubs. In 1933, a group of clubs broke away to form the Johannesburg African Football Association (JAFA) because of a dispute over gate-takings. This new 'African' association was formed within the ranks of the BSC. For both the new association and the BSC, this was an attempt to move away from municipal control. They accused the municipality of using 'municipal autocracy to maintain an official monopoly of all Bantu sport in the city'.[91] The substitution of 'African' for 'Bantu' was not accidental and it illustrates a broader struggle within the prevailing racial discourse.

While the Johannesburg Bantu Football Association (JBFA) continued its close ties with the NEAD, the Johannesburg African Football Association (JAFA) became an independent association. In deciding to take an autonomous route, the JAFA invited confrontation with the NEAD. The NEAD refused to provide the JAFA with any resources and did not allow them access to municipal soccer fields. They did not recognize the JAFA. In spite of this, the JAFA struggled on and by 1946, it was quite a large operation with two leagues and about 130 attached teams. At the height of the JAFA's success, the municipality established the Salisbury-Jubilee beerhall in a vacant lot near to the BSC. The beerhall became a further point of contention between JAFA management and the NEAD.[92] On a privately-owned narrow strip of land between the beerhall and the sports ground, illegal shebeen-owners set up shop. The strip, known as 'Magaba Nge Jubane', was a favourite among soccer patrons and players. With shebeens so accessible, players and spectators had ample opportunity to drink before, during and after matches. Once the beerhall and shebeens had been established, player and crowd behaviour became virtually uncontrollable, and assaults and fighting skyrocketed. Predictably, the incidence of violence and confrontations grew as the level of intoxication increased. Although violence had always been a part of Johannesburg's soccer clubs, in spite of strenuous efforts to control it by Ray Phillips and the NEAD, the availability of alcohol from the beerhall and the shebeens made a bad situation worse. Some referees refused to accept certain games because they felt they did not have adequate protection.[93] And referees were not the only target. Players and spectators also assaulted each other. The police had to be called regularly, especially towards the end of the season when excitement heightened with the approach of the finals.

By the late 1940s, the problem had escalated into a nightmare for the JAFA management. Despite regular raids, the illicit shebeen liquor trade was thriving. On the weekends players, spectators and referees spent the day drinking and playing. Games were interrupted by police chasing spectators across the soccer fields. On one occasion, several hundred Africans stoned police raiding the 'Magaba' area for beer. And, on another violent occasion, a police raid claimed the lives of three players who died from stray bullets. The fence between the beerhall and the BSC became increasingly fragile as spectators refreshed themselves. The hard implication of this was that the JAFA lost much needed gate-revenue. The JAFA appealed consistently to the District Commandant, the BSC Trustees and the municipality to remove the beerhall and the shebeens and repair the fence. A frustrated Dan Twala condemned the NEAD for raising revenue from an institution which promoted such disorder.[94] The location of the beerhall and the lack of municipal interest in dealing with these problems demonstrated the struggle for independence which the JAFA faced and which only ended with the move towards professionalism in the 1950s. Professionalism brought resources and as a result, the freedom of access to non-municipal facilities.

CONCLUSION

This period in the story of organized African sport ended with the Nationalist Government coming to power in 1948, with the barrage of Apartheid legislation requiring the forcible removal of many of Johannesburg's communities, with the relocation of African sport to the new dormitory suburbs and with an increasingly militant and oppositional population. As the society generally became more politicized under the new government, so too did African sport.

Why was organizing sport for Africans so important to the missionaries, the municipality and, for some time, to the African middle class? Their obvious intention was to combat the social problems – gambling, drinking, prostitution, crime and gang activity – which accompanied rapid African urbanization, high unemployment and growing political interest. Alongside systems of more coercive policing measures, these leisure activities were implemented to bring some order and social conformity to urban Africans. They were part of a much broader attempt by whites to control the social and cultural spaces of Africans in the city. Organized British- and American-style sports were intended to occupy Africans during their spare time and teach them 'respectable' values. Thus fortified, they would find jobs, earn money legally, spurn Communist Party propaganda, and abandon the immoral life that they were assumed to succumb to in the city. The organizers of sports for Africans also wished to promote a racial hegemony which would ensure the continued subordination of Africans with minimal resistance. Newly introduced traditions such as soccer or boxing, and re-created old traditions such as 'tribal' dancing, were part of the non-coercive tools of white domination. Institutions such as the Bantu Mens Social Centre and the Bantu Sports Club perpetuated the language, the idioms and the discourse of racial subordination and African political moderation.

Yet, like all attempts at domination, coercive or non-coercive, the process was never complete and never completely dualistic. The story of organized African sport in Johannesburg, it seems, is not a linear narrative but a collection of narratives. Depending on their position within the racial discourse and the prevailing discourses of power, the missionaries and municipality were at times aligned and at times in conflict. What about the Africans who were organized and controlled? Johannesburg's Africans accepted organized sports with enthusiasm and soccer, for example, developed a huge following. Yet it seems that the participants were able to enjoy the sport and embrace these 'new traditions' without succumbing to the controlling elements intended by the organizers. Organized sport in Johannesburg suggests a pattern of resistance to attempts to mould African cultural life into patterns made elsewhere. While the emphasis was to occupy as many people as possible at single events, large crowds of 'excited' Africans all gathered in one place were often much more problematic than the organizers had bargained for. In addition, the new traditions of 'fair play' and 'good sportsmanship' never entirely transferred into African sports. Politically, the efforts of the missionaries and the City Council to defuse passions served only to provide Africans with the structures, the space and the framework for collective organization and the growth of a political voice. There was clearly a huge gap between intentions and repercussions. Is this because in the realm of cultural traditions and memories there is more space for political manoeuvring? Mudimbe argues that as foreign imperialists invented an Africa that would serve their purposes, so must Africans invent a West which serves African purposes.[95] Perhaps this is what the story of (un)organized African sport in Johannesburg is all about?

NOTES

1. R. Archer and A. Bouillon, *The South African Game* (London: Zed Press, 1982), p.117.
2. In other parts of South Africa, particularly the Cape Province, African rugby and cricket had been organized to a certain extent.
3. C.M. Badenhorst and C.T. Mather, 'Tribal Recreation and Recreating Tribalism: Recreation on the Gold Mines, 1920–1950', *Journal of Southern African Studies*, 23, 3 (1997), 473–89.
4. P. Walshe, *The Rise of African Nationalism in South Africa* (Berkeley: University of California Press, 1970), notes, p.93; T. Couzens, 'Moralizing Leisure Time: The Transatlantic Connection and Black Johannesburg, 1918–36', in S. Marks and R. Rathbone (eds), *Industrialisation and Social Change in South Africa* (London: Longman, 1982), pp.315–37.
5. J. Simons and R. Simons, *Class and Colour in South Africa, 1850–1950* (London: International Defence Aid for Southern Africa, 1983), p. 267.
6. Y. Golombick, 'African crime', *City of Johannesburg Newsletter* 8, (Jan. 1946), 7.
7. See, S.H. Elliot, Report to investigate crime on the Witwatersrand and in Pretoria, 1942.
8. V.Y. Mudimbe, *The Idea of Africa* (Bloomington: Indiana University Press, 1994), p.129.
9. P. Brantlinger, 'Victorians and Africans: The Genealogy of the Myth of the Dark Continent', *Race, Writing and Difference* (Chicago: Chicago University Press, 1986), pp.185–221.
10. M.L. Pratt, 'Conventions of Representation: Where Discourse and Ideology Meet', in W. Van Peer (ed.), *The Taming of the Text* (London: Routledge, 1989), pp.15–34.
11. T.O. Ranger, 'Race and Tribe in Southern Africa: European Ideas and African Acceptance', in R. Ross (ed.), *Racism and Colonialism* (The Hague: Martinus Nijhoff Publishers, 1982), pp. 121–42.
12. J. Comaroff and J. Comaroff, *Of Revelation and Revolution: Christianity, Colonialism and Consciousness in South Africa* (Chicago: The University of Chicago Press, 1991), Volume 1, p.22.
13. Badenhorst and Mather, 'Tribal Recreation'.
14. S. Dubow, 'Race, Civilisation and Culture: The Elaboration of Segregationist Discourse in the Inter-War Years', in S. Marks and S. Trapido (eds), *The Politics of Race, Class and Nationalism in Twentieth-Century South Africa* (London: Longman, 1987), p. 72. For more detail on the discourse of race and segregationist policy in South Africa see also S. Marks and S. Trapido (eds), *The Politics of Race, Class and Nationalism in Twentieth-Century South Africa* (London: Longman, 1987); S. Dubow, *Racial Segregation and the Origins of Apartheid in South Africa, 1919–1936* (London: Macmillan, 1989).
15. A.G. Cobley, *Class and Consciousness* (New York: Greenwood Press, 1990).
16. Dubow, 'Race, Civilisation and Culture', p. 72.
17. M. Hunter, *Reaction to Conquest* (London: Oxford University Press, 1961, first edn 1936).
18. Ibid., pp.x, xii.
19. It is difficult to see any continuation between 'athletic' activities in traditional African societies and urban white (American and British) sports like soccer, cricket or boxing. Some extensions of traditional social activities which continued in the urban areas were 'stick fighting' and 'tribal (war) dances'. Both of these activities were shaped profoundly by the urban context and any 'traditional' elements came under attack from the missionaries, the municipality and the Chamber of Mines. The racial discourse in Johannesburg promoted new traditions for Africans, not a continuation of old ones. It is also difficult to find evidence of 'athletic' activities in traditional rural societies. Stick fighting and 'war' dances were social customs and not primarily leisure activities. Phillip Meyer did a study of the leisure occupation of traditionalists and mission-educated Xhosa migrants. He found that traditionalists spent their leisure time drinking and talking about home-affairs with other people from home. Mission-educated Xhosa participated in concerts, clubs and white sports. See P. Mayer, *Townsmen or Tribesmen* (Cape Town: Oxford University Press, 1961). In a society based on migrant labour the lines between urban and traditional are often very blurred because migrants travel back to their homes regularly. During the 1940s, for example, soccer teams in the urban areas were organized by players around home allegiances and the team's name usually reflected the district or family.
20. P. Rich, *White Power and Liberal Conscience* (Johannesburg: Ravan Press, 1984), p.11.
21. Natal Archives (Pietermartizburg), American Board Missions Collection A608 B/2/71,

'Return for Native Affairs Department of Mission work in Johannesburg', 1938.
22. R.E. Phillips, 'Social Work in South Africa', in J. Dexter Taylor (ed.), *Christianity and the Natives of South Africa* (Cape Town: Lovedale Press, 1928), p.183.
23. R.E. Phillips, *The Bantu in the City: A Study of Cultural Adjustment in the Witwatersrand* (Cape Town: Lovedale Press, 1938), p.xiii.
24. Phillips, 'Social Work in South Africa', p.197.
25. J. Dexter Taylor, *Social Work: Report of the National European-Bantu Conference* (Cape Town: Lovedale Press, 1929), p.195.
26. Phillips, *The Bantu in the City*, pp.ix–x; Phillips, 'Social Work in South Africa', p.183.
27. R.E. Phillips, *The Bantu are Coming* (Stellenbosch: Students' Christian Association of South African, 1930), p.62.
28. Ibid., p.98.
29. Dexter Taylor, *Social Work*, pp.195–6.
30. Phillips, *The Bantu in the City*; Phillips, *The Bantu are Coming*, p.68.
31. Phillips, 'Social Work in South Africa', p.146.
32. University of the Witwatersrand, Department of Historical Papers (UW), Phillips Papers A14444 File 1, American Board of Commissioners for Foreign Missions Newsletter entitled: 'Christianity versus African Heathenism, Ray Phillips' social service work', 1930.
33. Dexter Taylor, *Social Work*, p.196.
34. Phillips, *The Bantu are Coming*, p.103.
35. R.V. Selope Thema 'The Bantu and Bolshevism', *Umteteli Wa Bantu*, 9 Aug. 1924, 3.
36. Phillips, *The Bantu are Coming*, p.103.
37. Ibid., p.32
38. Phillips, 'Social Work in South Africa', p.150.
39. Phillips, *The Bantu are Coming*, p.52.
40. Dexter Taylor, *Social Work*, p.200.
41. Phillips, 'Social Work in South Africa', p.150.
42. Phillips, *The Bantu in the City*, pp.195, 245.
43. Ibid., p.246. See E. Hellmann, *Problems of Urban Bantu Youth* (Johannesburg: South African Institute of Race Relations, Monograph Series No. 3, 1940) pp.44–5.
44. Central Archives Depot (CAD), K26 NEC vol. 12: Statement by Archdeacon Hill, 1930–32.
45. Cobley, *The Rules of the Game*, p.25.
46. CAD, JUS 855 1/132/25, Conference on Urban Juvenile Delinquency, Johannesburg, 10–12 Oct. (1938). Paper by Dr Ray E. Phillips, 'A Survey of the Situation on the Witwatersrand'.
47. Dexter Taylor, *Social Work*, p.199–200.
48. 'Sportsmanship', *Umteteli Wa Bantu*, 10 Dec. 1930, 7.
49. 'Play Honest Game and Emulate the British Sportsmen', *Bantu World*, 30 Dec. 1933, 16; 'The Natives' Leisure', *Umteteli Wa Bantu*, 9 Aug. 1924, .2.
50. For more on the transfer of these ideals across the Atlantic, see C.M. Badenhorst, 'The Geography of Sport as a Cultural Process: A Case Study of Lacrosse', (unpublished MA thesis, University of British Columbia, Vancouver, 1988). For transfer of these ideals through British colonial Africa, see A. Kirk-Greene, 'Imperial Administration and the Athletic Imperative: The Case of the District Officer in Africa', in W.J. Baker and J.A. Mangan, *Sport in Africa* (New York: Africana Publishing Company, 1987), pp.81–113.
51. D.N. Murray, *Social Welfare Work in Johannesburg* (Johannesburg: City Council of Johannesburg, 1941).
52. *Annual Report of Manager*, Native Affairs, 1927; 1928.
53. *Annual Report of Manager*, Native Affairs, 1934.
54. *Annual Report of Manager*, Native Affairs, 1929.
55. *Annual Report of Manager*, Native Affairs, 1935.
56. *Annual Report of Manager*, Native Affairs, 1937; UW, Joint Councils AD 1433 G.2.1.17 file 2: Letter from G. Ballenden Manager NEAD Johannesburg to SAIRR, 11 Sept. 1937. Also CAD, GG 1569 50/1481, Letter from G. Ballenden, Manager NEAD to the Mayor, Town Hall, 3 Jan. 1933; Annual Report of Director of Social Welfare, 1939–40.
57. Municipal Reference Library, Johannesburg (MRL), MPam 326:352:45 (68221) JOH: Johannesburg Non-European Affairs Memorandum on the history of the NEAD, 1965.

58. NEAD become more involved in women's leisure-time activities from the time social welfare became a separate section, *Annual Report of Manager*, Native Affairs, 1944–48.

59. *Annual Report of Manager*, Native Affairs, 1936 (Quote); 1938–42.

60. *Annual Report of Manager*, Native Affairs, 1944–48.

61. MRL, MPam 326:352:45 (68221) JOH, City of Johannesburg Non-European Affairs Department, 1951. See also, UW, P.R.B. Lewis Collection A1132 A2/4 Pamphlet 'Happy Living' by NEAD, 1964.

62. 'Great Social Problem of Urban Native', *Star*, 14 Nov. 1938.

63. See *Annual Report of Manager*, Native Affairs, 1948–49.

64. Intermediate Archives, Johannesburg (IA), WRO 55/3: Letter from L.I. Venables, Manager NEAD to Mr J.F. Botha, National Advisory Council for Physical Education, Union Education Department, 5 Nov. 1948; IA, WRO 110/3: Letter from L.I. Venables, Manager NEAD, to Mej Louise Erasmus on the social services of the Johannesburg Municipality, 30 Aug. 1949; IA, WRO 110/3: Johannesburg Report on Native Services, 23 Aug. 1949.

65. For an example of the type of research see, IA, WRO 138/1: 'Report on Recreation in Johannesburg by Graham Young', Recreation Officer NEAD, 9 Jan. 1947.

66. *Annual Report of Manager*, Native Affairs, 1944–1948.

67. *Annual Report of Manager*, Native Affairs, 1949–50; MRL, MPam 326:352:45 (68221) JOH: Johannesburg Non-European Affairs Memorandum on the history of the NEAD, 1965.

68. 'To Remake Men', *Cape Times*, 9 Nov. 1943.

69. Ernst Jokl was a medical doctor who received a specialist's diploma in Physical Education in Berlin, Germany, before the Second World War. In the early 1940s he was involved in, and did research for, the National Advisory Council for Physical Education and, by the late 1940s, he was Physical Education Research Officer to the Union Department of Education.

70. E. Jokl, 'South African Natives Fall Short as Athletes', *The Forum* 2, 4 (1939), 18–19.

71. E. Jokl, *Manpower*, 2, 1 (1943), 1–46.

72. See E. Jokl, 'Physical Education, Sport and Recreation', in E. Hellmann (ed.), *Handbook on Race Relations in South Africa* (Cape Town: Oxford University Press, 1949), pp.442–64.

73. IA, JGE 361 16/16 B2496: Extract of agenda, 77th Ordinary Meeting of City Council, 25 Aug. 1942.

74. A.L. Saffrey, 'The Liquor Problem in Urban Areas', *Race Relations*, 7, 4 (1940), 88–94; J. Crush and C. Ambler (eds), *Liquor and Labor in Southern Africa* (Ohio: Ohio University Press, 1992), pp.214–34.

75. E. Hawarden, 'Municipal Policy and Native Welfare', *Race Relations*, 8, 4 (1941), 46–50; Hellmann, *Handbook on Race Relations in South Africa*, pp. 229–74.

76. Hawarden, 'Municipal Policy and Native Welfare', 47–9.

77. Hellmann, *Handbook on Race Relations in South Africa*, p.261.

78. '£121,477 made by City Council on sale of Kaffir Beer', *Star*, 23 Nov. 1945.

79. See Cobley, *The Rules of the Game*, for a discussion on the struggles the beerhalls system initiated between different groups of Africans and between Africans and the NEAD.

80. Saffrey, 'The Liquor Problem in Urban Areas', 92–3.

81. UW, AD 843/RJ Aa12.18.22: SAIRR report on the production and distribution of Kaffir Beer, n.d., c.1951.

82. P. Bonner, 'The Transvaal Native Congress, 1917–1920: The Radicalisation of the Black Petty Bourgeoisie on the Rand', in Marks and Rathbone (eds), *Industrialisation and Social Change in South Africa*, pp. 270–313, see especially p. 272; Cobley, *Class and Consciousness*, p. 9.

83. Rich, *White Power and Liberal Conscience*, pp.10–11.

84. Cobley, *Class and Consciousness*, pp.75–81

85. Walshe, *The Rise of African Nationalism in South Africa*, p.189; Bonner, 'The Transvaal Native Congress', p.305.

86. Walshe, *The Rise of African Nationalism in South Africa*; Simons and Simons, *Class and Colour in South Africa*; T. Lodge, *Black Politics in South Africa since 1945* (Johannesburg: Ravan Press, 1986); Cobley, *Class and Consciousness*, p.91.

87. CAD, VWN 523 SW 80/7/1 Vol. 1: BSC Annual Report, 1943.

88. Ibid.; UW, XUMS AD 843 ABX 430501G: May Day demonstration notice, 1 May 1943.

89. UW, SAIRR AS 843 B73.4.4: BSC Aug. Bulletin 1938.

90. CAD, VWN 523 SW 80/7/1 Vol. 1: BSC Annual Report, 1945. See also B. Hirson, *Yours for the Union: Class and Community Struggles in South Africa, 1930-1947* (Johannesburg: Witwatersrand University Press, 1990), p.47. He also mentions mass meetings on the BSC grounds held by the Council of Non-European Trade Unions, p.102, and worker riots and demonstrations, p.193.

91. 'Municipality and Native Sport', *Umteteli Wa Bantu*, 11 Feb. 1933, p.13.

92. CAD, KJB 406 N1/14/3: JAFA Annual Report 1946; UW, SAIRR AD 843 B73.3: JAFA Annual Report 1941.

93. UW, SAIRR AD 843 B73.3: JAFA Annual Report 1941; CAD, VWN 519 SW80/3/6: JAFA Annual Report 1944.

94. CAD, KJB 406 N1/14/3: JAFA Annual Report 1945, 1946, 1948: IA WRO 138/8 vol. 2: JAFA Annual Report 1950; UW, SAIRR AD 843 B73.3: JAFA Annual Report 1949.

95. V.Y. Mudimbe, *The Invention of Africa* (Bloomington: Indiana University Press, 1988), p.171.

6

Deconstructing 'Indianness': Cricket and the Articulation of Indian Identities in Durban, 1900–32

GOOLAM VAHED

Indian immigrants arrived in South Africa in two waves; approximately 150,000 indentured labourers imported between 1860 and 1911 were followed by traders from the west coast of India. Use of the term 'Indian' suggested that the attribute 'Indianness' united them as a group in opposition to Whites, Coloureds and Africans.[1] Indians were seen by Africans, Coloureds and successive white Natal governments as a distinct group on the basis of skin colour, 'strange' culture and foreign origin. This study of Indian cricket questions the notion of a homogeneous and self-contained community prevalent in early literature, and probes the true nature of Indian identity in South Africa.[2] While Swan demystified Gandhi,[3] and Padayachee and Vawda gave voice to Indian workers,[4] this study will explore race, class, caste, ethnic, religious and linguistic differences among Indians,[5] and how these were negotiated and articulated.[6] This survey will also consider the role of sport and popular culture in defining ethnic, racial and class identities. Did sport reinforce differential identities in a highly stratified society, or serve as a link between whites, Africans and Indians, as well as between working and middle classes? Did sport become the commonality between these divergent groups, based on merit rather than status, to break down barriers and forge a truly unique South African culture, or did sport reinforce and cement differences?

ARRIVAL AND SETTLEMENT OF INDIANS

The arrival of Indian indentured labour on the sugar plantations of Natal, a province of South Africa, had significant consequences. While the government expected Indians to return to India, about 60 per cent remained in the Colony after their contracts had expired. Traders, known as 'passengers' because they came at their own expense and initiative, gave permanence to the Indian presence. Most 'free' Indians, as those who had completed their indentures were known, grew fruit and vegetables for the local market on land rented or purchased from absentee landlords. Small numbers worked as shoemakers, clerks, cooks, domestics, laundry workers, plumbers, fishermen and tailors. Whites desired the outright coercion of Indians and became hostile as Indians challenged their dominance of local trade. White concerns increased as the numbers of Indians reached parity. By 1894, the Indian population of Natal of 46,000 exceeded the white population of 45,000.[7] Whites used their political clout to subdue and dominate Indians after they achieved self-government from Britain in 1893. The new government viewed town planning, public health, trade arrangements and other public issues in terms of racial distinctions.[8] Its objective was to force Indians to re-indenture or return to India upon completing their indenture, and to legally subordinate non-indentured Indians. The Indian Immigration Law of 1895 compelled Indian adults to pay an annual tax of £3, Act 8 of 1896 imposed franchise restrictions and the Immigration Restriction Act of 1897 gave the state power to control Indian entry.

Indian politics was dominated by trader elites. In 1894, they formed the Natal Indian Congress (NIC) whose strategy was primarily constitutional and consisted of issuing long petitions to private individuals and government officials. Most Indians could not afford the annual membership fee and 75 per cent of the NIC's members were merchants, the balance being the educated elite. The secretary of the NIC was the great Indian nationalist leader Mahatma Gandhi.[9] The 20-year struggle of Indians culminated in a national strike from October to December 1913. This was a spontaneous outburst against terrible working conditions, and a reaction to the realization that the poll tax meant perpetual indenture. Mass action was possible because merchants and workers shared a common position. Indians responded to the state's use of race to subordinate them by adopting a practice of resistance based on race. The Indian Relief Act of 1914 made some concessions to Indians but left many issues unresolved. Gandhi therefore considered the Act a 'Magna Carta' for the Indians, providing them with breathing space to resolve their outstanding grievances.[10]

For whites, race was the most effective political and ideological means of ensuring a cheap labour supply, and was used to separate Natal's

population into discrete groups by suggesting that Indians and Africans
were naturally different and inferior. The privileged economic position
of Indian elites was neutralized by their having to confront racism,
which placed them in the same situation as workers. In response,
middle-class Indians used the cause of their rejection, race, to formulate
a strategy of resistance. The formation of a racial organization, the NIC,
assisted in fostering and keeping alive a separate racial political identity.
As far as non-Indians were concerned, Indians constituted a homogeneous community; the reality was different, however, and this study
examines the relevance and importance of class, caste, ethnic, religious
and linguistic differences among the Indians.

TABLE 6.1
RACIAL COMPOSITION OF DURBAN'S POPULATION

Year	Whites	Coloureds	Indians	Africans	Total
1904	31,302	1,980	15,631	18,929	67,842
1921	46,113	4,000	16,400	29,011	95,524
1931	59,250	4,240	17,860	43,750	125,100
1936	88,065	7,336	80,384	63,762	239,547

Source: University of Natal, The Durban Housing Survey, 1952, p.35.

This study focuses on Durban, where most of Natal's Indians lived.
During the period under review, Durban was a town of approximately
13,000 acres. It was chiefly a port and commercial centre with rudimentary industrial development.[11] As late as 1914, the Umgeni Sugar
Company was planting cane on the 80 acre property 'Eastern Vlei', less
than two miles north of the city centre.[12] Industry consisted mainly of
metals and engineering firms which manufactured wagons and repaired
imported machinery on the sugar estates, coal mines and in the shipping
trade.[13] The chief exports were coal, wool, hides, wattle bark, maize and
whale oil.[14] The Natal economy relied greatly on railway traffic from the
Transvaal, and the trade from the mining centres of Transvaal and the
Orange Free State, customs duties and railway receipts accounting for 69
per cent of Natal's revenue in 1908–9.[15] Durban's economy was given
momentum by the First World War, when local industries were given a
fillip by restrictions on overseas trade and high freight costs, and
'enjoyed a high increase in their businesses'.[16] Wartime demand for soap,
matches, spirits, beer and explosives boosted industrial development,

while an oil refinery, flour mill and Hardening Works were started in 1915.[17] As a result of this rapid growth, the boundaries of Durban were extended in 1932 from 13 to 70 square miles, which resulted in the incorporation of an additional 101,786 people.[18] Indians made up a third of Durban's population during this period.

INDIAN STRATIFICATION

Indians comprised a diverse grouping. Durban was home to a large working-class Indian population, primarily employed by the Durban Municipality and Natal Government Railways, which performed unskilled work such as street-sweeping and grass-cutting. In 1949, for example, workers and their dependents totalled almost 10,000 when the Indian population in the Old Borough of Durban was 25,000.[19] Indian workers were among the lowest-paid in Durban and lived in appalling sub-economic municipal housing scattered across the city.[20] According to Councillor Knight, 'some Councillors have felt and said that the more wretchedly the Indians are housed and paid the more likely they will be willing to be repatriated' to India.[21] When Indira Gandhi, the future Prime Minister of India, visited Durban in 1935 she referred to working-class housing as 'Durban's feudal rat hovel'.[22] Indian traders occupied an important structural position. When they started to arrive in the 1870s, they could not compete with the established white businesses and built their shops and shacks on swampy land at the north-western periphery of the white business area, in the Grey-Victoria streets and Warwick Avenue areas. Later, as the Indian and white business areas expanded and impinged on each other, whites used the 1897 Dealer's License Act to restrict Indian traders to this area. Indians had greater access to capital and credit than Africans and dominated trade in this segregated Black business district.[23] The relationship between Indian traders and workers only went 'so far as trade and labour compelled them'.[24]

In addition to workers and traders, a third social group among Indians was a professional class, mainly teachers and clerks, which emerged in Durban from the 1890s as the result of English-language education provided by mission schools.[25] Their numbers were small because of the lack of facilities and the poverty of parents; the Natal Population Census of 1904 showed that only 5,211 of 100,918 Indians were literate in English. Most educated Indians were Christians, mainly

Roman Catholics, Anglicans and Wesleyan-Methodists, who valued western education. Church missions were already established when Indians arrived in Natal. The Roman Catholic Church built a mission in Durban in 1853 under Father Sabon, who opened the first Durban school for Indian children in 1867; the Wesleyan Mission under Reverend R. Stott in 1862 opened a school in 1867; Anglicans began the St Aidans Mission in 1884 under Reverend Dr Lancelot Booth. By 1896, the Mission ran 15 schools in Natal.[26] E.A. Hammick, Archdeacon of Durban, observed in 1901 that 'the Indian, by coming to Natal has thrown off caste restrictions ... he is very anxious to cease being an Indian and tries to become English in all ways'.[27] Prominent Christian Indian families emerged, such as the Lawrence, Gabriel, Royeppen, Lazarus, Godfrey and Sigamony families, who used their knowledge of English to assume leadership roles in the civil service, politics, sports and education.[28] V. Lawrence typified the educated elite. A teacher, he married Josephine Gabriel, whose mother, Amonee, had come to South Africa as an indentured worker in 1901. According to Sylvia Lawrence, her father's strong desire to escape the 'coolie' image resulted in his giving all ten of his children a sound education and making them proficient in western musical instruments such as the piano, violin and saxophone.[29]

THE VALUE OF SPORT

Durban's Indian elite saw sport as a means to instil discipline, implant a healthy value system and teach social values such as teamwork, allegiance to fellow players, respect for rules and authority and fortitude in the face of adversity. Joseph Royeppen, a colonial-born Indian who studied at Cambridge University, wrote in 1912 that sport had a 'greater purpose' than winning:

> The battles of England have been won on the playing fields of Eton. As yet there are little signs of our battles being won upon our playing fields of South Africa ... so long as young men follow sports without eye or ear to their final value for us in this our adopted land of one continued struggle for honourable existence, but merely for the passing excitement and intoxication of the thing, our playing fields must continue to be, not the school and the training ground to higher calls of life and duty, but scenes of our sure damage and loss.[30]

When Mahatma Gandhi was departing for India in 1914, he addressed the children at a farewell reception given in his honour. Gandhi said that the giving of prizes had a 'demoralizing' effect on children. He felt that sport was only beneficial when children competed 'to show that they had been endeavouring to keep the physical portion of their being in fit and proper state'. This would demonstrate the 'value of industry, the courage and the time that they put forth in a disciplined manner in order to gain that particular purpose in life'.[31] Manilal Gandhi, son of Mahatma Gandhi and editor of *Indian Opinion,* which Mahatma Gandhi had started in 1903, agreed that sport had a vital role to play in moulding the character of Indians:

> In South Africa, sports and athletics take a very prominent place in life … This is a good habit in a new country like South Africa where Nature herself is always telling us to be healthy and strong. Football and cricket have a special value of their own. They teach people to play together, to play for the team, and to endure hardship, without becoming angry and losing one's temper. All these things are of immense value in training people to be good South Africans.[32]

ESTABLISHING THE GAME

Cricket has old roots in India.[33] By the middle of the nineteenth century, Bombay was the centre of Indian cricket, mainly through the Parsees who excelled at the game. From the 1890s, annual matches were played between the Parsees and the English, who were joined by Hindus in 1907 and Muslims in 1912 in a Quadrangular tournament.[34] Cricket was familiar to Indians who arrived in Natal. In Durban they played both football and cricket on grounds provided by the Durban Town Council (DTC or Council) in the Botanical Gardens area in 1886.[35] Soccer was more popular because it was less costly and took less time, important considerations for working-class Indians. Formally organized cricket began with the formation of the Durban District Indian Cricket Union (DDICU or Union) in 1901. Educated Indians formed the early cricket teams in Durban. The Standard Cricket Club, for example, was formed in September 1901 by educated Christians at a meeting at the St Aidan's Boys Schoolroom, while the City Players Indian Cricket Club was formed in October 1901 by Reverend John Thomas, headmaster of the

Wesleyan School. These teams represented Anglican and Methodist Christians respectively. The chairman of the DDICU was A.H. Peters, a clerk at the Durban Court, and the secretary Frank B. Ernest, both Christians.[36]

Teams competed for the Pandays Shield and Peters Bowl. The Shield was sponsored by Lutchman Panday who was born in Durban in 1874 to indentured parents and educated at the Boys' Model School. He joined a firm of lawyers in 1888 and served for five decades. Lutchman played competitive football and cricket, and served as an official on many sports bodies.[37] The 'Peters Bowl' was named after A.H. Peters, first president of DDICU and a pioneer in Indian sports. Teams and players varied from year to year. In 1910–11, the members of the Union were Pirates of India (Pirates), Greyville, Natal Government Railways (Railways), Higher Grade School (School) and Overport. Ottomans joined in 1911.[38] In 1915, Overport and Railways became defunct due to their players' involvement in the First World War. Indian Teachers and Star of India joined in 1919, Moslems in 1924, Moonlight and Centrals in 1925 and Kismet in 1932. The number of players fluctuated from season to season but averaged around a hundred. For example, there were 106 players during 1912–13.[39] Matches were played from 2:30 p.m. to 6:30 p.m. over two Saturdays to accommodate Christians who refused to play on Sundays on grounds of religion. A Sunday League was formed in October 1926 for non-Christians.[40]

High registration fees constrained working-class participation, and made cricket an elitist undertaking. The annual subscription was £3.3.0 per team, which even trader and educated elites struggled to pay. In 1911, for example, School did not pay arrear registration fees until threatened with expulsion.[41] From December 1912, teams were fined for failing to pay registration fees.[42] In April 1913, £4.13.6 was owed to the Union.[43] The 1925 season began late because only two teams, School and Pirates, paid subscriptions.[44] While cricketers were denied equality with whites, this did not prevent them from mimicking the Colonial masters and behaving as gentlemen by observing the 'rules of the game'. Clubs were fined or points deducted if results were not submitted within 72 hours.[45] Schools and Ottomans, who played on 24 February 1923 without the sanction of the union, were warned not to organize matches without permission.[46] When the father of a Pirates player died, Greyville agreed to reschedule the match, but the Union refused.[47] In February 1926, clubs were advised to be clad 'in proper cricket costumes when playing for respective clubs and should this instruction not be adhered to, the defaulting club will be dealt with as the Committee think fit'.[48]

IMPACT OF WIDER DEVELOPMENTS

Cricket was closely bound to society and affected by wider developments. Fixtures were suspended from October to December 1913 because of a strike by Indians in support of Gandhi's passive resistance campaign against anti-Indian policies. Fixtures resumed on 17 January 1914, 'as soon as normal conditions resumed'.[49] Cricket was also disrupted during the First World War. The Indian commercial and educated elites, eager to prove their loyalty to the British because, in the words of the *African Chronicle*, 'better prospects are awaiting us, under the aegis of the same Empire when it has emerged triumphantly from the present ordeal',[50] declared their 'loyalty to the King-Emperor, and readiness to serve the Crown in defence of the country'.[51] An army camp was constructed in Stamford Hill Road for Indian volunteers who served as stretcher-bearers in East Africa. When Senator Marshall Campbell visited the camp in November 1915, he found the volunteers playing cricket. On 13 December 1915, a public meeting in the Town Hall bid farewell to the Bearer Corps. Cricketers Butler (Ottoman), Karrim (Ottoman), V.K. Naidoo (Railway), Anglia (Greyville), Thumbadoo and Sullaphen were part of the committee that arranged the farewell reception.[52] School and Railways withdrew from the Union because many of their players served in the war. The secretary of DDICU reported in 1917 that he 'could not find words adequate enough to express my sentiments about these patriotic men who have answered the call of duty. We are proud of them and if they do not come back their memories will be revered by us'.[53] The 1918–19 season started late because of the 'terrible visitation of this pestilence – the influenza which has engaged us most of the time'.[54]

Indian cricketers faced many problems, such as the lack of proper grounds, absence of grass wickets, torn and worn out mats and unmarked boundaries. There was no assistance from the Council. D. Kolipillai, an Indian teacher, reassured whites that Indian demands for better facilities 'do not advance any claim to political equality, but they do claim a treatment that will be kind, unselfish, just and tender – a treatment that will take into consideration what is best in them, and encourage them to make up what is lacking in them'.[55] Players had to mark pitches and boundaries, peg stumps and lay out mats. Since grounds did not have huts, players were forced to change in front of spectators; there was petty thieving due to the absence of secure storage facilities and spectators suffered in hot and wet weather because there was no covered seating.[56] When Essop Manjoo, captain of Kismet, visited India in 1934, he was amazed by the amenities, limited to whites in Durban, and wrote excitedly to team-mates:

> I saw one of the best grounds in the world, the Bombay Stadium, what a lovely ground and sitting accommodation, shelters all over, yes. I haven't seen one like that before in my life! I didn't know whether I was in India or America ... Another thing I saw which is unbelievable to your mind and eyes, unless you come and see for yourself, the Bombay Race Course, 3 stories and what a crowd and style.[57]

Indians formed the Durban United Indian Sports Association (DUISA or Sports Association) in 1911 to press the Council for a ground. When an Indian criticized the project because it implied that Indians would lose their right to use existing public facilities,[58] J. Royeppen of the Sports Association explained that although facilities were theoretically open to all, in practice they were restricted to whites. DUISA was campaigning for the same facilities that whites enjoyed: 'proper turfing, drainage, fencing, and a pavilion with the necessary conveniences'.[59] The Sports Association made little progress. *Indian Opinion* noted in 1915 that 'after a lapse of so many years the Corporation were bound, in bare justice and fairness to all concerned, to materialise their promises'.[60] Despite persistent appeals, the Council informed DUISA in December 1921 that it intended to give the site set aside for Indians in 1912 to whites, and offer Indians an alternative site.[61] A livid Royeppen wrote:

> The Indian community are not making any 'claim' as if from today. They made their claim ten years ago and that claim was recognized by your Council and the resultant right was vouchsafed to the Indians. It is that right Indian sportsmen are concerned about now.[62]

The Council eventually agreed in 1924 to lease 23 acres at the foot of Botanic Gardens. However, the 'onus of laying out and equipping the grounds be upon the Indian Sports Bodies'.[63] The new sports area was named Curries Fountain after Councillor H.W. Currie, town councillor of Durban from 1863–66 and Mayor in 1879–80. Currie's Fountain was only opened in 1932.[64] Generally, Indians did not receive formal coaching, or possess personal equipment, as was the case with white cricketers. Cricket gear was shared, irrespective of whether the fit of pads and gloves was precise. The lack of equipment and practice facilities, absence of coaches and coaching, and the deplorable state of the pitches hindered the development of the game. After playing and practising in India, Manjoo wrote enthusiastically: 'I have learnt a great deal – If I stayed back one season more, I should have mastered it'.

ADMINISTRATORS AND ELITISM

There was a close relationship between cricket and the trader and educated elites. While some administrators were well-known sportsmen, others occupied leadership positions because they were articulate in English or were respected politicians and businessmen. Most administrators held official positions in multiple social, religious, educational, economic and political organizations, which had a detrimental effect on Indian cricket. This manifested itself in an unwillingness or inability to attend meetings to fulfil the work of the Union. In 1913, for example, only five of 16 meetings were held; the rest were called off because of a lack of quorum.[65] Such tardiness resulted in the Union resolving in December 1922 that delegates failing to attend two consecutive meetings would lose their right to represent the club.[66]

Patrons of the Union, such as R.B. Chetty, J. Royeppen, Parsee and Sorabjee Rustomjee, R.K. Khan and J.K. Tandree, represented a 'Who's Who' of Indian society in Durban. The involvement of Parsee and Sorabjee Rustomjee was not surprising given their pre-eminence in trade and the fact that the small Parsee community were pioneers of cricket in India. Parsee Rustomjee, a general merchant, built an orphanage for children in 1903, was trustee of *Indian Opinion*, founder member of the Parsee Rustomjee Library, a prominent passive resister with Gandhi, and an outstanding sports leader: 'His house in Field Street was the house of the Indians and Indian sportsmen', remarked *Indian Opinion* upon his death.[67] Ramaswami Balaguru (R.B.) Chetty, who arrived from Mauritius in 1896, was proprietor of the Imperial Cigar Manufacturing and Trading Co. and Rex Printing Company. He was president of the Hindu Tamil Institute, donor to Sastri College and M.K. Gandhi Schools, as well as a senior member of the NIC.[68]

Albert Christopher and Shaik Emamally, presidents of DDICU, occupied prominent social, economic, political and religious roles in Indian society. Emamally, who arrived in Durban in 1880 at the age of two with indentured parents and died in 1927, was proprietor of the Mineral Water Works. He was secretary and vice-president of the NIC, treasurer of the Mahatma Gandhi library, trustee of the Sports Association and life trustee of the May Street Mosque.[69] Advocate Albert Christopher was educated at the Higher Grade Indian School and called to the Bar at Lincoln's Inn in England. He served in the First World War and was awarded the Distinguished Conduct Medal. He was president of many political, sports, cultural and welfare organizations.[70] These individuals dominated cricket during the early period, both from a playing and an administrative point of view. In addition to their multiple positions, administrators had to cope with the deep poverty of the fledgling Indian community and racist practices of the local state.

IDENTITIES: RELIGIOUS, ETHNIC, LINGUISTIC, RACE AND CLASS

Durban's Indian cricketers formed teams on the basis of commonalities. These mirrored local neighbourhood, religious and class identities. There were differences of hierarchy between traders and indentured Indians. Traders were considered by the state (and considered themselves) 'Arab' because they were Muslim and wore Middle Eastern garb.[71] Differences among Muslims based on language, region and class were reflected in the composition of teams. Ottomans was made up of Urdu-speaking traders and their shop assistants from Rander in Gujarat, India. In Natal, Urdu-speaking traders were known as *Miabhais*.[72] Ottomans was formed in October 1911 at the home of Shiaku Peerbhai (S.P.) Butler.[73] Shiaka Peerbhai, who had come to South Africa in 1896, opened a retail store at 474 West Street. He was later joined by his wife and three brothers from India, Ahmed Peerbhai (A.P.), Rahman Peerbhai (R.P.) and Karrim Peerbhai (K.P.) Butler. All were prominent in Ottomans, and held official positions in the Union. The main benefactor of Ottomans was Abdul Hack Kazi, known as 'Kwamdhlambuzi' (Zulu for 'goat') among Zulus because of his love for meat. Kazi was born in Rander in 1876 and came to South Africa at the age of 13. He was educated in Rander and Boy's Model Schools in Durban. He owned a retail store in Field Street as well as several branches throughout Natal. An indication of Kazi's wealth was that he was the first individual to own a Daimler in Durban, and was the envy of many whites. According to Mr Goolam Butler, grandson of S.P. Butler, most Ottomans' players worked for Kazi. In December 1914, for example, Ottomans requested that its fixtures be postponed because players were required to work late on Saturday due to Christmas shopping.[74]

Employers provided boarding and lodging for shop assistants from India, who were usually young and single.[75] According to Goolam Butler, Kazi formed Ottomans to occupy the leisure time of his employees and prevent them from getting involved in vices, such as gambling. Ottomans had a strong Muslim identity. Thus, for example, when Muslims beat Parsees in Bombay in 1913, the *Mercury* reported that the 'local Muslim community is exceedingly jubilant over the news of the victory. The Durban Ottoman Cricket Club dispatched a cable message to the Islam Gymkhana of Bombay conveying Durban Moslems congratulations to the distinguished winners.'[76] The multiple subject positions of Ottomans' players became manifest against Greyville. Although Greyville contained non-Muslim players, its founding members, officials and the majority of players were Muslims, such as Shaik Emamally, Mahendeally Thajmoon, Hoosen 'Sonny' Buckus and Chand Noor Mahomed (C.N.M.) Khan, who were descendants of indentured Muslims. Among traders, descendents of indentured Muslims were known pejoratively as *Calcuttias* if they were from northern India and *Hyderabadees* if from the south. In addition to obvious differences of class, there were also differences of language, since indentured Muslims initially spoke Bihari, Bengali, Tamil and Telegu as opposed to the Urdu spoken by traders.

Emamally arrived in Natal in 1880 at the age of two with his indentured parents from Gurakhpur, Uttar Pradesh. Buckus, his brother, was born in Natal. Thajmoon was born in Durban in 1877 and educated at St Aidan's school. Khan was born of indentured parents in Durban in 1889. Educated at St Aidan's School, he was variously a cartage contractor, proprietor of the Orient Cinema which brought the first Indian movie to South Africa in 1926, and partner in Radio Record Trading Co. in Victoria Street. While Ajam Haffejee, a prominent member of Greyville, was from Gujarat, he had lived in England for 13 years, where he studied and was a clerk at the War office in London. He married a white English woman which, according to Butler, made him an 'outcast' locally: 'He could not fit in with the Surtees because of this.' Intense rivalry between Ottomans and Greyville was connected to these class, ethnic and language differences. According to Butler:

> I don't want to be rude, but when we played Greyville we said that we were playing the thirty three and one-third's. You know, they were children of indentured Muslims. When indentured Indians came, the English, although they were Christian, sent one woman per three men. One woman was shared by three men, so the children could not know for sure who the father was. It had to be one-third, one-third and one-third. (interview, 25 January 2001)

Yusuf Emamally, whose father played for Greyville, recalled that players of Ottomans constantly reminded them of their indentured heritage:

> There was a lot of division among Muslims at the time. Ottomans did not like us because they thought that they were higher class. We also had non-Muslims like S. Shams, G.K. Singh and Jack Papa. They looked down on us. Even M.I. Yusuf did not escape this. When they could not get him out they would say 'Koja' (Black) to upset him, because most indentured Indians were from south India and darker. (interview, 13 June 2001)

Among traders, there were linguistic differences between Urdu and Gujarati-speakers. According to Goolam Butler, Gujarati Muslims displayed little interest in cricket until the 1920s, when 'old-man Akoojee', M.I.Badat, M.E. Jadwat, the Timols and Jeewas took up the game. Teams like Moslems and Kismet were not confined to Surtees. Kismet's 1932 constitution stated that membership was 'open to all Muslims of every class and sect, subject to rules'. However, 'the Committee shall have complete discretion either to accept or reject any application without assigning any reasons whatsoever'. They included Muslims from various language groups, but never non-Muslims. One informant recalled his futile attempt to get A. Stephens, regarded as the greatest Indian fast bowler, to join Moslems because he was not a Muslim. The category Muslim was thus not homogeneous. There was a hierarchy between indentured Muslims and traders, between Gujarati and Urdu-speaking Muslim traders, and between Miabhai and Hyderabadee Urdu-speaking Muslims.

Ottomans were consistently the most successful team. Between 1911 and 1926, the club won the Peters Cup six times in nine seasons and

Pandays Shield three times in eight seasons. In his Annual Report for 1912, the secretary of the Union reported that Ottomans was successful because it was the only team 'that consistently practiced'. Similarly, the secretary of Pirates blamed his team's failures on lack of practice: 'The members did not turn up to practice regularly last season, and that was the cause of their defeat, as it is evident that the upkeep of a team mainly depends on it.'[77] The secretary reported in 1926 that Ottomans won the Peters Bowl 'for a number of years and if this same enthusiasm is shown by other clubs, the trophy may change hands'.[78] Kazi built a practice net behind his store in Field Street where shop assistants, with little else to do, practised during evenings and on weekends. Joseph Royeppen described a typical practice net in a letter to the Council:

> A full size cricket pitch is laid out and is enclosed on both sides and the top portion by wire netting carried on wattle poles. The cricket pitch is 22 yards and the bowlers 'run' takes up the rest of the yard in line. The pitch is laid out in sand stone to take the cricket matting. (NAR, 30BN, 4/1/3/236, 17 July 1932)

According to Goolam Butler, as a result of this practice net:

> Ottomans had an advantage. They had the facilities and time and were the only ones to practise. Everything was found for them. They ate, slept, worked and played cricket. What else was there to do? Other Indians had to hunt for a living. (interview, 25 January 2001)

Latest reported in 1917 that 'since the advent of Ottoman in our Union they have evinced a keenness for the game which surpasses that of the other teams. They are punctual, attend to practice, and, above all, are fully equipped with the required gear.'[79] Patrons of other teams provided similar facilities in later years. This, together with other financial incentives, ensured that cricket was dominated by teams sponsored by traders. Writing about one of his key players, Essop Manjoo advised Kismet's secretary from India that I.A. Timol:

> is our right hand today – therefore I want you to look after him well during the off season, because this lad is young. Keep your eyes open on this boy. Please see that Timol gets something for his 100 wickets, a trouser and a boot will do. I hope you'll try for this, and give it from our club money. If I was there, I should have given him myself but now it is your duty to work for it, and give something

... For our good, I suggest that every month end our boys must try and have a good junk [party], and it will cost you 5/- extra a month. Invite all our players only for eats, and keep them together, it will help us a long way. It may look curious to others, but I know you'll agree with me.[80]

Class factors were pivotal in the success of Ottomans initially, and other Muslim clubs later. Class determined who could and could not participate in formal cricket. In November 1918, B. Nobin, M. Chinswami and T. Gabriel formed a cricket association for Durban's waiters who could not get time off on Saturdays to play in the regular league.[81] In 1922–23, Durban's waiters applied to join the Union. Their representative, Thomas Gabriel, requested that games be completed at 6:00 p.m. as waiters at leading hotels began work at 6:30 p.m. The Union, however, insisted that games finish at 6:30 p.m., forcing Gabriel and his band of working-class cricketers to withdraw their application.[82] Formal cricket was dominated by merchants and educated Indians who founded the earliest clubs and remained active as players and administrators.

According to Surendra Bhana, who has written extensively on Indians in South Africa, in the 'unique circumstances in which the notion of "Indianness" became crystallized in South Africa, it became racialized in the creation of White supremacist rule'.[83] The social structure in Natal militated against class organization. The racialization of class made race a point of reference in personal and group behaviour, and made race boundaries meaningful for members. Thus, when Coloured clubs Congella United, Union and Comets requested permission to use its ground in December 1912, DDICU's president R. Bughwan felt that although Coloureds had treated Indians 'very poorly' in sport, the Union should accede to the request to show them that 'we are not the same kind of sportsman as they are'.[84] From October 1914, Coloureds were barred from participating in the Union as members; in fact, all 'applications for registration from those not of Indian parentage as recognised by the law of the country be refused'.[85] In 1919, DDICU 'resolved that under no circumstances Coloureds be allowed to umpire matches'.[86] 'One of Your Readers' even complained to *Latest*:

I certainly do not appreciate the inclusion of Coloured sporting items in the Indian Sports Columns of 'The Latest' as I observed last week ... I feel that the publication of notes of the Coloured sporting bodies is a gross abuse of the Indian columns, and entirely uncalled for. Coloured sportsmen do not generally participate in or interest themselves in Indian sports, and a rowdy and boisterous section of the Coloured sporting community have at all times abused Indian sports, and never patronise our shows at any time. This being so, why should you publish their sporting news?[87]

Many Indians objected to membership by Malays. 'Malay' is a historical description that refers to Coloured Muslims of the Western Cape, a small number of whom made their way to Natal. Being 'Malay' distinguished them from the larger population termed Coloured, as well as from Indian Muslims who arrived in the nineteenth century.[88] In October 1914, Sigamony proposed that 'as a matter of privilege Malays be allowed to take part in one Union match'.[89] In October 1923, R.E. Moodley and S.L. Singh moved to have Malays barred from the Union, but their proposal was defeated. In November 1924, Singh proposed that Malays be allowed to participate in 1924 'as a concession', but be excluded from 1925. Delegates voted in favour. This shows the importance of race identity since nine of the 12 delegates were Muslims, but voted against other Muslims on the basis of race.[90] A resolution was adopted that the Union should be composed of Indians only.[91] The Natal Indian Cricket Union (NICU) voted against Malay participation in 1926,[92] while DDICU turned down an invitation to play a visiting Malay XI from Cape Town in January 1927.[93]

Indians flirted briefly with non-racialism in January 1913 when DDICU affiliated to the South African Coloured Cricket Board (SACCB), which had been formed in 1902. SACCB 'did not recognise any distinction amongst the various sporting peoples of South Africa, whether by creed, Nationality or otherwise'.[94] Teams competed for the Barnato Cup which had been donated by Sir David Harris, president of De Beers Consolidated Mines. DDICU sent a team to the 1913 tournament in Kimberley, which represented 'Natal'. A Finance Committee was formed under the chairmanship of Parsee Rustomjee, who urged local traders to contribute financially because the team represented 'the community' and it was the duty of merchants to 'assist it to do justice to the reputation of Natal Indians'.[95] Blazers were made compulsory for players, who had to pay for them or forfeit their place in the team. Lalla, Huck and Bughwan withdrew for financial reasons.[96] The blazer had a green body with gold braid, the national colours of white South African cricket.[97]

The tournament was dominated by Western Province, with Natal losing all its matches. The experience, according to a reporter, was 'an eye opener to almost all the Natal men who, because of an occasional score put together by them, have plumed themselves as cricketers of knowledge and experience'.[98] *Tsala Ea Batho*, a Kimberley newspaper, reported that the tournament,

> brought from Natal the finest type of British Indians, natives of Natal who ever graced any company with their presence. Sociable, refined, gentlemanly, scholarly, they seemed to combine these qualities in a manner which captivated all who came in contact with them, and could scarcely have had a more enthusiastic reception than was accorded these modest sons of tea and sugar planters.[99]

Players and officials were particularly touched by the kind gestures of the Indians of Kimberley. The Union's secretary, Mahabeer, remarked in his report that 'any reference to this tournament would be incomplete were no allusion made to the hearty hospitality of the good people of Kimberley to your men during their stay there'.[100] Bonds with Indians from other parts of South Africa were often enduring. In February 1914, a banquet was held in honour of Amod Mohammed of Kimberley when he visited Durban.[101] The Union affiliated to SACCB in 1914, with Sigamony and Christopher elected as its delegates. However, the SACCB meeting scheduled for November 1915 was cancelled because of the First World War.[102] Thus ended the brief flirtation of Durban's Indians with non-racial cricket.

While Indians did not forge a broader alliance with other Blacks in South Africa, many saw themselves as part of the British imperial order. Soodyall, who served in the First World War and managed a team of South African Indian sportsmen to India in 1922, attempted to get South African Indians to participate in the Quadrangular tournament. Soodyall explained why:

> Our mission to India is twofold; first to see more of our beloved Motherland and learn more of Englishmen, who are a very interesting race of people, and despite the fact that they rule India, we South Africans found them to be very impartial in their kindness and courtesy towards strangers. They showed us marked kindness and I personally feel that there are some very loyal and patriotic

Englishmen in India who really feel for India, and who are ready to shoulder the burdens of India and ready to assist Indians in every possible manner. Some Englishmen in India are the real gems of the English race. Anti-Indians of the 'Sahib' class are a very negligible quantity.

The second object is to create a really good relationship between Indians and the Englishmen on the pitch, learn more of the real game of cricket, how to field, keep wicket, bowl and learn the arts and rudiments of the game, as experts do before they become famous batsmen. We want to also be masters of this famous game. Englishmen have become famous throughout the world on account of their fine sporting qualities. We want Indian Hobbs and Meads, and we are going to have them.[103]

Britishness extended to language. For example, delegates refused permission to H. Dada to speak in Hindi at a Union meeting, which led to bitter discord. The chairman compromised by allowing Dada to speak in Hindi for that meeting only. Dada expressed 'regret that notwithstanding the members all understood the Hindi language yet they objected to him being heard in that language'. An angry Dada stormed out of the meeting without the sanction of the chairman and was prohibited from participating in future meetings.[104] Although Indians were denied equal rights, the Union sent a letter of congratulation to white Natal cricketer Herbie Taylor for scoring 250 against Transvaal in December 1913.[105] In July 1914, a letter was sent to the white Natal Cricket Association informing it of 'the appreciative sense of your Union relative to the great and only victory by Natal over England and for the magnificent batting and bowling by H.W. Taylor, A.D. Nourse and C.P. Carter'. This gesture was particularly striking given that Indians had been involved in a lengthy passive resistance campaign against the state from October to December 1913, and that Emamally and Christopher were active participants in that struggle. On 10 October 1914, the Union cancelled fixtures to allow members to participate in a sports meeting called by the Mayor to raise funds for the War.[106]

FOSTERING 'INDIANNESS'

'Indianness' was fostered in a number of ways. This included playing against Indians from other parts of Natal and South Africa as well as visiting India. For example, when Ottomans of Johannesburg toured Durban in February 1914, in addition to a formal banquet by the Union, officials also entertained the team individually.[107] Local Indian cricketers kept a keen eye on developments in the Indian world. In September 1915, the Union sent a telegram to Prince Ranjitsingh: 'Durban Indian cricketers sympathize with you in your sad accident. Hope well again in the best possible time.'[108]

The highlight for many Indians was a tour to India in 1922. Mahatma Gandhi, who departed from South Africa in 1914, sent a message that students at Indian colleges were keen to meet South Africans to find out more about the country.[109] The visit was delayed by the First World War but came to fruition in 1922 when a team visited Calcutta, Allahabad, Cawnpore, Aligarh, Delhi, Ajmere, Madras, Poona, Bungalow and Agra.[110] They took a letter from the Mayor of Durban, Fleming Johnston, testifying that they were 'respected not only by their fellow-Indians in the field of sport, but also by the European community'.[111] According to the manager, Soodyall, many of the best sportsmen could not tour because workers were unable to get leave for five months.[112] While the team lost most of its games, Albert Christopher was proud that they had 'shown to the Motherland that her sons away from home are doing everything to uphold its honour and ancient traditions'.[113] Indians continued to identify with India, as use of 'Motherland' by Christopher suggests. Essop Manjoo echoed similar sentiments when he wrote about a match between England and India in 1944:

> Many spoke for India, and said a lot about *our* cricketers, but I know why they lost. Look at *our* team. Names on the paper, *we* are very strong on paper but when *we* go to field, there is something wrong with *us*. [Author's emphasis] ... After my visit to the Motherland, I am coming home with tears in my eyes. I am leaving behind friends and relatives and my family here don't want me to leave. Anyhow, I am leaving them behind and God knows when I will see them again. (Manjoo Collection, see n57)

Durban's Indians played cricket informally with Indians in other parts of Natal, and attempted to establish a Natal union. In August 1913,

DDICU sent a letter to C. Nulliah and G. Narrandes of Pietermaritzburg proposing this but did not receive a reply.[114] In October 1914, Sigamony and Sullaphen of Durban arranged to meet B.M. Ally of Pietermaritzburg. However, the meeting did not materialize because Ally insisted that they meet in Pietermaritzburg, while Sigamony wanted the first meeting to take place in Durban, which he considered Natal's 'Sporting Centre'.[115] In December 1917 and September 1918, DDICU again wrote to Pietermartizburg but did not receive a reply.[116] A meeting eventually took place during a match between Pietermaritzburg and Durban at the Albert Park Oval on 5 April 1920, where Durban won 'by an innings and odd'. While the meeting failed to form a union, Shanker, DDICU's secretary, felt that 'matches of this nature should be encouraged as much as possible, as it will improve the standard of play and create friendly relationships between all concerned'.[117]

Delegates from Durban and Pietermaritzburg eventually formed Natal Union at the home of Parsee Rustomjee in 1923, with Albert Christopher elected president.[118] Annual matches between Durban and Pietermaritzburg forged unity. For example, when Durban played Pietermaritzburg in January 1926, a subscription list was opened amongst officials and clubs in Durban. Meals and socials that accompanied the matches forged close relationships.[119] In January 1926, Durban advised NICU that it could not play on Sundays because of its Christian players.[120] From 1925, champion teams from Durban and Pietermaritzburg competed for the Panday Shield.[121] There were regular games between Indians from Durban, Stanger, Dundee, Ladysmith, Newcastle and other parts of Natal.

CONCLUSIONS

This study has sought to unravel 'Indianness' and draw attention to the complexity of Indian identities in Durban. The thrust of the paper is that 'Indianness' did not identify who the Indians really were. Sometimes, Indians were Hindus, Muslims or Christians, sometimes they were Surtee or Calcuttia or Miabhai Muslims, sometimes they were workers or traders or educated elites, sometimes they were Tamils or Telegus or Gujaratis, sometimes they were Indians in relation to Whites, Africans, Coloureds and Malays, and so on. Indian cricket teams reflected particular identities. Greyville from central Durban and Sydenham to the west of the city reflected local neighbourhood identities; School was made up of the Christian educated elite who occupied a particular niche in the evolving class structure among Indians. Railways was made up of descendants of indentured Indians who had worked for the Natal Government Railways. Pirates of India and Ottomans reflected transnational identities and solidarity with India or the wider Muslim world. DDICU fostered a local identity by confining membership to players living within the official boundaries of Durban. M.H. Christian, for example, was de-registered in January 1918 because he had moved residence a few miles outside Durban.[122]

Cricket created and cemented race identity at local and national levels. During the 1913 tournament in Kimberley, for example, some Coloured players did not participate because they opposed the inclusion of educated Africans.[123] Coloured cricketers broke away from SACCB in 1926 and formed the South African Independent Coloured Cricket Board, which prohibited the participation of Indians, Africans and Malays. In 1932, SACCB was dealt another blow when Africans formed the South African Bantu Cricket Board. Thereafter SACCB only represented Malays. Indians formed the South African Indian Cricket Union in 1940 to organize matches between Indian provincial teams throughout South Africa. Cricket was thus divided racially and remained so until 1961 when Africans, Coloureds, Malays and Indians joined in a new body.

Sport was not a medium of cross-racial contact. It could not be in circumstances where the colonial census tagged Africans, Coloureds, Indians and Whites as 'races' and defined racial political identities through the force of law. In such circumstances, as Mahmood Mamdani, a specialist on East Africa, points out, identities become frozen; there are very clear differences 'between those who are said to belong and those who are said not to belong, between insiders entitled to rights and outsiders deprived of these rights'.[124] The attempts of Indian traders to protect class interests were rebuffed in a setting where the law treated them, divided them and categorized them on the basis of race. The construction of parallel forms meant that sport did not transcend the sectional divisions of Durban's social order. On the other hand, Indians were in contact with other Indians in Durban, Natal, South Africa and India. This is not to suggest that Indians constituted a homogeneous entity. There was conflict and tension among Indians, but they were 'Indians' in relation to other South Africans.

INTERVIEWS

There are very few informants surviving from the period studied, or even people who have a vivid recollection of these distant events:

Mr Goolam Butler, 25 January 2001. Mr Butler was born on 5 July 1912. His father was a founder member of Ottomans.

Mr Yusuf Emamally, 13 June 2001. Born 8 November 1917. His father was a founder member of Greyville and an official of DDICU.

Miss Sylvia Lawrence, daughter of V. Lawrence, 30 March 1989.

NOTES

1. Even though the author's position is that there are no biologically differentiated race groups to which we can attribute specific features, question marks have not been used for terms like 'race', 'African', 'Black', 'White', 'Coloured' and 'Indian'. While some of these terms may not have a foundation in social science they are used here because they have been widely internalized by most South Africans, are used freely in political discourse and debates, and continue to be accepted in official post-apartheid record keeping such as the census, applications for funding and jobs, and labour regulations.

2. See P.S. Aiyar, *The Indian Problem in South Africa* (Durban: African Chronicle Printing Works, 1925); G.H. Calpin, *Indians in South Africa* (Pietermaritzburg: Shuter and Shuter, 1949); P.S. Joshi, *The Tyranny of Colour. A Study of the Indian Problem in South Africa* (New York: Kennikat Press, 1973, original 1949); H.S.L. Polak, *The Indians of South Africa. Helots within the Empire and How They are Treated* (Durban: G.A. Natesan & Co., 1909).

3. M. Swan, *Gandhi. The South African Experience* (Johannesburg: Ravan Press, 1985). Mahatma Gandhi arrived in South Africa in 1893 to represent an Indian trader in a legal case against another Indian trader. Shortly after his arrival, the Natal and Transvaal governments, provinces within South Africa, passed restrictive laws against Indians. Gandhi was persuaded by Indians to lead their struggle against these laws. He remained in South Africa until 1914. Prior to Swan, most of the work was hagiographic and presented Gandhi as the champion of Indians of all classes. Swan, however, argues convincingly that Gandhi primarily protected the interests of Indian trading classes.

4. V. Padayachee and S. Vawda, 'Indian Workers and Worker Action in Durban, 1935–1945', *South African Historical Journal*, 40 (May 1999), 154–78.

5. Since there is constant reference to race, ethnicity, class and community, these will be defined for the purposes of this study. Differences of religion, language and customs are so great amongst Indians that it is more accurate to look at them as a racial group comprised of a number of ethnic groups. While race was an identity imposed on Indians by others, ethnicity was self-imposed and became relevant in relations amongst Indians. In this study, race and ethnicity are used interchangeably though clear differences exist. As far as class is concerned, as Cohen has noted, 'a person's class is established by nothing but his objective place in the network of ownership relations, however difficult it may be to identify such places neatly'. Community refers to both a sense of shared identity as well as a group with a fixed local territory.

6. The task of reconstructing the story of Indian cricket in Durban is arduous given the paucity of written records. This study is based on newspaper accounts, the few records that have survived and oral testimony. The richest source was *The Latest*, a little known sporting newspaper that existed from 1910 to 1927. Although its focus was primarily on white sports, *Latest* included a fortnightly article on 'Indian Happenings' from 1914. The minutes of meetings of the Durban and District Indian Cricket Union, 1911–26 was a rare and invaluable record that assisted greatly in this study.

7. C.G. Henning, *The Indentured Indian in Natal* (New Delhi: Promilla & Co., 1993), p.81.
8. M.W. Swanson, 'The Asiatic Menace: Creating Segregation in Durban, 1870–1900', *International Journal of African Historical Studies*, 16, 3 (1983), 421.
9. Swan, *Gandhi*, p.51.
10. Calpin, *Indians in South Africa*, p.36.
11. M. Katzen, *Industry in Greater Durban* (Durban: University of Natal Press, 1961), p.1.
12. B.S. Young, 'The Industrial Geography of the Durban Region' (unpublished Ph.D. thesis, University of Natal, 1972), p.72.
13. Katzen, *Industry in Greater Durban*, pp.33–85.
14. Standard Bank Archives (SBA), INSP 1/1/209, Durban 1905–29, July 1913.
15. B. Guest and J. Sellers, 'Introduction', *Receded Tides of Empire: Aspects of the Economic and Social History of Natal and Zululand since 1910* (Pietermaritzburg: University of Natal Press, 1994), p.2.
16. SBA, INSP 1/1/209, Durban 1905–29, 17 June 1916.
17. SBA, INSP 1/1/209, Durban 1905–29, 21 July 1915.
18. *Mayor's Minute*, 1933: p.62.
19. NAR, 3/DBN, 4/1/3/2052, City Health Dept. to Town Clerk, 9 Sept. 1949. The Old Borough refers to Durban before its boundaries were extended in 1932.
20. B. Freund, *Insiders and Outsiders. The Indian Working Class of Durban 1910–1990* (Pietermaritzburg: University of Natal Press, 1995).
21. *Indian Opinion*, 3 Dec. 1926.
22. *Indian Opinion*, 6 Aug. 1935.
23. Swanson, 'The Asiatic Menace: Creating Segregation in Durban, 1870–1900', 401–21.
24. Swan, *Gandhi*, p.4.
25. J. Brain, *Christian Indians in Natal* (Cape Town: Oxford University Press, 1983), pp.198–9.
26. J.B. Brain, 'Religion, Missionaries and Indentured Indians', in S. Bhana (ed.), *Essays on Indentured Indians in Natal* (Leeds: Peepal Tree Press, 1991), pp.219–23.
27. Synod Reports, Diocese of Natal, May 1901.
28. Brain, 'Religion, Missionaries and Indentured Indians', pp.219–23.
29. Interview with Sylvia Lawrence, daughter of V. Lawrence, 30 March 1989. Whites used 'coolie' to refer to Indians in a disparaging way. As Valentine Daniel has shown, 'coolie' is a mixture of Gujarati and Tamil terms that has to do with denial of personhood and suggestions of someone devoid of morals. V. Daniel and J. Breman, 'The Making of a Coolie', in H. Bernstein, E. Valentine Daniel and T. Brass (eds), *Plantations, Proletarians and Peasants in Colonial Asia* (London: Frank Cass, 1992), pp.268–95.
30. *Indian Opinion*, 5 Oct. 1912.
31. *Indian Opinion*, 2 Sept. 1914.
32. *Indian Opinion*, 18 Feb. 1927.
33. For a general discussion of the spread of sport during the imperial era see J.A. Mangan, *The Game Ethic and Imperialism: Aspects of the Diffusion of an Ideal* (London: Frank Cass, 1985).
34. M. Bose, *A History of Indian Cricket* (London: Andre Deutsch, 1990), pp. 32–3.
35. *Shaan*, March/April 1998.
36. *Colonial Indian News* (*CIN*), 1 Nov. 1901.
37. D. Bramdaw, *South Africa Indian WHO'S WHO and Commercial Directory 1936–37* (Pietermaritzburg: Natal Witness Ltd., 1935), p.153.
38. Annual General Meeting of DDICU (*AGM*), Oct. 1911.
39. *AGM*, 1915–16, 12 Sept. 1915.
40. *Latest*, 13 Nov. 1926.
41. Com. Meeting, 28 Oct. 1911.
42. Com. Meeting, 23 Dec. 1912.
43. Com. Meeting, 29 April 1913.
44. Com. Meeting, 29 Oct. 1925.
45. Com. Meeting, 23 Dec. 1912.
46. Com. Meeting, 28 Feb. 1923.
47. Com. Meeting, 26 March 1923.
48. Com. Meeting, 23 Feb. 1926.

49. *AGM*, 1914–15, 8 July 1914.
50. *African Chronicle*, 16 Oct. 1916.
51. *African Chronicle*, 2 Sept. 1914.
52. Com. Meeting, 17 Nov. 1915.
53. *Annual Report of DDICU (Annual Report)* 8 Dec. 1917.
54. Com. Meeting, 11 Dec. 1918.
55. *Indian Opinion*, 11 June 1910.
56. Com. Meeting, 20 Nov. 1912.
57. These letters form part of a collection of Kismet correspondence meticulously preserved by its former player and administrator, M.E. Jadwat. His son Baboo Jadwat allowed me to examine the material in Sept. 2001.
58. *Indian Opinion*, 11 May 1912.
59. Ibid.
60. *Indian Opinion*, 3 March 1915.
61. NAR (Natal Archives Repository), 3/DBN, 4/1/2/164, Letter from Town Clerk to A. Christopher, 2 Dec. 1921.
62. NAR, 3/DBN, 4/1/2/164, Royeppen to Town Clerk, 14 Dec. 1921.
63. NAR, 3/DBN, 4/1/2/1165, Extract from the Minutes of DTC Meeting, 6 March 1924.
64. Brochure commemorating installation of floodlights at Curries Fountain, Nov. 1964.
65. *AGM*, 8 Aug. 1914.
66. Com. Meeting, 6 Dec. 1922.
67. *Indian Opinion*, 27 March 1925.
68. Bramdaw, *South Africa Indian WHO'S WHO*, p.23.
69. *Indian Opinion*, 28 June 1927.
70. Bramdaw, *South Africa Indian WHO'S WHO*, p.76.
71. G.H.M. Vahed, 'The Making of Indian Identity in Durban, 1914–1949' (unpublished Ph.D. thesis, Indiana University, Bloomington, 1995), p.31.
72. The origins of this term are probably to be found in the fact that many of their first names included the suffix Mia such as Goolam Mia. *Bhai* means brother.
73. *African Chronicle*, 14 Oct. 1911.
74. *Latest*, 17 Dec. 1914.
75. K. Hiralal, 'The Natal Indian Trader – A Struggle for Survival' (unpublished MA thesis, University of Durban-Westville, 1991), pp.262–88.
76. *Natal Mercury*, 16 Sept. 1913.
77. *Natal Mercury*, 27 Sept. 1913.
78. Annual Report, 1925–26, 17 Aug. 1926.
79. *Latest*, 17 March 1917.
80. From Kismet correspondence; see Footnote 57 above.
81. *Latest*, 6 Dec. 1918.
82. Com. Meeting, 28 Oct. 1922.
83. S. Bhana, 'Indianness Reconfigured, 1944–1960: The Natal Indian Congress in South Africa', *Comparative Studies of South Asia, Africa and the Middle East*, 27, 2 (1997), 100–7
84. Com. Meeting, 23 Dec. 1912.
85. Com. Meeting, 8 Oct. 1914.
86. Com. Meeting, 5 Nov. 1919.
87. *Latest*, 22 July 1922.
88. S. Jeppie, 'Re-classifications: Coloured, Malay, Muslim', in Z. Erasmus, *Coloured by History, Shaped by Place. New Perspectives on Coloured Identities in Cape Town* (Cape Town: Kwela Books and SA History Online, 2001).
89. *Latest*, 29 Oct. 1914.
90. The 12 members were S. Emamally, S.L. Singh, M. Thajmoon, A. Haffejee, C.N.M. Khan, C. Rajpaul Singh, M. Johns, E.H.I. Motala, R.P. Butler, M.S. Badat, R.J. Moodley, A.I. Bux, and S.V. Rajah.
91. Com. Meeting, 11 Dec. 1924.
92. Annual Report, 1925–26, 17 Aug. 1926.
93. *Latest*, 8 Jan. 1927.

94. Com. Meeting, 24 Jan. 1923.
95. *Latest*, 8 March 1913.
96. Com. Meeting, 10 March 1913.
97. Annual Report, 1912–13, Aug. 1913.
98. *Latest*, 5 April 1913.
99. *Tsala Ea Batho*, 12 April 1913.
100. Annual Report, 1912–13, 9 Aug. 1913.
101. Annual Report, 1913–14, 8 July 1914.
102. Com. Meeting, 17 Nov. 1915.
103. *Latest*, 13 Dec. 1924.
104. Com. Meeting, 27 March. 1918.
105. *Latest*, 19 Dec. 1913.
106. Com. Meeting, 8 Oct. 1914.
107. Annual Report, 8 July 1914.
108. Com. Meeting, 9 Sept. 1915.
109. *Ind. Opinion*, 3 March 1915.
110. The contingent, known as 'Christopher's Contingent' after its manager, Advocate Albert Christopher, included Schraj Raj (teacher at Depot Road school); E. Sewsunkar Sham (headmaster at Umhloti School); A. Ramithlal (President of the Hindu Young Men's Society); J.M. Soodyall (Higher Grade School who served as a stretcher bearer during the First World War, being awarded a British War Star and Silver Badge); P. Moosa (St Aidan's School); A.H. Seedat (Higher Grade Indian School); R. Ramith (Government Aided School); A. Gafoor (Durban Government Elementary School); Ajmath A. Gany (Durban Government Elementary School); G. Doorsamy (Higher Grade Indian School); P.B. Singh (Higher Grade Indian School).
111. K. Reddy, *The Other Side: A Miscellany of Cricket in Natal* (Durban: KwaZulu-Natal Cricket Union, 1999).
112. *Statesman*, 15 Jan. 1922.
113. *Latest*, 15 April 1922.
114. Com. Meeting, 17 Aug. 1913.
115. Com. Meeting, 8 Oct. 1914.
116. AGM, 1 Oct. 1919.
117. Annual Report, 16 Oct. 1920.
118. Com. Meeting, 18 Dec. 1925.
119. Annual Report, 1925–26, 17 Aug. 1926.
120. Com. Meeting, 18 Jan. 1926.
121. Annual Report 1925–26, 17 Aug. 1926.
122. Com. Meeting, 30 Jan. 1918.
123. *Latest*, 3 May 1913.
124. M. Mamdani, 'Making Sense of Non-Revolutionary Violence: Some Lessons from the Rwandan Genocide', Frantz Fanon Lecture, University of Durban-Westville, 8 Aug. 2001, p. 47.

Cricket in India: Representative Playing Field to Restrictive Preserve

BORIA MAJUMDAR

As many as five players among the current cricketers playing for India at national level come from relatively modest backgrounds. Shiv Sundar Das, Harbhajan Singh, Zaheer Khan, Virender Sehwag and Sarandeep Singh are men from middle-class and relatively underprivileged backgrounds who have emerged as national icons in the years between 1998 and 2001.[1] The presence of five players from modest backgrounds in a team of 14 is significant, because Indian cricket, at national level, continues to be dominated by the economically privileged, affluent sections of society.[2] It may be noted that the economically privileged stratum has been for decades, and remains, upper-caste, a fact gleaned from analyzing the composition of India's national sides in the years since independence. The close connection between caste and class here is not special, for traditionally in India, caste and class status have in most cases tended to overlap. In cricket, this overlap has been noticeable since the inception of the game in the country from the middle of the nineteenth century.[3]

Contrary to arguments in existing historiography, wherein the game is believed to have been democratized in the decades after independence,[4] the history of cricket in post-independence India demonstrates that prior to the nation's triumph in the Prudential Cup of 1983,[5] the game was dominated by an affluent, educated, upper-caste elite. The victory in 1983 opened up among the middle-class and underprivileged sections of Indian society the possibility of cricket being a viable career option, allowing men like Vinod Kambli, Dodda Ganesh and David Johnson to come to the fore and don the national colours.[6] Close investigation, however, reveals that these men remain exceptions to the rule, with the game still dominated by men from the affluent, upper-caste echelons of society. Nevertheless, existing historiography has hailed post-1947 Indian cricket as being more democratic and representative when compared to the structures operative in colonial India. Contrary to assertions that the game was restricted to an English-speaking Indian aristocracy and the educated, affluent, middle classes in colonial India, cricket in colonial India was representative of Indian society as a whole. With players from underprivileged backgrounds emerging as leading stars at various points between 1890–1947, the game was not an elite monopoly.

A look at the history of cricket in the decades before independence shows that players from diverse economic and cultural backgrounds had made their way to the highest rungs of fame, for example, Palwankar Baloo, Palwankar Vithal, H.L. Semper, Lala Amarnath, Amir Elahi and D.D. Hindlekar, to name but a few.[7] Though the captains of the touring Indian teams, the Maharaja of Patiala in 1911, the Maharaja of Porbander in 1932, Maharajkumar of Vizianagram in 1936 and Iftikar Ali Khan Pataudi in 1946, were men from aristocratic families, the leading players in the teams, Palwankar Baloo in 1911, Mohammed Nissar and Amar Singh in 1932, Lala Amarnath in 1936, were men of humble origins, from lower-caste, economically underprivileged backgrounds. Their careers reveal that by the early years of the twentieth century, prowess in cricket had come to symbolize a ladder for social mobility among the relatively underprivileged. With mastery of the game holding out before them prospects of association with, and the opportunity of drawing benefits from, the ruling elite, cricket had already emerged as an attractive proposition for the lower–middle-class Indian.

Since the coming of *bhadralok*[8] and princely patronage in Indian cricket in the 1880s, the game had been considerably democratized. These patrons, aiming to form quality cricket teams, ones that could meet and defeat English sides, ignored caste, creed, colour and economic prejudices when recruiting players of merit. Men like the Maharaja of Natore, for example, harboured ambitions of defeating the English at their own game, viewing the game as a means for the assertion of indigenous strength.

The key to the democratic nature of the sport is also to be sought in the peer rivalries that dominated princely life in early twentieth-century India. It was to outdo his sworn rival, the Maharaja of Cooch Behar, that Jagadindranarayan Ray, the Maharaja of Natore, patronized talented cricketers from all parts of the country, disregarding their social status.[9] Similarly, the rivalry between the Maharaja of Patiala and the

Maharajkumar of Vizianagram, which manifested itself in the form of an ugly tussle for captaincy during the twin tours of Britain in 1932 and 1936,[10] led these aristocrats to patronize men from all walks of life.[11] Aristocratic patronage, rooted in political and commercial considerations, therefore, played a significant role in democratizing cricket in colonial India.

Alongside Indians, British patrons also contributed to making cricket democratic in early twentieth-century India. Looking upon cricket as an imperial tool, key to the colonial strategy of civilizing the natives, these men did much to promote the game in the educational institutions and Gymkhanas of the country.[12] In their official capacities, they encouraged cricket among the various Indian communities, providing land, initiating competitions and according patronage to talented men, irrespective of their backgrounds. This representative nature of the game between 1880–1947 underwent a gradual change with India's independence in 1947.

Key to this change was the altered nature of patronage. Corporate patronage, firmly entrenched in post-independence India, transformed the game into a preserve of the educated elite and the relatively affluent.[13] The companies which employed cricketers had clearly defined policies of recruitment. They were interested in employing educated cricketers, men who would not be liabilities to the concern after retirement. This policy made it impossible for relatively underprivileged Indians to play the game, often lacking opportunities for higher education. The cricket clubs and educational institutions, which emerged as centres of cricketing excellence in post-independence India, were also in most cases beyond the reach of the underprivileged. Charging high fees, these clubs, even if unconsciously, allowed economically-privileged groups to perpetuate their monopoly over the game. This monopoly was reinforced by the costly nature of the game, which prevented it from being adopted by relatively modest educational institutions. Lacking the finances necessary to purchase cricket gear and establish necessary infrastructure, these institutions gradually shifted towards promoting less costly games like football or hockey. With students from modest means attending such institutions, the assumption that cricket was the game of the elite, while football and hockey were to be played by the common man, gathered strength.

This study begins by tracing the nature of indigenous cricket from the close of the nineteenth century. As has already been stated, existing studies have focused on the aristocratic nature of the sport in colonial

India, ignoring the representative element, moulded by the assumption that democratization of the game was a post-colonial phenomenon.[14] This assumption, ignoring other, no-less-tangible historical realities, leads to the argument that post-independence Indian cricket was far more representative and democratic in character. It is my purpose to correct this weakness in existing studies by going beyond the assumptions and prejudices that have moulded it. The second section of the study demonstrates that post-independence Indian cricket was hardly democratic as has been stated in the conventional literature on the subject. Far from having been 'plebeianized' in post-colonial India, cricket continued to be monopolized by the affluent elite. Systems of corporate patronage and the policies of the Board of Control worked towards the perpetuation of this monopoly. A social history of cricket in India, it will be evident from this study, is hardly conceivable without taking into account the role of the Board of Control for Cricket in India. The Board, arbiters of the fortunes of the game since 1928, has done much to shape the character of the sport, especially after independence.[15]

In post-independence India, the nature of cricket had undergone a radical transformation. As Richard Cashman argues, there was a distinct change in the nature of the game's patronage after 1947. After independence, erstwhile princely patrons, men who had fallen from their positions of social and economic preeminence, 'were forced to prune their cricketing ventures, to dismantle their teams and to terminate cricketing appointments'.[16] Though some princes continued to accord patronage to cricketers, this was on a considerably reduced scale. The void left by the princes was filled by commercial establishments, corporate concerns which 'took over the role of patronage established by the princes'.[17] This shift, Cashman contends, 'has had a profound effect on Indian cricket both on and off the field. Above all it has provided a stability and continuity in which there could be cricket expansion.' Finally, Cashman declares that although corporate patronage helped to create a more educated cricketer, patronage was not lacking for gifted players from deprived backgrounds, or for those with limited education.[18]

Following Cashman, Sandeep Bamzai, in his recently published monograph on Bombay cricket, states that around the 1940s, an 'important paradigm shift was taking place in Bombay's cricket. From a predominantly south Bombay sport which had been controlled by the upper class Parsees and Gujratis, cricket was now moving towards the lower-middle-class Maharastrian stronghold of Dadar.'[19] He perceives the rise of lower-middle-class cricketers like Vijay Manjrekar and Subhas Gupte in Bombay as being indicative of this shift.[20] However, as Bamzai acknowledges, Manjrekar had to play as a professional for Bengal to make a living and was later on the payroll of the Maharana of Mewar.[21] Gupte too, failing to secure a sufficiently good job with an Indian concern, was forced to settle in the West Indies, working for a sugar concern in Trinidad.[22] This was natural because in post-partition India, non-cricketing, chiefly academic qualifications played an important role in determining a cricketer's remuneration, his level of appointment and future promotions. The policies adopted by commercial patrons made it mandatory for players to have completed a college degree. In its absence, the chance of securing employment was considerably reduced. Even if a player did find employment it would be at a far lower grade when compared to his educated counterpart, a significant transformation from earlier practice. Increased importance accorded to non-cricketing quali-fications, therefore, contributed to making cricket a preserve of the relatively affluent in post-independence India.

THE REPRESENTATIVE PHASE (1880–1940)

Bengal

This period witnessed a broadening of the games base, one that allowed players from underprivileged backgrounds to emerge as national figures. At the root of this change lay the alteration in the political equation of the province, when, in the post-Mutiny period, the educated Bengali middle-class found it imperative to devise effective strategies to counter colonial charges of effeminacy.[23] From the 1880s, this had, as Mrinalini Sinha demonstrates, come to acquire a more specific connotation when compared to the early nineteenth century. If in the past effeminacy loosely described all inhabitants of Bengal, in the second half of the century it was used specifically to refer to and degrade the Indian middle-class or a section of this class identified as *babus*.[24] As the Hobson Jobson, a glossary of British words and phrases in India compiled in the 1880s, suggests, in the popular colonial imagination the word *babu* was used with a hint of disparagement, characterizing a superficially culti-vated but often effeminate Bengali.[25]

The charge of effeminacy eventually led the middle-classes to shun an earlier aversion to physical culture, emerging as conscious patrons of activities rooted in physical prowess.[26] A realization that prowess in English games like cricket and football would allow them to challenge British superiority on the sporting field led the Bengalis to shun discriminatory practices in an effort to pick the best talent and promote these sports among the masses of the province. This development may be traced back to 1881–82. A figure such as Nagendraprasad Sarbadhikary epitomized this dual critique of caste and class. Nagendraprasad, who belonged to an orthodox Hindu family, ignored all caste prejudices while establishing a series of sporting clubs. His critique of such practices is clearest in the incident surrounding the induction of a potter's son into the Wellington Club.[27] The latter had a membership of nearly 500 from all classes of society. However, when Nagendraprasad wanted to induct Mani Das, the potter's son, the richer members of the club protested vehemently. Nagendraprasad refused to buckle underpressure, asserting that a sporting club was beyond any prejudice, eventually deciding to dismantle the Wellington Club.[28] Declaring that caste-based discrimination was similar to racial discrimination, Nagendraprasad was determined to make full use of Mani Das's potential. This attempt by Nagendraprasad to free sports of caste prejudices in the 1880s was the first of its kind in India.

Motivated by such efforts and determined to outdo his sworn rival, the Maharaja of Cooch Behar, the Maharaja of Natore, Jagadindranarayan Ray, invited Palwankar Baloo, a *chammar*[29] cricketer from Dharwad, to Bengal as coach of his team in the early twentieth century.[30] The Maharaja also recruited the other Palwankar brothers, Shivram, Ganpat and Vithal, forming one of the strongest cricket combinations of the country. At the turn of the century, the Natore team also included leading Muslim players, Razzak, Salamuddin and Zainulabad.[31] Mani Das, too, was part of the Natore side between 1901–14.[32] Among all the players to whom Jagadindranarayan extended patronage, Palwankar Baloo was his prized recruit and on many occasions received special gifts from the Maharaja. Vithal, Baloo's elder brother, also received a gold watch from the Maharaja. In a match at Natore Park, Vithal had taken a spectacular catch at the boundary. Although he fell over a chair, he managed to hold on to the ball. Congratulating him for this spectacular effort, the Maharaja rewarded him with a gold watch costing 550 rupees.[33]

Bombay

The best-known low caste/class achievers in Indian cricket were the Palwankar brothers, *chamaars* by caste, men who played for the upper-caste Hindu team in the Bombay Quadrangular tournament with distinction.[34] All four Palwankar brothers, Baloo, Vithal, Shivram and Ganpat, were noted cricketers and were recruited as professionals by patrons from all over the country. Even Baloo's son, Y.B. Palwankar, represented Bombay between 1944 and 1955 in the Ranji trophy. 'Antoo' as he was popularly known, was a good all-rounder, a left-hand attacking batsman and right-arm medium-pace bowler.[35]

Alongside the Palwankars was H.L. Semper. Semper, as the legendary Indian cricketer D.B. Deodhar recounts, was a fine all-rounder and had many noted performances to his credit. On one occasion, he scored a half-century in each innings of a match, a performance that won him a special award at the hands of Lord Willingdon, the Governor of Bombay.[36] Semper played for the Hindus between 1910 and 1915.[37] Among the Palwankars, Vithal went on to lead the Hindus for almost a decade, being carried off the ground on the shoulders of the high-caste Hindus after leading them to victory in the Quadrangulars of 1923.[38] However, these successes have failed to serve as models for later *dalit* cricketers and not many have followed in the footsteps of the Palwankars.

Palwankar Baloo, a *chamaar,* was born in Dharwad in 1875. His sporting prowess had induced the Brahmins of the Deccan Gymkhana – determined to beat the British Poona Gymkhana – to induct him into the Hindoo team in the late nineteenth century.[39] In early life, Baloo had worked as a groundskeeper at the European Gymkhana for a salary of three rupees a month. While working there, he had on one occasion bowled to the Europeans at the nets. Surprised by his talent, the Europeans asked Baloo to continue bowling. Subsequently, the Poona Hindus realized his potential and quickly made him a member of the Hindu club at Poona:

> The champion bowler of the Hindus is Mr. Baloo, a *chamaar.*
> Indeed it is not Bombay that rubbed off this caste exclusiveness.
> Years back Baloo was a bowler in the Poona European Gymkhana.
> The Poona Hindus who consisted mostly of upper-caste Hindus
> found that *chammar* though Baloo was his inclusion in the Hindu
> team would improve matters considerably. With the pluck and

spirit, which the Poona Hindus of the 1890s had, they admitted him as their member and so far as pollution from touch with a low caste went, the plucky Brahmins of Poona gave the slip to ortho-doxy.[40]

A few years later, the Bombay Hindu Gymkhana, 'with such an example from orthodox Poona, admitted him after pacifying a few Gujerati [*sic*] members as regards his admission. The Hindu Gymkhana went further and they openly began inter-dining with Baloo. [Soon] Shivram, Baloo's brother, was admitted without the least scruple.'[41] Commenting on Baloo's rise in an India driven by caste prejudices, the *Indian Social Reformer* wrote in 1906: 'The history of the admission of these Chamaar brothers in the Hindu Gymkhana is a credit to all and has done far more to liberalize the minds of thousands of young Hindus than all other attempts in such spheres.'[42] It went on to conclude that it was a:

> landmark in the nation's emancipation from the old disuniting and denationalising customs … Hindu sportsmen in Poona and Bombay have shown … that, where national interest required, equal opportunity must be given to all of any caste, even though the offer of such opportunity involved the trampling of some old prejudices. Let the lesson learnt in sport be repeated in political, social and educational walks of life. Let all disuniting and denationalising customs disappear and let India cease to be the laughing stock of the whole world.[43]

Among the Palwankar brothers, Baloo had won considerable social acclaim and had initially served as a great inspiration for B.R. Ambedkar.[44] However, friendship between the two was short-lived and Baloo, in later life, went on to contest an election against Ambedkar. The *Free Press* journal reported in 1931 that 'a large section which embraces the vast majority of the Depressed Classes Community', under the leadership of 'P. Balu, B J Deorukhakar and Mr. Patel', repudiated Ambedkar's position on separate electorates and special representation and declared their faith in the Congress and Mahatma Gandhi.[45] Following this, in September 1932, he acted as a mediator in the Poona Pact from the Congress side. In 1933–34, Baloo fought a by–election for a seat in the Bombay municipality and lost to a Parsiee doctor, Homi F. Pavri.[46] Three years later, he was the Congress candidate, pitted against Ambedkar in the elections of 1937 to the 'E' and 'F' wards of the

Bombay city. Ambedkar had rejected the Poona Pact and was standing as a Scheduled Caste Federation candidate. Baloo obtained 11,225 votes, Ambedkar 13,245. Baloo's chances were affected by a Congress rebel's contesting the elections as an independent candidate.[47] The closely contested election is proof enough of the social acclaim achieved by Baloo. His confidence of facing Ambedkar in electoral battle is a telling comment on his popularity.

Besides Bengal and Bombay, other regions also witnessed extensions of patronage to relatively underprivileged sections by the 1920s. As Vasant Raiji states:

> Jamnagar was a small state but its ruler hired a foreign coach, A.F. Wensley, and good players from other states. Cricket in Saurashtra, Baroda and the Western Indian States Cricket Association also enjoyed princely patronage. Players were provided with jobs and well looked after. The princes themselves often played the game and were members of the state teams.[48]

Patiala

The Maharajas of Patiala, who had taken to cricket patronage in the late nineteenth century, looked upon cricket to assert equality with their colonial masters. With this end in view, they formed their own cricket grounds at Patiala and Chail.[49] Maharaja Rajendra Singh initiated cricket patronage at Patiala, which has given India a number of its leading cricketers since the 1890s.

As Richard Cashman declares, no ruler had recruited cricketers on the scale begun by the Maharaja of Patiala since 1895.[50] Merit, as is evident from the lists of the players he employed, was the primary consideration, deemed more important than motives of caste, creed, or economic background. Maharaja Bhupinder Singh, son of Rajendra Singh, continued this tradition of patronage after his father's death at the premature age of 28. It was due to his efforts that great Indian cricketers like Lala Amarnath, Anwar Hussain, Lall Singh and Nazir and Wazir Ali were able to do justice to their talent. They were patronized by the Patiala Darbar, which absorbed 'any sportsman who had made a name for himself at cricket, wrestling, athletics or some other sport, into the state service'.[51] While some of these sportsmen were given positions of responsibility, such as Colonel Mistry, most were not and were left free to pursue their careers in sport.[52] In recognition of his patronage to cricket, Maharaja Bhupinder Singh was appointed the first President of the Cricket Club of India in 1937.[53] He was also nominated President of the Indian Olympic Association in 1939 and held this position until 1960, when his younger brother Raja Bhalindra Singh succeeded him.

At Patiala, royal patronage was also extended to athletics, hockey and polo. A number of athletes who have represented India in the Olympics have enjoyed the patronage of this house. Note must also be made of the National Institute of Sports at Patiala, which houses one of the country's best sports museums and is still among the country's foremost sporting centres.

Gujrat

Cricket in Gujrat was concentrated in Rander, a little town in the vicinity of Surat.[54] Cricket was introduced in Rander in the 1880s. However, it was only in the early twentieth century that the sport gained a firm foundation, with locals establishing the Rander Islam Gymkhana. Soon after its establishment, cricket among the Muslims gathered momentum, with the Gymkhana producing cricketers who represented the Muslim team in the Bombay Quadrangular. During the years 1914–19, the Gymkhana was at its best, according patronage to a number of talented Muslim cricketers. With its finances being satisfactory – its annual income was 10,000 rupees with expenditure not exceeding 8,000 rupees – it was able to play a leading role in grooming cricketers from modest backgrounds.[55] Among the cricketers patronized by the Gymkhana was Casam Ahmad Moorad, invited by the Maharaja of Mymensingh in 1916 to play for his team. Pleased with his performance, the Maharaja rewarded him handsomely.[56] M.E. Sheikh was another cricketer from a relatively modest background patronized by the Gymkhana.[57]

CRICKET IN THE EDUCATIONAL INSTITUTIONS

The princely patrons did much to stimulate development of school and college cricket, enabling children from relatively modest backgrounds to play the game. Receiving handsome donations from royal houses, the educational institutions did not charge high fees for setting up necessary infrastructure, allowing students from modest backgrounds to play the game. The Maharaja of Gondal took a keen interest in improving the standard of school cricket, and the institution of the Harris Shield school cricket tournament in Bombay in 1896, patronized by the rich and the affluent, generated considerable excitement.

Alongside Indian patrons, British officers and viceroys also played a significant role in promoting cricket in the educational institutions. Guided by imperial notions of civilizing the natives, they attempted to use cricket as a tool in this project, promoting the sport from the 1870s.[58] In Dhaka, development of native cricket owed much to the patronage of local European administrators and it was from their European teachers that Indian boys got their first lessons in the game.[59] In Bombay, Lord Harris was instrumental in initiating the Presidency matches between the Parsees and the Europeans in 1892.[60] He allotted land to the three Indian communities, the Hindus, Muslims and Parsees in the 1890s, to form their respective Gymkhanas. Further, as W.D. Begg mentions:

> It was during the reign of Lord Irwin that the foundation of the Central Board of Cricket Control in India has been laid under his direct patronage while F.S. Jackson, the Governor of Bengal, had shown keen interest in promoting the game soon after he had arrived in India.[61]

The history of school cricket in Bombay goes back to the 1880s. Until the 1890s however, the structure of the sport in the schools was 'crude and indefinite'. It was under Sir Dorab Tata that the initiative to form the Bombay High School Athletic Association was launched.[62] Wishing to eliminate differences of colour, caste and creed on the sporting field, he tried to unite the various local clubs in the city, promoting notions of fair play among the young boys. At first the success of the scheme seemed doubtful. This was because it was not known whether the European schools would join native schools to form the union. However, with Mr Savage of the Cathedral school joining hands with Sir Dorab Tata, success was assured and the Association came into existence in 1893.[63]

The chief obstacle towards establishing school cricket on a firm footing was the paucity of playgrounds in late nineteenth- and early twentieth-century Bombay. This led to the levy of a games fee in most high schools, but it was specified that students from modest backgrounds would not have to pay this levy.[64] With aristocratic and upper-class patronage coming their way, many schools revoked this levy in course of time.

That these initiatives yielded results is evident from an analysis of the list of the award winners in school cricket competitions. Representing

New High School, Vithal Palwankar was awarded the gold medal for best performer among school students in 1904. His brother, Ganpat, repeated the feat in 1909. P.N. Polishwalla, one of India's earliest commentators on cricket, in his account on schools and colleges in the country hailed the achievements of both brothers, naming them as stars of their school, an institution that had the distinction of winning the Harris Shield four times in a row between 1896–99.[65]

In colonial Bengal, cricket was not confined to the schools and colleges in the metropolitan centres, but had spread to many parts of the province by the turn of the century. Cricket tournaments for schools were organized as part of annual fairs in East Bengal, contests that, records reveal, generated considerable excitement. In 1890, four school teams from small district towns in East Bengal, Senhati, Comilla, Bagerhat and Khulna, took part in one such contest at Khulna, with Senhati emerging as the eventual winner.[66]

That the Bengali patrons attempted to spread the game among the masses is discernible from the tenor of vernacular writings on the game. Cricket was compared to the indigenous Indian game of *gilli danda*, played by most young boys in both rural and urban Bengal.[67] In Calcutta, Indian patrons in collaboration with their British counterparts made every effort to promote the game among the rank and file. Prizes were instituted in every department of the game offering incentives capable of attracting students from diverse backgrounds to play. In the Vidyasagar College, the value of such prizes amounted to 160 rupees, a considerable sum in contemporary India.[68] Besides Bengal and Bombay, college cricket had achieved considerable progress in parts of North and Central India. The accounts of the Elphinstone College tours undertaken between 1903–13 to different parts of the country are proof that college cricket across the country was of a fairly developed nature.[69]

Among North Indian colleges, the Aligarh College had achieved high standards of cricketing prowess by the early twentieth century. Performances of the Aligarh team at Simla, Patiala and Bombay reflected of this. Aligarh also had one of the finest hockey teams in the country.[70]

THE CORPORATE PHASE (1947–)

However, as mentioned earlier, not many from the economically under-privileged groups and lower castes have followed the footsteps of their illustrious predecessors in post-independence India. The reasons behind this anomaly are rooted in a social analysis of the game, in the changing nature of cricket patronage over time.

Corporate patronage, which emerged as the dominant structure in post-independence India, did little to alleviate the instability of players from economically underprivileged sections of society, players with little formal education beyond their training in the game. This was because the companies preferred to employ cricketers from educated backgrounds, men who would be able to serve them after retirement. It was a conscious policy to encourage recruitment of cricketers with a minimum level of education. As Richard Cashman asserts, 'When G. Sunderram joined BEST in 1956, having already represented his country, he was informed by the General Manager that it was the policy of the agency to employ cricketers but they must meet the minimum requirements for a position'.[71] Even the Tata Company, the firm that has played a pioneering role in sports promotion in the country, preferred to recruit graduates, hoping that they would not be a liability for the company after retirement.[72] Academic qualifications played an important role in the determination of a player's salary and level of appointment and rank at the Tata Company:

> A non-matriculate would be employed usually in the factory as a security officer; a matriculate would generally secure a position as a clerk with rather limited prospects of rising to the officer cadre; graduates could expect to become officers though some have had to work their way up from clerk status.[73]

The mandate adopted by the Tatas was a model for most commercial patrons of post-independence India, a model that made it essential for cricketers to have minimum formal education if they were to be employed by well-known concerns. This ensured that men from affluent and educated backgrounds had a head start over other less-privileged sportsmen, who were also in most cases members of the depressed castes.

Even the parent body, the Board of Control for Cricket in India, was hardly conscious of the problems faced by the cricketers and refused to come to terms with the crisis brewing in Indian cricket. Accounts in contemporary newspapers indicated that the Board was responsible for transforming the game into a preserve of the affluent elite by raising the cost of tickets and the guarantee money due to be paid by a centre hosting an international encounter.[74] The sudden increase in the cost of tickets provoked widespread outrage from ordinary people, who, reports suggest, were unable to see matches given the increased price of tickets. It was reminisced that in the days of the Pentangular, all the small clubs with practice nets on the maidan were given tickets at subsidized rates for members.[75] There was also a grandstand for the public, admission to which was affordable to most. Twelve days of the Pentangular could be enjoyed, with all ancillary facilities of transport, refreshments, etcetera, for a payment of not more than 10 rupees per head.[76] Even for the Gymkhana stands, the price of a season ticket was not more than 10 rupees per person.[77]

Following the increase, the Bombay Cricket Association was expected to pay the Board 30,000 rupees as guarantee money and 40,000 from ticket sales (at the rate of 4 rupees per ticket), forcing them to price tickets at amounts beyond the reach of the ordinary enthusiast. They were also expected to pay Indian players 250 rupees per head as the match fee and bear the expenses of hosting rival teams. This situation led the *Free Press Journal* to comment:

> The stage is definitely reached when it would be advisable to consider whether it is worthwhile to have a foreign side playing in Bombay, which costs the city not less than 100,000 actual expenditure. If only 10 per cent of the total expenditure were to be utilized for providing sporting facilities to students, we would probably get much more results.[78]

This price hike provoked considerable unrest as is evident from a series of letters published in the *Free Press Journal*:

> Enhanced Rates: I read your comment re. the entrance rate for the big cricket matches, I too join in drawing the attention of the authorities. If this rate, as you state, is fixed by the CCI after 'full consideration', I should say that they have lost sight of the economics of 'little purse' as well as defeating the very purpose, namely, making the common people cricket minded. In whose welcome participation lies the success of cricket, football and sports in India? Don't you think that as the rate stands today, only one man will enter grudgingly where three more would have ungrudgingly done, had the rates been brought down?[79]

Disregarding such unrest among the public, the BCCI, in an effort to facilitate the MCC's visit to India in 1951–52, opted to shelve the

Schools Cricket Championship for two years at the first instance. The argument put forward by the BCCI was that the championship was doing no good:

> The schools cricket tournament 'is doing no good', according to Mr. A S De Mello, President of the board, who is sponsoring the move to abandon the championship for two years in the first instance. Lack of interest among schools authorities, it is learnt, caused great difficulties in completing the early rounds, and last year the semi finals were not played.[80]

The Board also wished to shelve the Ranji trophy tournament temporarily.[81] These attempts provoked widespread anxiety among cricket enthusiasts in all parts of the country. Commenting on these proposals the *Times of India* reported:

> Nothing could be more harmful to the interests of cricket in India than the move to replace the Ranji trophy competition with a zonal tournament. Ostensibly this change is intended to meet the exigencies of the forthcoming MCC tour. The glamour of sponsoring tours at home and abroad appears to have overcome the highly susceptible pundits of the Board of Control for Cricket in India … What Indian cricket needs is not glamourisation but consolidation and the Board of Control's lack of interest in the constructive side of the game was represented by the Schools' Championship of India, the Inter University Championship and the Cricket championship is greatly to be deplored.[82]

It concluded by saying that the decision on the national championship would indicate whether the BCCI was committed to a policy of fostering the game in the country or whether it preferred to sponsor tamashas.[83]

The rise in the cost of tickets, contemporary newspaper reports noted, significantly altered the nature of spectatorship, making the cricket stadium the preserve of the affluent. The disappearance of the common man from the grounds caused much disillusionment among noted commentators of the game:

> Candidly, our present crowds give me a pain in the neck. Not one in ten comes to the cricket for the game, and only one in ten knows anything about its finer points. I hear it is the same all over the

country these days, as it is in Bombay, the cricket crowd being composed largely of noisy, oily tamasha mad people, one or two names of stars on their lips, understanding that one team is leading the other in the score books. Fat and greasy nouveau riche men, with fat and greasy spouses and fat and greasy brats turning the stands into a common bazar, a mohalla, anything but a refined cricket arena.[84]

The problems of underprivileged cricketers were further compounded when the Government decided to reduce its annual sports grant to schools in Western India, money intended to promote development of cricket in these institutions. This resulted in a decreased budget for cricket promotion in high schools by over 50 per cent, which forced the authorities to run one team only, instead of dividing the boys into senior and junior sides.[85] Accordingly, schools and colleges that played key roles in cricket promotion from the 1950s were those which could, by themselves, afford the infrastructure required for the game. The costly nature of the game acted as a detriment to its development and prevented cash-strapped educational institutions from promoting it. The privileged, with the opportunity of attending premier educational institutions, ones with the necessary infrastructure, were therefore able to perpetuate a monopoly over the game.

A study of the composition of national teams of the 1960s, 1970s and 1980s demonstrates that the game was an upper class/caste affair. In the 1978 team that played against the West Indies, S.M.H. Kirmani and Bishen Singh Bedi were the only players who were not upper-caste Hindus (see Table 7.1).[86] In the 1982 team that played England at Lords, all the players except Azharuddin were brahmans or other upper-caste Hindus.

CONCLUSION

As mentioned at the start of this essay, existing historiography has looked upon colonial Indian cricket as a sport dominated by the aristocracy and the affluent upper classes. This has led to the articulation of the view that while cricket was the game of the elite, soccer and hockey, the two other most important sports in the subcontinent, were played by Indians from relatively modest backgrounds. However, having noted the representative nature of cricket in colonial India, it may be argued that this hierarchization of sport was a post 1930s phenomenon. Statistics reveal that till the 1930s many of India's noted footballers and hockey players were also noted cricketers, a feature fundamentally transformed in post-independence India. This contention is best supported by the histories of sport in educational institutions of the country. In these, students made no distinction between games and indulged in all forms of physical activity until the end of the 1930s. This explains the simultaneous formation of soccer and cricket clubs in leading Indian colleges from the late nineteenth century.[87] Cricket grounds were also used for playing football and hockey, the same group of students often engaged in playing all three games.

The representative nature of cricket in colonial India indicates that

TABLE 7.1
THE 1978 INDIAN TEAM

Player	Caste/Religion/Social status
S.M. Gavaskar	brahman
C.P.S. Chauhan	upper caste
M. Amarnath	son of Lala Amarnath, one of India's leading players in the 1930s and 1940s. Though Lala was the son of a farmer, he had been able to make his fortunes from the game in colonial India.* Not only had he captained India, but had also served as chief selector for a number of years after independence. Thus when Mohinder came to play for the country the Amarnath's were socially mobile upper-class men.
G.R. Vishwanath	upper caste
D.B. Vengsarkar	brahman
S.M.H. Kirmani	muslim
N.Kapil Dev**	jat
K.D. Ghavri	upper caste
S. Venkatraghvan	upper caste
B.S. Bedi	sikh
B.S. Chandrasekhar	brahman; Chandra however is an exception, having faced considerable financial difficulty after his career had ended. This crisis was partly overcome after the BCCI organized a benefit match for him in the 1990s.

Source: *Himal*, Feb. 2002.

* That Lala Amarnath had achieved financial stability as a cricketer is evident from a peculiar event documented in the *Times of India*, which reported that Amarnath's first wife had filed a legal case demanding compensation from her husband. The petitioner had submitted that she was married to Amarnath in 1935 and alleged that after four years of marriage her husband had maltreated her and turned her out of the house. She added that Amarnath had already married another girl. According to her estimate Amarnath was earning 1,000 rupees per month. The court gave its verdict on 13 March 1939. Accepting that Amarnath was earning substantial money he was ordered to pay compensation of 15 rupees a month to his first wife. This event reveals that Amarnath, a farmer's son, had by 1939 made a considerable fortune from cricket.

** Kapil Dev and Eknath Solkar may be regarded as exceptions. They were men from relatively modest backgrounds who rose to the highest rungs on the game in India. Solkar's achievement is creditable for he was also from a low caste background.

class antagonism was, in many cases, overcome by pressing social, political and economic concerns, this cohesion finding articulation on the sporting field. Indigenous club, school and college cricket promoted cohesion across the lower and middle classes. There were calls for a dilution of caste and class status from the educated members of society, calls that brought about cooperation between the elite and underprivileged segments. Such evidences of cohesion on the sporting field have been ignored in discourses on social reform in India.

The representative nature of the game in colonial India also brings to light instances of cohesion between the middle classes and the princely aristocracy. Clubs dominated by men from the educated middle classes often received patronage from the aristocracy. Ignoring such pointers, existing histories continue to look upon princely aristocracy and the middle classes as social groups at loggerheads with each other so far as the nationalist project was concerned.

Collaboration between the princely aristocracy and the *bhadralok* on the sporting field was, however, a thing of the past in post-independence India. Norms governing corporate patronage may be identified as instrumental in this dissociation. Cricket in post-independence India, governed by institutionalized norms of patronage, made the sport a monopoly of the relatively privileged, as discussed earlier. This transformation may also explain changes in the nature of spectatorship in Indian cricket. Studies of spectatorship in India have tended to ascribe the volatility of audiences in post-independence India to the game's democratization in a post-colonial context. Such explanations often obscure the reality of the situation. Crowd unrest cannot simply be explained by suggesting that violence is a product of the plebeianization of the crowd. In all domestic and international matches in the 1930s and 1940s, the crowd was divided into small compartments separated by ropes. Many of these enclaves were led by the unemployed youth of various localities, elements who were no longer able to afford tickets in post-independence India. The glamour associated with the game from the 1950s and 1960s made entry into the cricket grounds a symbol of social status, a badge of the socially mobile.

Accordingly, the relatively underprivileged spectator's access to the cricket stadiums was increasingly restricted from the 1950s, with their dominions usurped by the moneyed, college-going 'educated', jingoistic youth. Spectator violence, a recurrent phenomenon from the 1950s and 1960s, is the expression of this privileged lot, the educated elite, who had monopolized cricket grounds in post-independence India. The critical question, which now confronts us, is 'why did this educated elite take to hooliganism?' After having spent a substantial sum in procuring tickets, or in securing membership of the cricket association, this crowd demands their money's worth. For them cricket matches are arenas of 'spectacle', sites for the demonstration of national strength. This often leads many of the educated elite to flex their muscles on the cricket field, their only available respite.

NOTES

I would like to thank Dr David Washbrook and my supervisor, without whose help, guidance and inspiration this essay could not have been written. Sharmistha Gooptu found time from her own work to go through earlier drafts of this paper. Anandji Dossa, Vasant Raiji, K.N. Prabhu and Theo Braganza in Mumbai have been most helpful in giving their time.

1. Among them Harbhajan Singh's case is most interesting. Having almost single-handedly won the series for India against Australia in Feb.–March 2001, Harbhajan suddenly became the target for sponsors. Upon being asked what he would do with the huge amounts earned from endorsements, he replied that he would use the money to marry off his sisters. This reply, typical of a son in a traditional Indian household, is a reflection of his economic background.

2. The large amounts spent by the rival factions during the Board's elections testify to this point. In the election for the post of President in 2001, the two candidates, Jagmohan Dalmiya and A.C. Muthiah, were said to have spent more than 10 million rupees.

3. The history of Indian cricket goes back to the 1840s, to the establishment of the Oriental Cricket Club in 1848. This was followed in the 1850s by a series of other Parsee cricket clubs, Jupiter, the Rising Star, Herculean, Mars and Spartan Cricket Clubs. The naming of the clubs was significant, drawing attention to the elite nature of the game in the 1850s and 1860s. Most of the Parsees styled their clubs after the appellations of Greek gods. The reason, as Shapoorjee Sorabjee states, was that, in those days the history of Greece was generally taught in the schools which could afford classical education. The youth attending these schools were from the higher orders among the Parsees and were inspired by the exploits of the Greek gods, thus naming their cricket clubs after them. For details on the early Parsee clubs and their social base, see S. Sorabjee, *A Chronicle of Cricket amongst Parsees and the Struggle: Polo Versus Cricket* (Bombay, 1897).

4. Most published works on Indian cricket have portrayed the game in these terms, for example: E. Docker, *History of Indian Cricket* (Delhi: Macmillan, 1976); R. Cashman, *Patrons, Players and the Crowd* (Calcutta: Orient Longman, 1979); S. Bamzai, *Guts and Glory: The Bombay Cricket Story* (New Delhi: Rupa, 2002).

5. India's victory in the Prudential World Cup in England in 1983 is justifiably regarded as a watershed in the history of Indian cricket. This win increased cricket's popularity greatly and made it the country's foremost national passion.

6. All these players are from lower castes and from modest economic backgrounds. Kambli, who belonged to the fisherman caste, lived in a Bombay slum, while Ganesh, a member of the Gowda caste, lived in a small town some hundred miles of from Chennai.

7. While Baloo, Vithal and Semper were economically underprivileged *dalits*, Amarnath was the son of a farmer and Amir Elahi was the son of a butcher. Faced with severe financial crisis, Elahi had to bowl in local matches for the payment of one rupee. Hindlekar, India's wicket keeper in the 1936 tour of England, also came from a poor Bombay family.

8. The historical data provided by scholars like S.N. Mukherjee provide room for the argument that the category *bhadralok* refers to both a class of aristocratic Bengali Hindus, the *abhijata*

bhadralok, and more middle-income groups. The latter group surpassed the *abhijats*, in numbers and correspondingly in social influence, from the second half of the nineteenth century due to large-scale immigration. The *abhijat sreni* was made up of men who had moved into the city of Calcutta around the mid-eighteenth century. While some of them had made their fortunes through service to the Mughals, most of them 'rose from poverty to wealth' in businesses and occupations as varied as shipping, indigo plantation, *banyans* to the British, and purchasing *zamindaris* and flour mills. Below this group were the large shopkeepers, small landholders and white-collar workers in commercial and government houses, teachers, 'native doctors', journalists and writers. This group was referred to as the *madhyabit* in early nineteenth-century Calcutta. S.N. Mukherjee, *Calcutta: Essays in Urban History* (Calcutta: Subarnarekha, 1993).

9. In his memoirs, the Maharaja of Natore mentions that the cricket team formed by the Cooch Behar Maharaja hardly contributed to the improvement of indigenous cricket in Bengal. This was because he recruited British and European players. To remedy this deficiency and ensure an improvement in Indian cricketing standards, the Maharaja of Natore decided to recruit Indian players from all parts of the country. His covert intention in doing this, it may be surmised, was to prove that he was a greater patriot than his Cooch Behar counterpart.

10. In both these cases, the issue of captaincy resulted in a dispute between the two princely patrons. In 1932, Patiala successfully outmanoeuvered Vizzy, pushing him into the peculiar position of Deputy Vice Captain. In 1936, Vizzy took his revenge, claiming the captaincy, despite being the worst player in the touring party.

11. For a detailed description of this rivalry see; M. Bose, *History of Indian Cricket* (London: Andre Deutsch, 1990).

12. An Indian term for clubs. In pre-partition India, such clubs were community-based and cricket was organized along communitarian lines.

13. Corporate patronage means patronage by leading commercial corporations of the country, for example, the State Bank of India, Tatas, Indian Railways, Food Corporation of India.

14. All hitherto published works on Indian cricket have portrayed the game in these terms; Docker, *History of Indian Cricket*; Cashman, *Patrons, Players and the Crowd*; Bose, *History of Indian Cricket*; Bamzai, *Guts and Glory.*

15. 1928 is accepted as the year of the Board's establishment. No authentic data is yet available to point the specific date as to when the Board was founded. For detailed analyses on the date of the Board's establishment, see Docker, *History of Indian Cricket.*

16. Cashman, *Patrons, Players and the Crowd*, p.48.

17. Ibid.

18. Ibid., p.55.

19. Bamzai, *Guts and Glory*, p.74.

20. Ibid., p.76.

21. Ibid., pp.76–9.

22. Cashman, *Patrons, Players and the Crowd*, p.59.

23. Mutiny here refers to the Sepoy mutiny of 1857, perceived by historians as the first major Indian upsurge against British rule. The revolt was brutally crushed, making the British Raj more secure than ever in the closing decades of the nineteenth century.

24. M. Sinha, *Colonial Masculinity: The Manly Englishman and the Effeminate Bengali in the Late Nineteenth Century* (Manchester: Manchester University Press, 1995), p.16.

25. H. Yule and A.C. Burnell (eds), *Hobson Jobson* (Delhi: Munshiram Manoharlal, 1968), pp.44–5.

26. Newspaper reports and other evidence show that until the 1850s, the middle classes hardly indulged in any form of sporting activity. They organized competitions in which their servants fought against each other amidst great excitement and enthusiasm.

27. S.K. Ghosh, *Krida Samrat Nagendra Prasad Sarbadhikari 1869–1940* (Calcutta, 1964), pp.118–19.

28. Ibid.

29. A low caste person. In colonial India men from the higher castes considered a *chamaar* as an untouchable. His touch was considered as polluting.

30. For a detailed description of the cricketing involvement of the Maharaja of Natore, Jagadindranarayan Ray, see J. Ray and P. Mukhopadhyay (eds), *Manasi o Marmabani* (Calcutta,

1925–26); In a series of articles published in the magazine, leading players of Bengal described how the efforts of the Maharaja gave a great fillip to Bengal cricket. These articles throw considerable light on Bengal's cricket history between 1890–1920, a chapter that has been little noticed in existing works on Indian cricket.
31. Ray and Mukhopadhyay, *Manasi o Marmabani*, p.517.
32. Ibid.
33. K. Roy and J. Smriti in Ray and Mukhopadhyay, *Manasi o Marmabani*, pp.615–26.
34. The Bombay Quadrangular, later Pentangular was the most popular cricket tournament in pre-partition India. It had its inception in the Presidency matches of the 1890s, played between Europeans and the Parsiees. Gradually these matches expanded into the Pentangular with the inclusion of the Hindus in 1907, the Muslims in 1912 and the 'Rest' comprising mainly Christians and Anglo-Indians in 1937. It continued despite considerable opposition until the 1940s, to be finally abolished in 1946.
35. V. Raiji, 'Palwankar Brothers', in B. Majumdar (ed.), *Vasant Raiji on Indian Cricket* (Mumbai: Marine Sports, forthcoming).
36. D.B.. Deodhar, *Looking Back: An Autobiography, A Sport and Pastime Serial* (IOL-T27059) p.69.
37. Ibid.
38. B. Majumdar, *Hulla Baloo* in P. Gym, *Outlook* (23 April 2001).
39. By the 1890s, defeating the English in sport had acquired great significance. This explains the Brahmin keenness to achieve such a feat.
40. Hindu Cricket (Contributed), *The Indian Social Reformer* (1906), pp.292–4.
41. Majumdar, *Hulla Baloo*.
42. *The Indian Social Reformer*, pp.292–4
43. Ibid.
44. In the absence of many *dalit* men of renown, it was natural for Ambedkar to hail Baloo's achievements as symbolic of *dalit* prowess. Baloo's achievements were a marker that the *dalits* were in no way inferior when compared to the high caste Hindus.
45. Quoted in E. Zelliot, *From Untouchable to Dalit* (New Delhi: Manohar, 1996), p.104.
46. B. Majumdar, *The Caste of Cricket, The Dalit* (Chennai: Dalit Murasu, 2002).
47. Ibid.
48. Oral interview with V. Raiji (Mumbai: Aug. 2001); see also an interview by V. Gangadhar in www.clickcricket.com (Mumbai: April 2000).
49. W.D. Begg, *Cricket and Cricketers in India* (Ajmer: publisher by the author, 1929), pp.161–3; for a detailed description on cricket patronage by the Maharaja's of Patiala see also Cashman, *Patrons, Players and the Crowd*, pp.48–73.
50. Cashman, *Patrons, Players and the Crowd*, p.28.
51. Ibid., p.31.
52. Ibid.
53. *Indian Cricket* (Mumbai: Cricket Club of India, 1937); this journal published for five years between 1934–39 by the Cricket Club of India was one of the most authoritative publications on Indian cricket.
54. Begg, *Cricket and Cricketers in India*, pp.36–41, gives a detailed description on cricket in Gujrat which includes player profiles, statistics, a brief history of clubs and patrons.
55. Ibid., p.37.
56. Ibid., pp.37–8.
57. Ibid., p.41; Sheikh first represented the Rander Gymkhana A team in 1915. Noted for his fielding, he later began to bowl medium pace and was a member of the Gymkhana team during its All-India tours in 1915–16. In 1919 he was selected to play in the Bombay quadrangular and distinguished himself as a splendid fielder. In 1920 he was invited to play for the Rangoon Mohammedan cricket club in the Rowe Challenge Shield. After his return to Rander he was again invited by the Bombay Islam Gymkhana to play in the quadrangular matches but owing to ill health he failed to perform creditably.
58. For details on the efforts of British officers to promote cricket in India see Begg, *Cricket and Cricketers in India*, pp.80–84.
59. M. Mamoon, 'Dhakar Cricket', in M. Mamoon (ed.), *Dhakar Tukitaki* (Dhaka, 1998), pp.40–5.

60. For details on the introduction of the Presidency matches see V. Raiji and M. Menon, *The Story of the Bombay Tournament: From Presidency to Pentangulars* (Mumbai: Ernest Publications, 2000).

61. Begg, *Cricket and Cricketers in India*, p.i; in his tribute to Lord Irwin, Begg mentions that under his patronage the MCC team visited India in 1926–27 and opened a new chapter in the annals of Indian cricket.

62. M.E. Pavri, *Parsi Cricket* (Mumbai: J.B. Marzban and Company, 1901), pp.189–96.

63. Even when Mr Savage had joined Dorab Tata and when the schools Association scheme had started being viewed as a viable proposition, it was believed in some high European circles that the Union could only interest native schools. Accordingly, attempts had started to form an independent European Schools Association. Justice Fulton and Archdeacon Louis were considering the latter scheme. Knowing about this, Mr Tata and Mr Savage approached the men in charge, proposing a joint movement. After much deliberation the idea of a perfect union was agreed upon and a joint circular signed by the four men was issued to invite all Bombay schools to form an Athletic Association.

64. P.N. Polishwalla, *School and College Cricket in India* (Mumbai, 1921), p.11.

65. Polishwalla, *School and College Cricket*, pp.16–17.

66. *Sakha* (Calcutta: Feb. 1891); These matches were limited overs matches. In the finals Senhati scored 94 runs, in reply to which Khulna were all out for 78. The umpire was an Englishman, a person who had taught the Khulna players the basics of the game. However, contrary to the spirit of the game, the players were involved in an ugly fight after the final was over. This brawl led the author to comment that the natives should aim to learn the game together with the codes considered integral to the game.

67. S. Ray, Cricket Khela, *Mukul* (Calcutta, 1899); Reprinted in S. Ghosh and P. Ray, *Majar Cricket* (Calcutta: Saibya Prakashani, 1999).

68. *The Vidyasagar Sagar College Magazine* (1925–26).

69. J.D. Antia, *Elphinstone College Tours* (Bombay: 1913); in this monograph, Antia, who was a student at the Elphinstone College, describes in detail the tours undertaken annually by the college between 1901–12. These tours were organized to all parts of India and involved a series of matches played against regional, club and college teams.

70. Polishwalla, *School and College Cricket*, p.28; among the noted cricketers of the college were Syed Mohamed Khan, Ashan Al Hak and Shafkat. Touring Bombay in 1903, the Aligarh team beat the Hindu Gymkhana and the Parsee Gymkhana. Their only defeat was at the hands of the Elphinstone College team. For information on Cricket at Aligarh see also D. Lelyveld, *Aligarh's First Generation* (New Delhi: Oxford University Press, 1996), pp.287–92.

71. Cashman, *Patrons, Players and the Crowd*, p.52.

72. Ibid., p.54.

73. Ibid., p.55; This policy led educated cricketers to seek employment with the Tatas. Sudhir Naik, an M.Sc. in Chemistry, mentioned this stating that the Tatas had offered him a job in the research department while any other concern would have employed him as a Public relations officer or in some other branch of the company's administration.

74. The BCCI had levied a tax of four annas per seat per day for matches against the Commonwealth cricket team that toured India in Nov. 1949; *Times Of India*, 8 Sept. 1949.

75. Ibid.

76. *Free Press Journal*, 18 Oct. 1950.

77. Oral interview with V. Raiji. Even for the best seats, a few rows of sofas near the fencing, the prices were a reasonable five rupees per day during the days of the Pentangulars. For the international engagements the sofa would cost ten rupees per day. With four persons accounted for by one sofa the price per individual came to 1.25 rupees for the Pentangulars and 2.50 rupees for international matches. V. Raiji, a student at the time of India's first test match on home soil in Mumbai against Jardine's team was rewarded by his father, who had bought him a sofa for the whole match in 1933–34.

78. *Free Press Journal*, 18 Oct. 1950; the author mentions in the same report that Bombay has served host to Gilligan's team in 1926–27, Jardine's team in 1933–34 and the Australian side brought out by the Maharaja of Patiala. But for all these matches the cost to Bombay as a whole was nowhere near the figure that was now claimed by the BCCI for the one seat allotted to Bombay.

79. *Free Press Journal*, 13 Oct. 1950.
80. *Times Of India*, 22 July 1951.
81. Ibid. This proposal was mooted by the President of the Board Of Control for Cricket in India, A.S. De Mello, who thought that whenever any foreign team visited India, the Ranji trophy matches were delayed and the completion of the tournament was a matter of grave concern. It was a matter of inconvenience for players and posed great difficulty to the host centre.
82. *Times Of India*, 1 Aug. 1951.
83. Ibid.
84. *Free Press Journal*, 14 May 1950.
85. *Times Of India*, 28 April 1952; though the Club of Maharastra and the P.Y.C. Hindu Gymkhana came forward to help the schools after the government's decision was announced, their efforts were hardly sufficient. The club of Maharastra charged a fee of 25 rupees for its coaching camp, a sum that was beyond the reach of the underprivileged cricketers.
86. S. Anand, 'Eating with our Fingers, Watching Hindi Cinema and Consuming Cricket', *Himal South Asian Journal* (Feb. 2002).
87. On many occasions the clubs were formed for both cricket and football. In the Presidency College Calcutta, a cricket and football club was formed in 1891 under the superintendence of Professor Bipin Behari Gupta. In the Vidyasagar College also, a cricket and football club was formed under Professor Saradaranjan Ray in the late nineteenth century.

8

'Physical Beings': Stereotypes, Sport and the 'Physical Education' of New Zealand Māori

BRENDAN HOKOWHITU

The writer commodifies [them] so that [they] can be exploited more effectively by the administrator. Exploitation is the reality behind the rhetoric.[1]

This study examines how sport, state education and physical education have contributed to the suppression of the indigenous New Zealand Māori.[2] It demonstrates that historical vestiges of Māori savagery and physicality have been perpetuated through a racist state education system, and by limiting Māori achievement and the integration of *tikanga Māori* (Māori culture) to physical arenas, such as sport and physical education. The article begins by examining the historical underpinnings of the stereotype of Māori as a physical people, particularly how the control of power/knowledge by the colonizer combined racial superiority and social Darwinism to construct Māori culture as encumbered within a primitive physical world. As I then explain, this history helped found a racist education system that, by denigrating Māori culture, justified the banishment of Māori physical practices. Later, the state employed the Māori physicality stereotype to channel Māori into physical, as opposed to academic, realms of life. A shift in attitude occurred in the inter-war years; state physical education became the first subject area to make inclusivist overtures to Māori. In analysing this shift more closely, I focus on Philip Smithells, the inaugural Dean of the School of Physical Education at the University of Otago in Dunedin. Smithells placed *tikanga Māori* in the New Zealand physical education curriculum, but arguably his attempts at cultural inclusiveness further oppressed Māori by perpetuating their physical stereotype. Lastly, the article deconstructs representations of Māori as naturally athletic. The article concludes that the naturalization of Māori as sportspeople contributed to the colonization process by assimilating Māori in a very limited way; Māori are successful only in areas of society that do not threaten their dominant representation as a physical people.

HISTORICAL BACKGROUND

Racial representations 'need to be located squarely with respect to contested interpretations of power', where power 'functions through the disciplinary procedures and self regulation of everyday life'.[3] As French philosopher Michel Foucault asks: 'If power was never anything but repressive, if it never did anything but say no, do you really believe that we should manage to obey it?'[4] In other words, dominant racial ideals and other social constructions are powerful because they are disciplined norms that one willingly acts out or obeys. Power's ultimate authority, Foucault challenged, was not in its monolithic or repressive form but rather in its power to discipline through construction. That is, to create a 'normal' representation of a person based on historical constructions of race, class, gender and age. Such 'normal' depictions of Māori are undoubtedly tied to a bio-racist history contrived by colonizer privilege, as Sue Tait points out,

> Representations of black bodies remain inscribed with the fantasies and anxieties of our racist histories ... biology it has been assumed accounts not only for physical variations like skin colour, but also qualities like intelligence, behaviour and ability ... there remains vestiges of its assumptions – for example, a warrior instinct 'in the blood' ... or sporting or muscular ability among blacks due to 'natural rhythm'.[5]

Racism in the colonies did not develop because of simple ignorance or hatred for an alien culture; rather it emerged because colonization was justified through discourses on race and Europeans' right to rule.[6] Biological differences between races confirmed the natural power structure of colonialism: '[Europeans] liked to see colonialism as a moral statement on the superiority of [their] culture and the inferiority of others.'[7] Travellers, missionaries and early settlers constructed Māori as physical, unintelligent and savage.[8] Early depictions of both Māori and Pākehā (the common name for New Zealanders of European ancestry, literally meaning 'foreign') became 'icons of representation' that mirrored the power relationship between the two, and invariably led to 'an appropriate vocabulary and a set of verbal images depicting significant difference... Stylized figures rather than real people were created'.[9] One stylized configuration of Māori was the physical/unintelligent dolt. A physical/intellectual dichotomy, that would limit Māori throughout colonial history, emerged in the grand colonizing era of the eighteenth and nineteenth centuries. The eighteenth-century notion of the primitive 'Other' derived from the idea of the 'Great Chain of Being', the belief that god had created all living things and organized them into a hierarchy of existence.[10] As the nineteenth century approached, Enlightenment theories of the progress of humankind, and corresponding evolution theory, gave credence to the concept of hierarchical racial division. The application of evolution theory to explain power disparity between races produced social Darwinism. Social Darwinism provided scientific evidence to fragment the human continuum into a hierarchy of races. Science validated arbitrary differences between the European and the Other; races became facts based on 'primarily biological and natural difference[s] which w[ere] inherent and unalterable'.[11]

In the New Zealand context, social Darwinism validated the common-sense claims that Māori were less intelligent than the advanced settlers: 'British political and economic might ... [was] an indication of the "survival of the fittest"'.[12] Moreover, social Darwinism was closely linked to the belief in a natural dichotomy between Māori and the civilized European: Māori belonged to the unconscious physical realm, while the European belonged to the realm of western enlightenment. Descartes' claim that the soul, including morals and intelligence, was somehow divorced from the extended material or mechanics of the body created Cartesian dualism, later employed to cast the physicality of people of colour as unenlightened and, thus, uncivilized.[13] According to Ernesto Laclau, the colonized peoples were essentially history-less or, in other words, incapable of universal thought.[14] Eighteenth- and nineteenth-century translators circulated indigenous mythology in the West, describing it as 'irrational fairytales produced by unconscious history, meant for savages and children'.[15] European philosophers such as Hegel described the primitive Other as generically possessing a 'character of spirit in a state of dream', as incapable of action and therefore 'pre-historical', and in turn facing the necessary fate of European subjection.[16]

European missionaries, travellers and philosophers depicted Māori thought and culture as primitive: located somewhere between that of the civilized European and the ape – deceptive, delusional and child-like.[17] Referring to the raised pole seen in *morere* (swing), traveller William Wade describes 'boys and girls, stark naked, and the women with only a rough garment around the loins, run[ning] up the pole as readily as monkeys'.[18] Similarly, Edward Wakefield in 1845 believed the Māori passion for storytelling had all the sensibility of a primate: 'Nothing can remind one more forcibly of the monkey who has seen the world, than a Māori thus relating news.'[19] Frederick Maning in 1863 likened *kapa haka* (any form of dance accompanied by singing or chanting) to a 'dance and capper' performed by 'mad-monkeys'.[20] Others employed 'scientific' methods to demonstrate the lack of evolution in Māori intelligence. In his *The Story of New Zealand: Past and Present, Savage and Civilized*, Arthur Thomson, an early traveller, exploited craniometry to demean Māori intelligence:

> It was ascertained by weighing the quantity of millet seed skulls contained … that New Zealanders heads are smaller than the heads of Englishmen, consequently the New Zealanders are inferior to the English in mental capacity … The memory they possess is the memory of boyhood; and their minds may be compared to mirrors … incapable of retaining any trace of the past … The faculty of imagination is not strongly developed among them, although they permitted it to run wild in believing absurd superstitions … This analysis shows the New Zealanders have the minds of children.[21]

Early nineteenth-century Pākehā perceived Māori as having the capacity to reach 'civilization' eventually. Indeed, Māori were often referred to as the most civilized of all savages, or as Jock Phillips puts it, the 'Aryan Māori', a concept suggesting Māori, of all the indigenous peoples, 'were most like us'.[22] Within a few decades, however, Māori were being cast as a hindrance to the social and economic development of the new colony. The change in attitude occurred just before the civil land wars, precisely as settler impatience with Māori refusal to sell their land peaked. Accordingly, anthropological and other scientific findings increasingly depicted Māori as 'inherently inferior'.[23] The ensuing genealogy of representation these images created effectively limited Māori access to the privileges enjoyed by Pākehā. The following section discusses how, first, missionary education employed the abhorrence of Māori physicality to prohibit Māori physical cultural practices; second, how state education applied the naturalness of Māori physicality to limit Māori to a 'physical' education; and third, why State physical education was perceived as an appropriate subject area for the incipient inclusion of *tikanga Māori*.

MISSIONARY EDUCATION

In 1808, Samuel Marsden recommended the construction of missionary schools for 'a nation who have derived no advantages hitherto either from commerce or the Arts of Civilization, and therefore must be in a state of Heathen Darkness and Ignorance, in which every nation must unavoidably be, who has no connection with the Civil Religious and Commercial part of Mankind'.[24] Thus, guided by righteous intent, the first missionaries, led by Marsden, arrived in 1814 to replace Māori cultural institutions with civilized European faculties.[25] Marsden's assimilation philosophy encouraged Māori to adopt European customary, moral and commercial practices as a 'fitting preparation for receiving the Christian gospel'.[26] Such a policy was congruent with the beliefs of most missionaries who deplored Māori values, attitudes and perceptions, and who, consequently, attempted to squash *tikanga Māori*. Missionary education imposed on Māori an alternative way of understanding the world. For example, Brian Sutton Smith suggests that missionary intervention detrimentally impacted on students' concepts of physical activity. According to him, while missionaries banned many Māori 'games' outright, they showed more lenience towards 'pastimes that they recognized as the pastimes of "civilized" and not just "heathen" children'. Thus, Māori children were explicitly encouraged to continue playing games that were 'intelligible to the European way of life'.[27] In the late 1940s, Sutton Smith found games such as knucklebones, stilts, whip tops and string games in some Māori communities and that they all had 'counterparts in the unorganised play of Pākehā children'.[28]

What Sutton Smith fails to recognize is that the cultural customs that accompanied such Māori physical practices did not survive the missionary onslaught. For example, Europeans viewed death and 'play' as incongruous, yet Māori used *pōtaka tākiri* (spinning tops) and other physical practices in the contexts of both death and leisure:

> When a clan had been defeated in battle and visitors came to condole with them, all assembled on the plaza of the village, and there chanted the lament of the dead. At the conclusion of each

couplet of the song, many tops were spun, and these wailing tops helped to avenge the defeat.[29]

More than likely, Māori associated *pōtaka tākiri* with breath: 'The humming tops that remained spinning for a considerable time were said to possess a long breath, which was considered desirable'.[30] The inclusion of 'games' in the spiritual realm appeared barbaric to Christian missionaries, who outlawed them. As a Māori elder testified: 'we were much puzzled about the new laws made for our people. We were not to spin humming tops on Sunday'.[31] In 1839, the American voyager, Charles Wilkes, confirmed the *kaumātua* (respected elder) complaint: 'social amusements are prohibited by severe penalties, although the people are evidently fond of them'.[32]

In 1845, the missionary William Brown described Māori dancing and singing but noted with pride that 'amongst the missionary natives they are entirely discontinued'.[33] Tīmoti Kāretu lamented the effect of missionary policy on *kapa haka*, noting that many tribes performed them less as the influence of missionaries intensified.[34] Accordingly, *kapa haka* became obsolete in some tribes. For instance, one tribe had to be taught *kapa haka* by another so that they were able to host the 1934 Waitangi celebrations.[35]

The state neither officially sanctioned missionary practices before 1847, nor did they put in place checks. British representatives viewed missionary education of Māori as a cheap means of social control.[36] Politicians only officially approved the civilizing doctrine of mission schools after initial Māori acceptance of the missionary movement began to wane. Many Māori initially viewed missionary settlements as a means to attain certain skills (such as literacy)[37] necessary to deal with Pākehā. Yet, Māori resistance (or 'apathy' as it was, and is, commonly described) to mission schools grew as Māori became increasingly aware of missionary repression and constrictions of their teachings. The failure of missionary schools to convert the majority of Māori eventually led to the introduction of state education for 'natives'.

THE GENEALOGY OF STATE EDUCATION

Until 1867, missionaries provided the entire European education of Māori. Parliamentarians who debated the 1867 Native Schools Act clearly feared that Māori who were not educated by Europeans were more likely to revolt against colonial practices. Henry Carleton, the Under-Secretary of the Native Department, insisted that 'the traditional Maori lifestyle could not be tolerated to continue ... things have now come to pass that it was necessary either to exterminate the natives or to civilize them'.[38] The parliamentary debates on Native education put more emphasis on 'the assimilation of Maori children into European culture and society'[39] than humanitarian duty. In short, education was seen as an agent of social change for Māori that would benefit the colony. The 1867 Native Schools Act placed Māori education under the juris-diction of the Department of Native Affairs, and replaced mission schools with a national system of secular Māori village day-schools.

Representations of Māori as savage shaped New Zealand's educa-tional policy. As J.A. Mangan says, 'ideology shaped the fiction and fiction, in turn, formed the ideology'.[40] Early settlers portrayed educa-tion as part of an evangelical duty to advance Māori away from their heathen culture and into modern civilization. Educational policy, there-fore, was founded on a 'contrived moral doctrine'.[41] Settlers and the embryonic New Zealand government hoped that by educating Māori, they would avoid what would ultimately occur if all else failed – exter-mination![42] Yet, such hopes were based on appeasing British liberals aware of the atrocities that had occurred in other colonies, rather than empathy for New Zealand's natives. The following discussion demon-strates how misrepresentations of Māori savagery and physicality within educational discourses initially justified the State education of Māori.

REINFORCING STEREOTYPES

Dominant vocabularies mould the way groups of people perceive each other, with the outcome being an interaction that stabilizes 'the taken for granted world'[43] of the dominant. Imperial education perpetuated the racial images of the early travellers and propagated racist scientific theory. Its main purpose was 'to appropriate attitudes of dominance and deference ... to shape the ruled into patterns of proper subservience and "legitimate" inferiority, and ... to develop in the rulers convictions about the certain benevolence and "legitimate" superiority of their rule'.[44]

The perception of Māori culture as barbaric and, hence, in need of a civilizing education appears in the following quote by one parliamen-tarian:

The 'Haka' is an exposé of the evil which really lies at the root of their present prostrate condition, an exhibition of the substratum of utter immorality, depravity, and obscenity, which forms the ground work of their race; and in spite of the veneering with which we clumsily cover the rough wood, we shall do nothing until we alter their entire character, by taking in hand the education, per force of the young growing saplings.[45]

New Zealand school textbooks commonly contrasted the superiority of the British race with weaker races to foster imperialistic nationalism. For instance, a geography text records that: 'Whites form by far the most important race, for they have the best laws [and] the greatest amount of learning.'[46] Standard explanations of racial differences attributed them to either geographical location and climatic variation, or degree of white blood. In the case of the former, 'the tropics bred feckless indolence ... location and relief of particular temperate regions ... produced sub-races'.[47]

Images of Māori in school texts around the turn of the twentieth century regurgitated familiar travellers' tales that were, in some cases, over 100 years old. Māori were represented as aggressive: 'At last they saw the North Island ... Angry brown men came rushing down with spears to drive them back.'[48] The myth surrounding the Chatham Island Moriori continued to appear in schoolbooks in the 1920s.[49] Māori were depicted as a violent people who savagely disposed of 'a weaker, darker race'.[50] The same myth still endures especially among 'redneck Pakeha's spluttering over Maori land claims'.[51] Māori were also represented as naive, confused or disobedient children: 'Maoris were very troublesome, and tried to steal anything to which they took a fancy';[52] 'they found the people there were just like children ... men of war, and yet pleased with beads and dolls ... like naughty children, too, the natives would steal and tell lies, and threaten mischief with spears'.[53] School texts depicted *tikanga Māori* as fanciful myth. The foremost myths, still favourites in classrooms today, were presented as a series of Māori stories titled 'Maoriland fairy tales'.[54]

The most common portrayal of Māori, in the decades following the turn of the twentieth century, was the 'noble savage'. As Māori survived their predicted natural death,[55] the settler population found itself amongst native neighbours. Māori were now suddenly the most sophisticated of barbarians. In accordance with the assimilation policy of the day, the 'new age' Māori appeared capable of performing most Pākehā functions. Textbooks implicitly distinguished between the 'real Maori' of the past and the 'brown–skinned citizens' of today. The former were 'romantic, cloaked, tattooed warriors, poets and hunters ... Maoris had done so well for savages that their achievements could be compared with those of the British in the remote past',[56] for they had demonstrated 'a greater aptitude for civilization than any other barbarous race'.[57] The widely-used education resource series, *Imperial Readers*, stated that 'Maori were savages but noble savages'.[58] The following discussion demonstrates that although notions of the savage and physical Māori initially justified the State's philosophy of a civilizing education, a racist curriculum would restrict the 'noble savage' to the physical world.

THE 'PHYSICAL EDUCATION' OF MĀORI

The idea of an agricultural British paradise in the South Seas required a school curricula to teach manual, technical and agriculture skills. Māori, in particular, received a state 'physical education' that limited their access to the skills and qualifications necessary to compete in the profes-sional workplace. An egalitarian rhetoric of universal education for all underpinned the provision of free education. The upshot of a 'free education' was, however, a docile labour force designed to secure the interests of the middle-class, white establishment. With most of the land owned by Pākehā, training Māori in farming skills can only be viewed as the training of workers to increase profits. The education provided for Māori largely enclosed them in rural areas as subsistence labourers. Education was used to discipline Māori, that is, to deny, exclude, marginalize and enclose: 'this form of discipline worked at the curricu-lum level ... as a mechanism for selecting our "native" children and girls for domestic and manual work'.[59]

John Barrington's discussion on educational policy and Te Aute College, a Māori denominational boarding school, provides unsettling reading. Under headmaster John Thornton, Māori boys achieved at a level equal to anyone in the country in math and science. But Māori academic achievement alarmed James H. Pope, the inaugural Inspector of Native Schools. In 1866, he suggested that Te Aute should teach Māori boys 'agriculture, market gardening, stock farming, poultry keeping and bacon curing'. Pope particularly resented the resources of the estate 'being diverted to literary work'.[60] George Hogben, the

Inspector General of Schools, took up the issue with representatives of Te Aute and demanded that the latter drop Latin, Euclid and Algebra from the curriculum.

From the 1880s through to the 1940s, educational policies reflected 'a narrow and limited view' of Māori potential and their role in New Zealand society.[61] Ministers of Education deemed Pākehā education 'too academic' for Māori. In 1905, compulsory schooling for Māori children was introduced two years after William Bird succeeded Pope as inspector. The following year Bird declared that Māori were inherently unsuited to academic subjects: 'The natural genius of the Maori in the direction of manual skills and his natural interest in the concrete would appear to furnish the earliest key to the development of his intelligence.'[62] Bird believed that education should not prepare Māori to compete with Europeans in trades and commerce. By 1913, Bird's beliefs had been fully realized:

> In none of the secondary Māori schools … is there any attempt or desire to give what is usually understood by a 'college' education … the girls schools afford further training in English subjects and in various branches of domestic duties – cooking, sewing and dressmaking, housewifery, nursing and hygiene; the boys schools in English and manual training – woodwork, elementary practical agriculture and kindred subjects and that is all.[63]

The Rev. Butterfield, headmaster of a Gisborne Māori boarding school, agreed; telling the Young Māori Party in 1910 that Māori were not fitted to the various professions:

> About 999 out of 1000 could not bear the strain of higher education. In commerce Maori could not hope to compete with the Pakeha. In the trades the Maoris were splendid copyists, but not originators. As carpenters they would cope under a capable supervisor but not otherwise. Agriculture was the one calling suitable for Maoris … it was therefore necessary to teach them the 'nobility of labour'.[64]

Thomas Strong, the Director of Education from the late 1920s to the mid-1930s, was surprised and disturbed to find Māori learning 'the intricacies of numerical calculations' in some schools. He warned that educating 'the dark races' and 'encouraging pupils to a stage far beyond their present needs or their possible future needs' is a 'fatal facility'.[65] In

1941, Thomas Fletcher, the Inspector of Native Schools, identified home-making, building, furniture making, cooking and child rearing as the staple curriculum in the newly established Native District Secondary Schools.[66] With no School Certificate courses in Native District Secondary Schools, pupils were unable to gain the qualifications necessary to compete in the broader workplace.[67] Fletcher's philosophy was similar to that of his predecessors and formed the core of Māori educational policy in the early twentieth century: 'To lead the Maori lad to be a good farmer and the Maori girl to be a good farmer's wife.'[68]

Urbanization in the mid-twentieth century precipitated a greater emphasis in the Māori boys' curriculum on trade training for jobs in cities. The search for employment forced many young Māori men and women, and consequently young Māori families, to leave their *hapū* (sub-tribe). Māori were no longer needed as farmers and farmers' wives, rather they were needed as carpenters and carpenters' wives.[69] The next section examines state physical education's innovation as the first subject area to include Māori culture. But it questions whether this benefited Māori or further perpetuated their stereotype as a physical people?

STATE PHYSICAL EDUCATION AND MĀORI

It must be stated, first and foremost, that the Western State's adherence to the classical Greek education model of 'subjects, disciplines and syllabi as sets or provinces of meaning'[70] undermined the holistic nature of *mātauranga Māori* (Māori knowledge and systems of learning). The imperial system of fragmentation denigrated Māori understandings of the world.[71] The breaking down of Māori life into sections, subsections and categories that aligned with European perceptions of the world violated Māori knowledge. As a distinct subject area, physical education, for example, contrasted a Māori holistic view of health and physical activity.[72]

Initially, physical education in New Zealand (for the working classes at least) was military-based. In 1901, the Public and Native Schools Act made physical drill for boys and girls, eight-years-old and over, mandatory. Partly a reaction to a sense that New Zealanders should protect their own shores, the new physical education curriculum ironically ignored the ingenious and tactical successes of Māori in battles with British troops.[73] Even Native schools accorded Māori military and weaponry drills no recognition. Demonstrating the extent that physical education was tied to an Imperial world-view, physical educationalists of this time dismissed anything Māori; Māori could not possibly offer anything to the modern world, especially if those offerings contradicted British notions of superiority.

In 1909, the English Board of Education syllabus of physical exercises provided the first official 'clearly defined space' in the curriculum for physical education. Its introduction marked the increasing awareness that exercise could facilitate mental aptitude and signalled a shift away from military drill.[74] But the reference to holistic health completely ignored *tikanga Māori*. Among Māori, health stems from the complex idea of *mauri* (life principle) which includes *hauora* (literally 'life-breath' but commonly referred to as holistic health), and in turn is regulated by *whenua* (relationship with the land), *wairua* (the spiritual element), *hinengaro* (the mental element), *whānau* (the family element) and *tinana* (the physical element). Such a philosophy was consistent with the basic assumption that informed physical education policy and practice in New Zealand, 'A healthy body breeds a healthy mind',[75] and, therefore, could have been integrated into the curriculum.

By the 1930s, however, the perception of Māori culture as completely irrelevant to the 'modern' world changed. In the inter-war years Pākehā society increasingly recognized the adaptive powers of Māori, as well as their pride as a people. To some degree, the Māori cultural renaissance of the 1930s, led by Sir Apirana Ngata,[76] was acknowledged by mainstream society. Moreover, Māori became to be accepted as fellow citizens. The school journals increasingly described an egalitarian society in which Māori neighbours had been assimilated: 'We are accustomed to seeing Maoris sitting at tables with Europeans, talking to them in the street and competing on equal terms in various sports and occupations. The good Maori stands as high as the good Pakeha and the bad Pakeha sinks as low as the bad Maori'.[77] Note the word 'various', meaning in some areas of life but not all!

Concomitant with the notion of the Māori 'neighbour' was a developing sense of cultural obligation. Appropriate sites where *tikanga Māori* could be integrated into mainstream environments were sort. Consequently, state education 'had perforce' to ally itself with Ngata's cultural renaissance.[78] The introduction of *tikanga Māori* into Native schools was limited to primary schools and included only non-threatening aspects, such as 'song, crafts, art, story, and dance'.[79] This signalled the state system's initial use of things Māori as instruments of adornment to create an atmosphere of artificial culture, while ignoring *tikanga Māori* of any substance, such as language.

A large part of the Māori content taught in Native schools was considered physical education. Māori culture was perceived as a 'doing' culture and, consequently, physical education was deemed an appropriate subject area for its integration:

> Each pupil balances mental with physical exercise and offsets both with a certain period of relaxation. Physical education classes are held first in the morning. The play interval is devoted to agility exercises and games, including Maori games such as homai, stick games, top spinning, and string games ... At the end of the afternoon, when the children are becoming mentally tired, we have a further fifteen-minute period for gardening, or pois [a ball connected to a string to give suppleness and dexterity to the wrists and hands], action songs ... to offset the mental fatigue and to release of the pent-up physical energy ... In terms of modern educational theory the Native craft work fits into the 'doing' programme, the appealing and important aspect of any school ... As a 'golden fringe' to the busy activities come the poi, haka, and the action songs. All of these exhibit remarkable rhythmic features.[80]

At the same time, mainstream education also began to feel culturally obligated to introduce *tikanga Māori* into its curriculum. Like Native schools, mainstream schools deemed physical education to be the appropriate site for its inclusion. Phillip Smithells is generally heralded as the crusader for the introduction of *tikanga Māori* into state physical education. He has been credited as the first educationalist to make 'overtures to Maori teachers and students, since the inception of formal education'.[81] The following discussion examines the affects that Smithells' actions had on Māori.

The Department of Education employed Smithells (a member of the English upper-class and educated at Cambridge) to implement the 1933 English physical education syllabus in New Zealand schools. Smithells 'endeavoured to promote a uniquely New Zealand version of the English dictates'.[82] A decade later, Smithells became Dean of the School of Physical Education at the University of Otago, Dunedin. Consequently, from the 1930s until his retirement in the 1970s, Smithells exerted immense influence on the direction of physical education in New Zealand.

Smithells began his quest of developing a physical education programme unique to New Zealand by recruiting selected men and women to train teachers in the new system.[83] By 1947, between 70 and 80 trained organizers promoted Smithells' vision of physical education, which included Māori practices. In an interview in the 1970s, Smithells summarized his concept:

> My idea from the start was to try and find out what would suit New Zealand, drawing on ideas from several countries and also on anything indigenous which was valuable. Early in 1940 I realised that many Māori physical activities were excellent in themselves and peculiar to New Zealand ... [from 1941] onwards [men and women] were trained in Māorii activities as an essential part of Physical Education.[84]

Smithells saw educational value in 'Māori rhythmic' games and 'sought to revive these for the use in both Māori and Pākehā schools'.[85] He instructed staff to 'collect activities or photograph them' as they travelled around the country to train teachers. He later claimed that his staff 'rescued' 'many games and activities'.[86]

The dominant discourse surrounding Smithells' relationship with Māori celebrates Smithells as a visionary. According to Bob Stothart, Smithells initiated a 50-year alliance with Māori movement:

> The great and gentle Philip Smithells intuitively recognised the importance of Māori movement during the 1940s and he encouraged the advisers ... to photograph and gather information. New Zealand physical education publications have consistently carried a Maori dimension resulting directly from Smithells' early interest.[87]

Likewise, Mike Boyes, a current member of staff at the School of Physical Education describes a durable relationship between physical education and *tikanga Māori* inaugurated by Smithells:

> For nearly 60 years Physical Education teachers have taken a strong interest in Maori physical activities. Philip Smithells in the 1940s actively promoted the collection and valuing of these activities and for decades New Zealand school children have enjoyed and been challenged by learning through this movement context.[88]

According to Annette Golding, Smithells bought about recognition by physical educationalists of 'the many games and dances of the Maori people. Since then, teachers, specialists and students have had access to a considerable repertoire of hand, string and stick games, poi dances, action songs and hakas'.[89] Maharaia Winiata, among other Māori, 'publicly congratulated [Smithells] on many *marae* [community meeting place] for the work he did in gathering and preserving'.[90]

The New Zealand physical education profession, thus, prided itself as 'Native friendly' and as the discoverers and rescuers of Māori physical activities:

> This game [titi tūrea] has an interesting history of which our profession may well be proud. Up to 1945 it was not a Maori stick game that was known at all widely. It was discovered at a small one-teacher Maori school, Kokako – a mile or two on the Wairoa side of Waikaremoana. June White who was the assistant organiser in Gisborne at that time and who was particularly interested in Maori games, recognised it as being essentially different from Maori stick games we knew of ... June taught it to the Education Department Physical Education Staff at a Refresher Course in Wanganui at the beginning of 1947, since when it has spread all over the dominion. This is just one example of several indicating how physical educationists in this country have kept alive a part of Maori culture that might have died out.[91]

It is commonly accepted by New Zealand physical educationalists, therefore, that Smithells was 'pro-Māori'. While this seems correct, especially in the context of New Zealand State education in the 1940s, questions remain concerning the affects of Smithells' actions on Māori, particularly the perpetuation of Māori physical stereotypes and misrepresentations.

Smithells nearly always described Māori physical activities in terms of their reproduction to bring about Western outcomes. Lisette Burrows sees two dominant discourses surrounding the value of physical education in the 1940s. The first was a child-centred, problem-solving approach, emphasizing 'freer, less dictatorial modes of teaching and the promotion of human creativity'.[92] This is clearly evident in Smithells' work:

> The Maori can give the Pakeha as much useful healthy gymnastic movement as the Pakeha can give the Maori. For this reason ... the simpler type of Maori rhythmical activity should become a basic

part of physical education ... it will give a new type of exhilaration, pleasure, and refreshment that every one may experience ... these games are fun to learn.[93]

A second discourse emphasized the progressive scientization of physical education and the 'categoris[ation], measure[ment] and control [of] body movement'.[94] In an article entitled 'Māori Rhythm', Smithells confines *tikanga Māori* within western scientific constructs: 'The bending of the knees in the Māori form gives a better pelvic position than the usual formal position with straight legs ... A detailed anatomical analysis of all the positions used in Māori activities shows that the positions used are corrective and developmental ones.'[95]

The point of this discussion is not to bemoan Smithells' recognition of Māori culture, nor to suggest that he should have understood *tikanga Māori*. Indeed, Smithells stepped outside the parameters of his contemporaries and New Zealand society. Yet, he only appreciated the rudimentary functions of Māori physical practices. They were defined within western constructs and, hence, their cultural underpinnings ignored. From a Māori perspective, Smithells' actions were as suppressive as the total concealment of Māori culture. It is one thing for westerners to ignore others' culture as irrelevant to modernity; it is something else to have one's culture 'Othered'. It is not my intention to villainize Smithells, rather my objective is to voice the reality for Māori: the actions of 'Māori friendly' Pākehā also had consequences. Anne Salmond claims that the 'absence of any serious attempt to discover how Maori material could be ordered in Maori ways... answers the Western demand for orderly descriptions of "areas" of life, but it also cuts across tribal ways of understanding the past... [which] are organised along very different lines'.[96]

Smithells' classification of Māori cultural practices as 'Maori Rhythm', demonstrates to Māori, at least, that he did not understand how Māori conceived their world and so, whether intentionally or not, he fragmented the Māori world to resemble, as closely as it could, his European world and his misunderstandings of Māori culture: 'The Taiaha [close-quarters weapon] routines – some of them extremely rhythmical – are accompanied by what appear to be curses upon the enemy, gesticulations, grimaces, and that ever present protrusion of the tongue which the Māoris loves to use and which appears again and again in his fascinating carvings.'[97] Herein lies the problem of Pākehā classifications of things Māori. While *poi*, *taiaha* and *mau rakau* (stick activities) may have appeared as rhythmical pastimes to Smithells, Māori conceived them differently. Contrast Smithells' understanding with that of prominent *kapa haka* analyst, Tīmoti Kāretu: 'the tongue is the avenue whereby the thoughts of the mind is conveyed to the audience. It is, therefore, correct that the tongue should be so honoured as it is in carvings of male ancestors ... Like pūkana [dilation of the eyes], whētero [protrusion of the tongue] is used to emphasise certain words, phrases or references'.[98]

Māori researcher Peter 'Te Rangihiroa' Buck alerts us to the fact that no cultural practice can survive in a decontextualized vacuum. What Smithells imparted into mainstream curricula and what was to be the trend in physical education and education in general, was not *tikanga Māori* – it was merely a few Māori words and actions:

> The old Maori games have practically disappeared and have been replaced by games learnt from Pākehā children ... Tops have survived because they are used by European children but the old chants which accompanied them have been forgotten. Adults no longer take interest in them because the social usages with which they were connected have died out. Kites, if they exist at all, take the Pākehā form of construction, and the priests who used them for divination are extinct as a class.[99]

Thus, while Smithells dreamed of a physical education seasoned by indigenous movements, Māori saw no point in pursuing activities that lacked the other essential elements, which combined to form a holistic philosophy. The least important aspect of *poi*, *mau taiaha* or stick games was the physical.[100] Incantations and stories that surround these activities allowed for the regeneration of *whakapapa* (genealogy) and *tikanga*.

Smithells' decontextualized versions of *tikanga Māori* did not propagate Māori culture within dominant society, nor did it bring about a better understanding of Māori culture among educationalists, much less the lay public. As attested to by Moana Nepia's reluctance to participate in some activities during her physical education in the 1950s because they were culturally inappropriate: 'One of the games that used to make us really *whakamaa* [belittled] was tunnel ball. And leapfrog. I couldn't bring myself to do it. We were made to do it by teachers yet we couldn't go and explain because we would be accused of wanting to dodge Phys. Ed.'[101] Similarly, Rewiti Webster found that his educators were less than sympathetic to *Māori* physical practices:

it soon became very clear to me that things Māori were not things
to be proud of. We were told not to speak Māaori in the
playground, we were strapped ... I used to make tops ... and take
my flax whip to school. I thought I'd introduce this game to them.
The teacher ... said, 'What sort of a Māori game is that?'[102]

The acceptance of *tikanga Māori* within the physical education curriculum by the Department of Education in Smithells' time was consistent
with a growing empathy for certain aspects of Māori culture (that is,
practices within the physical realm that were non-threatening and non-
academic). A similar degree of cultural obligation to include Māori
content in curricula can be seen in the Native school[103] (see p.207). The
inclusion of Māori culture in physical education was an ideal solution to
cultural obligation because physical education was considered non-
academic; it was also in keeping with the stereotype of Māori as a
physical people. The following section explores how sport, like physical
education, became an acceptable arena for Māori achievement due to its
location in the physical realm.

THE NATURALIZATION OF THE MĀORI ATHLETE

Māori have achieved more in sport than in any other area of New
Zealand society. Sport was the only mainstream activity where Māori
could achieve success and compete with Pākehā on an 'even playing
field' and, accordingly, could gain *mana* (respect/esteem) in the Pākehā
world. Initially, Māori leaders saw sport as a way to embellish their own
culture while integrating themselves into the dominant society. At the
beginning of the twentieth century, with their culture on the brink of
extinction and subjected to explicit racism in nearly all walks of society,
sport offered Māori something of a salvation. Furthermore, given the
national hysteria for rugby throughout the twentieth century and the
consequent status of the game, it is not surprising that Māori placed
mana on being 'great footballers'. One need only look at the obituaries in
Mana Magazine[104] to see how Māori eulogize sporting feats.

Māori, like various colonized groups, have had conditional access to
the colonist's world. For example, Māori men, as warriors, 'showed
themselves to be good at those things which Pakeha men [were also]
proud of. Maori men were good at war and they were damn good at
playing rugby, so they took on a special status of being Kiwi males with

a slightly exotic flavour.'[105] Yet, war and rugby were two of the few sites where Māori men were able to enter into the Pākehā domain on a 'level playing-field'.[106] Māori gained access to these arenas because they were 'damn good' but, more importantly, because representations of Māori athletes or Māori warriors did not conflict with stereotypes of Māori as a physical and savage people: 'Maori, by their savage nature, were supposed to fight – in war or its peacetime substitute, rugby football. Neither required intellect.'[107] Rugby and war require physical prowess and can be brutally violent, especially where Māori are typically found: the engine rooms of the scrum and the trenches of the battle-field.[108]

The athleticizing of Māori began as a commentary on the 'noble savage'. A significant minority of commentators, such as Rousseau, believed the savage Other morally superior because they lived closer to nature.[109] However, Rousseau's notion of the noble savage was a critique on the state of civilized society, rather than a suggestion that modern society should revert to the savage ways of the Other. Correspondingly, many early travellers romanticized the savage as part of a 'natural world' filled with 'innocence and purity', as opposed to the 'corruption and decay' of the developed world.[110] By romanticizing the noble savage in instances of extraordinary athleticism, western representations of Māori offered a humanistic account of a beautifully naive, simple and mystical life prior to the reasoned life imbued by the scientific revolution. An early traveller to New Zealand, for example, relates an invigorating tale of the 'bronzed Māori' competing in a long lost primordial battle against nature:

> The canoe was now rushing through the tide … its expert helms-
> man, as rigid as one cast in bronze … The most lasting impression
> made on my mind in this surfing incident, was that of the poise and
> skill of Te Rangi Tuataka Takere, the high born Rangatira [chief],
> as he sat statue like, steering-paddle firmly grasped, his fine
> muscular figure and clean cut tattooed features, reproducing … a
> grand picture of pure Maoridom as it had been for centuries prior
> to AD 1884. Alas! That we were to witness such a scene never
> again.[111]

The uptake of European sports by Māori served two functions for the dominant group. Firstly, sport was undoubtedly a form of social control: 'rugby and cricket, famously described as "Britain's gift to the World", marked out the contours of Empire. Sport became seen as essential preparation both for character and service in Empire.'[112] Māori sportspeople were the greatest trophies of colonization; the disciplined brute – his/her aggression and savagery confined to the sporting arena. Indeed, the British Press depicted the first national New Zealand rugby team to tour Britain, the 1888–89 Native Team, as a circus sideshow exhibiting tamed savages from the South-Seas.[113] New Zealanders felt the actions of the 1888–89 Native Rugby team could 'make or break the wider reputation of the young colony', and it was with satisfaction that New Zealanders heard of their own colonizing successes. The *Daily Telegraph* (London) reported, 'The Maoris have certainly progressed since Captain James Cook· ... found the finely painted and neatly tattooed ancestors of our visitors eating each other in the bush'.[114] *The Times* (London) offered: 'it is a tribute to our colonising faculty. The colonising race that can imbue the aboriginal inhabitants of the colonised countries with a love for its national games ... Wherever the Englishman goes he carries the bat and the goal posts.'[115]

Secondly, it ingratiated Māori to the Pākehā public. The athleticizing of Māori aided the colonial project by providing a bridge for the dominant culture to recognize some good in their darker brethren. Māori were assimilated into society through physical pursuits, whether that was through war exploits, physical labour, physical education, sport or through their aptitude with physical activity. Māori were endeared to the general public because, in Smithells' words, they had 'rhythm':

> By countless years of experience, trial and error these rhythmic activities have evolved with the purpose of giving quickness of hand and eye, rhythm, anticipation, and the strengthening of certain muscle groups. Besides the direct physical effects of greater motor control, there is the joy and exhilaration that comes from such control and from the body moving rhythmically, whether in the wild sweeps of the taiaha, the staccato beat of homai [handgame], or the continuous smooth rhythm of the stick games.[116]

Smithells presented Māori as masters of movement: 'The Pākehā may have taught the Māori many games but he has taught him little about movement ... we can try to learn from the Māori some of the basic factors in movement, rhythm, relaxation, and co-ordination about which he knows so much.'[117] Conversely, he decreed the clumsy Pākehā as the antithesis of Māori: 'The Pakeha, who is often slower in anticipation and, because of muscle tension and other factors, is much less rhythmical than his Maori countrymen.'[118] While seemingly complimentary, from a Māori perspective, such notions merely reinforced prevailing stereotypes that Māori lacked the psychology of a white person, which in turn gave them 'natural ease'. Such a construction is implicitly linked to the Cartesian claim that civilized reason had to be impartial and thus separate from the passions of the body, while the unconscious 'flow' of the Māori athlete was symptomatic of deriving from a more primitive culture.

And, thirdly, representations of the natural Māori athlete perpetuated stereotypes of Māori savagery, aggression and physicality. The discourse surrounding the success of Māori in sport was linked closely to social Darwinism that validated colonization based on humanitarian ideals. According to this discourse, Māori sportspeople achieved because they had yet to completely evolve out of the physical realm of the animal world, and into the echelons of the enlightened European. For example, Gordon Slatter describes the great Māori and All Black flanker, Waka Nathan, as a sleek animal-like predator who had a 'great instinct' and 'great natural ability' embodied in a 'splendid physique', 'dark rippling muscles' and 'lithe speed' earning him the nick-name of the 'Black Panther'. Slatter goes on to justify the pseudonym by quoting the *Encyclopaedia Britannica*: 'The leopard, pard or panther are quick and graceful, obtain[ing] its prey by springing upon it from ambush or by a stealthy stalk. Never had [Waka Nathan's] nickname, the Black Panther, suited him better then when he suddenly appeared from nowhere to capture the Ranfurly Shield.'[119] Such a construction, while overtly positive, is implicitly linked to the nineteenth-century soulless animal discourse.

Complicit with the idea that Māori sportspeople are handed rewards on a genetic plate, is the caveat that natural physical ability is paralleled by an inherent lack of mental resolve. This concept developed from the notion that Pākehā intelligence and fortitude alone has led to New Zealand's economic and cultural development; a discourse still clearly evident in this commentary by New Zealand's most celebrated sports broadcaster, Murray Deaker: 'I think it is fantastic that we have this wonderfully athletic group of people that can help us develop our sport … But I also want the hard, tough white farmer to be a part of my All Black side … [The type of player who is] there for 80 minutes in a ruthless uncompromising way.'[120] Ex-All Black, Grant Fox suggests that 'Polynesian players were naturally superior to us in talent, but a lot of them aren't there now because they didn't have the discipline for physical conditioning. They lacked the right kind of mental attitude. They'd just turn up and play.'[121] While Auckland club rugby coach, Dale Atken, suggests that 'the Polynesian boys are athletically explosive and that's paralleled [by] their concentration as well. When you make the comparison with the white guys, well they are 80–minute toilers. They are the workers.'[122] Just as State education gave Māori only those physical skills necessary to provide labour on Pākehā lands, so too are Māori only credited for having natural athleticism; for, according to the above analysis, it was the intelligence and integrity of Pākehā that developed New Zealand into the country it is today, just as it is the dogged determination of Pākehā that will win games for the All Blacks in the future. Although the Māori sportsperson acts as an exemplar of a subject within an egalitarian state who has triumphed over adversity, the representation can also be employed to implicitly suggest that Māori lack a work ethic, are lazy and fickle.

CONCLUSION

Constant representations over time cause what Foucault calls the 'exhibitionary regime of truth'. As Edward Said argues, colonialism 'can create not only knowledge but also the very reality [it] appear[s] to describe'.[123] In general, the genealogy of representing Māori as physical people has created a New Zealand culture that channels Māori into the physical realm; the Māori athlete and manual labourer represents 'that part of the past that is still operative in the present'.[124] Yet, stereotypes of Māori are not dangerous because they are false representations of a given reality; they are dangerous because they are 'an arrested, fixated form of representation that, in denying the play of difference, constitutes a problem'.[125]

The stereotype of Māori as physical people continues unabated. Recently, Farah Palmer found that many secondary school teachers viewed Māori achievement purely within the physical or sporting realm. One teacher said 'there is a certain stereotype for Māori and Pākehā that you have to face up to ... Māori are good at PE ... [We need to] ensure that the structure of courses are shaped around their interests, such as sport, so there is a *practical* application they can relate to' (emphasis added).[126] Another teacher based her opinions of Māori on their sporting success: 'I like the Māori students because they are good at sport and they are enthusiastic about their sport.'[127] Generally, teachers believed Māori students possessed natural attributes to be 'good athletes' but had 'very low expectations of Māori students' academic capabilities'.[128] For Māori sport has become a proxy for the stylized physical labourer construction that limited their fathers, grandfathers and great-grandfathers to lackeys in Pākehā businesses.

Historical vestiges of Māori savagery and physicality have been promulgated through State education, physical education and sport. The three arenas have culminated along with other institutions, such as the media, to form a powerful construction of the Māori as a physical being. While education initially justified its civilization of the savage Māori by representing them as a physically barbaric people, Māori physicality was later used to ingratiate Māori to the Pākehā public through physical education and sport. There is no mistaking the reason that physical education was the only subject area in State education for over three decades (1940s–70s) to carry Māori content: laying in the physical/non-academic realm made it, by design, the only appropriate subject area for the inclusion of *tikanga Māori*. Similarly, sport has, for over a century, remained the only institution (apart from entertainment) where Māori successes have gained consistent mainstream representation. The naturalization of Māori as physical people has become an exhibitionary regime of truth, where Māori successes on the sports field, on the farm or within physical education continue to justify the representation of Māori as a physical people.

NOTES

1. J.A. Mangan, 'Images for Confident Control: Stereotypes in Imperial Discourse', in J.A. Mangan (ed.), *The Imperial Curriculum: Racial Images and Education in the British Colonial Experience* (London: Routledge, 1993), p.9.
2. The word Māori is both plural and singular, thus one can say, 'Bob is a Māori', while one can also say, 'those children are Māori'. There is no 's' in the Māori language and it is incorrect to employ 'Māori' as a plural form. I avoid employing the phrase 'the Māori' because it suggests that Māori are or were a homogenous group of people, which is clearly not the case.
　　Māori is a generic word that initially meant 'normal' but has come to incorrectly represent the tribal-based indigenous peoples of the Pacific Islands, now called New Zealand. Mason Durie has this to say about being Māori: 'Before European contact, the word Māori simply meant normal or usual. There was no concept of a Māori identity in the sense of cultural or even national similarities ... The original inhabitants of New Zealand did not refer to themselves as Māori; rather they were Rangitāne or Ngāti Apa or Tūhoe or any of 40 or more tribes', *Te Mana, Te Kāwanatanga: The Politics of Māori Self-Determination* (Auckland:

Oxford University Press, 1998), p.53.

3. A. Cornwall and N. Lindisfarne, 'Dislocating Masculinity: Gender, Power and Anthropology', in A. Cornwall and N. Lindisfarne (eds), *Dislocating Masculinity: Comparative Ethnographies* (New York: Routledge, 1994), pp.37–8.
4. M. Foucault, *Discipline and Punish: The Birth of the Prison*, A. Sheridan (trans.) (London: Tavistock, 1977), p.36.
5. S. Tait, 'Advertising, Cultural Criticism and Mythologies of the Male Body', in R. Law, H. Campbell and J. Dolan (eds), *Masculinities in Aotearoa/New Zealand* (Palmerston North: Dunmore Press, 1999), p.207.
6. G. Bederman, *Manliness and Civilization. A Cultural History of Gender and Race in the United States, 1880–1917* (Chicago: University of Chicago Press, 1995).
7. A. Nandy, *The Intimate Enemy* (Oxford: Oxford University Press, 1983), p.100.
8. L.T. Smith, *Decolonizing Methodologies: Research and Indigenous Peoples* (London: Zed, 1999).
9. Mangan, 'Images for Confident Control', pp.8–10.
10. R. Miles, *Racism* (London: Routledge, 1989).
11. Ibid., p.70.
12. J. Simon, 'The Place of Schooling in Māori-Pākehā Relations' (unpublished Ph.D. thesis, University of Auckland, 1990), p.56.
13. R. Descartes, *Meditations on First Philosophy* (Melbourne: Cambridge University Press, 1996).
14. E. Laclau, *New Reflections on the Revolution of Our Time*, J. Barnes (trans.) (London: Verso, 1990).
15. Nandy, *The Intimate Enemy*, p.60.
16. G. Hegel, *The Philosophy of History*, J. Sibree (trans.) (New York: Colonial Press, 1899), pp.204–25.
17. B. Hokowhitu, 'Te Mana Māori – Te Tātari i ngā Kārero Parau' (unpublished Ph.D. thesis, University of Otago, 2002).
18. W. Wade, *A Journey in the Northern Island of New Zealand* (Christchurch: Capper Press, 1977), p.157.
19. Cited in E. Best, *Games and Pastimes of the Māori* (Wellington: The Board of Māori Ethnological Research, for the Dominion Museum, 1925), p.120.
20. F. Maning, *Old New Zealand* (Christchurch: Whitcombe and Tombs, 1956), p.44.
21. A. Thomson, *The Story of New Zealand: Past and Present, Savage and Civilized. Vol. 1* (London: John Murray, 1859), pp.81–4.
22. Cited in R. Schick and J. Dolan, 'Masculinity and *A Man's Country* in 1998: An Interview with Jock Phillips', in Law, Campbell and Dolan (eds), *Masculinities in Aotearoa/New Zealand*, p.56.
23. Simon, 'The Place of Schooling in Māori-Pākehā Relations', p.85.
24. Cited in P. Harvard-Williams, *Marsden and the New Zealand Mission: Sixteen Letters* (Dunedin: University of Otago Press, 1961), p.115.
25. Simon, 'The Place of Schooling in Māori-Pākehā Relation'.
26. Ibid., p.51.
27. B. Sutton Smith, 'The Meeting of Māori and European Cultures and its Effects upon the Unorganized Games of Māori Children', *Journal of the Polynesian Society*, 60, 2/3 (1951), 319.
28. Ibid.
29. E. Best, *Games and Pastimes of the Māori* (2nd edition. Wellington: A.R. Shearer, Government Printer, 1976), p.161.
30. Ibid., p.157.
31. Cited in Best, *Games and Pastimes of the Māori* (1st edition, 1925. 2nd edition, 1976), p.15.
32. C. Wilkes, *Narrative of the United States Exploring Expedition During the Years 1838, 1839, 1840, 1841, 1842* (Philadelphia: Lea and Blanchard, 1845), p.175.
33. Cited in Best, *Games and Pastimes of the Māori*, p.15.
34. T. Kāretu, *The Dance of a Noble People* (Auckland: Reed Books, 1993), p.35.
35. Refers to the celebrations commemorating the signing of the 1840 Treaty of Waitangi between Māori and Pākehā. The Treaty of Waitangi is recognized as New Zealand's founding document.
36. Mangan, 'Images for Confident Control'.
37. See Simon, 'The Place of Schooling in Māori-Pākehā Relations', for her discussion on Māori

literacy in these early days. For a number of years Māori literates outnumbered European literates. There are several accounts of Māori learning to read and write English in a mere few days. Of course such facts are largely unknown, as they do not accede to the dominant stereotypes of Māori.

38. Ibid., p.102.
39. R. Harker and K. McConnochie, *Education as Cultural Artefact: Studies in Māori and Aboriginal Education* (Palmerston North: Dunmore Press, 1985), p.92.
40. Mangan, 'Images for Confident Control', p.10.
41. Ibid., p.11.
42. J. Barrington and T. Beaglehole, *Māori Schools in a Changing Society: An Historical Review* (Wellington: New Zealand Council for Educational Research, 1974).
43. G. Esland, 'Teaching and Learning as the Organisation of Knowledge', in M. Young (ed.), *Knowledge and Control* (London: Crowell, Collier, and Macmillian, 1971), p.81.
44. Mangan, 'Images for Confident Control', p.6.
45. Cited in Simon, 'The Place of Schooling in Māori-Pākehāa Relations', p.86.
46. M.J.B. Ward, *The Child's Geography for School and Home Tuition* (London: John Murray, 1879), p.44.
47. C. McGeorge, 'Race, Empire and the Māori in the New Zealand Primary School Curriculum', in J.A. Mangan (ed.), *The Imperial Curriculum*, p.67.
48. New Zealand Education Department, *The School Journal*, 2, 1 (1908), 135.
49. The Moriori were a Māori tribe who lived off the coast of New Zealand on the Chatham Islands. Between 1790 and 1840 their tribe were ravaged by European diseases, the loss of their basic food supply due to the extermination of seals by European hunters, and killing by invading Taranaki tribes. The myth suggests that Māori killed off a darker and weaker race for land, and in so doing, justified the usurpation of New Zealand by Pākehā (that is, a lighter and more powerful race). In reality, however, the Taranaki tribes killed only 226 Moriori, whereas the European effect (as it was on all Māori) on the demise of the Moriori was vastly more significant. R. Walker, *Ka Whawhai Tonu Matou* (Auckland: Penguin, 1990), pp.39–42.
50. McGeorge, 'Race, Empire and the Māori', p.77.
51. Ibid., p.77.
52. New Zealand Education Department, *The School Journal*, 136
53. Ibid., pp.24–5.
54. Ibid., p.29.
55. It was commonly thought, in the mid to late-nineteenth century, that Māori would die a natural death *vis-à-vis* the evolutionary 'survival of the fittest' philosophy. Māori extinction was considered as an unfortunate but natural phenomenon: 'Just as the Norwegian rat has displaced the Māori rat, as introduced plants have displaced native plants, so the white man will replace the Māori' (Unknown, cited in Durie, *Te Mana, Te Kāwanatanga*, p.30).
56. McGeorge, 'Race, Empire and the Māori', p.69.
57. J.A. Cornwell, *School Geography* (London: John Murray, 1881), p.330.
58. *The Imperial Readers* (Christchurch: Whitcombe and Tombs Ltd, 1899), p.83.
59. Smith, *Decolonizing Methodologies*, p.68.
60. Ibid., p.47.
61. J. Barrington, 'Learning the "Dignity of Labour": Secondary Education Policy for Maoris', *New Zealand Journal of Educational Studies* 23, 1 (1988), 45–58.
62. Cited in Simon, 'The Place of Schooling in Māori-Pākehā Relations', p.98.
63. Barrington, 'Learning the "Dignity of Labour"', 53.
64. Ibid., p.49.
65. T. Strong, 'The Problem of Educating the Māori', in P.M. Jackson (ed.), *Māori and Education: On the Education of Natives in New Zealand and Its Dependencies* (Wellington: Ferguson and Osborn, 1931), p.194.
66. Simon, 'The Place of Schooling in Māori-Pāakehā Relations'.
67. Ibid.
68. Cited in Harker and McConnochie, *Education as Cultural Artefact*, p.95.
69. P. Ramsay, 'Māori Schooling', in S.J. Havill and D.R. Mitchell (eds), *Issues in New Zealand Special Education* (Auckland: Hodder and Stoughton, 1972), pp.68–80.

70. M.F.D. Young, 'An Approach to the Study of Curricula as Socially Organized Knowledge', in M.F.D. Young (ed.), *Knowledge and Control* (London: Collier-Macmillion, 1971), p.27.

71 Smith, *Decolonizing Methodologies*.

72. M. Durie, 'Kaupapa Hauora Māori: Policies for Māori Health', paper presented at the Te Ara Ahu Whaka mua, Māori Health Decade Hui, Te Papa i Ouru Marae, Ohinemutu, Rotorua, 1994.

73. J. Belich, *The New Zealand Wars and the Victorian Interpretation of Racial Conflict* (Auckland: Penguin, 1988).

74. A.P. Roydhouse, 'Thirty Years Ago', *New Zealand Physical Education Society Bulletin*, 2, 4 (1947), 155–7.

75. L. Burrows, 'Mapping Discourses of Physical Education in New Zealand: 1877–1960' (unpublished Ph.D. thesis, University of Otago, 2000), p.206.

76. One of the most significant and effective Māori leaders in the first half of the twentieth century, gaining plaudits and positions of power in both the Māori and Pākehā worlds.

77. New Zealand Education Department, *The School Journal*, 3, 3 (1909), 115–16.

78. D.G. Ball, 'Māori Education', in I.L.G. Sutherland (ed.), *The Māori People Today: A General Survey* (Wellington: The New Zealand Institute of International Affairs and The New Zealand Council for Educational Research, 1940), p.300.

79. New Zealand Department of Education, 'Native Education', *Education Gazette*, 20, 10 (1941), 190.

80. Ibid., 195.

81. Burrows, 'Mapping Discourses of Physical Education in New Zealand', p.216.

82. Ibid.

83. B. Stothart, *A Brief History of the Physical Education Advisory Service* (Wellington: Bob Stothart, 1996), p.16.

84. Cited in B. Ross, 'President's Column: Kia Ora Katou!' *Journal of Physical Education New Zealand*, 31, 1 (1998), 3.

85. Sutton Smith, 'The Meeting of Māori and European Cultures and its Effects upon the Unorganized Games of Māori Children', 318.

86. Stothart, *A Brief History of the Physical Education Advisory Service*, p.18.

87. B. Stothart, 'A Landmark Conference: Te hui o te reo kori', *New Zealand Journal of Health, Physical Education, and Recreation*, 25, 2 (1992), 4.

88. M. Boyes, 'Editorial', *Journal of Physical Education New Zealand* 31, 1 (1998), 1.

89. A. Golding, 'Maori Activities in Physical Education: Part 1', *New Zealand Journal of Physical Education* 17 (1959), 3.

90. Stothart, *A Brief History of the Physical Education Advisory Service*, p.4.

91. New Zealand Physical Education Society, 'Titi Torea Poi', *New Zealand Journal of Physical Education* 9 (1956), 28.

92. Burrows, 'Mapping Discourses of Physical Education in New Zealand', p.187.

93. P. Smithells, *Philip Smithells' Papers* (Archiveal material Dunedin: Hocken Library), p.205.

94. Burrows, 'Mapping Discourses of Physical Education in New Zealand', p.188.

95. P. Smithells, 'Māori Rhythm', *Education Gazette* 20 (1941), Inset.

96. A. Salmond, 'The Study of Traditional Maori society: The State of the Art', *Journal of the Polynesian Society*, 92 (1983), 318.

97. Smithells, 'Māori Rhythm', .7.

98. Kāretu, *The Dance of a Noble People*, pp.29–31.

99. P. Buck, *The Coming of the Māori* (Wellington: Maori Purposes Fund Board/Whitcombe and Tombs, 1949), p.250.

100. Hokowhitu, 'Te Mana Māori'.

101. Cited in J. Metge, *In and out of Touch: Whakamaa in Cross Cultural Context* (Wellington: Victoria University Press, 1986), p.64.

102. Ibid., pp.49–50.

103. J. Simon (ed.), *Ngā Kura Māori: The Native Schools System 1867–1969* (Auckland: Auckland University Press, 1998).

104. A glossy monthly dedicated to Māori issues, events and stories.

105. J. Philips, cited in Schick and Dolan, 'Masculinity and *A Man's Country* in 1998', p.56.

106. M. MacLean, 'Of Warriors and Blokes: The Problem of Māori Rugby for Pākehā Masculinity in New Zealand', in T. Chandler and J. Nauright (eds), *Making the Rugby World: Race, Gender, Commerce* (London: Routledge, 1999), pp.1–26.
107. Ibid., p.21.
108. B. Hokowhitu, 'Māori Masculinity, Post-structuralism, and the Emerging Self', *New Zealand Sociology*, 18, 1 (2003).
109. Miles, *Racism*.
110. Smith, *Decolonizing Methodologies*, p.49.
111. W. Skinner, 'Surf-riding by Canoe', *Journal of the Polynesian Society*, 32 (1923), 35–7.
112. J. Beynon, *Masculinities and Culture* (London: Open University Press, 2002), p.42.
113. G. Ryan, *Forerunners of the All Blacks* (Christchurch: Canterbury University Press, 1993).
114. Ibid., pp.44–5.
115. Ibid., p.50.
116. Smithells, 'Māori Rhythm,' Inset.
117. Smithells, *Phillip Smithells' Papers*, p.205.
118. Smithells, 'Māori Rhythm,' Inset.
119. G. Slatter, *On the Ball; The Centennial Book of New Zealand Rugby* (Christchurch: Whitcombe and Tombs, 1970), pp.83–4. Refers to the famous try Nathan scored to win the Ranfurly Shield for Auckland against Canterbury in 1960. The Ranfurly Shield is New Zealand's most coveted national sporting trophy.
120. Cited in J. Matheson, 'So What's the White Answer?' *NZ Rugby World*, 47 (2001), 32.
121. T. Hyde, 'White Men Can't Jump: The Polynesianisation of Sport', *Metro*, (1993), 67.
122. Cited in Matheson, 'So What's the White Answer?', 32.
123. E. Said, *Orientalism* (New York: Vintage Books, 1978), p.94.
124. T. Niranjana, *Sitting Translation: History, Post-structuralism, and the Colonial Context* (Berkeley: University of California Press, 1992), p.37.
125. H.K. Bhabha, 'The Other Question', *Screen*, 24, 6 (1983), 27.
126. Cited in F. Palmer, 'Māori Girls, Power, Physical Education, Sport, and Play: 'Being Hungus, Hori, and Hoha' (unpublished Ph.D. thesis, University of Otago, 2000), p.275.
127. Ibid., p.276.
128. Ibid., pp.309–10.

9

Institutionalized Discrimination against Japan-born Korean Athletes: From Overt to Covert Discrimination

HARUO NOGAWA

Discrimination, the unfavourable treatment of a person or a group, is not a new phenomenon. Social problems exist in most societies, including Japan. Japanese society was an exclusive, simple-ethnic stock and a homogeneous society until the turn of the twentieth century. A recent increase of foreign labour from Southeast Asian, South American, and Middle-Eastern countries has made Japan an increasingly multi-ethnic society.

A large number of Koreans migrated to Japan between 1910 and 1945, most involuntarily. The total number of Korean immigrants working in the mines and mills reached a peak of two million during the Second World War.[1] The end of the War brought independence to Korea and nearly 1.4 million Koreans returned home. But about 600,000 Koreans decided to remain in Japan for several reasons, and various kinds of discrimination, both overt and covert, have been directed at those 600,000 Koreans since 1945.[2]

A 1995 Japanese governmental report disclosed that 1,320,768 alien residents were living in Japan in 1994.[3] Of this number, approximately 690,000 (52 per cent) were Koreans and 150,000 (11 per cent) were Chinese. Among the 690,000 Koreans, 620,000 possessed permanent alien residency and 70,000 had alien residency for the purpose of business, higher education, technical training and entertainment. Those 620,000 permanent Korean residents have experienced numerous types of discrimination in terms of naturalization, housing, loans, education, occupation and marriage.[4] And discrimination directed at permanent Korean residents has become pervasive in the Japanese sport scene.

More than 85 per cent of the Korean permanent residents are estimated to have been born in Japan, according to Kan and Kim.[5] Numerous studies have been conducted to investigate discrimination against Japan-born Koreans on the basis of occupation, marriage, education, housing and citizenship.[6] Nevertheless, very little is known about discrimination against Koreans in Japanese sports, either domestically or internationally. This neglect is due to the minimal interest in the field of sport among social scientists in Japan. Furthermore, ethnic and racial issues are politically-charged topics in the area of sport and leisure studies in Japan.

This study mainly focuses on Japan-born Koreans.[7] In-depth information on the historical background of discrimination against Japan-born Koreans in the sport scene is included. Some socio-political factors, which counteract discriminatory practices against Japan-born Koreans, will be discussed. Finally, the author will address the issue of racial discrimination against foreign athletes in the Japanese sports world in general.

HISTORICAL OVERVIEW OF KOREANS IN JAPAN

From the dawn of Japanese history, a close relationship has existed between Japan and Korea. Korean settlers brought Chinese civilization and crafts to Japan. Koreans and Japanese share a common Mongolian racial heritage and are physically indistinguishable from each other.[8]

After the Meiji Restoration, the Japanese government invaded Korea in 1905 and annexed it in 1910. The government of Japan adopted the French assimilation policy that was to force Koreans to speak only Japanese and to make the use of Japanese surnames mandatory.[9] Many Koreans were forced to immigrate to Japan between 1910 and 1945 (see Figure 9.1). Involuntary Korean immigrants worked in the mines and mills as virtual slave labourers, and the total number of Korean immigrants reached a peak of two million during the Second World War.[10]

The majority of Koreans returned to their homeland after the War. Yet approximately 600,000 Koreans decided to remain in Japan in 1947 because of the unstable economic conditions in Korea, and for various other reasons.[11] After the War, however, Koreans found themselves stateless, losing their Japanese citizenship. The Japanese government established alien registration and immigration laws which reclassified Koreans as 'alien residents' in 1947 and stripped them of most of their previous rights in 1952.[12] Alien residents would have no citizenship, no voting rights and no protection against occupational and educational discrimination for the next 30 years. The alien registration and immigration laws were designed to exclude Koreans and Chinese from Japan, yet

FIGURE 9.1
MARRIAGES OF JAPAN-BORN KOREANS (1915–1948)

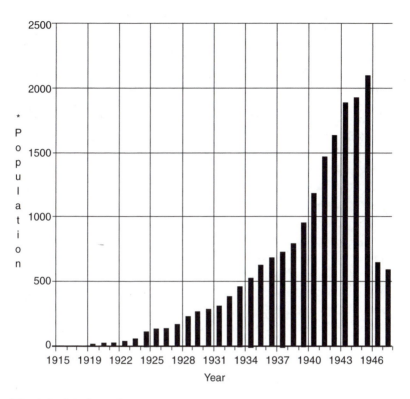

* Population is in thousands.

Source: Kan and Kim (1989).

these very same people had been brought to Japan to perform forced labour during the colonial era.[13]

The Japanese government employed a harsh policy of assimilation against minority groups such as the Koreans and the Chinese.[14] The assimilation policy forced members of minority groups to lose their language and ethnic identity. The Japanese government not only denied the accreditation of Korean ethnic schools, but also forced many of them to close down in 1949.[15] Up to the present day, only four Korean ethnic schools (affiliated with South Korea) have been accredited and received financial support from the Japanese government. But the remaining 155 schools, those affiliated with North Korea, have not received any financial support or accreditation from the Japanese government.[16] The North Korean affiliated ethnic schools are free to establish their own curricula and use the Korean language to teach all subjects except Japanese. Students in these schools suffer disadvantages such as no student discount rate on public transportation, no free textbooks and no high school diploma to advance to college, all of which their Japanese counterparts receive.[17] There are approximately 150,000 Korean children attending schools in Japan. Fewer than 15 per cent of them attend Korean ethnic schools and the rest are students of regular Japanese schools which provide no exposure to Korean language, history or literature. Min has shown that Japan-born Koreans have lost much of their cultural repertoire and have suffered from a negative ethnic identity.[18] Several studies have blamed the Japanese educational system as well as the minority policy for Japan-born Koreans' ignorance of their ethnic language and lack of awareness of their ethnic identity.[19]

The alien status of Koreans did not stop at first-generation immigrants. It has included their Japan-born children and grandchildren, the second and third generations. Unlike the US government, the Japanese government did not grant automatic citizenship to Japan-born children of alien residents. From cross-ethnic marriage, acquisition of citizenship for Japan-born Koreans came only if the father was Japanese up to 1985; since then Koreans born with a Japanese parent have been granted Japanese citizenship.[20] Even though Korean alien residents have had the right to apply for Japanese citizenship through naturalization since 1952, they have had to meet several conditions, such as giving up their Korean name in order to use a Japanese surname, and having to be interviewed and investigated by security officers.[21] This alien registration law was slightly liberalized in 1985, at which time alien residents were not required to change their surnames when they became citizens of Japan.[22] Some 23,180 Japan-born Korean permanent alien residents acquired citizenship through naturalization between 1992 and 1994.[23] Thus, a total of 233,920 were naturalized from 1952 to 1999. An increase in the number of naturalized citizens has naturally resulted in a decrease in the number of Korean alien residents. Some statisticians forecast that there will be very few Japan-born Koreans with permanent alien residency by the year 2050.[24]

Until the late 1980s, Korean alien residents could not work as public school teachers or government officials and had to carry an alien registration card at all times or risk serious criminal penalties.[25] But in the past

FIGURE 9.2
MARRIAGES OF JAPAN-BORN KOREANS (1960–1990)

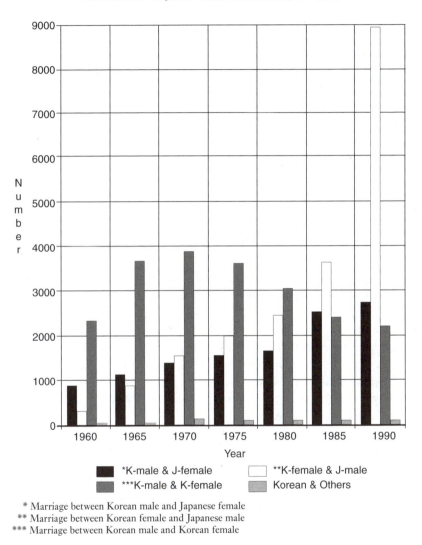

* Marriage between Korean male and Japanese female
** Marriage between Korean female and Japanese male
*** Marriage between Korean male and Korean female

Source: Ministry of Welfare Population Statistics (1992) in Fukuoka, *Koreans in Japan* (1993).

two decades, the Japanese government has removed many of the legal-
ized forms of discrimination, so that conditions for Koreans have
improved significantly.[26] They are eligible for most forms of social
welfare, pension benefits and public employment, and are no longer

required to be fingerprinted in order to register as residents.[27] However, Japan-born Koreans still face overt prejudice and discrimination when they look for work and when they wish to marry Japanese.[28] The majority of Koreans, both naturalized and alien residents, are reluctant to use their ethnic names and still adopt Japanese surnames. In fact, Sklar reported that less than 5 per cent of Koreans used their own names in business dealings; Koreans adopt Japanese surnames in public to conceal their ethnic background, thus avoiding possible encounters with prejudice and discrimination.[29]

The maintenance of intra-ethnic marriage is one important indicator of ethnic survival for a minority group in any society. About 66 per cent of Japan-born Koreans' marriages were intra-ethnic in 1960, and marriage between Japan-born Koreans occurred in the majority of cases in the 1960s. But the rate of intra-ethnic marriage dropped to 56.3 per cent in 1970, 42.2 per cent in 1980, and 15.8 per cent in 1990.[30] Figure 2 shows that inter-ethnic marriage has been increasing over the last 30 years, whereas intra-ethnic marriage has decreased. Although marriage between Japanese women and Japan-born Korean men occurs less often than marriage between Japan-born Korean women and Japanese men, younger Japanese are more willing to accept both inter-ethnic marriage (see Figure 9.2) and Koreans in general. In fact, on the basis of a telephone survey, a Japanese weekly magazine *Aera* reported that the younger generation of Japanese, particularly males, had no qualms about marrying Koreans, and vice versa.[31] A dramatic increase was found in marriage between Korean females and Japanese males in 1990. Fukuoka asserted that in 1990 nearly 4,000 of the 8,940 marriages which took place between Japanese men and Korea-born Korean women were arranged through matchmakers. In fact, fewer than 18 per cent of Japan-born Koreans' marriages were intra-ethnic in the 1990s; Fukuoka estimated that nearly seven out of every ten marriages of Japan-born Koreans was inter-ethnic marriage with Japanese partners.[32]

A BRIEF REVIEW OF ETHNIC STUDIES IN SPORT

Allison has suggested that sport is 'a vehicle through which minority members can learn the value orientations of the dominant culture (achievement, competition, etc.)'.[33] Sport has shown itself to be a factor in forming a point of contact between the mainstream and ethnic groups who find themselves living in close proximity.[34] Nevertheless, very little research has been carried out on the use of sport or games as an agent of the adaptation process into the core society. To this writer's knowledge, there has been no empirical research study conducted on Koreans in Japan in the area of sport and race/ethnic relations. This paper will attempt to describe the inequalities afflicting Japan-born Koreans in the area of ethnicity and sport. The majority of ethnic studies in sport have been carried out in the United States and this literature helped to develop the study of ethnicity and sport in Japan.[35] Thus, a brief review of related studies in American ethnic studies will be introduced here.

Numerous ethnically-related studies have been conducted to investigate African Americans in the field of sport in the United States. However, very little is known about sport and ethnicity among much smaller minority groups like Asian Americans. Apart from racial discrimination, ethnicity and sport research has been conducted into two typical cases. The first case focuses on the relationship between soccer, a sport foreign to most Americans until the 1980s, and the members of immigrant groups, and attempts to determine whether participation in foreign sports promoted or retarded the assimilation process of immigrant groups. The second case scrutinizes the relationship between basketball, an indigenous American sport, and ethnic group members. Earlier research studies attempted to ascertain whether participation in indigenous sport promoted or retarded the acculturation process of ethnic members who were of non-European descent.[36]

Pooley investigated the assimilation process among members of ten urban-area ethnic soccer clubs in Milwaukee, Wisconsin, the players being of European ethnicity. Pooley concluded that club policies regarding recruitment of members were largely responsible for inhibiting the structural assimilation of club members.[37] As pioneer research in a neglected area, Redmond described Pooley's study as an important landmark.[38] In the 1970s, two Canadian researchers stimulated by Pooley's work, Day and McKay, took Pooley's recommendations into their research designs, modified several research instruments and replicated his framework in two different cities of Ontario, Canada. In contrast to Pooley, both Day and McKay found that involvement in ethnic sport clubs in Toronto and London, Ontario, appeared *to promote* the structural assimilation of club members into the host society.[39]

On the basis of three years of direct observation and interaction, Blanchard found that participation in basketball did not play a significant role in the acculturation of the Rimrock Navajo, a native-American people, in New Mexico.[40] Tindall conducted research on the psycho-cultural orientations of two different ethnic groups in the game of basketball, studying Anglo-Mormon and Ute-Indian male high school students in Utah. Tindall reported that basketball clubs and leagues in both communities were exclusive ethnic structures for their members. However, in contrast to Blanchard's study, Tindall indicated that the game of basketball itself partially served as a vehicle for the accultura-tion of the Utes.[41]

Nogawa and Suttie conducted research to determine whether partic-ipation in a Japanese-American community basketball league affected the rate of assimilation of Japanese-American high school-aged males into the dominant culture of the United States. On the basis of the results from a written questionnaire, formal and informal interviews and direct observation, they found that strict club policy with regard to membership recruitment played a major role in retarding the structural assimilation of its members into the host society. They concluded that participation in ethnic sport clubs was apparently not a causal factor favouring the assimilation of Japanese-American high school males, but rather an index of establishing and maintaining ethnic solidarity.[42]

COMMON DISCRIMINATORY PRACTICES IN SPORT

Three types of discriminatory practices have been common in the Japanese sport world. The first type, the main theme of this paper, is discrimination against permanent alien residents of Japan. This kind of discriminatory practice consists of a total exclusion on the basis of citizenship and school affiliation. Japanese sports organizations excluded permanent alien residents attending non-Japanese schools and non-accredited schools, mostly Japan-born Koreans, from participating in official inter-high school and inter-collegiate competitions. Japan-born Koreans have to clear three hurdles to get an equal opportunity to compete against their Japanese counterparts: citizenship, school affilia-tion and membership status. A similar prohibition, though more subtle, has also affected foreign nationals in elite sports such as soccer, baseball, sumo, basketball, ice hockey and volleyball.

The second type, a formal quota system on the basis of citizenship, has existed in most sports leagues and associations. For example, the Professional Football League, the so-called J-League, and the Professional Baseball League have established a by-law which states that 'no more than three non-Japanese players can be in the game for one team at any given time'.[43] The sports leagues, both amateur and professional, basically have to abide by the rules and regulations of their parent associations, such as the Japanese Football Association and the Japanese Baseball Association. Occasionally, corporate sports leagues in basketball, ice hockey and volleyball have banned foreign nationals from their rosters. The reason for this restriction in most sports is identical: foreign nationals have dominated crucial positions within each sport resulting in a weakening of the national team.

Personal discrimination against foreign athletes, the third type, has been observed in the professional sport scene from time to time. Foreign athletes have been labelled as 'Gaijin' (foreign) and have received different treatment than their Japanese counterparts.[44] A recent controversial racial issue in the Japanese sport world occurred in sumo wrestling. A Samoan-American sumo wrestler, Salevaa Atisanoe, whose Japanese name is Konishiki, was not promoted to the level of grand champion, *Yokozuna*, although he met most qualifications. Konishiki was the first non-Asian to reach *Ozeki* (champion), sumo's second highest rank. An *Ozeki*'s promotion to the rank of *Yokozuna* rests in the hands of the Advisory Council for *Yokozuna* Promotion. The council's recommendation is based on an *Ozeki*'s cumulative record of three consecutive tournaments; out of 15 bouts in a tournament, he must win 13 or 14 in each tournament. The council also evaluates the candidate's character, which should demonstrate actions which have the dignity befitting a grand champion.[45] Konishiki had the best recent record at that time. He won two of his last three tournaments, even though he did not win two in a row. *Nihon Keizai Shimbun*, a leading financial newspaper, quoted Konishiki as saying, 'Bluntly speaking, it is racial discrimination ... There is only one reason why I did not make it to *Yokozuna*. It's because I'm not Japanese.'[46]

After coverage in the *New York Times* brought this issue from the domestic to the international arena, the issue of Konishiki's fate moved quickly from the sports pages to Parliament.[47] The matter was considered so dangerous that political leaders up to the level of Prime Minister denied that the Japanese Sumo Association would discriminate against non-Japanese wrestlers. The Foreign Minister, Michio Watanabe, was worried about the remarks attributed to Konishiki and told a Diet committee that the affair should not to be allowed to develop into a big issue. Watanabe was reported to have said irritably – 'It is really bothersome when a really small thing turns into a ruckus based on misunderstanding.'[48] The Sumo Association was also very upset that Konishiki spoke so openly to the press and with his charges of xenophobia. The head of the Sumo Association quickly dealt with Konishiki and warned him 'not to make careless comments'.[49]

Faced with this embarrassing development, the Japanese Sumo Association reacted in classic Japanese style: they draped the issue in ambiguity and dealt with the facts in an indirect, inexact way. In effect, sumo's top brass created a public drama that left Konishiki weeping apologetic tears and the public in doubt as to what really had been said. Konishiki called on the head of the Sumo Association and declared that he had not made the charges printed in the *New York Times*. The head of the Sumo Association pronounced himself pleased with this explanation. Thus the question of whether the powerful American had actually been a victim of Japanese racism remains to be answered.[50]

Subsequently, Konishiki did not make it to *Yokozuna*, but got demoted from *Ozeki* after his peak. He became a crowd favourite later on and eventually retired after he obtained the right of stable master to remain in the sumo world. His follower, American-born Akebono (Chadwick Rowan), became the first non-Asian to be promoted to *Yokozuna* ten months after the Konishiki incident. Akebono's ascent to *Yokozuna* met with little opposition from the Advisory Council for *Yokozuna* Promotion. His acceptance was partly due to his unquestionable performance in the last three tourneys and Konishiki's previous bitter experience.[51]

DISCRIMINATION AGAINST JAPAN-BORN KOREANS

The height of imperialism emerged in the late nineteenth century. Military strength appeared to the Japanese to be as essential as industrial power to guarantee security and a place in the sun. Korea was perceived as a dagger pointed at the heart of Japan if it should be in the hands of a hostile power. Japan fought two wars over its control of Korea and won both. The result of these wars was the emergence of Japanese imperialism, which colonized Korea, Taiwan, the southern tip of Manchuria, and the southern half of Sakhalin in the early twentieth century.[52] Discrimination and prejudice toward Koreans seemed to stem from this era. Japan treated Koreans and Taiwanese as second-class, 'colonial' citizens. A former United States ambassador, Edwin Reischauer, who was born and raised in Japan, tried to analyse the deeper psychological reasons for the perpetuation of Japanese discrimination against Koreans:

There is no feeling of closeness and warmth between Japanese and Koreans. The latter remember Japan's past colonial exploitation of them ... (Their) deep resentments, however, are paralleled by unspoken admiration ... The Japanese for their part tend to be contemptuous of Koreans. They think of Korea as a backward country they once ruled and Koreans as a troublesome minority in Japan. Koreans in Japan do have more than their share of crime and dubious business practices. Korea is to the Japanese a problem ... a semi-permanent irritant.[53]

A significant number of Japan-born Korean athletes have succeeded in at least three sports, baseball, sumo and professional wrestling. A winning 400 metre hurdler Masaichi Kaneda, a hitting wizard Isao Harimoto and the founder of Kyokushin Karate Masu Ohyama, to name just a few, are all Japan-born Koreans. However, most of them use their Japanese surnames and have concealed their ethnic identity. They look Japanese and have a Japanese life-style, but the Japanese do their best to keep them from obtaining managerial jobs.[54]

The majority of non-Japanese schools are Korean ethnic schools, so that the main objectives of this discriminatory practice is to target Japan-born Koreans, the largest minority group among permanent alien residents in Japan. The majority of Koreans living permanently in Japan are North Korean and have established their own cultural schools for their descendants in order to preserve their own language, cultural traditions and ethnic identity. The Ministry of Education, Science, Sport and Culture did not recognize these schools and they were not allowed to participate in any official athletic tournaments by the Japanese Amateur Sports Association (JASA) until 1993. The JASA, the Japanese version of the Amateur Athletic Union (AAU), is the umbrella organization governing all sport associations in Japan and is under the control of the Ministry of Education, Science, Sport and Culture. This institutionalized exclusion of non-Japanese high school students from inter-scholastic athletics became a controversial issue in the 1970s and the Ministry of Education, Science, Sport and Culture and JASA were finally forced to change their policies slightly from the beginning of the 1994 academic year.[55]

Institutionalized discrimination against Japan-born Koreans and other alien permanent residents on the basis of school affiliation is displayed in Figure 9.3. Regardless of citizenship, students of non-Japanese high schools (mostly Japan-born Koreans) were excluded from all official athletic tournaments between 1947 and 1993. In contrast, permanent alien residents and even foreign exchange students attending regular Japanese high schools have been allowed to participate in all official interscholastic athletic competition since 1947, with one exception, the National Sports Festival. This discriminatory practice has prevented Japan-born Korean students from interacting with Japanese high school students. Under the influence of the Ministry of Education, Science, Sport and Culture, JASA excluded permanent alien residents from the National Sports Festival from 1947 to 1981. Thus, non-Japanese high school students with Chinese citizenship like Sadaharu Oh, an ace pitcher of the All Japan High School baseball championship team in 1957 and the Japanese version of Babe Ruth later on, were not permitted to participate in the National Sports Festival until 1981.[56] Permanent alien residents in Japanese colleges have been eligible for the National Sports Festival since 1990. The mass media and Korean residents repeatedly criticized institutionalized discriminatory practice against permanent alien students. But efforts to eliminate the discriminatory practice by the people inside sports circles were rare.

The year 1981 was a turning point for Japan-born Koreans. The Japanese government signed the International Refugee Treaty in 1981. This international political act was originally designed to guarantee that refugees from Indo-China received the same civil rights as their Japanese counterparts. This law became effective in 1982 and affected the treatment of non-Japanese permanent residents significantly, both directly and indirectly.[57] In fact, in the fall of 1981, the Japanese Amateur Sports Association quickly altered its by-laws to allow permanent alien residents attending Japanese high schools to participate in the National Sports Festival.[58] Since then, Japan-born Koreans have been able to take part in all official athletic tournaments with the one condition; that the student must have attended Japanese high schools. Thus, institutionalized discrimination against Japan-born Koreans in Japanese high schools was ultimately removed in 1981. Nevertheless, discrimination on the basis of school affiliation still endured against Japan-born Koreans in ethnic schools for the next 13 years. Students of non-Japanese high schools did not receive the same rights or the same treatment as Japanese students and they continued to suffer total exclusion from interscholastic athletics up until 1994.

FIGURE 9.3
INEQUALITY OF ATHLETIC PARTICIPATION ON THE BASIS OF
SCHOOL AFFILIATION

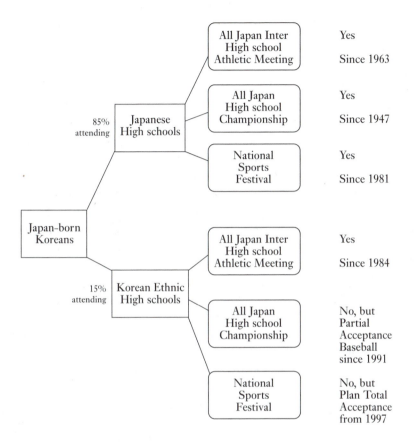

Students of non-Japanese high schools have been denied inclusion in Japanese sport associations since the Second World War. In March 1991, the Japanese High School Baseball Association decided to grant permits to non-Japanese high schools as well as non-accredited schools, allowing them to participate in official interscholastic tournaments, with the possibility of accepting them as formal members of the association in the future. This was the first major breakthrough towards obtaining equal athletic opportunity for Japan-born Koreans attending ethnic schools. Following this declaration, the Osaka Middle School Sport Association granted non-Japanese middle schools formal permission to participate in any official sports tournament.[59] There were mixed reactions among officials of sport organizations and associations, and these changes had a tremendous impact on public opinion. The mass media reaction was very positive and interpreted these changes as a gigantic step toward solving inequalities in the sports world.[60] Eight years later, in 1999, the Korean ethnic high school in Kyoto, the Kyoto Korean School, was finally permitted to become a formal member of the Japanese High School Baseball Association. Of the 12 Korean ethnic high schools, only the Kyoto Korean School applied for formal membership.[61] There were two reasons for this, a sharp decline in the numbers of Japan-born Koreans in ethnic schools and the fact that baseball was a somewhat minor sport (compared with soccer) at ethnic high schools. In fact, the number of students in the Kyoto Korean School totals only 32, 19 boys and 13 girls. But a number of Japan-born Koreans were delighted with this inclusion and donated money and baseball equipment to the high school.[62] The media reaction again was quite positive and explained this inclusion as a positive by-product of the 2002 Soccer World Cup match between Korea and Japan.

In November 1993, the Japanese High School Sports Association (JHSSA), the governing body of interscholastic athletics, decided to grant students of non-Japanese institutions and non-accredited schools permission to take part in the All Japan Inter High School Athletic Meeting, one of the three major athletic events for high school students in 1994.[63] This was the first major step for Japan-born Koreans from ethnic schools towards being accepted by the mainstream culture, although their membership status within the JHSSA was still withheld.[64] Their participation in other official tournaments, such as the National Sports Festival and the national high school championships in all sports were still denied until 1997 (see Figure 9.3). The membership status of Korean ethnic schools has become a controversial issue among sports organizations at national and prefecture levels.[65] The Japanese Volleyball Association made a positive decision to grant the formal inclusion of Korean ethnic schools from March 1995. But other sports organizations have not lifted the rule of membership exclusion against Korean ethnic schools. Thus, the membership status of Korean ethnic schools varies from one sports organization to another, and from national level to prefecture level.

Further major progress was the recent announcement that all high school students would be able to participate in the National Sports

Festival starting in 1997, regardless of citizenship and school affiliation. Foreign nationals graduated from Japanese secondary schools have been allowed to participate in the National Sports Festival since 1997. However, those who graduated from ethnic school and non-accredited schools have still been refused participation in that event. A third generation Japan-born Korean, Ms Sadako Eke, was able to take part in the National Sports Festival for the first time since she was a high-school student. At the age of 32, Ms Eke confessed her frustration at having been denied participation in that event after her graduation from high school.[66] It took nearly 13 years to remove this inequality based on citizenship for students of Korean ethnic schools, but the inequality based on school affiliation was perpetuated in the National Sports Festival. The other main interscholastic tournament, the National High School Championship of all sports, was eventually opened up to students of Korean ethnic schools since 1997. The most recent developments are the inclusion of Korean University in the Kanto (Tokyo metropolitan region) Intercollegiate Rugby Conference and the inclusion of permanent alien residents' soccer teams in the Japanese Soccer Association in 2001.[67] The Korean University was the only ethnic college for Japan-born Koreans in Japan. Even though the inclusion movement has been accelerated, the membership status of Korean ethnic high schools has not yet been finalized. In fact, although students of ethnic schools and non-accredited schools were allowed to participate in most official athletic championships since 1997, the JHSSA has still refused to grant formal membership to them. Another encouraging incident, and the slow but steady change was affected by people inside sports circles. If the membership status of Korean ethnic schools remains the same as now, being special members, this will lead to another inequality. Without a full-membership status, Korean ethnic schools will have no voting right, no right to become board members and therefore no way to obtain a power position in sports organizations. A significant way to stop these institutionalized inequalities would be to grant formal membership status in the JHSSA to Korean ethnic schools. This may happen very soon as the International Football Association (FIFA) has decided to allow Japan and Korea as co-host nations to stage the so-called Korea-Japan World Cup in the year 2002. Nevertheless, these institutionalized inequities directed at Japan-born Koreans did not become serious obstacles to collaboration.

Institutionalized discrimination against non-Japanese has been perpetuated beyond high-school athletics (see Figure 9.4). The crucial

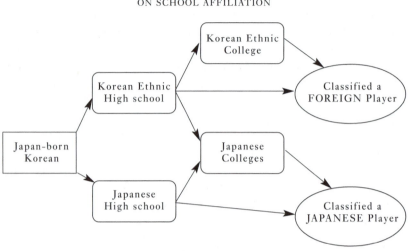

distinction is whether a non-Japanese athlete belongs to a regular Japanese high-school or college. As Figure 4 shows, permanent alien residents graduating from ethnic high schools and colleges are classified as foreign players, both in professional and amateur sport leagues.[68] These sports leagues have their own by-laws which limit the number of foreign players, making teams reluctant to recruit and develop non-Japanese high school graduates to fill the limited number of spaces allowed to foreign players. Japan-born permanent residents graduating from regular Japanese high schools or colleges are classified as special players, not foreign players. However, sports associations like the Japan Football Association (soccer) officially limit the registration in all leagues to only one special player per team.[69] Unless this institutionalized discrimination is abolished, students and graduates of ethnic high schools and ethnic colleges will continue to be restricted from sharing athletic experiences with their Japanese partners.

CONCLUSIONS

Upon reviewing the historical background and discriminatory practices against Japan-born Korean athletes, the following conclusions may be drawn:

1. Slow but significant progress has been made to overcome partial inequalities directed against permanent alien residents in the Japanese sport world. This progress has continued even after FIFA Korea-Japan World Cup 2002.

2. Membership policies on the basis of affiliated schools, whether Japanese schools or non-Japanese schools, have engendered severe inequalities between Japanese and non-Japanese as well as among non-Japanese high-school students. An important way to solve this institutionalized discrimination against Japan-born Korean athletes is in the hands of the Ministry of Education, Science, Sport and Culture who should deregulate this membership rule.

3. Basic civil rights of Japan-born Koreans have been violated for nearly half a century. The right to participate in the National Sports Festival has also been violated. Participation in interscholastic athletics seems to have been a matter of privilege rather than a right within the Japan High School Sports Association. The mentality of Japanese sports organizations must be changed.

4. Total exclusion policy is the main discriminatory practice against Japan-born Korean athletes, whereas the formal quota system is employed against foreign athletes in the Japanese sport scenes. The formal quota system will be continuously employed against foreign athletes in the Japanese sport scenes. However, the total exclusion policy against Japan-born Koreans will become minimized because of severe criticism from the Japanese and Korean mass media.

NOTES

1. D. Sneider, 'Korean Minority Battles for Basic Civil Rights, Cultural Identity', *Christian Science Monitor*, 21 Nov. 1985, 32.
2. K. Oguri, 'Resident Koreans Are Native Speakers Too', *Japan Quarterly* (Oct.-Dec. 1990), 424–31.
3. Management and Coordination Agency, *Statistics of Japan* (Tokyo: Government Printing Office, 1995), p.30.
4. A. Fukuoka, *Koreans in Japan* (in Japanese) (Tokyo: Chuko Shinsho, 1993); C. Kim, *Centennial History of Permanent Korean Residents in Japan* (in Japanese) (Tokyo: Sangokan Publishing, 1997).
5. J. Kan and D. Kim, *Koreans in Japan: Their History and Future Implications* (in Japanese) (Tokyo: Rodo Keizaisha, 1989).
6. Discrimination on occupation, see C. Cho and Y. Han, 'Reality and Issues regarding Teacher Employment of Foreign Nationals at Municipal Government Level', (in Japanese) *Urban Issues* [*Toshi Mondai*], 84, 11 (1993), 53–62; I. Kaminaga, 'Reality and Future Issues of Hiring Civil Servants on the Basis of Nationality at Municipal Government Level', (in Japanese) *Urban Issues* [*Toshi Mondai*], 84, 11 (1993), 29–40; M. Kwon, 'Significance of Attaining Civil Servant Positions for Resident Japan-born Koreans', (in Japanese *Urban Issues* [*Toshi Mondai*], 84, 11

(1993), 41–52. Discrimination on marriage see Fukuoka, *Koreans in Japan*; Kim, *Centennial History of Permanent Korean Residents in Japan*, pp.229–32. Discrimination on education is found in Kan and Kim, *Koreans in Japan*. Discrimination on citizenship see Y. Kim, *Naturalization of Koreans in Japan* (in Japanese) (Tokyo: Akashi Shoten, 1990); K. Nakai, *Permanent Alien Residents and Their Rights to become Public Servants* (in Japanese) (Tokyo: Tsuge Publishing Co., 1989); S. Tsurushima, 'Human Rights Issues and the Status of the Burakumin and Koreans in Japan', in G. De Vos (ed.), *Institutions for Change in Japanese Society* (Berkeley: Institute of East Asian Studies, University of California, 1984), pp.83–113.

7. The term 'Japan-born Koreans' is used in this study rather than Korean-Japanese. 'Japan-born Koreans' refers to descendants of Korean immigrants who decided to stay in Japan without Japanese citizenship as permanent alien residents after 1945. The ethnically oriented term 'Korean-Japanese' is inappropriate in Japan, since naturalized Koreans are not classified as an ethnic group by Japanese society. See A. Fukuoka, *Koreans in Japan*.

8. Sneider, 'Korean Minority Battles for Basic Civil Rights', 32.

9. T. Oka, 'Japan's Korean Minority', *Christian Science Monitor*, 8 Jan. 1993, p.18.

10. C. Lee and G. De Vos, *Koreans in Japan: Ethnic Conflict and Accommodation* (Berkeley: University of California Press, 1984); Sneider, 'Korean Minority Battles for Basic Civil Rights', p.32.

11. Sneider, 'Korean Minority Battles for Basic Civil Rights', 32; Fukuoka, *Koreans in Japan*.

12. Nakai, *Permanent Alien Residents*; P.G. Min, 'A Comparison of the Korean Minorities in China and Japan', *International Migration Review*, 12, 1 (1992), 4–21.

13. Kan and Kim, *Koreans in Japan*; Lee and De Vos, *Koreans in Japan*; Fukuoka, *Koreans in Japan*; Kim, *Naturalization of Koreans in Japan*.

14. Min, 'A Comparison of the Korean Minorities in China and Japan', 4–21.

15. Kan and Kim, *Koreans in Japan*.

16. Fukuoka, *Koreans in Japan*.

17. Ibid.

18. Min, 'A Comparison of the Korean Minorities in China and Japan', 4–21.

19. See more information in Min, 'A Comparison of the Korean Minorities in China and Japan', 4–21; Fukuoka, *Koreans in Japan*; Kan and Kim, *Koreans in Japan*.

20. Kan and Kim, *Koreans in Japan*; Nakai, *Permanent Alien Residents*; Sneider, 'Korean Minority battles for Basic Civil Rights', 32; Min, 'A Comparison of the Korean Minorities in China and Japan', 4–21.

21. Kim, *Naturalization of Koreans in Japan*.

22. Kan and Kim, *Koreans in Japan*; Nakai, *Permanent Alien Residents*; Sneider, 'Korean Minority battles for Basic Civil Rights', 32.

23. Fukuoka, *Koreans in Japan*; Kim, *Centennial History of Permanent Korean Residents in Japan*, p.237.

24. H. Kan, *Why Japan-born Koreans are Superior in Sports* (in Japanese) (Tokyo: KK Best Sellers, 2001), pp.162–4.

25. D. Sklar, 'Testing Japan's Anti-Korean laws', *Nation*, 25 June 1990, 886, 888–90.

26. Nakai, *Permanent Alien Residents*; Sneider, 'Korean Minority battles for Basic Civil Rights', 32.

27. Oka, 'Japan's Korean Minority', 18.

28. S. Chira, 'They Call Japan Home, but are Hardly at Home', *New York Times*, 1 Feb. 1988, A4.

29. Sklar, 'Testing Japan's Anti-Korean Laws', 886, 888–90.

30. Kim, *Centennial History of Permanent Korean Residents in Japan*, pp.229–30.

31. Y. Usanami, 'A Decrease of Hatred against Japan among Younger Korean Generations', (in Japanese) *Aera*, 24 Jan. 1994, .6–9.

32. Fukuoka, *Koreans in Japan*; Kim, *Centennial History of Permanent Korean Residents in Japan*, pp.229–30.

33. M.T. Allison, 'On the Ethnicity of Ethnic Minorities in Sport', *Quest*, 31, 1 (1979), 53.

34. H. Nogawa, 'A Study of a Japanese-American Basketball League and the Assimilation of its Members into the Mainstream of United States Society' (unpublished Ph.D. dissertation, Oregon State University, 1983).

35. R.D. Day, 'Ethnic Soccer Clubs in London, Canada: A Study in Assimilation', *International Review of Sport Sociology*, 16, 1 (1981), 37–50; A.G. LaFlamme, 'The Role of Sport in the

Development of Ethnicity: A Case Study', *Sport Sociology Bulletin*, 6, 1 (1977), 47–51; J. McKay, 'Sport and Ethnicity: Acculturation, Structural Assimilation, and Voluntary Association Involvement among Italian Immigrants in Metropolitan Toronto' (unpublished M.A. thesis, University of Waterloo, 1975); J.C. Pooley, 'Ethnic Soccer Clubs in Milwaukee: A Study in Assimilation' (unpublished M.A. thesis, University of Wisconsin, Madison, 1968).

36. K. Blanchard, 'Baseball and the Cultural-Change Process: The Rimrock Navajo Case', *Council of Anthropology and Educational Quarterly*, 5, 4 (1974), 8–13; H. Nogawa and S.J. Suttie, 'A Japanese-American Basketball League and the Assimilation of its Members into the Mainstream of United States Society', *International Review for Sociology of Sport*, 19, 3/4 (1984), 259–71; H. Nogawa and K. Ikeda, 'Ethnic Sport Leagues and Reverse Discrimination', *Bulletin of Tokyo Gakugei University Section*, 5, 39 (1987), 159–66; B.A. Tindall, 'The Psycho-Cultural Orientation of Anglo and Ute Boys in an Integrated High School' (unpublished Ph.D. dissertation, University of California at Berkeley, 1973).

37. J.C. Pooley, 'Ethnic Soccer Clubs in Milwaukee: A Study in Assimilation' (unpublished M.A. thesis, University of Wisconsin, Madison, 1968).

38. G. Redmond, 'Sport and Ethnic Groups in Canada', *CAHPER Sociology of Sport Monograph Series* (Calgary: The University of Calgary, 1979).

39. Day, 'Ethnic Soccer Clubs in London, Canada: A Study in Assimilation', 37–50; McKay, 'Sport and Ethnicity'.

40. Blanchard, 'Baseball and the Cultural-Change Process: The Rimrock Navajo Case', *Council of Anthropology and Educational Quarterly* 5, 4 (1974), 8–13.

41. Tindall, 'The Psycho-Cultural Orientation of Anglo- and Ute Boys in an Integrated High School'.

42. Nogawa and Suttie, 'A Japanese-American Basketball League', 259–71.

43. 'Membership Registration Rule', (in Japanese) *Japanese Football League Newsletter*, 104 (Feb. 1993), 33.

44. R. Whiting, *The Chrysanthemum and the Bat* (Tokyo: Saimaru Publishing, 1979); R. Whiting, *Jesse and Sale: A Story of Foreign Sumo Wrestlers* (translated to Japanese by Midori Matsui) (Tokyo: Chikuma Publishing, 1989).

45. L. Sharnoff, 'Foreigners Making Their Mark in Sumo', *Japan Quarterly* (April–June 1990), 169.

46. 'Konishiki says he Faces Racism', *Japan Times*, 22 April 1992, 4.

47. D.E. Sanger, 'American Sumo Star Denies Accusing the Japanese of Racism', *New York Times*, 24 April 1992, A11.

48. 'A "Bothersome" Thing', *Japan Times*, 24 April 1992, 3.

49. 'Sumo Group Issues Warning', *Japan Times*, 24 April 1992, 3.

50. T.R. Reid, 'Wrestling with Weighty Matters', *Washington Post*, 27 April 1992, A13.

51. T. Koike, 'The Dawning of a New Age of Sumo', *Japan Quarterly* (April–June 1993), 193–8.

52. E.O. Reischauer, *The Japanese* (Cambridge: Harvard University Press, 1980), pp. 336–7.

53. Ibid., pp.415–16.

54. Kan, *Why Japan-born Koreans are Superior in Sports*, pp.132–5.

55. Ibid., pp.71–2.

56. H. Tanaka, *Alien Residents in Japan* (in Japanese) (Tokyo: Iwanami Shinsho, 1991); Kan, *Why Japan-born Koreans are Superior in Sports*, p.109.

57. Tanaka, *Alien Residents in Japan*; Kan and Kim, *Koreans in Japan*.

58. Y. Kobayashi, *Korean Japanese Power* (in Japanese) (Tokyo: Soyosha, 1988), p. 229.

59. 'Major Breakthrough for Japan-born Korean High School Athletes', *Asahi Shimbun*, 18 (March 1991).

60. J. Takahashi, 'Even Soccer Players want to Participate in an Official Tournament', (in Japanese) *Aera*, 19 March 1991, 72.

61. 'Inclusion of Ethnic Schools and Non-Accredited Schools to National High School Baseball Association', (in Japanese) *Asahi Shimbun*, 16 May 1999.

62. 'Welcome Greetings from all over Japan to a Korean Ethnic School of Kyoto', (in Japanese) *Kyoto Shimbun*, 7 July 1999.

63. 'New Era of Inter-High School Athletic Championships (Part 1)', (in Japanese) *Yomiuri*, 29 July 1994, 13.

64. Ibid., 14.
65. Ibid.
66. 'Participating in the National Sports Festival after a 15–Year Absence', (in Japanese) *Kobe Shimbun*, 27 Oct. 1997.
67. 'Inclusion of Korean Ethnic University to the Kanto Intercollegiate Rugby League', (in Japanese) *Yomiuri Shimbun*, 6 March 2001; 'Inclusion of Permanent Alien Residents' Soccer Teams into the Japan Soccer League', (in Japanese) *Tokyo Shimbun*, 16 Jan. 2001.
68. 'Membership Registration Rules', (in Japanese) *Japanese Football League Newsletter*, 104, (Feb. 1993), 33.
69. Ibid.

10

Cricket and Calypso:
Cultural Representation and Social History
in the West Indies

DOUGLAS MIDGETT

'What do they know of cricket who only cricket know?' is the rhetorical question posed by C.L.R. James in the Preface to *Beyond a Boundary*, his comprehensive treatise on cricket, West Indian social history, English letters and class struggle. In the book he provides something of a response, explaining the importance of cricket in the West Indies for a people who have everything to do in constructing a national identity:

> English people ... have a conception of themselves bred from birth which ... constitutes a national tradition. Under-developed countries have to go back centuries to rebuild one. We, of the West Indies, have none at all, none that we know of.[1]

He goes on to emphasize how significant cricket, and especially successful competition at the international level, has been for the definition of a West Indian consciousness.

This study explores the role of cricket in West Indian society and looks at it as a metaphor for West Indian conceptualizations of who they are and how they position themselves in a globalized world.[2] It also examines another central Caribbean performance form, Trinidadian calypso. Calypso has long been an important medium of popular expression in Trinidad and the eastern Caribbean, carrying messages of love and hate, colonial and global politics, local scandal, and the fortunes of the West Indies cricket team. Three calypsos are analysed, written at different periods, which take cricket as their subject. In a broad sense, this study examines how culture and social history are reflected in these two modes of popular expression.

Any examination of West Indian culture and society in the second half of the twentieth century must consider the linked issues of colonialism and nationalism. Anthropological writing has recently shown more awareness of the links between cultural expression and colonialism. Dirks suggests that, apart from wealth, power and military conquest, colonial domination 'was also based on a complexly related variety of cultural technologies'.[3] Additionally, in a movement away from narrowly confined 'small society' studies, themes of globalization, nationalism and identity have become prominent anthropological concerns.[4] While these considerations are relevant to the present study, they are hardly novel approaches for the student of Caribbean social history. As Mintz has suggested, the islands of the Caribbean constitute the world's first 'modern' societies, formations linked through trade to the centres of Europe and structured as commodity producers by overseas European capital.[5] The construction of 'cultural technologies', emphasizing these links, contributes to our understanding of this process.

Cricket is a particularly compelling subject for such an examination, because it allows us to look at a public drama that has captured the West Indian imagination for decades. James has stated the case quite clearly: 'Cricket is first and foremost a dramatic spectacle'.[6] He explains and amplifies this assertion, arguing that among sporting events, only baseball can compare in this regard. The dramaturgical aspects of cricket have also been recognized by other observers.[7] As a dramatic event, the cricket match becomes a site for examining social and cultural phenomena, an exercise which students of Caribbean life and social history have recognized.[8]

The history of cricket in the British West Indies and its relationship to the region's colonial history is well documented.[9] Briefly, the elements are these. Brought to the Caribbean by British colonial functionaries and military personnel, the game was adopted by the sons of colonial officials and the gentry. It was promoted through clubs, the most prominent of which became the ruling bodies in the larger territories, much as the Marylebone Cricket Club (MCC) did in England.[10] The game became known to the masses partly through the employment of black West Indians as bowlers to their white countrymen in the practice nets. Various writers have noted how the introduction of the game was accompanied by a code and culture embodied in the phrase – 'it's not cricket' – which imposes the ethos of the colonial master through its internalization by the colonial subject. In its expression in the Caribbean colonies, however, cricket changed; it developed into a street and beach game, played by the emerging, post-emancipation proletariat, appropriated by them, and bearing the stamp of their own cultural expression.[11]

The development of cricket as a cultural expression contributing to West Indian self-definition is paralleled by its importance for West Indian nationalism. If there is anything approaching a sense of West Indian community as elaborated in Benedict Anderson's formulation – particularly an attachment to cultural representations – it must include the identification with the West Indies cricket team.[12] The assembling of the team to compete internationally at the highest level predates, by nearly two decades, the founding of the University of the West Indies and serious discussion of a federated nation-state. Moreover, where the state failed to survive and the University has often been subjected to the pull of national interests in the three islands where its campuses are located, the integrity of the cricket side has never seriously been threatened by insular particularism.

Calypso, in its Trinidadian birthplace, and in the other islands of the eastern Caribbean, has long been a medium for the expression of popular commentary on all manner of public events and figures.[13] Because cricket has come to occupy such an extraordinary place in the imagination of West Indians, it is entirely predictable that it should become the subject of numerous calypsos. A compilation of cricket-oriented calypsos includes mention of most of the great or near-great cricketers over the past half-century, and many songs discuss critical matches and other events that have impacted the cricket scene. Moreover cricket, as a site for contestation and political expression, is occasionally treated in calypso renditions as metaphor, where the elements of the game stand for other issues. Most prominent calypsonians, assured of the likely popularity of the subject, have penned a few cricket calypsos, and the three calypsonians examined here are members of the pantheon of performers, three of the greatest of their respective eras.[14]

The three periods which will be examined are 1950, the West Indies' first test match win in England; 1965, the occasion of their first win against Australia under a new captain, Gary Sobers; and 1987, an ignominious defeat in cricketing's World Cup, following a decade of world dominance. The social and political events leading up to the period in question are briefly sketched, the fortunes of the West Indies team prior to the cricket event are discussed, and the event and calypso rendition focusing on it are examined.

1950. VICTORY AT LORD'S – 'CRICKET, LOVELY CRICKET'

Society and Politics

In 1950, the British territories in the Caribbean were approaching the latter stages of their long colonial existence. Nascent impulses towards political sovereignty had begun as early as 1932 with a conference in Roseau, Dominica, attended by representatives from most of the islands of the eastern Caribbean, including Trinidad and Barbados. Representative Government Associations had formed in many territories to advance the cause of greater autonomy. In Roseau, conference delegates worked to formulate strategies to appeal to the British government to gain self-rule and establish some kind of political confederation. A telling feature of the conference was that the participants could not agree on a principle of universal adult suffrage as a basis for new representative arrangements, an impasse which reflected the elitist nature of some of them.

The islands had not long to wait, however, before matters were taken in hand by some of their humbler citizens. Beginning in 1935 in St Kitts, labour disturbances occurred in most of the British Caribbean, from Jamaica to British Guiana, the culmination of a lengthy period of deprivation created by the global capitalist depression that had begun in the Caribbean in the 1920s. In territory after territory, spontaneous eruptions signalled that the West Indian working-class was ready to assert itself, challenging a status quo which had prevailed for a post-emancipation century.

The turmoil of the 1930s prompted the British government to send to the Caribbean a Royal Commission headed by Lord Moyne to engage in a comprehensive study of social and economic life in the British West Indies. The Commission undertook its work in 1938–39 and published its report in 1945. The members of the Moyne Commission visited all the British Caribbean territories and British Guiana and their report stands as an encompassing portrait of the region around 1940.[15]

Among the recommendations of the Report are that the islands be set on a constitutional path ultimately leading to dominion status. It was recognized that the future of the Caribbean territories must be charted finally by their residents. Although this decision was reached shortly after the study was concluded, the Report was not published until after the Second World War for fear of destabilizing repercussions in the region. Another direction indicated in the Report, one that was instituted almost immediately, was the creation of new trade union legislation. Before this time, workers in most of the territories were effectively prohibited from engaging in trade unionism or other industrial action, and the 1930s upheavals and representation of workers by some individuals and organizations such as the Workers' League in St Kitts indicated to commission members that responsible trade unionism needed to be instituted. Indeed, one of the commission party, Sir Walter Citrine, Secretary of the British Trade Union Council, conducted meetings with prospective unionists in the islands during the Commission's travels. The result was that by 1940 all of the territories had new ordinances which allowed for the organization of unions and permitted industrial action without threat of prosecution.

In 1947 the Colonial Office instigated a 'Conference on the Closer Association of the British West Indian Colonies'. Held in Montego Bay, Jamaica, it represented the first step initiated by Great Britain toward political unification of the territories, with the ultimate goal of dominion status. Two years earlier, representatives of most of the territories, as well as delegates from the Dutch colony of Surinam, had convened in Barbados at a meeting of the Caribbean Labour Congress where the issue of federation was raised.[16] The Montego Bay conference was significant in that the delegates accepted the principle of federation and constituted a 'Standing Closer Association Committee' with a charge to undertake a number of initiatives, including the drafting of a federal constitution. Thus, by 1947, procedures were set in motion designed to bring to fruition a long-standing dream of West Indian nationhood.

With the institution of universal adult suffrage, first in Jamaica and Trinidad and Tobago, and by 1951, in the remaining territories, the electorate was vastly expanded, introducing an era of mass participation in politics. The islands had embarked on a trajectory that led in new directions with regard to their identity and political future.

Cricket

Although teams from the West Indies toured England as early as 1900, the West Indies cricket team came of age in 1928 with the first test series competition against an English side. The debut was inauspicious. The West Indies received an innings defeat in each of the three tests and only two batsmen scored as much as a half-century; but as Manley notes, this marked the first time that black competitors played in an international test match.[17]

In 1930, an English team embarked on a Caribbean tour and in four matches each side claimed a victory with two matches drawn. Thus – and thanks to some heavy rains in the fourth test – the West Indies played the visitors even. The series also saw the emergence of the great Jamaican batsman, George Headley, who laid waste to English bowling with three centuries and a match-saving double-century in the fourth test.

The following year, the West Indies team toured Australia with results similar to the first English tour, although they salvaged one win in the five-match series. Headley had some moments, but the pattern of batting collapses continued to indicate that the West Indies had some distance to go before competing on the level of the world's two premier sides.[18] Another trip to England in 1933 resulted in defeat with only a draw to interrupt British dominance. And then in March 1935 at Sabina Park, Kingston, Jamaica, the West Indies concluded a winning series against England with an innings victory. Headley made his highest test total, 270 not out, as the home side won two matches to one, with a draw.

In 1939 there was an inconclusive result as three of the four matches were drawn after England won the first. It was the last test series until after the Second World War, and for George Headley it was the end of the productive part of his career. He would return for a few post-war matches against England and India in 1948, but he was then nearing 40 and was no longer the fearsome sight at the wicket he had been. George Headley retired from test cricket having made ten centuries in fewer than 40 innings, the first of the West Indian cricketing heroes embraced throughout the Caribbean territories.

The post-war fortunes of the West Indies team improved. In 1948 they defeated England in the Caribbean, taking two tests after drawing the first three, and a trip to India resulted in a one-match victory in a series dominated by the West Indies. The scene was set, therefore, for their first post-war visit to England, seat of the empire and the birthplace of cricket.

The team that travelled to England resembled many of those that had preceded it. It was composed of a rather even mix of black and white West Indians, out of proportion to their numbers in the region. The captain, as he had always been, was white – the Barbadian, John Goddard, who had led the victorious sides in 1948. The team included three black Barbadians, all in their mid-20s, who had come to prominence during the 1940s, and were to be the mainstays of the team for the next decade. They were Frank Worrell, Everton Weekes and Clyde Walcott, forever to be known as the 'Three Ws'. The side also included a pair of unlikely bowling stars, Alf Valentine, from Jamaica, and Sonny Ramadhin, from Trinidad, who were just 20 when the series began. The unlikely aspect was that both were spin bowlers, a departure from the pattern in a region that throughout most of its cricket history has been known for intimidating pace bowling.

The Test Series

The series began inauspiciously for the West Indies when, at Old Trafford in Manchester, England won by 129 runs despite effective bowling by Valentine and Ramadhin. Thus, the West Indies came to Lord's, the home of the MCC and hallowed ground of cricket, still looking for their first test win in England. Goddard won the coin toss and the West Indies opened the batting. They scored 326 with Allen Rae, the opener, making 106 and Weekes and Worrell, half-centuries. In the England first innings the Valentine/Ramadhin duo gave an indication of things to come, taking nine of the ten English wickets for 114 runs. England were all out for 151 after their openers had put up 62 for the first wicket.

In the West Indies' second innings the star was Walcott who batted until the declaration, scoring 168 not out. Weekes had another half-century and the West Indies lead was 600 runs. In the English second innings the opener, Washbrook, hung on for 114, but his support evaporated and the side were all out for 274, defeated by 326 runs. Ram and Val again took nine wickets between them, bowling an incredible 231 overs for the match with 145 maidens. The great feat had been achieved; the West Indies had come to England and beat the Mother Country on its most sacred piece of home cricketing soil.

The next two tests had similar outcomes. The West Indies, having broken through at Lord's, won in Nottingham by ten wickets and at Kennington Oval by an innings and 56 runs. The West Indies batting shredded English bowling and the two spin bowlers continued to befuddle English batsmen. By the end of the series Valentine and Ramadhin had bowled more than 790 overs, taken 59 of the 80 English wickets and compiled superb averages of 20.42 and 23.31 runs per wicket. It was certainly great material for a calypso.

The Calypso

Lord Beginner had come to England in the late 1940s, a calypsonian of the first rank since the mid-1920s. His great cricket song, with the mundane original title, 'Victory Test Match Calypso', is typical of compositions that took the sport as subject.[19] It is a straightforward commentary on the Lord's match, locating the test, the captains, and the result in the first verse. King George VI's presence is noted – 'The king was there well attire, so they started with Rae and Stollmeyer' – and a summary of the match is given, extolling the exploits of Rae, Stollmeyer and Walcott, and featuring the heroic work of the 'little pals of mine, Ramadhin and Valentine'.[20]

The unusual fact of the dominance of two spinners in a West Indian side has already been noted. Ram and Val bowled extensively in the match, a pattern which would continue throughout the series and in subsequent ones – to the extent that Michael Manley criticizes the West Indian captains for overworking the pair, contributing to their somewhat early retirements. Without doubt, the 1950 test series was their finest hour. Never again were they able to effect the sustained bowling dominance exhibited there.

There was another appealing aspect to the performance of the two bowlers, one that did not escape Beginner. When he refers to his 'little pals' in each of the first three one-line choruses, Beginner emphasizes their diminutive aspect. Ramadhin was a small man; Valentine was taller, although very slim. It was not their size, though, but rather the nature of their success that was significant. Unlike the frightening domination of West Indian fast bowlers, spinners must win by cleverness and decep-tion. The ball does not intimidate by sheer pace; rather the batsman must be fooled, made to play shots that are beaten by the unexpected turning of the ball. The bowlers, then, are the cricketing equivalent of tricksters – Anansi figures in West Indian folklore – who defeat batsmen wielding willow clubs, not by overmatching them with power, but by out-manoeuvring them with spin.[21]

This imagery which Beginner captured and emphasized in his chorus seems entirely appropriate for its time. The colony side comes to the colonial centre and wins with guile and trickery. Notice also that, although the West Indian batting bludgeoned English bowling in the last three tests, not much is made of this except to mention Walcott's magnificent innings – 'Walcott licked him [the English bowler, Jenkins] around'. The song departs from the pattern of many in that it is not a boasting calypso. While celebrating the achievement of this victory the song does not rub it in. It is almost polite in expressing the joy of West Indians: 'Hats went into the air, people shout and jump without fear.'

1965. THE DEFEAT OF AUSTRALIA – 'SIR GARFIELD SOBERS'

Society and Politics

By 1965, the citizenry of the British West Indies were perhaps a sadder but wiser political constituency. The Federation, with its great promise of a West Indian nation that would take its place alongside other nations, had been born in 1958 and died within four short years. In the aftermath, the largest units of the Federation, Jamaica and Trinidad and Tobago, had become independent. Barbados and British Guiana – the latter had stayed out of the Federation – were about to embark on independent nationhood. The remaining eastern Caribbean territories had seen the failure of a subsequent attempt at unification – the 'Little Eight' – and their political future in 1965 was unclear.[22]

The late 1950s and early 1960s was also a time of demographic upheaval in the West Indies. Beginning in the post-Second World War years, West Indians began to travel to England in search of economic opportunities. Although this was hardly the first of such migrations out of the region, it soon became the largest. By 1962, when the British government effected the Commonwealth Immigrants Act, hundreds of thousands of colonial citizens from the Caribbean had made the trip to the Mother Country. The effects for the islands have been manifold and long-standing and those for England no less significant. One significant result was that English cricket fans witnessed the completely different approach of an audience to the game when the West Indies played in front of their compatriots at Lord's or the Oval.

Elsewhere in the Caribbean, events transpired which thrust the region into the spotlight of international superpower confrontation. The triumph of the Cuban Revolution in 1959 and the subsequent missile crisis in 1962 revealed to West Indians a world more fraught with danger than even that of the 1939–45 struggle. Cuba's experiment with socialism caught the imagination of some regional politicians, a compelling model in a region preparing to throw off colonial shackles.

Other anti-colonial struggles, the fall of the French in Indo-China and strivings in Africa, were newspaper copy in the West Indies, and the cold and hot wars in Europe and Korea continued to portray a divided world in which anti-colonial issues were often recast into the bipolar struggle that dominated. Over 30 newly independent nations emerged in Africa between 1956 and 1964, but the West Indies, fragmented and with uncertain direction, continued to be partly colonial.

Cricket

In the years between the West Indian victory at Lord's in 1950 and the arrival of the Australian team in the West Indies for a five-match test series in 1965, West Indian cricket had undergone some significant changes. Following the victorious series in England the impulse, long stifled, to name a black West Indian captain mounted. The teams that succeeded the 1950 side were led by Goddard, Jeff Stollmeyer, Denis Atkinson, Goddard, again and Gerry Alexander, all white West Indians from Barbados, Trinidad and Jamaica. The fortunes of the team fluctuated during this time. The promise of 1950 was not realized, for during the next decade, five test series were won and five lost with one drawn. More to the point, four of the losses came at the hands of the English and Australians and the wins were against teams of lesser calibre such as New Zealand, India and Pakistan.

By the time of a 1958–59 tour of India and Pakistan, the West Indian side had been largely reconstituted. Walcott and Weekes had retired and Worrell did not make the trip. A new set of stars had arrived, the most promising of them Gary Sobers and Conrad Hunte from Barbados and Rohan Kanhai of British Guiana. Facing a touring Pakistan side in Jamaica in early 1958, Sobers made a test record of 365 (not out) to announce his arrival as the greatest cricketer of his time. With the addition of the fast bowlers Wes Hall and Roy Gilchrist and the spinner, Lance Gibbs, West Indians had reason to believe that they would at last become the undisputed premier world side.

The Indian series seemed to confirm this. Three victories and two draws in which they dominated indicated a team that played to its potential. But a three-match series in Pakistan suggested otherwise. Batting collapses in the first two matches led to defeats, and the team was unsettled by the disciplinary dismissal of Roy Gilchrist, who was sent home before the series. The West Indies salvaged a measure of pride in the third test, with an innings victory when Kanhai scored 217, and they returned to the Caribbean to await an English tour in early 1960.

The series with England was unsatisfactory and troubling. The unsatisfactory part was in the result, a defeat for the West Indies resulting from a single English victory and four drawn matches. West Indian battling was at times careless and the bowling was rarely able to contain English batsmen. The troubling part came in Trinidad during the second test. Already convincingly beaten in the match, the West Indies were simply playing out their last remaining wickets when Ramadhin, a batsman of no stature, was declared out, lbw (leg before wicket). The crowd erupted and a bottle-throwing mêlée ensued, suspending play for the rest of the day. On the face of it the outburst is inexplicable, but in a perceptive analysis C.L.R. James has suggested the underlying causes for West Indian dissatisfaction with the way the West Indian team was selected and managed.[23]

Part of the cause of the Trinidad uprising he attributes to the treatment of the Gilchrist case, but more significantly, he cites the continuing failure of the West Indies Cricket Board of Control to appoint a black captain. With the West Indies preparing a tour of Australia in 1960–61, the campaign for a black captain grew stronger, led by James' strident editorial advocacy in the *Nation,* the newspaper of the People's National Movement, Trinidad's government party. James pushed for Frank Worrell's captaincy, and there was little doubt that he had earned it and that he was qualified. When Worrell was finally named to lead the side for the Australian tour, it marked a turning point in the way selection and composition of the team would be handled. It is important to note that this momentous decision was made during the brief existence of the Federation, the only time when West Indian political unity ever approached the regional unity behind their cricket team.

The team played well in Australia, although they once again lost when the home side won the last test by two wickets. After the Australian tour, the team hosted India in 1962 and delivered an inhospitable 5–0 defeat to the tourists. A tour of England followed in 1963, with the West Indies winning three matches to one, their first victory over England since 1950. The English tour also marked the end of Worrell's captaincy and his test career. Nearing 40, he had confirmed all that had been said or written about his abilities as a leader. He had taken a troubled but talented side, brought it to its potential and had done everything but defeat Australia. That task would fall to his successor, Gary Sobers.

The Test Series

Garfield (Gary) Sobers' assumption of the captaincy of the West Indies side marked another milestone. Although Frank Worrell had been the first black man to lead the side in test series, his selection to that honour was almost a foregone conclusion. He became a great leader and source of West Indian pride, but Worrell was anything but a plebeian hero. He was of middle-class origins, had attended elite schools and studied at Manchester University before being called to the captaincy. Maurice St. Pierre has compared Worrell to the West Indian 'middle-class hero' politicians of the 1950s who were acceptable as leaders precisely *because* they so much resembled their white/English predecessors.[24]

The contrast with Sobers is instructive. Gary Sobers was an ex-policeman whose cricketing skills had been noticed as a boy in Barbados. He became the greatest of cricketing all-rounders, and his fame stems primarily from his brilliance as a player. Sobers' reputation, which continues to shine, does not rest on his leadership, which pales next to Worrell's. In 1965, however, Gary Sobers became the captain of a great cricketing side. Worrell had succeeded in making a team out of a collection of highly skilled individual athletes. They would now face the best team in the world on the basis of recent performances, an Australian side that they had yet to beat.

The series was by no means decisive in its outcome. The West Indies took the first test, Hunte top-scoring with 81 in the second innings. Wes Hall and Charlie Griffith menaced Australian batsmen into a measure of submission and the West Indies won by 179 runs. The second test was a draw as both sides made big scores, Australia closing their first innings for 516. Hall and Griffith were not particularly effective. The West Indies won the third test in British Guiana by 212 runs when the visitors could not reach 200 runs in either of their innings. The damage was done by the spinner, Lance Gibbs, who took nine wickets for only 80 runs.

The West Indies began the fourth test needing only a draw to win the series and the recently-named Worrell trophy. They got the draw when, again, both sides scored prolifically, combining for over 1200 first innings runs. Having won the series the West Indian batsmen, aside from Hunte and Kanhai, took a holiday in the fifth test, and the Australians saved a little face with a ten-wicket victory. With the win under their new captain, the West Indies could claim to be the world's best in 1965.

The Calypso

Beckles and Walcott have noted how 'Sir Garfield Sobers' departs from the commentary narrative form of cricket calypsos.[25] The Mighty Sparrow had been a calypsonian of the top rank for nearly a decade by 1965; his 'Obeah Wedding', composed that year, remains one of the most popular of all time, its lyrics familiar to many not even born when it was written. Thus, as the commercial he made for Phosphorene used to say, 'If Sparrow say so, is so.' It was true of this most famous cricket calypso, for it was Sparrow who originally *knighted* Sobers. Eventually the Queen would get around to it, bestowing the title on him in 1975 for 'contributions to cricket'. But for West Indians the title became part of Gary Sobers' name after Sparrow's declaration.

Apart from his audacity in dubbing Sobers 'the greatest cricketer on Earth or Mars', Sparrow's song is a celebration of what it meant to West Indians to partake in that series. Federation may have been dead – he commented on that in another song – but in 1965 the West Indies stood at the top of the cricket world, without peer, and Sparrow proclaimed them 'the greatest team on Earth, who else but the West Indies?'. This is a boasting calypso, quite unlike the almost apologetic tone of Beginner's praise song. The chorus rubs it in – 'I say you lost and you know you lost' – and the Australian Captain, Bobbie Simpson, comes in for opprobrium for his whiny claim that Griffith 'chucked' – bowled with an illegal motion. The Australian side is denigrated: 'We prove that Australia was strong, but only on paper.' And finally, Sparrow delivers a gratuitous piece of advice: 'You lost, better luck next time.'

An interesting feature of 'Sir Garfield Sobers' is that it is not quite an accurate representation of the test series. The West Indian victory was hardly a comprehensive drubbing; Hall and Griffith, while sometimes effective, did not dominate as Ramadhin and Valentine had done in 1950, and Sobers himself did not have a good series with the bat (see Appendix 2). Nevertheless this is a great calypso, combining all of the musical and poetic attributes of a genius like Sparrow, rhyming 'Mars/Sobers,' 'helmet/Griffith,' and 'Jamaica/on paper.'

It is more than that, however. At a time when the idea of West Indian nationhood was at a low ebb, when the future of many of the islands was uncertain, the cricket victories of the mid-1960s team and the style they exhibited were rallying points for regional pride. West Indians used to have a word, 'flash', which defined a quality of male audacity and style that was universally recognized.[26] One has only to look at a photo of Kanhai batting, or of Hall in full flight preparing to bowl to understand the nature of 'flash'.

1987. THE END OF AN ERA? –
'RALLY ROUND THE WEST INDIES'

Society and Politics

In the years after 1965 the tendency to imprint the East-West struggle on every issue, especially in the developing world, continued to accelerate. The Vietnam War was not only experienced by West Indians through their news media, but many families had a son in combat there, caught up in the US Army after he had migrated north in search of a job or an education. This most imperialist of American wars was hard to read for West Indians, whose attitudes toward the US had tended to be positive, born of admiration for a place that had long been a destination for those seeking to better their lives.

In the 1970s, many West Indian states discovered just how vulnerable they were in a world where they had little control over forces that could impact on them profoundly. The OPEC-instigated petroleum crisis hit energy-poor countries with devastating suddenness. Small nations and near-nations attempting to modernize and extend services to their citizens found these innovations priced almost out of reach as a result of their increased dependence on petroleum products. Only Trinidad among the West Indies was not completely dependent on foreign energy sources.

Finally, from the late 1960s to 1983, the small islands of the eastern Caribbean went through successive constitutional changes that eventually brought political independence to Grenada, St Vincent and the Grenadines, St Lucia, Dominica, Antigua and Barbuda, and St Kitts-Nevis. These changes were accompanied by movements seeking to relieve these societies from some of the baggage of colonialism and the hegemonic shadow of the US. Radical impulses, influenced by the North American Black Power movement, intellectual Marxism, and varieties of populism, all created an atmosphere of flux and experimentation during this period of waning colonial influence and uncertain national emergence.

Grenada's revolution in March 1979 thrust that small island into the middle of global Cold War politics, and for the next few years interest in the strategic implications of West Indian allegiances ran high. The Grenadian revolutionary experiment, the antagonism it engendered from the US and the final implosion and US invasion signalled a new chapter in the history of the region's relationships with imperial powers. The reality of these small places as occasional pawns in the games of international politics and business was revealed with great clarity.

Cricket

In the years after the triumph over Australia by the Sobers-led team, West Indian cricketing fortunes went into one of those declines that seem periodically and inevitably to affect all great teams. They defeated England in the summer of 1966, confirming their claim to global superiority and beat an Indian side in 1966–67. In 1968, however, entertaining a touring English side, an event took place which haunted Sobers from that day.

After drawing the first three tests of a five-test series, the teams moved to Queen's Park Oval in Trinidad. The West Indies had not played especially well in the first three matches and were fortunate still to have a chance for victory in the series. In Trinidad, batting first, they put up their largest score of the series, 526 runs for seven wickets, and Sobers declared, sending the English in to bat. They answered with 404 and the West Indies had a lead of 122 as they came out to bat for the second time. With less than a day remaining in the match, another draw appeared almost certain. The West Indies batsmen scored 92 for the loss of just two wickets bringing the lead to 214 with only 165 minutes left to play. Sobers then confounded observers by declaring his innings closed, sending the English back to the crease with enough time to win. They proceeded to do just that; the match was lost, and when the fifth test was drawn, the West Indies had lost on their home turf.[27]

The 1968 series loss is important, for it marked a turning point in West Indies cricketing fortunes. They did not win another test series until 1973, when they took two matches in England in a short three-match series. The record during that interlude is depressing: Australia, loss; New Zealand, draw; England, loss; India, loss; New Zealand, draw; Australia, loss. Sobers retired as captain after the second New Zealand draw, his position taken by Kanhai for the next three test series. His record as captain after the victories against Australia, England and India shows just two test match wins, eight losses and 16 draws.

The mood in the West Indies must be assessed in light of the successes of the Worrell and early Sobers years. The team had emerged as the world's best, and had demonstrated what its supporters had imagined all along, that they were the world's best cricketers. The failures of the 1967–73 period, therefore, were cause for greater concern than their earlier ineptitude. It was in the midst of this regional despair that Clive Lloyd of Guyana assumed the captaincy.

Lloyd had first been named to a West Indian test side at the age of 22 for the Indian tour of 1966–67. He had proved to be a prolific scorer and an occasionally useful left-arm bowler. By 1974, he had played in ten tests and demonstrated to selectors the qualities which made him the West Indies' greatest captain, leading a team which had the longest sustained run of excellence of any side in modern cricket history. In his first series as captain of a side which toured India in 1974–75, he celebrated by scoring 636 runs with a 79.5 average and a top score of 242 not out.

Lloyd's success was not all about leadership. He was fortunate to be assuming the captaincy of a team which, despite recent failures, was poised for greatness. Already on the side were the exceptional batsmen, Roy Fredericks, Laurence Rowe and Alvin Kallicharran, and the team was joined on the Indian tour by Gordon Greenidge and the Antiguan, Vivian Richards, who would become the West Indies' greatest scorer in test cricket, eventually surpassing Sobers. Add to this Andy Roberts, the first of a set of overwhelming fast bowlers who made their appearance during Lloyd's reign, and a team came into being fully capable of the kind of sustained excellence to which West Indian fans became accustomed over the next decade.

This success did not happen at once; in his third series as captain Lloyd saw his team soundly beaten by Australia, 5–1. But over the next ten years, from 1976 to 1985, the West Indies, under his captaincy, won 13 series and lost one. In test matches in which he appeared as captain they won 32, lost 7, and drew 22. When Lloyd retired after a successful test series in Australia in 1984–85, he had established an enviable record, unlikely to be equalled soon.

During Lloyd's captaincy events occurred which changed the face of international cricket. In 1977, Kerry Packer, an Australian media owner, sought to televise test cricket in Australia. When the Australian Board turned down his bid in favour of the state-owned Australian Broadcasting Corporation, Packer set about signing up most of the world's best cricketers to engage in what was billed as a 'World Series of Cricket', to be played in Australia and covered by his television station. The pay he offered was astounding in a sport in which competitors were notoriously underpaid, and when the news of Packer's coup surfaced, the inner sanctums of cricket were sent reeling. The Packer scheme, if played out according to plan over the next few years, would have reduced international test cricket to a shambles.

As it turned out, Packer was really interested in seeing his media empire expand and through the cricket ploy, he was able to do this. For the cricketers, however, the furore occasioned by Packer's dealings was a godsend. As Manley points out: 'On the players' side … the chance to break with tradition and open up the possibility of new levels of remuneration were the central, directing thoughts operating in cricketers' minds.'[28] He emphasizes how important the Packer episode was in marketing cricket and creating the structure of corporate sponsorship which now operates in the sport. The Packer experiment and the rise of one-day matches also meant much more cricket for participants, and for the West Indies, the need for more rigorous training if they were to succeed. All of this contributed to the triumphs of the Lloyd years.

Clive Lloyd retired as captain of the West Indies side in 1985, to be succeeded by Viv Richards. Although there may have been questions about Richards's leadership potential and some lingering reluctance to name a captain from a 'small island' for the first time, there was little doubt that he had earned the position.[29] Already one of the most prolific scorers in cricket history, the 'Master Blaster' was acknowledged as the best batsman in the world. Surrounded by the fast bowling contingent assembled during the Lloyd years and joined by his countryman Richie Richardson, another in the line of superb run-producers, Richards' job looked secure.

It appeared at the outset that the Richards years would be an uninterrupted continuation of his predecessor's prosperity. In his first two matches as captain, the team defeated New Zealand and then wiped out England 5–0, a repeat of their victory in 1984. In the next two tests, however, on tour against Pakistan and New Zealand in 1986–87, the West Indies could manage only draws in three-match series. Pakistan, especially, was a poor series, with inept batting by both sides. In New Zealand, after winning the second test, a complete batting collapse in the first innings of the third test spelled defeat for the West Indies. Were there 'chinks in the armour', as David Rudder's calypso suggests? The next big competition would be the cricket World Cup, a competition the West Indies had dominated in its first years of existence.

The 1987 World Cup

In 1975, the first of a quadrennial competition took place in England. The cricket World Cup, roughly modelled on the FIFA football competition, was inaugurated as a tournament consisting of one-day matches pitting national teams in two groups, producing four semi-finalists and an eventual final match. Public interest was high. One-day matches had become very popular alternatives to the five-day test matches, and were a feature of every tour. The West Indies swept through the first World Cup without a loss and repeated their victory four years later, solidifying their claim to world superiority.

In 1983, they entered the tournament as heavy favourites, but lost to India in the final, the last World Cup side that Clive Lloyd led. In 1987, the competition was held for the first time outside England. India and Pakistan would host, with matches being played at venues split between the two countries.[30] The West Indies were placed in Group B, set to play two matches each against England, Sri Lanka and Pakistan.

What happened during the first three weeks of the competition confirmed the fears of West Indians who felt that their hold on cricketing superiority was slipping. In their first match, the side appeared to have England on the ropes, but the generosity of West Indian bowling allowed England to score 36 runs in the last three overs for the win. In the next match, Richards scored 181 for a World Cup record, as the side demolished Sri Lanka. Next, a very close match went to Pakistan by one wicket and the West Indies had completed the first set of three matches, winning only one. They began the second round by scraping past Sri Lanka and then took their third loss, again at the hands of the English. With only a match against Pakistan, the West Indians had to win and hope that somehow Sri Lanka, without a win in the competition, could beat England. They defeated Pakistan, but the victory was hollow when England won. Thus, the favourites to win the tournament had not even made the semi-finals.

The Calypso

David Rudder's calypso, rather than celebrating West Indian victories, like the two others examined here, exhorts West Indians to get behind their declining side in its moment of need. It is significant that this cricket calypso has had more staying power than any other. It has become the anthem of West Indian cricket, played and sung by fans whenever the team plays. It was recently – with some lyrical alterations – the official song of the team which competed in the 1999 World Cup.

Perhaps the popularity of 'Rally Round the West Indies', is at least in part attributable to its use of cricket as metaphor, addressing issues, current and historical, that extend well beyond a narrow focus on the game. It is a richly nuanced lyric, worthy of the reputation Rudder has built for writing pieces that transcend the commonplace and the mundane themes of many calypsos. In the first verse we are given a history lesson about renewal: 'When the Toussaints go, don't you know the Dessalines come', evoking the heroic aspects of the Haitian revolution. Again, in the second verse, there is an allusion to slavery as a lingering contribution to Caribbean 'confusion'. In the third verse we are treated to an ironic reference to the ethos of cricket – 'this is just not cricket' – linked to a literary reference to James' masterpiece, *Beyond a Boundary*, and the highlighting of the plight of mini-states in a globalized system that 'don't need islands no more'. Thus, Rudder completes the portrait of a region which, despite its brutal history and resource limitations, has produced the glories of West Indian cricket.

'Rally Round the West Indies' is a calypso for the 1980s and 1990s. It engages themes of colonialism, neo-colonialism, identity and impotence in an era of global dominance by a single superpower and unfettered capitalist exchange. It continues to speak to the situation of small island states whose economic viability can be threatened by forces like the recent US-instigated World Trade Organization challenge to the European Union's adherence to a policy of subsidies for Caribbean bananas. Its enduring relevance makes this calypso a thoroughly contemporary expression, reflecting the confusion and trepidation of those caught up in a world out of their control, but affirming their intention to make their place in that world: 'Little keys (islands) can open up mighty doors.'

CONCLUSION: CRICKET, CULTURE, IDENTITY

This study has focused on two areas of popular culture in the West Indies and examines the representation of sporting, regional and global themes. The way in which a people culturally represent themselves and their world can be revealed by the ways in which they play and organize their performances. Cricket and calypso are two of the most compelling performer–audience activities for West Indians, and consequently provide sites for the examination of contestation, resistance, artistic expression and representation of those who participate. When the intersection of these two forms is considered, an area of heightened meaning for residents of these places is encountered, a conjuncture which enables a deeper understanding of the forces, historical and contemporary, which shape their lives, and of the various ways in which they respond to and seek to influence those forces.

Various writers have agreed on the importance of a consideration of cricket and calypso for an understanding of West Indian society and culture, and this often involves some discussion of West Indian response to historic hegemonic domination. With respect to cricket, the works of Beckles and St. Pierre examine the game as cultural resistance, a vehicle for contesting the relationship of colonial and post-colonial subordination. Similar arguments have been made for calypso.[31]

Beckles asserts that West Indians have 'promote[d] cricket as an agent in the dismantlement of the imperial order and a symbol of liberation'.[32] As evidence, he refers to the views of English observers whose expressions in regard to Caribbean cricketers indicated that they saw something, if not revolutionary, at least profoundly disturbing to the colonial order. This is a telling point, for in order to locate a confrontational activity we must become aware of how it is evaluated by those to whom it is addressed, whether this evaluation reflects the intent behind its production or not. This requires greater attention to the historical moment within which the activity occurs, including the changing nature of hegemonic relations over time. Confrontational rhetoric by colonized politicians could be dismissed as innocuous in a colonial context where the power differential was unquestioned, but not in a post-colonial situation where the fiction of sovereign equality has prevailed.[33]

Another theme sounded here is that of nationalism. One must first notice that this is a confused issue, for there is not now, and there has only briefly been, a West Indian nation. Thus, when Burton writes of 'a need felt by West Indians, thirty years and more after formal independence, that their cricketers continue to humiliate the ex-colonizers', he must recognize that independence never came to a *West Indian* nation, that their 'collective selfhood' is completely bound up in their devotion to their cricket teams.[34] There is simply no other institutional symbol which compels this kind of affiliation and identity as 'West Indian' rather than 'Jamaican', 'Barbadian', etcetera. There is no flag, no territorial definition, no head of state.

In conclusion, I think we can locate the meaning of cricket by reminding ourselves of some facts of Caribbean history, distant and recent. The commonality of most Caribbean peoples – and this, of course, extends beyond the Commonwealth Caribbean – includes a history of economic servitude, whether slave or indenture. With respect to cricket, Beckles notes that its politics coincided with those of post-emancipation social formations, to maintain the subordination of black West Indians.[35] In a present world that apparently 'don't need islands no more' the past injuries of colonialism are quite possibly of less concern than the present steamroller of global capitalism. In the face of this latter kind of threat the cricket team may continue to be an entity to 'rally round'. If this seems a heavy load for a set of sportsmen to carry, it may be that the burden is even greater. For, I would contend that the pride and identification that West Indians hold for their cricket team is not dependent just on its competing on the world's pitch, but on its consistent success. It may well be the case that West Indian cricket depends upon some enduring sense of West Indian community, and that that identity in turn requires West Indian cricket, cricket played at the highest level of competitive excellence.

APPENDIX 1 - CALYPSOS

Lord Beginner (Egbert Moore) – 'Cricket, Lovely Cricket' (original title, 'Victory Test Match—Calypso') Melodisc 1133

Cricket, lovely cricket, at Lord's where I saw it
Cricket, lovely cricket, at Lord's where I saw it
Yardley tried his best, but Goddard won the test.
They gave the crowd plenty fun, second test and West Indies won.

(chorus) With those little pals of mine, Ramadhin and Valentine

The king was there well attire, so they started with Rae and Stollmeyer.
Stolly was hitting balls round the boundary but Wardle stopped him at
 20.
Rae had confidence so he put up a strong defence.
He saw the king was waiting to see, so he gave him a century.

With those little pals of mine, Ramadhin and Valentine

West Indies first innings total was 326 just as usual,
When Bedser bowled Christiani the whole thing collapse quite easily.
England then went on and made one hundred and 51.
West Indies then had 220 lead, Goddard said that is nice indeed.

With those little pals of mine, Ramadhin and Valentine

Yardley wasn't broken-hearted when the second innings started.
Jenkins was like a target, getting the first five into his basket.
But, Gomez broke him down, while Walcott licked him around.
He was not out for 168, leaving Yardley to contemplate.

The bowling was superfine, Ramadhin and Valentine.

West Indies was feeling homely, their audience had them happy.
When Washbrook's century had ended, West Indian voices all blended.
Hats went into the air, people shout and jump without fear.
So at Lord's was the scenery, it bound to go down in history

After all was said and done, second test and West Indies won.

b) The Mighty Sparrow (Slinger Francisco) – 'Sir Garfield Sobers' from 'The Calypso Genius', National NLP 8420

Who's the greatest cricketer on Earth, or Mars?
Anyone can tell you it's the great Sir Garfield Sobers.
This handsome Barbadian lad really knows his work.
Batting or bowling, he's the cricket king. No joke.
Three cheers for Captain Sobers!

Win or lose, the spectators are always please(d)
With the greatest team on Earth, who else but the West Indies?
Men like Butcher, Joe Solomon, Kanhai, and Davis
And Nurse, Rodrigues, Conrad Hunte and White, Gibbs
And the wicket keeper, Hendricks.

(chorus)Australia you loss, the West Indies is boss, the trophy
belong to us.
I say you lost and you know you lost.
Australia speak your mind, Australia don't grind,
You lost, better luck next time.

Them Australian jokers send down crash helmet,
To protect their batsmen from Hall and Charlie Griffith.
I feel so sorry for Simpson. He tried but in vain.
With Griffith and Hall, wickets start to fall, like rain.
Three cheers for Hall and Griffith!

Only when Australia making big riot.
When he facing Griffith, he so bloomin' quiet.
When only real fast bowling is to see him duckin'.
And the very guy, telling so much lie,
Telling the world that Griffith chuckin'.

   (chorus)

From the time the series start in Jamaica,
We prove that Australia was strong, but only on paper.
The fourth test in Barbados they full up the scoreboard.
But Rohan and Seymour, carry up we score, oh Lord.
Three cheers for Nurse and Kanhai!

Special praise to Conrad Hunte our opener.
Brian Davis, Solomon, Lance Gibbs, Hendricks and Basil Butcher,
All the boys fought gallantly under Sobers' captaincy.
So hip hip hip hooray! hip hip hip hooray!
For a glorious victory.

   (chorus) Australia you loss, the West Indies is boss, Worrell trophy
   belong to us.
   etc.

c) David Rudder – 'Rally Round the West Indies' from 'Haiti', Sire Records 9 25723–4

For ten long years we ruled the cricket world.
Now the rule seems coming to an end.
But down here just a chink in the armour
Is enough to lose a friend.
Some of the old generals have retired and gone,
And the runs don't come
As they did before.
But when the Toussaints go, don't you know the Dessalines come.
We've lost the battle

But we will win the war.
(chorus)Rally Rally round the West Indies
Now and forever.
Rally Rally round the West Indies

Never say never.
Pretty soon the runs are gonna flow again like water,
Bringing so much joy to each and every son and daughter.
Say we gonna rise again like a raging fire,
As the sun shines you know we gon' take it higher.
But we gotta

Rally Rally round the West Indies
Now and forever.
Rally Rally round the West Indies
Stoke up the fire.

Way down under a warrior falls.
Michael Holding falls in the heat of the battle.
'Michael shoulda left long time,' I heard an angry brother shout.
Caribbean man, that, that is the root of our trouble.
In these tiny theatres,
Of conflict and confusion,
Better known as the isles of the West Indies,
We already know who brought us here
And created this confusion.
So I am begging my people, please,

    (chorus)

Now they making restrictions and laws to spoil our beauty.
But in the end we shall prevail.
This is just not cricket, this thing goes beyond the boundary.
It's up to you and me to make sure they fail.
Soon we must take a side
Or be lost in the rubble,
In a divided world that don't need islands no more.
Are we doomed forever
To be at somebody's mercy?
Little keys can open up mighty doors.

    (chorus)

APPENDIX 2 – MATCHES

West Indies in England, 1950

1st Test: Manchester – Old Trafford, 8–12 June
England wins by 202 runs
England, 1st innings: 312; Evans 104, Bailey 82 n.o.
    Valentine 8–104, Ramadhin 2–90
West Indies, 1st innings: 215; Weekes 52
England, 2nd innings: 215; Edrich 71
    Valentine 3–100, Ramadhin 2–77
West Indies, 2nd innings: 183; Stollmeyer 78.

2nd Test: London – Lord's, 24–29 June
West Indies wins by 326 runs
West Indies, 1st innings: 326; Rae 106, Weekes 63, Worrell 52
England, 1st innings: 151; Washbrook 36, Hutton 35 (62 1st wicket
partnership)
    Valentine 4–48, Ramadhin 5–66
West Indies, 2nd innings: 425–6; Walcott 168 n.o., Gomez 70, Weekes
    63
England, 2nd innings: 274; Washbrook 114
    Valentine 3–79, Ramadhin 6–86
    Valentine bowled 75 maidens in the match, Ramadhin, 70.

3rd Test: Nottingham – Trent Bridge, 20–25 July
West Indies wins by 10 wickets
England, 1st innings: 223; Shackleton 42
    Valentine 2–43, Ramadhin 2–49
West Indies, 1st innings: 558; Worrell 261, Weekes 129 (283 partner
    ship)
England, 2nd innings: 436; Washbrook 102, Simpson 94
    Valentine 3–140, Ramadhin 5–135
West Indies, 2nd innings: 103–0; Rae and Stollmeyer opened and
finished match.

4th Test: London – Oval, 12–16 August
West Indies wins by an innings and 56 runs
West Indies, 1st innings: 503; Worrell 138, Rae, 109

England, 1st innings: 344; Hutton 202 n.o.
   Valentine 4–121, Ramadhin 2–49
   2nd innings: 103; Sheppard 29
   Valentine 6–39, Ramadhin 3–38

Australia in the West Indies, 1965

1st Test: Kingston, 3–8 March
West Indies wins by 179 runs
West Indies, 1st innings: 239; White 57 n.o., Hunte 41
Australia, 1st innings: 217; Hawke 45 n.o.
   Hall 5–60, Griffith 2–59
West Indies, 2nd innings: 373; Hunte 81, Solomon 76, Butcher 71
Australia, 2nd innings: 216; Booth 56
   Hall 4–45, Griffith 2–36

2nd Test: Port-of-Spain, 26 March–1 April
Draw
West Indies, 1st innings: 429; Butcher 117, Hunte 89, Sobers 69
Australia, 1st innings: 516; Cowper 143, Booth 106
   Hall 2–104, Griffith 3–81
West Indies, 2nd innings: 386; Davis 58, Hunte 51, Kanhai 51

3rd Test: Georgetown, 14–20 April
West Indies wins by 212 runs
West Indies, 1st innings: 355; Kanhai 89
Australia, 1st innings: 179; Cowper 41
   Hall 2–43, Griffith 1–40, Gibbs 3–51
West Indies, 2nd innings: 180; Sobers 42
Australia, 2nd innings: 144;
   Spin attack; Gibbs 6–29 (Hall and Griffith bowled only 8 of 58.2
   overs)

4th Test: Bridgetown, 5–11 May
Draw
Australia, 1st innings: 650; Lawrey 210, Simpson 201 (partnership
382), Cowper 102
   Hall 2–117, Griffith 0–131
West Indies, 1st innings: 573; Nurse 201, Kanhai 129, Hunte 75,

Griffith 54
Australia, 2nd innings: 175–4; O'Neill 74 n.o.
  Hall 1–31, Griffith 0–38
West Indies, 2nd innings: 242–5; Hunte 81

5th Test: Port-of-Spain, 14–17 May
Australia wins by 10 wickets
West Indies, 1st innings: 224; Davis 121
Australia, 1st innings: 294; Simpson 72, Cowper 69, Hall 0–46,
Griffith 6–46
West Indies, 2nd innings: 131; Hunte 60
Australia, 2nd innings: 63–0; Lawrey and Simpson openers

World Cup – 1987, Group B Matches

England vs. West Indies, 9 Oct.
England wins by 2 wickets
West Indies: 243 for 7 (50 overs); Richardson 53
England: 246 for 8 (49.3 overs); Lamb 67 n.o.; Hooper 3 for 42

Sri Lanka vs. West Indies, 13 Oct
West Indies wins by 191 runs
West Indies: 360 for 4 (50 overs); Haynes 105, Richards 181
Sri Lanka: 169 for 4 (50 overs); Ranatunga 52 n.o.; Hooper 2 for 39

Pakistan vs. West Indies, 16 Oct
Pakistan wins by 1 wicket
West Indies: 216 all out (49.3 overs); Simmons 50, Richards 51
Pakistan: 217 for 9 (50 overs); S. Yousuf 56; Walsh 4 for 40

Sri Lanka vs. West Indies, 21 Oct
West Indies wins by 25 runs
West Indies: 236 for 8 (50 overs); Simmons 89, Logie 65 n.o.
Sri Lanka: 211 for 8 (50 overs); Ranatunga 86 n.o.; Patterson 3 for 30

England vs. West Indies, 26 Oct
England wins by 34 runs
England: 269 for 5 (50 overs); Gooch 92; Patterson 3 for 56
West Indies: 235 all out (48.1 overs); Richardson 93, Richards 51

Pakistan vs. West Indies, 30 Oct

West Indies wins by 28 runs

West Indies: 258 for 7 (50 overs); Richardson 110, Richards 67

Pakistan: 230 for 9 (50 overs); R. Raja 70; Patterson 3 for 34

NOTES

1. C.L.R. James, *Beyond a Boundary* (Hutchinson, London: 1963), p.225.
2. When I use the terms 'West Indies' or 'West Indian', I am referring to the territories in the Caribbean region which are former colonies of Great Britain.
3. N.B. Dirks, 'Introduction: Colonialism and Culture', in N.B. Dirks (ed.), *Colonialism and Culture* (Ann Arbor: University of Michigan Press, 1992), p.3.
4. B. Anderson, *Imagined Communities* (London: Verso, 1991).
5. S.W. Mintz, 'Goodbye Columbus: Second Thoughts on the Caribbean Region at Mid-Millenneum', Walter Rodney Memorial Lecture, Centre for Caribbean Studies, University of Warwick, 1993.
6. James, *Beyond a Boundary*, p.192.
7. See R.D.E. Burton, 'Cricket, Carnival and Street Culture in the Caribbean', *British Journal of Sports History*, 2 (1985), 179–97; R.D.E. Burton, *Afro-Creole: Power, Opposition, and Play in the Caribbean* (Ithaca: Cornell University Press, 1997); F. Manning, 'Celebrating Cricket: The Symbolic Construction of Caribbean Politics', *American Ethnologist*, 8 (1981), 616–32; O. Patterson, 'The Ritual of Cricket', *Jamaica Journal*, 3 (1969), 22–5.
8. See H. Beckles, 'The Political Ideology of West Indies Cricket Culture', in H. Beckles and B. Stoddart (eds), *Liberation Cricket: West Indies Cricket Culture* (Manchester: Manchester University Press, 1995), pp.148–61; M. St. Pierre, 'West Indian Cricket Part 1: A Socio-Historical Appraisal', *Caribbean Quarterly*, 19, 2 (1973), 7–27; M. St. Pierre, 'West Indian Cricket as Cultural Resistance', in M.A. Malec (ed.), *The Social Roles of Sport in Caribbean Societies* (Amsterdam: Gordon and Breach, 1995), pp. 3–84; K. Yelvington, 'Cricket, Colonialism, and the Culture of Caribbean Politics', in Malec (ed.), *The Social Roles of Sport*, pp.13–51; James takes the point even further suggesting that: 'A great West Indies cricketer in his play should embody some essence of that crowded vagueness which passes for the history of the West Indies' (*Beyond a Boundary*, p.13). He illustrates this in his portrait of Rohan Kanhai, 'Kanhai: A Study in Confidence', *New World Quarterly*, 3, 1 (1966), 13–15.
9. Beckles and Stoddart (eds), *Liberation Cricket*; M. Manley, *A History of West Indian Cricket* (London: Andre Deutsch, 1994); M. St. Pierre, 'West Indian Cricket Part 2: An Aspect of Creolization', *Caribbean Quarterly*, 19, 3 (1973), 20–35. The work by Michael Manley is a wonderfully comprehensive history of West Indian cricket, told by one who was witness not only to hundreds of matches, but to the modern history of the region.
10. James, *Beyond a Boundary*, pp.55–71.
11. Burton's suggestion that the skill of West Indian batsmen has its precursors in stickfighting, a practice pretty much exclusive to Trinidad, is highly fanciful (*Afro-Creole*, p.177). A more useful account of early cricket days and the development of skills in Barbados is provided by Walcott, 'The Home of the Heroes', *New World Quarterly*, 3, 1/2 (1966–67), 51–3. See also B. Stoddart, 'Cricket, Social Formation and Cultural Continuity in Barbados: A Preliminary Ethnohistory', in Beckles and Stoddart (eds), *Liberation Cricket*, pp.61–88.
12. Anderson, *Imagined Communities*, pp.9–36.
13. See P. Hylton, 'The Politics of Caribbean Music', *The Black Scholar*, 7, 1 (1975), 23–9; F. Manning, 'Challenging Authority: Calypso and Politics in the Caribbean', in M.J. Aronoff (ed.), *The Frailty of Authority* (New Brunswick, NJ: Transaction Books, 1986), pp.167–79; G. Rohlehr, 'An Introduction to the History of the Calypso', in *The Social and Economic Impact of Carnival* (St Augustine, Trinidad: Institute of Social and Economic Research, University of the

West Indies, 1984), pp.42–120; K. Warner, *Kaiso! The Trinidad Calypso: A Study of the Calypso as Oral Literature* (Washington: Three Continents Press, 1982).

14. I am greatly indebted to Graham Johnstone, whose knowledge of calypsos, especially those of the Mighty Sparrow, enabled me to reproduce the lyrics of Beginner's and Sparrow's songs.
15. *West India Royal Commission Report*, Cmd. 6607 (London: HMSO, 1945).
16. Colonial Office, *Conference on the Closer Association of the British West Indian Colonies, Montego Bay, Jamaica, 11th–19th September, 1947* (London: HMSO, 1948); Caribbean Labour Congress, *Official Report of Conference Held at Barbados from 17th to 27th September 1945* (Bridgetown: Advocate Printers, 1945).
17. Manley, *A History of West Indian Cricket*, p.462. The selection of the 1928 side reflected the racism of the period in that the team left out some prominent black cricketers, a situation on which Lord Beginner commented in his calypso extolling the talents of Learie Constantine:

    > Learie Constantine
    > That old pal of mine
    > Though the selection was more than bad
    > There was one good man from Trinidad
    > Who was he? Learie Constantine
    > That old friend of mine.

    (R. Quevado, *Atilla's Kaiso: A Short History of Trinidad Calypso* St Augustine: University of the West Indies, Extra-Mural Department, 1983], pp. 98–9). Beginner obviously recycled the last line in 'Cricket, Lovely Cricket'.
18. Kamau Brathwaite has captured this tendency in his famous poem, 'Rites', with the concluding lines: 'when things goin' good, you cahn touch/we; but leh murder start/an' ol man, you cahn fine a man to hole up de side …', *Islands* (London: 1969), p.46.
19. The form of this calypso is of interest in that it employs the eight-line structure of an earlier oratorical (*sans humanité*) mode, but follows a later narrative progression typical of the calypsos which emerged in the 1940s. See Rohlehr, 'An Introduction', pp.84–97.
20. The line is not 'those *two* little pals of mine, …' as it has often been reproduced. I thank Graham Johnstone for this observation.
21. Anansi is the spider-man trickster figure found in many West Indian and West African (Akan) stories. Small and physically impotent, he succeeds against formidable opponents by his wits and audacity, see I. Treitler, 'Br'er Anansi: Individual and Cultural Expressions in Antigua, West Indies', in S. Thomas and W. Evans (eds), *Studies in Communication, Vol. 4: Communication and Culture: Language, Performance, Technology and Media* (Norwood, NJ: Ablex Publishing, 1990), pp.134–40; K. Yankah, 'The Akan Anansi Cycle: Continuities in the New World', in J. Peters, M.P. Mortimer and R.V. Linneman (eds), *Literature of Africa and the African Continuum* (Washington: Three Continents Press, 1989), pp.115–28.
22. J. Mordecai, *The West Indies: The Federal Negotiations* (Evanston: Northwestern University Press, 1968); W.A. Lewis, *The Agony of the Eight* (Bridgetown: Advocate Printing, 1964)
23. James, *Beyond a Boundary*, pp.217–43.
24. St. Pierre, 'West Indian Cricket Part 1', p.22.
25. 'Redemption Sounds', in *Liberation Cricket*, p.378.
26. 'Flash' seems to me to be the physical equivalent of the verbal and performance characteristics that Roger Abrahams describes for the West Indian 'man of words'. See *The Man of Words in the West Indies: Performance and the Emergence of Creole Culture* (Baltimore: Johns Hopkins University Press, 1983). It is also reminiscent of reputation-defining aspects of behaviour as elucidated by P. Wilson, 'Reputation and Respectability: A Suggestion for Caribbean Ethnology', *Man*, ns 4 (1969), 70–84.
27. Sobers suffered the criticism of numerous West Indian commentators and fans for years until, at a gathering assembled for the first Frank Worrell Memorial Lecture, he disclosed that the decision had been much more a collective one by the team and management than anyone had supposed (Manley, *A History of West Indian Cricket*, pp.362–3).
28. Manley, *A History of West Indian Cricket*, p.276.
29. These issues are summarized in R. Ford, 'Life after Lloyd', http://www-uk1.cricket.org/link_to_data998/MAY/FORD_ON_RICHARDS_11MAY1998. html. (originally published in *The Cricketer International*, Feb. 1986). See also, P. Adrien,

Cricket and Development (Basseterre, St Kitts: Adrien Enterprises Ltd, 1999), pp.104–7.

30. An extraordinary feature of sport is that these two countries, seemingly forever involved in hostilities, could agree to conduct a major competition like this. They did not play each other, however, being placed in different groups. Nonetheless, it could have happened in the semi-final or the final.

31. Beckles, 'The Political Ideology of West Indies Cricket Culture'; St. Pierre, 'West Indian Cricket as Cultural Resistance'; Manning, 'Challenging Authority: Calypso and Politics in the Caribbean'. In contrast to this view Burton has drawn a distinction between what he refers to as cultures of resistance and cultures of opposition, arguing that West Indian cricket constitutes an oppositional practice, as distinguished from one that is fundamentally revolutionary of West Indian Cricket Culture (*Afro-Creole Power, Opposition and Play in the Caribbean*, pp.177–86.)

32. Beckles, 'The Political Ideology of West Indian Cricket Culture', p.149.

33. D.K. Midgett, 'Anansi vs. The Crown: The Politician as Trickster in a Colonial Situation', unpublished manuscript.

34. Burton, *Afro-Creole Power, Opposition and Play in the Caribbean*, p.186.

35. Beckles, 'The Political Ideology of West Indian Cricket Culture', p.150.

From the Gridiron and the Boxing Ring to the Cinema Screen: The African-American Athlete in pre-1950 Cinema

CHARLENE REGESTER

When black boxer Jack Johnson defeated his white opponent Jim Jeffries on 4 July 1910, two new relationships were born, one between the black athlete and the cinema industry, and the other between blacks and whites.[1] The Johnson-Jeffries fight became a prototype in America for a racial division with a new component. It introduced a kind of black empowerment, rendered through physical prowess. Johnson's defeat of Jeffries became ingrained in the public consciousness, exacerbating white fear of blacks and of blackness.

Perhaps the media itself influenced Johnson, who is reported to have prolonged the agony of his opponent for the benefit of the movie cameras,[2] which depicted such a public humiliation of a white athlete that there was a demand to suppress the exhibition of the fight pictures.[3] But the excitement the pictures ignited was the very reason they attracted spectators. The black athlete, in all of his violence, aggressiveness, and threatening behaviour, became a spectacle to be exploited for financial purposes, and there were repeated calls for the black athlete to return to the screen. Beginning in the early 1900s, African-American athletes who excelled in football also began making the transition from the gridiron to the cinema screen. Their overwhelming size, physique, and aggressive behaviour rendered them threatening, while at the same time, positioned them as desirable.

This essay will discuss the early twentieth-century transformation of the black athlete on screen. Interest was concentrated mainly in the sports of football and boxing, with the earliest transformation occurring in the Johnson-Jeffries fight. Unfortunately, while black athletes in the early 1900s made a considerable contribution to the black screen image, there is a paucity of available early screen representations. Therefore, while this essay provides a rather extensive representation of some of the better-known athlete/cinema performers, it will be limited to an overview of others about whom less original material is available.

As the black athlete was transformed on screen, he represented both danger and desire – binary opposites, resulting in a problematized image. Attesting to the duplicitous image of the black athlete in the media, television and film scholar Herman Gray suggests that the athlete is regarded in the same manner as the jazz musician – both are

> policed as much as … celebrated and exoticized by white men and women alike. Policed as a social threat because he transgressed the social role assigned to him by the dominant culture, and celebrated as the 'modern primitive' because he embodied and expressed a masculinity that explicitly rejected the reigning codes of propriety and place.[4]

Film scholar Steve Neale contends that 'Narcissism and narcissistic identification both involve phantasies of power, omnipotence, mastery, and control'.[5] Expanding on his views, he adds that 'the narcissistic male image – the image of authority and omnipotence – can entail a concomitant masochism in the relations between the spectator and the image, and further that the male image can involve an eroticism.'[6] Yet,

> the erotic elements involved in the relations between the spectator and the male image have constantly to be repressed and disavowed. Were this not the case, mainstream cinema would have openly come to terms with the male homosexuality it so assiduously seeks either to denigrate or deny.[7]

Thus, when the black male athlete was utilized by the cinema industry because he signified masculinity, he would prove to be a viable commodity. Film scholar Leger Grindon argues that regardless of the athlete's ethnicity, because of his body he became a signifier of power, privilege and beauty.[8] Therefore, black athletes who, because of their race, were reduced to the body became viable commodities to be exploited by the cinema industry. Moreover, scholar Chris Holmlund affirms that the 'constant framing, muscles bulging, in doors, mirrors … leaves no doubt that these are men who are meant to be looked at, by men as much if not more than by women. Clearly they are spectacles as well as actors.'[9] According to Holmlund, blackness was 'already coded in terms of spectacle'.

Yvonne Tasker notes that in action films in which the black male athlete is likely to be centred, the 'action heroes and heroines are cinematically constructed almost exclusively through the physicality, and the display of the body forms a key part of the visual excess that is offered in the muscular action cinema'.[10] The black male athlete was a natural for the role of action hero. Tasker concludes that the black hero 'who refuses the stereotypes of hyper-(hetero)sexuality ... [is instead reduced to] the monstrous within the film's symbolic hierarchy. These two elements actually work together, with the latter in some senses making space for the former.'[11] Film scholar Todd Boyd affirms that 'the constant proliferation of African American male imagery in popular culture, which references the most threatening aspects of this legacy, [attest to] making this a very profitable venue for all involved'.[12]

Of the black athlete it has been suggested that: 'Whether he is hero, anti-hero, or hero's foil, he stands tall and muscular, exudes overstated masculinity and is usually more accustomed to trotting his rugged good looks around [the sports arena than parading across the cinema screen]'.[13] The African-American athlete as actor became an embodiment of sexuality, while at the same time he symbolically represented danger because of his imposing size, stature and blackness, but 'almost always [he was] either at the service or under the control of white institutional power and authority'.[14]

While the scholars quoted above have formulated critiques for contemporary representations of masculinity as embodied in the black male athlete, this essay focuses on an earlier period, emphasizing the fact that the black athlete in the past has been utilized in much the same manner and for many of the same reasons. It thus appears that the black male athlete has always been a viable commodity and a point of exploitation for the cinema industry. Black athletes who were a dominating force in sports such as boxing and football before the 1950s used their physical prowess as a marketable commodity and managed to join the ranks of motion picture stars, whether or not they were talented actors. Because of their bodies, these African-American athletes were transformed on the screen; white film-makers inscribed their own concepts of black masculinity in their construction of the black male screen image. African-American athletes recruited as actors because of their bodies became objects of both danger and desire.

FOOTBALL

Paul Robeson was the quintessential athlete who made the transition from the football field to the cinema screen. One report noted: '[Robeson] was built so beautifully. He moved so gracefully. He was simply a very attractive man ... [There was] something unavoidably present about him.'[15] Robeson, a graduate of Rutgers University, had been a football star, but it was his physical attributes that first attracted stage and screen directors. It is true that Robeson later exhibited considerable talent as an actor and singer, but initially it was his body which made him a commodity to be exploited on stage and screen. To reconstruct Robeson's screen career and to demonstrate how he personified the duplicitous representation of the black male athlete when transformed on screen, this analysis separates Robeson's films into two categories: firstly, those films that primarily reflect his on–screen subject position as revealed through the interiority of his characterizations, character roles defined by inward behaviour and psychological dilemmas (for example, *Body and Soul*, 1924, and *Emperor Jones*, 1933); and, secondly, films that primarily reflect his on–screen subject position as revealed through the exteriority of his characterizations, roles defined by outward behaviour (for example, *Sanders of the River*, 1934, and *Big Fella*, 1937). According to this paradigm, his roles allowed for either pyschological development and introspection or were devoid of psychological development and introspection and thus, were defined primarily by their outward behaviour.[16]

Even before white film-makers in Hollywood recruited Robeson for the screen, African-American film-maker Oscar Micheaux recognized Robeson's potential as a commodity for the cinema industry – mainly because of his sexual appeal. But Micheaux also recognized Robeson's talent as an actor. Micheaux, the first film-maker to transform Robeson on the screen, cast him in the film *Body and Soul* (1924) in dual roles – one as the Revd Jenkins, a jackleg (unscrupulous) preacher, and the other as the preacher's brother Sylvester, a virtuous role-model. When the film was released, it was promoted as having the potential to attract audiences who would witness the combination of brains and art being transformed in the all-black cast film.[17]

In both roles – the good and the bad – Robeson became an object of danger and of desire. Robeson, as Isiah Jenkins, is a convict who is being extradited from Tatesville, Georgia, to England to face a variety of

FIGURE 11.1
Paul Robeson

criminal charges. Prior to his extradition, he assumes a number of aliases, including the title of Reverend as he poses as a minister. As the Revd Jenkins he engages in sinister activities, vices such as gambling, drinking, deception, assault, rape and even murder. With this character-ization, Micheaux, superimposing his own personal angst on the film, strategically conveyed 'images of black manhood as threat and dread [that] not only work to disturb dominant white representations of black manhood, they also stand in a conflicted relationship with definitions of images of masculinity within blackness.'[18] This essay asserts that there is a marked difference between the way in which black and white film-makers transformed black males on screen in the early twentieth century. And an example of this position might be Micheaux's presentation of the black male in *Body and Soul*. Micheaux targets an evil in a specific segment of the black population, whereas white producers' films, by not singling out specific population segments, may leave the impression of evil as being endemic to the race.

In the role of Revd Jenkins, Robeson extorts money from one of his most faithful church members, Sister Martha Jane, who symbolizes the mirror image through which Jenkins examines his evil soul. But Martha Jane is unable to see Jenkins as the evil man that he is because she is so blinded by her religious fervor, and this man-of-the-cloth impostor takes full advantage, even victimizing her daughter Isabelle. Film scholar Charles Musser affirms that: 'In this case the film viewer comes to want the dreamer (Martha Jane) to stop dreaming, to see clearly and to face reality',[19] and indeed, at the end of the film the viewer discovers this was only a dream. In addition to identifying the evil-doer as belonging to a particular segment of the black population, Micheaux could not allow this jack-leg preacher to represent reality. The representation of evil even in a 'bogus' preacher would have invited disapproval in the African-American community, which would not tolerate anything less than prestige for a black minister.

Whether playing the role of the evil Reverend Jenkins or of the paragon of virtue, Sylvester, Robeson was used for his masculinity – a masculinity associated with sexuality. According to film scholar Richard Dyer, who suggests that in *Body and Soul* Robeson's body signified black masculinity: 'We are repeatedly encouraged by the film to feel that sex appeal.'[20] Dyer says that we even see the evil Isiah Jenkins (Robeson) as attractive, and that the only other attractive man in the film, Sylvester, the man Isabelle wishes to marry, is also played by Robeson. Dyer sees Robeson's power as located in his sex appeal.[21]

In white Hollywood, Robeson was cast in a film based on the play *The Emperor Jones*, by Eugene O'Neill. In *The Emperor Jones* (1933), Robeson plays Brutus Jones, an escaped convict who becomes the emperor of a small island and is so consumed with the abusive power he has appropriated that he ultimately contributes to his self-destruction. In the film, Robeson is often paraded on the screen shirtless, so that his muscles protrude from his chest, eliciting the gaze of spectators. In this use of the term, 'gaze' can be thought of both in the literal sense – of a steady, almost hypnotically fixed look, and in the theoretical sense – of a look that has malicious overtones of reducing the character being portrayed from a *person* to a *body*. Film scholar Ed Guerrero observes that: 'These topless scenes uphold the enduring practice of focusing black male representation on the body and sensuality, as opposed to the white antonyms [or signifiers] of intellect and reason.'[22] Robeson's large size and stature are accentuated throughout the film – a film that depicts a huge black man, a one time Pullman car porter, now an escapee from prison. Killing a white prison guard, he stages an escape, swimming magnificently from a steamship across the ocean to a small island. Upon reaching the island, the former convict, a signifier of black masculinity, presents himself as invincible. Exploiting, deceiving and intimidating the islanders with the assistance of a questionable white partner, Mr Smithers, he achieves total power and pronounces himself emperor.

The film can be seen as exploring the internal struggles of the character. Blackness and maleness combine to problematize him. To draw upon Freudian psychology, Brutus Jones launches a journey in search of a 'normal' phallus – his sexuality is distorted in that he is hypersexualized. In order for him to achieve some level of normalcy regarding his sexuality, he embarks on a journey to explore his inner self. But his quest is never resolved or fulfilled. At the end of his journey, Jones remains problematized and forever internally conflicted. He is depicted as both dangerous – a self-appointed 'emperor' who abuses his power, and yet desirable – a sexual beacon. The criticism Robeson received from the black press was loud and disapproving. One critic wrote:

> Paul Robeson, once a credit to, and an idol of the colored people, is today considered a disgraceful skunk in the hearts of many members of his race who saw the picture *Emperor Jones* ... Personally, I never thought that Paul was so hungry for either money or fame as to accept and perform such a low part, so disgraceful to his race.[23]

Robeson apparently took such criticism to heart and conceded that his portrayal was a disservice to blacks.[24]

Disillusioned with Hollywood, and in defiance of white film-makers whose racial and sexual attitudes determined how black males were portrayed on the screen, Robeson turned to the British cinema.[25] It was his hope that he might escape having his physique and race used to entice an audience. In 1934, Robeson was cast in *Sanders of the River* (also titled *Congo Raid*), a film that reflected his on-screen subject position through the exteriority (outward behaviour) of his character as Bosambo, leader of an African village, who is used as a pawn of British imperialism. Robeson is placed in a role that requires him to murder opposing African rulers who are deemed threatening to colonial rule. But once again, the white male film-makers lay claim to his black body; Bosambo (Robeson), adorned in loin cloths, is paraded bare-chested and bare-legged through much of the film. Attention to his genitalia is designed to elicit the gaze, literally and theoretically.

In *Sanders of the River*, Robeson as Bosambo epitomizes the black male athlete's personification of both danger and desire. In this particular film, his murder of other African rulers to support British colonialism shows him as a male of fearsome courage and brutal strength. Depicted as hypersexualized, Robeson is again reduced to the body, and constructed as an object of the gaze, except that in this case, the critics introduced a caveat, with the word 'culture'. For example, the *Literary Digest* thought that: 'Physically, Robeson is the picture of a native chief; but the plot gives him the advantage of a government schooling, his cultured sonorous voice destroys the illusion created by his physique.'[26] One critic charged: 'It is most unfortunate that Paul Robeson was trapped by producers into playing the shameless Uncle Tom role of Bosambo' – no doubt a name derived from the Sambo stereotype – and an indication of how Robeson allowed himself to be compromised on the screen.[27]

Seeking improved screen roles, Robeson appeared in *Big Fella* (1937) as a dock worker who became involved with an estranged youngster. According to biographer Martin Duberman, while the film 'constructed Robeson as an ordinary black man who functions well in a contemporary European setting', he could not escape being marginalized because of his race and sex.[28] Film-makers minimizing Robeson's importance because of his race forced him to sing in dialect, as he did in a song like 'Lazin'.[29] And as expected, his body – its size and height – were used to convey his character, accentuated by his name, Big Fella.[30]

In *Big Fella*, Joe (Robeson) is recruited by police authorities to assist in solving the alleged kidnapping of the son of an aristocratic white family. It is hoped that because of his association with the underworld, he can locate the kidnappers. However, Joe discovers that the white youngster has not been kidnapped, but has run away. Joe forms a strong bond with the runaway. Joe, initially constructed as an underworld character, takes on the responsibility for the youngster's return, persuading him that happiness can replace the boredom of his privileged life. The two present an interesting contrast: the young white male is an aristocrat, privileged, intelligent and articulate. Diametrically opposed is Joe, a wayward black male who is unprivileged, speaks in dialect, suggests low intelligence and has no work skills. The theme, simplistically stated, seems to be that the encoded differences in society can be decoded, thereby creating a better society for both blacks and whites.

But the more compelling interpretation is that white film-makers deliberately infused Joe with immature characteristics, the exact opposite of what Robeson symbolized in real life – size, power, presence, intelligence and social stature.

In *Big Fella*, when the man and the youngster are juxtaposed, there is a fusion, a complicated overlapping of codes and classes. In theoretical studies of this period in American history, the terms 'Other' and 'Otherness' mean more than simply different – they connote inferiority by race. In this case, because of the overlap and resulting fusing of these codes, the white child emerges empowered because he has gained from his exposure to blackness, and he reaches a state of completeness and happiness through the efforts of the black Other. Unfortunately, however, the black character does not fare as well; while blackness may be empowering for whites, whiteness is not so empowering for blacks. In *Big Fella*, the handsome, virile black athlete is constructed as an object both of danger and of desire – dangerous in that he is associated with the underworld, and desirable in the power he exerts over the runaway. As previously noted, Richard Dyer contends that Robeson's 'size evoked in the title of *Big Fella*', is a subtle attempt to conflate his title with his sexuality.[31]

No other black athlete/film star of the early twentieth century approached Robeson's success and standing. Little is known about some of his competitors, but a few were similarly revered in the cinema world and deserve mention. Striving to rival Robeson's popularity, Woody Strode, a UCLA football player and Los Angeles Rams player, was another athlete turned actor. According to writer Frank Manchel, Strode's body was 'so impressive [that] … the controversial German film-maker, Leni Riefenstahl, during a good will tour in California, used him as a model for a painting commissioned by Hitler for the 1936 Olympics in Berlin'.[32] Strode's athletic build and physique became such a marketable commodity in Hollywood that he was cast in several films during the 1940s, including *Sundown* (1941), *Star Spangled Rhythm* (1942) and *No Time For Love* (1943). In these films, Strode often paraded only partially clothed. It was not until 1959, when he was cast in *Pork Chop Hill*, that Strode was reported to have worn clothes for the first time on the screen.[33] Commenting on the demand created by Hollywood film-makers for his body, Strode once commented: 'What [Hollywood] needed were some African warriors, and because of my physical presence, I fit the role better than the actors.'[34]

Strode appeared in more than 50 films during his career, which lasted from 1941 to 1985. In his 'muscle roles', Strode signified black masculinity. Many of his early screen appearances remain inaccessible, and not until 1960 was there sufficient documentation of his more powerful visual representations. Among Strode's later films are *Sergeant Rutledge* (1960), in which he was cast as a sergeant accused of murdering a white female, and *Spartacus* (1960), where he plays a gladiator who elicits the gaze of white women and is selected by them to engage in battle with Spartacus, played by Kirk Douglas, a less capable gladiator, but one to whom Strode concedes defeat.[35]

In *Sergeant Rutledge*, Strode manages to supersede the commodification of the dangerous black male athlete, for he is depicted simultaneously as both desirable and yet of strong moral character. Accused of raping and murdering a white female – signifiers that make him both dangerous and desirous – he is defended by his commanding officer, a young, intelligent, skilful, white attorney. The accused middle-aged black male, Sergeant Rutledge, is exonerated, but his heroism is somewhat deflated by the way in which his white defender's strong oratory and intelligence overshadow his heroism. In contrast, during the trial proceedings, Rutledge's strength is reduced to his body, his physi-

FIGURE 11.2
Woody Strode

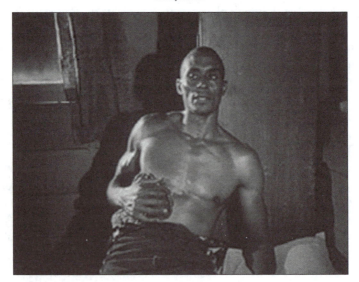

cality, as his resistance is eroded by the racial abuse he is forced to endure. Rutledge's reliance on his defender suggests that the strong white male has rescued the weak black male, who is disempowered and unable to defend himself. There are further complications before the real murderer emerges. But the essential point is that the black male must initially be held responsible for the rape and murder of the white female victim.

That Rutledge is represented as both dangerous and desirable is apparent in an early scene. Sergeant Rutledge arrives at an abandoned train depot in search of Apache Indians. He finds a lone white female (Mary Beecher) and the body of a white male train attendant. Rutledge removes the body and suggests that they seek refuge in the train station. Suffering from a gunshot wound, he removes his shirt and then he slowly releases his gun holster, which drops to the floor as his muscles glisten in the dimly lit room. Beecher attempts to attend to his wounds, but he makes it clear that he is unwilling to risk being discovered alone with a white female, especially since he has already been accused of murdering another white female. Strode is shown in the film as being desirable as his body becomes the object of the camera's gaze, but at the same time he is the embodiment of danger because he is fleeing from a murder accusation.

This film epitomizes the way in which the black male athlete was constructed when transformed on the screen. After the scene just described, the camera cuts back to the courtroom in one of a series of flashbacks. Here we see Mary Beecher testifying on the witness stand, maintaining Rutledge's innocence. But the prosecuting attorney interrogates her, asking whether she had been threatened, harmed or raped by Rutledge. The camera cuts to Rutledge – who is depicted as large, tall and muscular. In uniform, his commanding presence combines with his blackness to imply that he has the *potential* to be a murderer. Thus, the racial politics of the film are ignited and Rutledge's position as the black male who is both dangerous and desirous is established.

HISTORICAL OVERVIEW OF FOOTBALL PLAYERS IN PRE-1950 CINEMA

While Robeson and Strode were two former football players who had a major impact in the evolution of the black athlete/actor in this pre-1950 period, there were also others who contributed to the screen image of the

black male athlete. African-American football players who were transformed on the screen included Al (Iron Man) Duvall, Joe Lillard, and
Kenny Washington. Duvall, a former all-American football player at
UCLA, attracted the attention of film producers as early as 1935. He
was described as 'six feet two inches tall, weighs 210 pounds and ... of
perfect build'.[36] Duvall's screen career landed him a small role in *Jungle
Jim* (1937), in which he was cast as Kolu, appearing on screen according
to the usual formula as a scantily clad native.[37] The films *Murder on the
Mississippi* (1936) and *Gorgeous Hussy* (1936) allowed him only minor
appearances, the latter being a political drama about a Presidential candidate, with Duvall cast simply as a subservient black. Former NFL
football player, Joe Lillard, also made the transition from athlete to actor
in the Mae West films *Now I'm A Lady* (1935), *Cleopatra* (1934) and *Ali*
(1936), in which he was hired as a stock man in a jungle scene.[38]

Capitalizing on the trail already blazed, Kenny Washington, a former
running back for UCLA and later for the Los Angeles Rams, also
became an actor. He was cast in several films, including *Thousands Cheer*
(1940), an all-black cast film in which he plays a college athlete lured by
gangsters who coax him into fixing the outcome of a game or assume the
responsibility for a murder;[39] *Foxes of Harrow* (1947), in which he plays
a slave, Achille, who serves as the romantic lead to black actress Suzette
Harbin; *Rogues Regiment* (1948), in which he plays the role of a member
of the Foreign Legion; *Interference* (1949), in which he is cast as an
athlete;[40] and *Rope of Sand* (1949), where he was one of 'the authentic
muscle-men ... chosen for this brawling epic of the African desert'.[41]

These athletes paved the way for a later generation of football players
transformed on the screen. More recently, Jim Brown is well known as
an action hero whose roles (including *Dirty Dozen* – 1967, *100 Rifles* –
1968, *Riot* – 1968, *Ice Station Zebra* – 1968, *I'm Gonna Get You Sucka* –
1988) were always infused with the defiance he exhibited on the field;
Fred Williamson is frequently associated with the black male action
heroes who emerged on screen (in films such as *Black Caesar* – 1973,
Legend of Nigger Charley – 1972, *Three the Hard Way* – 1973). And of
course there is also O.J. Simpson, who was first cast in the television
mini-series *Roots* (with film appearances in *Klansman* – 1974 and
Towering Inferno – 1974), but has since become an icon in American
popular culture for the real life drama in which he was acquitted of the
murder of his former wife and her associate.[42] Similarly displaying their
athleticism on the screen, Bernie Casey has appeared in a large number

of films (including *Black Gunn* – 1972, *Cleopatra Jones* – 1973, *Cornbread, Earl and Me* – 1975, *I'm Gonna Get You Sucka* – 1988, *Another 48 Hours* – 1990, *Once Upon a Time When We Were Colored* – 1995) as has Carl Weathers (cast in *Rocky* – 1976, *Close Encounters of the Third Kind* – 1977, *Rocky II* – 1979, *Rocky III* – 1982, *Rocky IV* – 1985, *Predator* – 1987, and *Action Jackson* – 1988). More recently, Lawrence Taylor has played small screen roles (*Shaft* – 2000, *Any Given Sunday* – 1999), but has displayed the same level of invincibility on screen that he projected on the football field.

BOXING

Jack Johnson, the champion heavyweight boxer, was the first African-American athlete to be transformed on the screen, and several other black boxers were to follow in Johnson's footsteps. But according to film historian Thomas Cripps, Johnson's boxing appearances were among the most exciting black appearances on screen.[43] On 4 July 1910, Jack Johnson defeated his white opponent Jim Jeffries. Whites considered the outcome of this fight a public humiliation, and an attempt was made to halt the exhibition of these fight pictures.[44] Johnson's victory was significant racially, giving him a chance to vent his anger and assert his dominance in the ring. It is not difficult to understand how the African-American athlete's body, with its size and physical strength, became an object-of-the-gaze, first in the sporting arena (the boxing ring or the football field), and later, in cinema. In addition, however, to being attractive and eliciting the gaze in an innocent manner, the black male athlete's body soon took on other connotations as well. To the pleasure of beholding its physical beauty, an additional connotation was soon added – that of sexuality.

It was not long before film-makers recognized the marketability of exhibiting these men, and their success, to satiate the appetites of spectators. The industry realized that through objectification of the body an audience could be generated. Thus, critics began using the word 'gaze' in a pejorative sense. As well as Jack Johnson there were other examples of black athletes of similar physical strength and attractiveness. Joe Louis, heavyweight boxing champion, was often regarded as a parallel to Jack Johnson. Scholar Art Evans has suggested that the two were inextricably linked in the response they elicited from white America.[45] Louis was also attracted to the cinema, appearing in several films other

FIGURE 11.3
Joe Louis

than his fight films. Both men were rendered as objects of the gaze on screen.

Louis, referred to as the 'Brown Bomber', first appeared in a feature film in the all-black cast production of *The Spirit of Youth* (1938), a film based on Louis's own life. Although praised by the press, it was not a success because Louis, as an actor, lacked sex appeal. According to one critic, in this film 'Joe Louis tells the world in the same short, one-syllable word sentences that have characterized what few speeches he has made – that he is a great fighter, and a grand guy, but as a screen lover a dud, with a capital D'.[46] In *The Spirit of Youth*, in spite of Louis' lack of sex appeal, he is constructed as an object of the gaze. The black spectators identified with Louis, and it is not difficult to understand their excitement as he battered a train of white opponents on screen – opponents who were symbols of the white privilege and power that had been denied to blacks in the real world of the 1930s. His victories allowed black spectators to see Louis's power as their own. Bell hooks contends that 'as spectators, black men could repudiate the reproduction of racism in cinema and television, the negation of black presence, even as they could feel as though they were rebelling against white supremacy by daring to look, by engaging phallocentric politics of spectatorship'.[47] Therefore, black male spectators who were gazing at black athletes could identify with the symbolic power these athletes possessed to 'repudiate' or repel the racism projected onto them as black males.

The black press also praised *The Spirit of Youth* as a positive representation for black audiences because it was devoid of the racial epithets and caricatures that customarily characterized other all-black cast films.[48] However, there were those who thought that the film was a flop, and that without Louis in the leading role, it would have had no appeal.[49] Referring to Louis's limited acting ability, one review noted that 'Joe himself is no Robert Taylor on the screen, but the audience was kindly disposed to him despite his lack of histrionic ability. The most complimentary thing that can be said about his acting is that it was not affected. He was very real and natural.'[50] Speaking of his sex appeal, this reviewer thought that 'there is nothing about [Louis] except his physique to make feminine hearts flutter'.[51] A mainstream publication such as *Time* magazine, noting that at the end of *Spirit of Youth*, Louis spoke in dialect at a celebration after his victory in a championship fight, seemed to be pointing out how all-black cast films stereotyped blacks.[52] This may have been a subtle way of legitimizing Hollywood's continual misrepresentation of blacks. The film depicts a young boxer who is distracted by women, parties or bookies, who bet on his performances in the ring, on his rise to success. Joe Louis, in the role of Joe Thomas, has a side-kick played by Mantan Moreland. Thus the film resembles what is known as a 'buddy' film, one in which the 'buddy' is strategically positioned to enhance or elevate the protagonist's character. Although Louis is commodified to represent both danger and desire, because it is an all-black cast film, it escapes much of the racialization associated with mainstream cinema.

Louis's popular appeal allowed him an easy transition from all-black cast films to more mainstream pictures. In the role of a military officer in *This Is The Army* (1943), a war propaganda film strategically released during the height of the Second World War, it was politically correct for African Americans to appear as soldiers. Louis was recruited for the picture by the War Department primarily 'for story purposes and to head the production number, "What the Well Dressed Man in Harlem Will Wear"'.[53] As Louis's boxing career began to decline, his screen roles multiplied. When he was cast in *Joe Palooka Champ* (1946), Louis was described as 'still no terror as a thespian, [as he] punches a bag for the cameras'.[54] In 1947, he appeared in *The Fight Never Ends* (1947), an all-black cast film produced by William Alexander which focused on juvenile delinquency.[55] None of these films, however, allowed him to appear on screen in a leading role as he had in the *Spirit of Youth*.

Less known as a boxer than as an actor was welterweight fighter Canada Lee, formerly known as Lionel Canegarta. Lee appeared in several pictures such as *Keep Punching* (1939), an all-black cast film; *Lifeboat* (1944); *Body and Soul* (1947); *Roosevelt Story* (1949); and *Lost Boundaries* (1949). Lee's role in *Lifeboat* and *Body and Soul*, films regarded as significant for a black actor during this period, exemplify how he reconstructed black masculinity on the screen in mainstream cinema.

In Lee's transition to screen actor, his first role of importance was in *Lifeboat* (1947), directed by Alfred Hitchcock, and featuring white actress, Tallulah Bankhead. Canada Lee, in the role of Joe, once again demonstrates how the black male athlete is constructed as both dangerous and desirable. Here he is marginal in the film's plot, but still vital to the character development of the white stars with whom he interacts. The film focuses on ten survivors (white Americans, a black ship steward and one German POW) stranded at sea, crowded into a life boat after an ocean liner has been torpedoed. The survivors must reconcile their differences while they wait to be rescued. The film opens with Connie (played by Tallulah Bankhead) sitting in a lifeboat on a sea filled with debris described by *New Republic* film critic Manny Farber, as 'a crate of oranges, a copy of *The New Yorker*, some currency, a deck of cards slowly fanning out, and a Nazi's dead body'.[56] In the midst of this destruction, Connie is in full makeup, wearing a mink coat and a Cartier bracelet and equipped with her typewriter. Two other survivors are the Nazi prisoner and the former ship steward, who is black and referred to, disturbingly, as Charcoal-Joe, played by Canada Lee.[57]

In *Lifeboat*, the German prisoner is helpful, performing surgery on a wounded passenger, but the others soon realize that he has been hoarding water, and also that he has deceived them by using a hidden compass which he relies on to misdirect them in navigating the boat. Farber notes that

> the film's design is to show how this Nazi, by taking advantage of the others' humanity, sense of fair play, divided aims and general

FIGURE 11.4
Canada Lee

physical and mental debility, gains control of their boat, their minds and bodies and stabs them all in the back. This [is] intended [to] parallel the way the Nazis came into power.[58]

Yet, by the film's end, the lifeboat members collectively force the German prisoner off the boat. The film represents an interesting study of Otherness in that while relegating fellow passengers to the status of Otherness, each of the survivors is actually in the position of being an Other him/herself. Race is an Otherness *sine qua non*, as always, and yet in this case, the (white) prisoner is positioned as Other because he is a Nazi, and the (white) amputee is an Other because of his disability. Even the (white) women are Other because they are in the minority on this lifeboat. And of course, the black male is Other because of his race.

The film also introduces a subtext of some of the issues complicating democracy. The survivors on the lifeboat try to employ democratic principles, attempting to save even the German prisoner's life, but they have to abandon this ideal when it becomes obvious that he presents a threat to their very survival. When the time comes for them to vote, the black character, Joe, wonders whether or not he will be allowed to vote, a not so subtle reference to the fact that blacks were denied voting rights. But although Joe's role is small, he personifies the image of the black male athlete as dangerous and desirable. The physically domineering presence of Joe, a black male, suggested to white viewers that he was dangerous. While Joe is not overtly constructed as desirable in the usual cinematic hypersexual manner, his courage reveals him as an Other who is heroic.

In 1947, Lee was transformed as Ben Chaplin, a middle-weight champion, in *Body and Soul*, a role for which it was rumoured that he might be considered for an Academy Award.[59] His athletic build and his experience as a fighter allowed him to bring a realism to his role that few others could provide. As Ben, Lee is cast with white actor John Garfield playing the part of Charley Davis, a white champion who compromises his moral principles by participating in fights manipulated by people associated with the mob. Even though Charley knows that Ben is suffering from life threatening injuries (a blood clot received from a previous fight), he fights Ben purely for financial gain. When Ben loses the fight, in an attempt to ease his conscience, Charley hires Ben to work for him as a trainer. In this pairing of a white champion boxer who has sold his soul to the devil by participating in fixed fights and an injured black former champion boxer whose moral conscience remains intact, Ben becomes the mirror image through which Charley examines his 'dark' soul. It almost seems that the two represent both sides of the same self – Charley, the up-and-coming champion boxer who negotiates with crooked promoters to both lose and win fights for the sake of financial gains, sees himself in Ben, the former champion boxer who although in declining health, remains morally intact.

The film opens with Charley waking from a nightmare after Ben's death. It ends with Charley coming to terms with Ben's death as he decides to take the high moral ground and refuses to participate in another fixed fight. The decision is, of course, the end of his boxing career, but it represents the restoration of his moral conscience. Charley can now be seen as a moral person by his mother and his fiancée, the death of Ben has signalled the death of that part of Charley's self that is corrupt and immoral. Ben's death restores Charley to morality, and he becomes complete and whole. However, it is impossible to escape the film's racial politics. The portrayal of Ben as weak and almost emasculated by the injuries he has received suggests a disempowered and weak black male. More specifically, while Charley has a family, a fiancée and women, Ben is denied sexuality, he has no romantic partner or family and is seemingly disconnected from the black community. Ben is racially denigrated: when money is thrown on the floor, the black former boxing champ is asked to lower himself to retrieve it. Additionally, Ben personifies the black male athlete as an object of danger and desire, dangerous because he inflicts injuries and desirable because he creates popular appeal. Although Ben's appearances in the film are limited, his role is important and central to the development of the white protagonist, the white champion boxer Charley, who locates himself through his black Other. Lee's acting career was short-lived because of political views which resulted in his being barred from the industry, and he died an untimely death.[60]

Both Canada Lee and Joe Louis demonstrate how the black boxer was utilized on screen. Following in the paths of other boxers who had already made the transition to the screen in lesser parts, these two paved the way for a number of other boxers to be successfully transformed on screen.

HISTORICAL OVERVIEW OF BOXERS IN PRE-1950 CINEMA

With the exception of *Madison Square Garden* (1932), most of Jack Johnson's screen acting occurred in productions not made by Hollywood. Instead, pictures such as *For His Mother's Sake* (1921), a film that reportedly depicted the 'ex-champion in action. Close-ups of his great muscles and masculine body of steel, responding instantaneously to perfect control of mind over action', *As the World Rolls On* (1921); and *Black Thunderbolt* (1922) were all-black cast pictures.[61]

Heavyweights Joe Jeannette and John Lester Johnson captivated audiences on the screen as they had in the ring. Both Jeannette and Johnson appeared in *Square Joe* (1921); while Jeannette's screen career was limited, Johnson's was illustrious. He appeared in *Flames of Wrath* (1923), *The Criminal Code* (1930), *Lawyer's Secret* (1931), *Radio Patrol* (1932, a film that 'showed the public that a Colored man can play a dignified and manly role'),[62] *Hollywood Party* (1933), *Wild Man From Borneo* (1933, a picture that prompted one critic to exclaim that 'Johnson's histrionic interpretation of the wild man is destined to be the best comedy incentive seen here in years'),[63] *Bargain With Bullets* (1937, an all-black cast film), *Ali Baba Goes to Town* (1937), and *Tarzan's Revenge* (1938).

Making the transition from boxing to acting was 'Battling Siki' who was also known as Louis Phal of Senegal. Siki's acting career was short-lived due to his untimely death, yet he appeared in an unnamed film in

1923,[64] was interviewed for a role in an episode of *Tarzan of the Apes* (1926) and Cecil B. DeMille's *King of Kings* (1927)[65] – a film for which DeMille searched for the 'finest specimens of manhood' and for which Siki, along with boxer Sam Baker, was rejected because he was considered too large, in spite of the fact that they had been used by many studios because of their bodies.[66]

Sam Baker, also a former heavyweight champion, worked as an extra in films such as *Old Louisiana* (1927), *Grandmother Bernle Learns Her Letters* (1927), *Diamond Handcuffs* (1928) and *Jungle Mystery* (1933). In *The Mississippi Link* (1926), Baker landed the role of a gorilla – which required him to wear a costume that cost $1,000,[67] a role which film scholar James Snead contends blatantly links the idea of the black with that of the monster.[68] Baker's role in *Women of All Nations* (1931) attracted criticism from the black press; it was regarded as immoral because Baker and other 'colored giants' were cast as harem guards.[69]

Making his mark on the cinema world, Vic Alexander, described as a one-time leading black Western heavyweight, appeared in *Trader Horn* (1930).[70] He later landed a role in an unnamed MGM production,[71] and it was in *I Love You Wednesday* (1933) that he managed to negotiate a contract with First National and obtain employment with Fox Studios.[72] On the heels of Alexander, Henry Armstrong, who held three world championships – featherweight, lightweight and welterweight – turned from athlete to actor in the 1930s, first appearing in the Hollywood-produced picture *What Price Hollywood* (1932).[73] Armstrong's own life was depicted in an all-black cast film, *Keep Punching* (1939), a film that surprised 'several [reviewers who] actually admitted their bewilderment at Armstrong's fine dramatic ability. They knew he could fight, as he demonstrates on the screen, but they did not know he was a polished actor'.[74] These roles were followed by others in *The Pittsburgh Kid* (1941), *Joe Palooka Champ* (1946), and *A Song Is Born* (1948).

These athletes carved a niche for a later generation of boxers to be transformed on the screen, for example, Ken Norton (who appeared in *Mandingo* – 1975, *Drum* – 1986), Muhammad Ali (*The Greatest* – 1977, *Body and Soul* – 1981, *When We Were Kings* – 1996), Joe Frazier (*When We Were Kings* – 1996), Sugar Ray Robinson (*The Detective* – 1968, *Paper Lion* – 1968), George Foreman (*When We Were Kings* – 1996). Because of their popular appeal and because they were spectacles both in the ring and on the screen, these black athletes continued to be a viable commodity for the cinema industry.

CONCLUSION

Collectively, the black football players and boxers turned actors described here played an important role in America's cultural history. Objects of the gaze in the sporting arena, they became marketable commodities on screen. The film industry eagerly reached out to them to capitalize on their popular appeal and, whether or not they had acting ability, they were cast in more important roles than the humble 'extra' roles most blacks were limited to as they tried to infiltrate the cinema industry. Recognizing their talent and popular appeal, Hollywood capitalized on the black athlete's strength and bodily beauty, realizing that just as they had captivated spectators in the sporting arena, they would continue to do so on screen. But when black athletes were transformed on the screen they were transformed into objects of both danger and desire because of their blackness and their sexuality, becoming symbols of masculinity for both black and white spectators.

In sports, these black athletes had been 'contained' because they were provided with a forum within which to channel their aggressive behaviour, but once they were transformed on the screen, they became figments of Hollywood's imagination as objects of desire, danger and, ultimately, derision. Such perceptions have been superimposed, in a more general sense, onto black males in American society and can be felt outside the sports arena and the screen. While this article is limited to examples and discussion of the pre-1950 period, equally deserving of study is the transformation of the black male in the post-1950 period. In both cinema and in sport in America, black males have continued to be viewed as objects of desire and of danger. With the increased media exposure, the problem has indeed been exacerbated. A few, but only a few, have managed to maintain their good reputations without the inscribed violence or distorted sexualizing.

The unfortunate result is that the viewing of those black males whose appeal has been physical has translated into the viewing of *all* black males as objects of desire, danger and derision, thus perpetuating an untenable construction. This construction, based on a myth that can be traced to sports and the cinema in the early years of the twentieth century, must be acknowledged for historical purposes, but must be overcome for America's future cultural wellbeing. At the beginning of the twenty-first century, we should engage in a new reconstruction of the black male.

NOTES

1. T. Cripps, *Slow Fade to Black: The Negro in American Film, 1900–1942* (New York: Oxford University Press, [1977] 1993), p.18. Cripps contends that Johnson's boxing appearances were among the most exciting black appearances on screen.

2. L. Bennett, 'Great Moments in Black History No. VIII, Part 2: Jack Johnson and the Great White Hope', *Ebony*, 31 (Oct. 1976), 76.

3. D. Streible, 'A History of the Boxing Film, 1894–1915: Social Control and Social Reform in the Progressive Era', *Film History*, 3, 3 (1989), 248–9. According to Streible, Johnson's defeat of his white opponent and the public exhibition of this defeat had far-reaching implications for audiences, as whites were concerned that this fight would lead African Americans to try to exert their dominance in other aspects of American life.

4. H. Gray, 'Black Masculinity and Visual Culture', *Callaloo*, 18, 2, (1995), 401.

5. S. Neale, 'Prologue: Masculinity as Spectacle', in S. Cohan and I.R. Hark (eds), *Screening the Male* (New York: Routledge, 1993), p.11.

6. Ibid., p.13.

7. Ibid., p.19.

8. L. Grindon, 'Body and Soul: The Structure of Meaning in the Boxing Film Genre', *Cinema Journal*, 35, 4 (Summer 1996), 55, 60.

9. C. Holmlund, 'Masculinity as Multiple Masquerade', in Cohan and Hark (eds), *Screening the Male*, p.220.

10. Y. Tasker, *Spectacular Bodies: Gender, Genre and the Action Cinema* (New York: Routledge, 1993), p.35.

11. Ibid., p.53.

12. T. Boyd, 'The Day the Niggaz Took Over: Basketball, Commodity Culture, and Black Masculinity', in Aaron Baker and Todd Boyd (eds), *Out of Bounds: Sports, Media and the Politics of Identity*, (Bloomington: Indiana University Press, 1997), p.141.

13. 'Football Heroes Invade Hollywood', *Ebony*, 24, 12 (Oct. 1969), 196.

14. E. Guerrero, *Framing Blackness: The African American Image in Film* (Philadelphia: Temple University Press, 1993), p.79.

15. M. Duberman, *Paul Robeson: A Biography* (New York: Ballantine, 1989), p.55.

16. Many of these films could be placed in both categories, but for the purposes of discussion, they are assigned to one category or the other to lend credence to the idea that Robeson's screen characterizations were limited to one of these two types.

17. 'Film Tips: Paul Robeson and All-Colored Cast at Royal', *Afro-American*, Baltimore, 26 Dec. 1925, 4.

18. H. Gray, 'Black Masculinity and Visual Culture', *Callaloo*, 18, 2 (1995), 403.

19. C. Musser, 'To Redream the Dreams of White Playwrights: Reappropriation and Resistance in Oscar Micheaux's *Body and Soul*', *Yale Journal of Criticism*, 12, 2 (1999), 323.

20. R. Dyer, *Heavenly Bodies: Film Stars and Society* (New York: St Martin's Press, 1986), p.112.

21. Ibid., p.114. Robeson again represented black masculinity in *Borderline* (1930). (This was a film shot in Switzerland; it also featured Robeson's wife, Eslanda Goode Robeson.)

22. E. Guerrero, '*The Emperor Jones*', *Cineaste*, 21 (1995) 101.

23. 'Thirty-Three Insults Listed in Paul Robeson Film', *Afro-American*, Baltimore, 30 Sept. 1933, 1.

24. T. Cripps, 'Paul Robeson and Black Identity in American Movies', *Massachusetts Review*, 11, 3 (Summer 1970), 476–9.

25. Later, towards the end of Robeson's screen career, he was cast in *Tales of Manhattan* (1942). At this point he was so frustrated with the cinema industry and had become such a target of adverse criticism that he threatened to extricate himself from the industry. In fact, the *New York Amsterdam News* declared that Robeson's 'acceptance of [the *Tales of Manhattan*] role, that of a simple minded, docile sharecropper, leads one to wonder whether Robeson is abandoning his lot as a martyr, though he hasn't exactly starved, for an easier path' ('Paul Robeson, Ethel Waters Let Us Down', *New York Amsterdam News*, 15 Aug. 1942, p.15). Disturbed with his own portrayal, Robeson threatened that if New Yorkers picketed the film, he would join the picket lines ('Robeson Adds Protest to *Tales of Manhattan* Film', *Afro-American*, Baltimore, 5 Sept. 1942, p.10).

26. 'On the Current Screen', *Literary Digest*, 120, 1 (1935), 29.
27. 'An Actor Cannot Eat His Ideals, Is Robeson's Defense of His Playing the Uncle Tom Role in London Film', *Afro-American*, Baltimore, 12 Oct. 1935, Tuskegee Newsclipping File.
28. Duberman, *Paul Robeson: A Biography*, p.208.
29. 'London Writer Lauds Robeson', *Afro-American: A Biography*, Baltimore, 9 Oct. 1937, 1.
30. Dyer, *Heavenly Bodies*, p.134.
31. Ibid., p.134.
32. F. Manchel, 'The Man Who Made the Stars Shine Brighter: An Interview with Woody Strode', *Black Scholar*, 25, 2 (1995), 37–9.
33. W. Strode and S. Young, *Goal Dust: An Autobiography* (Lanham: Madison Books, 1990), 194.
34. Ibid., p.183.
35. Ina Rae Hark, in a discussion of masculinity and sexuality associated with gladiators in *Spartacus*, observes how Strode is objectified by the female characters in this film. Hark asserts that 'Helena insists on Draba [Woody Strode] because "I want the most beautiful. Give me the big, black one". Then she asks that the men be spared their "suffocating tunics' and clothed only in enough 'for modesty"', 'Animals or Romans: Looking at Masculinity in Spartacus', in Cohan and Stark (eds), *Screening the Male: Exploring Masculinities in Hollywood Cinema*, p.154.
36. L. Lautier, 'Feature Al Duvall, Grid Star in Big Film', *Chicago Defender*, 28 Nov. 1936, 11.
37. 'Football Star in Movie Featured Roles', *Pittsburgh Courier*, 5 Dec. 1936, 8 and Lautier, 'Feature Al Duvall', 11.
38. H. Levette, 'Coast Codgings', *Chicago Defender*, 23 Feb. 1935, 7, and 'Ralph Cooper, Joe Lillard Sign for Big Flicker *Ali*', *Chicago Defender*, 19 Sept. 1936, 11.
39. 'Kenny Washington in Regal's Film', *Chicago Defender*, 26 Oct. 1940, p.13.
40. 'Hollywood Turns to Gridiron As Talk of Robinson, Baseball, Cools', *Chicago Defender*, 7 Aug. 1948, 28.
41. 'Kenny Washington Given Big Role in Film *Rope of Sand*', *Chicago Defender*, 27 Aug. 1949, 27.
42. See Linda Williams' discussion of Simpson and the racial implications of his representation in contemporary popular culture in her book *Playing the Race Card: Melodrama of Black and White From Uncle Tom to O.J. Simpson* (Princeton: Princeton University Press, 2001), pp.252–95.
43. Cripps, *Slow Fade to Black*, p.18.
44. Streible, 'A History of the Boxing Film, 1894–1915', 248–9.
45. A. Evans, 'Joe Louis As a Key Functionary: White Reactions Toward a Black Champion', *Journal of Black Studies*, 16, 1 (Sept. 1985), 100–103.
46. G. Murphy, Jr., 'Kids'll Love Him, But the Ladies – Brown Bomber Proves Two-Fisted Fighter Who Finally Wins Girl', *Afro-American*, Baltimore, 8 Jan. 1938, 1.
47. bell hooks, *Black Looks: Race and Representation* (Boston: South End Press, 1992), p.118.
48. Murphy, 'Kids'll Love Him'.
49. L. Johnson, 'Light and Shadow: Spirit of Youth Could Have Been Saved', *Afro-American*, Baltimore, 6 April 1940, 13.
50. 'Joe Louis Picture Coming to Royal Theatre Beginning Midnight, Feb. 3', *Afro-American*, Baltimore, 29 Jan. 1938, 11.
51. Ibid.
52. 'Joe Thomas by Joe Louis', *Time*, 31 (31 Jan. 1938), 37.
53. '*This Is The Army* With Soldiers in Cast, at Met', *Chicago Defender*, 11 March 1944, 9.
54. 'Film Parade: *Joe Palooka, Champ*', *Ebony*, 1, 5 (1946), p.38.
55. 'Joe Louis' Picture Lacks Solid "Punch"', *Chicago Defender*, 13 March 1948, 29. The making of this film is described in R. Koszarski's, 'Joseph Lerner and the Post-War New York Film Renaissance', *Film History*, 7, 4 (1995), 457–9.
56. M. Farber, 'Among the Missing: Hitchcock', *New Republic* 110, 4 (1944), 116.
57. 'Author at Odds With 20th Over Filming of *Lifeboat*', *Afro-American*, Baltimore, 29 Jan. 1941, 8. Lee attempted to have this racially derogative name changed, but 'his protest … failed when he was informed that re-shooting of the scene would cost thousands of additional dollars'. He did succeed in having a number of lines in the film changed – lines he saw as demeaning to African Americans.
58. Farber, 'Among the Missing: Hitchcock', 116.

59. 'Lee Academy Award Talk in New Film', *Afro-American*, Baltimore, 11 Oct. 1947, 6.
60. G. Gill, 'Canada Lee: Black Actor in Non-Traditional Roles', *Journal of Popular Culture*, 25, 3 (1991), 85–9.
61. 'Jack Johnson Ex-Heavyweight Champion in *As the World Rolls On*', *Afro-American*, Baltimore, 24 Feb. 1922, 6. In checking films and athletes mentioned in this essay, H. Zucker and L. Babich, *Sports Films: A Complete Reference* (Jefferson: McFarland, 1987) proved to be a valuable resource.
62. 'Carl Laemmle Is For Race Actors', *Chicago Defender*, 17 Sept. 1932, 7.
63. L. Lamar, 'Johnson Ring Star in Movie', *Chicago Defender*, 28 Jan. 1933, 7.
64. 'Siki in the Movies', *Afro-American*, Baltimore, 23 Feb. 1923, 15.
65. 'Another Tarzan Picture Calls For Race Actors', *Pittsburgh Courier*, 9 Oct. 1926, 10, and 'Selects Race Athletes For New Biblical Production', *Pittsburgh Courier*, 21 Aug. 1926, 10.
66. 'Selects Race Athletes for New Biblical Production', 10.
67. 'Warner Raises Pay of Twenty-Nine', *Afro-American*, Baltimore, 16 Oct. 1926, 13.
68. J. Snead, C. McCabe and C. West (eds), *White Screens, Black Images: Hollywood from the Dark Side* (New York: Routledge, 1994), p.7.
69. H. Levette, 'Gossip of the Movie Lots', *Afro-American*, Baltimore, 3 Oct. 1931, .9, and *Afro-American*, Baltimore, 14 Nov. 1931, 9.
70. H. Levette, 'In Hollywood', *Afro-American*, Baltimore, 11 March 1933, 9.
71. 'This Ring Film Needs Old Jack', *Chicago Defender*, 30 Sept. 1933, 8.
72. 'Work for Movie Extras Jump', *Afro-American*, Baltimore, 10 June 1933, 9 and H. Levette, 'In Hollywood', *Afro-American*, Baltimore, 27 May 1933, 11.
73. 'Henry Armstrong', George P. Johnson Film Collection.
74. 'Henry Armstrong's Film to Regal Jan. 26', *Chicago Defender*, 20 Jan. 1940, 10.

Snowshoeing and Lacrosse: Canada's Nineteenth-Century 'National Games'

GILLIAN POULTER

It is firmly established in contemporary Canadian popular culture, and in the Canadian popular imagination, that ice hockey is the Canadian national game.[1] One need only watch an hour or two of television in Canada, or leaf through a few magazines and newspapers, to receive confirmation of this fact. Successful advertising campaigns regularly trade on the idea that to be Canadian is to love hockey. However, this was not always the case. In the latter part of the nineteenth century, when ice hockey was a brand-new sport, snowshoeing was already a distinctively Canadian winter activity and lacrosse was the national game.

In an 1863 article for *The British American Magazine*, W. George Beers, one of Canada's first sports journalists, distinguished between imported winter sports such as skating and curling, and home-grown sports such as snowshoeing, tobogganing, ice-boating, and moose and bear hunting, which he called 'our own Canadian originals'.[2] In subsequent articles he built on the distinction between imported (British) and indigenous (Canadian) sports, and reports about Canadian winter sports by Beers and other writers appeared in abundance in newspapers and magazines at home and abroad.[3] Sport historian D. Brown has argued that these articles helped to promote the idea that winter sports were 'peculiarly Canadian', and that through them the notion of Canadians as a hardy, northern race given to outdoor winter sports became familiar to American and British readers.[4] Through repetition, the linked themes of distinctive sports, wintery climate and northern geography became distinguishing characteristics of Canadian-ness which were reiterated in the political sphere by Canadian nationalists such as Robert Grant Haliburton and the members of Canada First.[5] Snowshoers certainly saw themselves as being engaged in a 'thoroughly national sport', and by 1886 American readers had evidently accepted this formula.[6] Under the heading 'Our Winter Sports. How they are Becoming Popular in Uncle

Sam's Domains – An American Picture of Our Leading Pastimes', a Montreal newspaper published an article by Newel B. Woolworth of the Saratoga Toboggan Club, who explained that:

> the hardships and physical exercise of early Canadian life gave little time or inclination to the people to use the snowshoe and toboggan for pleasure. It was not until some forty years ago that a leisure class having developed, the Anglo–Saxon element, with their Norseman blood and natural love of out of doors sports, seized upon the Indian snowshoe and toboggan wherewith to utilize for sport the deep snows of the long Canadian winter.[7]

The seasonal counterpart to snowshoeing and tobogganing was the indigenous summer sport of lacrosse. It too became associated with Canada and Canadians largely owing to the promotional work of Beers. As well as being a sports journalist, W. George Beers was a prominent Montreal dentist and avid sportsman. He was an active snowshoer and a long-time goal-keeper and captain of the Montreal Lacrosse Club team. Moreover he was a Canadian nationalist, dedicated to the promotion of the interests and prestige of Canada and Canadians, which he furthered through the medium of sport. In his mind, indigenous Canadian sports distinguished Canadians from the Americans and the British; he argued that Canadian prowess in vigorous outdoor sports like lacrosse demonstrated the superiority of Canadian health and fitness over their dissipated southern cousins. Furthermore, he claimed that indigenous sports did not suffer from the 'bar-room associations' and 'the beastly snobbishness' of imported British sports such as cricket and curling.[8] Beers was also the author of *Lacrosse: The National Game of Canada* (1869) a history and analysis of the game, and he wrote the rules of lacrosse adopted by the National Lacrosse Association, which he played a key role in forming in 1867. Beers led lacrosse teams on two exhibition tours of the British Isles and was so successful in his enthusiastic championing of lacrosse that it was popularly known as 'the National game' and erroneously believed to have been designated as such by an Act of Parliament shortly after Confederation.[9]

SPORT AND IDENTITY

The use of sport as a national signifier is not unique to Canada. In fact, as Eric Hobsbawm has argued, sport was 'one of the most significant of the new social practices of the late nineteenth century', and provided a means of national identification through the 'choice or invention of nationally specific sports'.[10] Cricket was firmly established as the British game, and the Turnen movement in Germany was strongly identified with nationalism and nationhood. Baseball was being called the American national game by the late 1850s, and between 1876 and 1926 a national sporting culture was established in the United States which was influential in the production of a modern national identity.[11] Brown has called lacrosse Canada's 'Imperial sport' since teams toured England, France, New Zealand and America, and played several times in front of members of royalty.[12]

It seems 'natural' that Canada should be linked with winter sports, given the climate and its importance as a national signifier, yet lacrosse is a summer sport, so why did Beers extol its virtues as 'the National game'? The answer to this question lies in the contemporary claim that: 'One of the characteristics of our best Canadian sports is that they are identified with the Indians.'[13] Before ice hockey, the sports identified as distinctively Canadian were indigenous; by taking over Native activities colonists put themselves in the place of the indigene, thereby taking on the identity of native-Canadians. Thus, identity was created not just through association with climate and geography, and created not just on an intellectual level by politicians, journalists or 'organic' nationalists, but was acted-out by ordinary members of the middle classes. These immigrant and Canadian-born professionals, merchants and small businessmen adopted and adapted Native activities and clothing, and performed their new identity on the streets and playing fields of the city. Snowshoeing across country provided an indigenizing experience with the landscape and thereby legitimized their claim to be native-Canadians, while performing these Native activities allowed the colonists to link themselves back into the historical and mythological origins of the continent.[14]

The promotion of indigenous sports as a national signifier illustrates the process by which identity could be negotiated in white-settler colonies such as Canada, Australia, New Zealand and South Africa. Colonists of these imperial outposts were faced with the problem of constructing for themselves a distinctive identity which, on the one hand, would retain the essential markers of civilized behaviour, and yet, on the other, distinguish them enough from their home land to provide a basis for their claim to new nationhood. There were a number of sports which instilled 'manly' Victorian values (notably, of course, cricket) but it was the indigenous sports – snowshoeing and lacrosse in particular – which demonstrated Canadian distinctiveness, and it was these which were displayed in civic celebrations, royal visits, parades, winter carnivals and on international tours. Explaining why snowshoeing was a distinctively Canadian activity, and why lacrosse became known as the Canadian national game, illustrates the ways in which a putative national identity was constructed and negotiated in Canada in the Victorian era, long before the harrowing experience of war in Europe which is generally considered so seminal to the creation of Canadian identity. Also demonstrated is that national identity is not purely a political construct or a mere reflection of political ideology, but is also actively produced in the cultural sphere.[15]

Identity formation is a multi-phased process in which the individual is both actor and spectator. Identity itself is always multiple because the identities of, for example, class, race and gender, are not discrete entities – one does not precede the other, rather, they are affected by and dependent upon each other. My interest in this essay is to foreground national identity, but much can also be said about the other dimensions of this putative nineteenth-century Canadian identity which was overwhelmingly masculine, anglophone and middle-class.[16] The process of national identity formation involves certain behaviours or attributes becoming identified as Canadian through being performed by individuals and acclaimed as such by spectators. Others emulate these performances and modify them; members of the audience enact the performance themselves in order to take on the identity. These performances are meaningful for the audience and for the actors, who feel internally what it is to be 'Canadian' through embodying that identity, as for instance on the sports field or race track. When the individual's performance is made available as a public performance, the identity is further confirmed through the recognition it receives from the audience. In fact, the audience authorizes and constrains the performance because the limits of what is acceptable behaviour are established by the audience's reaction.[17] Thus the construction of identity is a dialectical process which oscillates between actor and audience, embodiment and display.

Although the nature of identity might be posited on a political, ideological or intellectual level, it does not *become* an identity until it is realized through cultural practices such as sport, which in turn construct identity. Therefore, the *performative* aspect of sport, and the experience of both performer *and* audience, should be considered when attempting to understand how meaning is represented and received, even though they have often not been recognized in the numerous claims made for the role of sport in society. Play, games and sports have social importance beyond the epiphenomenal status commonly ascribed for them. A cultural approach takes seriously the significance of performance and the idea that sports produce meaning; sport and games are 'meaningful dramatizations of reality' in which the values of the community are represented and contested, and in which people are active agents in the making of their own identity.[18]

SNOWSHOEING

In taking up snowshoeing, Montrealers were engaging in a Native activity which dated back further than the recorded history of the continent and had strong links to the French Regime as well as to the history of the British in North America. Early French explorers who arrived in the New World were at first startled by the strange 'gutted shoes' worn by Native peoples, but quickly realized what an efficient method of transportation they had devised. During the French Regime, the military, French-Canadian *habitant* farmers, fur trade *voyageurs*, and the independent French traders known as the *coureurs de bois* all used snowshoes as a matter of course.[19] Thus, when British merchants and settlers arrived after the Conquest, snowshoes to their eyes were as much an attribute of French-Canadian culture as they were of Native peoples, and they considered both groups as native.[20] By learning snowshoeing and other native skills, the British merchants, clerks and factors connected with the fur trade – the Nor'Westers – were able to live in the *pays d'en haut* during the winter season, and could claim to be 'North Men', a new type of native-Canadian.

The men who formed the Montreal Snow Shoe Club (MSSC) in 1843 were of the generation of the sons and grandsons of the original Nor'Westers, and some, like Col. Ermatinger, the Club's first President, had worked in the North West themselves.[21] But by that time the era of the fur traders was dying and their merchant successors had become 'river barons' who led a far less active and adventuresome life. At this time too, the valley of the St Lawrence was becoming increasingly settled, with a network of roads making the cart or sleigh a popular and viable means of transport. Snowshoes, the indispensable winter tool of the Nor'Westers, were already becoming an anachronism in the developing urban areas, and were no longer a necessity but a divertissement.[22]

During the next two decades, ten or more snowshoe clubs were formed, although several, like the Beaver, Aurora and Dominion clubs, had a fleeting existence of only a few seasons. Enthusiasm for the sport increased and several more clubs were formed in the 1870s; by the 1880s snowshoeing was at the peak of its popularity in Montreal, Quebec City, Ottawa, Toronto, Winnipeg and the Maritime provinces. In the mid-1880s there were approximately 25 clubs in Montreal, and the MSSC alone had 1,100 active members, who were predominantly drawn from the Anglophone professional and commercial middle-classes.[23] Beers claimed that the snowshoe clubs attracted many of 'the leading spirits of the day', including men from 'our legislative halls, counting houses, banks, bench and bar' – a claim which is born out in the club membership lists.[24] For a variety of reasons, few Francophones joined the clubs, and women and the working-classes were excluded.[25]

The large number of clubs in Montreal meant that every evening of the week one or more groups would muster for a tramp over Mount Royal, and several clubs would gather on Saturday afternoons for longer and more challenging excursions to an inn or hotel in one of the rural communities outside the city. Since the clubs adopted similar uniforms, this regular routine made snowshoers a common sight on the streets of Montreal. The snowshoe outfit consisted of a white blanket coat tied with a long sash, complemented by a wool tuque, plus leggings and moccasins. By the 1870s each club had its own distinctive colours, used for epaulets or trim on the coats and for the tuque and stockings. Beers, for instance, was photographed in the Notman Photographic Studio wearing the uniform of the St George's Snow Shoe Club: white coat with distinctive membership badge, purple epaulets and purple and white tuque (see Figure 12.1). Since the snowshoe clubs from time-to-time made rules regulating the colour, style and detailing of their apparel, and stipulated when it should be worn, it is clear that these clothes were not just everyday winter wear, but actually a special uniform which one wore when snowshoeing.

In donning their uniforms, the snowshoe club members were dressing up as composite native-Canadians: the moccasins and leggings were aboriginal, the sash was a French-Canadian *ceinture flèchée*, the tuque was a French liberty cap, and the blanket coat resembled typical *habitant*

FIGURE 12.1
'Dr Beers on snowshoes, Montreal, QC', 1881, II-60469 Notman Photographic Archives,
McCord Museum of Canadian History, Montreal

FIGURE 12.2
Millicent Mary Chaplin, 'Canadian Farmer', c. 1840, watercolour C-866 National Archives of Canada

winter clothing.[26] Extensive transcultural borrowing had occurred between *voyageurs, coureurs de bois, habitants* and Native peoples since the sixteenth century. Both *habitants* and *voyageurs* had adopted elements of aboriginal clothing, particularly in foot and leg wear; both used pipes and beaded tobacco pouches and, of course, both had adopted aboriginal means of transport – birch-bark canoes, snowshoes and toboggans. A watercolour entitled 'Canadian Farmer' painted in 1840 by Millicent Mary Chaplin, a British visitor, illustrates that the clothing of a typical rustic figure no longer made it possible to distinguish between Native and French Canadian – a generic native/woodsman/farmer figure stood for all (see Figure 12.2).[27] The snowshoe outfit also bore a close resemblance to the winter dress of the other 'composite natives', the Red River Métis, as depicted by an 1851 traveller (Figure 12.3). The uniform chosen by the snowshoe clubs was therefore remarkably similar to the winter clothing worn by these 'Canadians of old'.[28] The sight of snowshoe club members clad in their blanket coats with snowshoes slung over their shoulders, trudging through the streets to their club rendezvous, was considered novel and picturesque and constituted a distinctively Canadian 'look' which was photographed extensively.[29] William Notman and other Montreal photographers produced hundreds of portraits of snowshoers for composite club portraits, as well as hundreds more souvenir photographs of visitors dressed in winter clothing.[30] These were distributed widely at home and abroad and exhibited at international exhibitions. The strength of the association between Canada and the snowshoe club outfit is demonstrated by an 1883 *Punch* cartoon lampooning Lord Landsdowne, the newly appointed governor general, dressed in 'his new Canadian costume adapted to remaining for some time out in the cold' (Figure 12.4).[31]

Apart from the snowshoe outfit being a distinctive visual attribute which conjured up memories of Canada's 'olden days', the performance of snowshoeing enacted a cultural fiction which allowed colonists to link themselves back to the fur trade and the aboriginal and French-Canadian past of the continent.[32] By taking on the rustic persona of the Nor'Westers, *voyageurs* and *coureurs de bois*, they displayed themselves as 'sons of the soil' – like Native peoples, closely linked with nature and the land. They positioned themselves within an invented mythological national past and appropriated the visual attributes of both 'real' Canadian natives in order to do so. In this way, organized club snowshoeing functioned to usurp and erase the Native *and* French-Canadian

FIGURE 12.3
Frank Blackwell Mayer, 'Winter dress of Red River Half Breeds', 1851, Ayer Art Mayer Sketchbook #44, The
Newberry Library, Chicago

histories of snowshoeing, obscuring the fact that snowshoeing was not
just part of the *British* history of Canada, but was also part of the
French-Canadian and Native histories of Canada. Performing an indigenous activity indigenized or naturalized snowshoe club members as a
new type of 'native-Canadian', whether they were Canadian-born or not.
In symbolic terms, the snowshoe club expeditions can be seen as ritual

FIGURE 12.4

'Lord Lansdowne in His New Canadian Costume, Specially Adapted to Remaining For Some Time Out in the Cold', *Punch*, 2 June, 1883, p.262. Photograph courtesy of Toronto Public Library, Toronto, Ontario

PUNCH'S FANCY PORTRAITS.—No. 138.

LORD LANSDOWNE,

IN HIS NEW CANADIAN COSTUME, SPECIALLY ADAPTED TO REMAINING FOR SOME TIME OUT IN THE COLD.

journeys, a simulation of the Nor'Westers' expeditions. These journeys, performed in 'Indian-file', accomplished a national task by conquering the 'wild' terrain, mapping it and possessing it.[33]

LACROSSE

Winter sports like snowshoeing and tobogganing connected colonists with the Canadian climate and landscape, but the category of indigenous sports also included the summer sport of lacrosse – a game favoured by the Anglophone professional and commercial middle classes in cities and towns in eastern and central Canada, and promoted tirelessly as the 'National game' by Beers.[34] Playing lacrosse was an appropriation and secularization of a significant aboriginal ritual. Unlike snowshoeing, it was not so much about dressing-up to become a distinctively Canadian figure as it was a means by which British colonists could prove their claim to be Canadian through supplanting the original Canadian *ethnie*. Both strategies were part of a subtle racial attack – a means by which colonists could subordinate and replace indigenous peoples by usurping their most distinctive activities. This was justified by the belief that Native peoples were a dying race, doomed to cultural assimilation. The transformation of *baggataway* into lacrosse was an act of power contested unsuccessfully by Native peoples who were gradually excluded from the game.[35]

As early as 1844, a team of white players competed against a Native team in Montreal, and subsequently occasional matches were played. The game was taken up seriously by whites when the Montreal Lacrosse Club (MLC) was formed in 1856 by members of the Montreal Snow Shoe Club and a disbanded athletic club. Interest grew further after the 1860 exhibition match played before the Prince of Wales by the Montreal Lacrosse Club and a Native team from Caughnawaga. After the formation of the National Lacrosse Association in 1867, there was a sharp surge of interest in the sport, by which time 80 clubs had been formed in central and eastern Canada, with over 2,000 members. By 1884, lacrosse clubs had been organized in the West and 20,000 players were registered.[36] Snowshoeing was ideal winter training for lacrosse and there was a great degree of cross-over in membership between the snowshoe clubs and the lacrosse clubs; consequently, the same values and ideals applied to snowshoeing were applied to lacrosse. Organized and regulated by the middle-class community, the two activities were complementary, both requiring strenuous activity, endurance and pluck, as well as discipline and moral character. With the large number of people playing, and crowds of 5,000–9,000 for major games, lacrosse was a cultural activity through which colonists could construct, witness and perform a putative national identity.

For centuries, versions of the Native game of *baggataway* or *tewaarathon* were played widely by Native peoples throughout the North American continent. Because of their proximity to Montreal, the game played at the First Nations' settlements at Caughnawaga and St Regis (present-day Kahnawake and Akwesasne Reserves) became the model for the westernized version called lacrosse. The transformation of *baggataway* into lacrosse was accomplished by the formulation of rules and regulations which imposed order and imbued the game with the 'gentlemanly' values already defined by the snowshoe clubs. For example, the Native game was traditionally played over fields of various dimensions and by any size of team; in addition, the game might last from a few hours to several days.[37] But these indeterminate and unstandardized spatial and temporal boundaries were impractical if the game was to be played in an urban environment, within the time constraints of an industrializing society. Similarly, the dictates of punctuality and standardization demanded that common rules had to be established in order that clubs could play each other without going through time-consuming pre-game negotiations.[38] Rules governing these aspects of the game were therefore instituted. They not only provided the necessary elements of discipline and fair play, but also brought the game under colonial control, and affirmed the importance of punctuality, standardization and private property. As Beers remarked, 'The white game differs from the red, in being restricted by that mark of civilization and trespass, the fence'.[39]

Beers was convinced of the potential of lacrosse as a distinctively Canadian game. He argued that:

> It may seem frivolous, at first consideration, to associate this feeling of nationality with a field game, but history proves it to be a strong and important influence. Cricket and curling have their national and nationalizing influences on their respective admirers, and so may Lacrosse … If the Republic of Greece was indebted to the Olympian Games; if England has cause to bless the name of cricket, so may Canada be proud of lacrosse.[40]

It was necessary, however, to purge the undesirable primitive aspects of the Native game through the imposition of rules and regulations. To demonstrate that the game had been ordered and 'civilized', it was necessary for the white game and players to look different from their Native counterparts. This was accomplished by distinguishing white players from Native players through a series of visual oppositions: the white teams wore special club uniforms, they played 'scientifically' rather than 'innately', they made changes in positioning and equipment, and they restricted and regulated the amount of physical contact and violence tolerated. These changes, in effect, invented a new sport and justified the claim that it was 'our' game. In appropriating and regulating lacrosse, the British colonists could claim to have 'invented' the game; all previous history of lacrosse could be relegated to a twilight pre-historical period when it was 'primitive' and 'savage'.[41] It also meant that Native players were forced to adapt their traditional style of play to suit the white game, thus 'taming' the Natives by making them behave according to white standards. Beers, the person who beyond all others was responsible for the appropriation and transformation of lacrosse, showed that he understood this when he wrote that,

> the Indians' old fierce *baggataway* has shared the fate of the Indian himself in having become civilized almost out of recognition into a more humane sport. It has lost its wild and wanton delirium, and though restless under regulations, has become tamed into the most exciting and varied of all modern field sports.

In the early years of club lacrosse, Native teams were indispensable. They provided the only challenging competition and were the source of all white knowledge about the game.[42] As soon as a critical mass of white teams had been formed, their importance as players waned, and the amateur rules adopted in 1880 virtually excluded them from club play.[43] However, they have never been totally dispensable as signifiers of Canadian identity. In the nineteenth century, important exhibition matches, major holiday games, and civic and state occasions such as the visits of the Prince of Wales in 1860 and Prince Arthur in 1869, included an appearance by a Native team.[44] In playing the westernized game of lacrosse, First Nations people were objectified as signifiers of Canada, and because the white Canadian teams played lacrosse with Native players, they also became part of a string of equivalents by which lacrosse itself came to signify 'Canada'.[45] When Native teams were invited to these events, to exhibitions or to the Montreal Winter Carnivals which were held in the 1880s, they were present as colourful, nostalgic reminders of the pre-historic existence of indigenous peoples in Canada, an essential part of its myth of origin.[46]

When Beers took white and Native teams to England for a tour in 1876, the 'Indianness' of the Native players, denoted by their 'primitive' activities and costume, was used as an advertising gimmick for the matches. He capitalized astutely on the exotic spectacle of Native dress and tradition, recognizing that it was the image of the 'barbarous savage' which created excitement and anticipation in spectators – or at least in the popular crowd. During the games, the Caughnawaga team wore bright colours – red and white striped jerseys and knickers and white hose, or red and yellow striped knickers (Figure 12.5). For the pre-game 'war dance' they also wore blue caps overlaid with ornamental bead work and scarlet feathers, along with tight fitting sashes and waist belts of blue velvet with a large 'C' on the front (Figure 12.6).[47] Morrow claims the 'C' stood for Caughnawaga, which no doubt it did; but it would also have denoted 'Canada' in the minds of the English audience unfamiliar with aboriginal names.[48] Along with their earrings and finger rings and the between-game antics they were required to perform, the Native players presented a stereotyped figure of 'Savage Indians'.[49] In restrained and 'civilized' contrast, the MLC team wore white jerseys, grey tweed knickers and dark brown hose (Figure 12.7). However, by the time Beers led teams on a second tour abroad in 1883, white players presented themselves as native-Canadians. The white team of 'Canadian Gentlemen' was dressed much more spectacularly than before in bright blue with a white maple-leaf crest on the jersey, on which was emblazoned a 'C' for Canada. This time, the Native players were dressed in contrasting scarlet.[50]

The way in which the 'primitive' Native game of *baggataway* was transformed into the 'modern' white game of lacrosse was, Beers claimed, through the diligent application of 'science'. This was a crucial concept because it rendered the game as 'civilized'; and because it legitimized the gradual exclusion of Native players from the game on the grounds that it was 'only the whites who can develop its science'. Beers claimed that:

> Science in a sport implies training and education of the intellect, a high use of the reasoning faculty, and a capacity to experiment and

FIGURE 12.5

'Caughnawage lacrosse team, Montreal, QC, 1876', II-41679 Notman Photographic Archives, McCord Museum of Canadian History, Montreal

FIGURE 12.6
'Wishe Tasemontie, Michael Dellebault, lacrosse player, Montreal, QC, 1876', II-41675 Notman
Photographic Archives, McCord Museum of Canadian History, Montreal

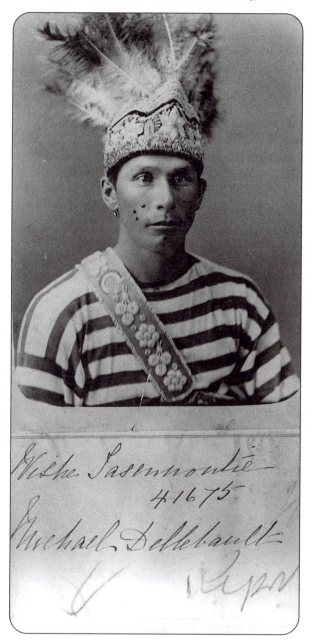

FIGURE 12.7

'The Canadian lacrosse team at Kennington Oval, London, 1876', Reproduced in J.A. Mangan (ed.), *The Cultural Bond: Sport, Empire, Society*
(London: Frank Cass, 1992), fig. 14

improve, and impart principles of knowledge to another ... The theory of Lacrosse is its science – the practice is its art.[51]

Native players were admired for their skill and physical capacities, but were considered inferior to white players since these were said to be *innate* abilities unrelated to the intellect.[52] 'Scientific play' elevated the game by heightening the mental requirements and putting greater emphasis on the actual performance of the players during the game than on winning.[53] Tactical play proved the superiority of the whites, and the failure of Native teams to demonstrate an understanding of strategy proved their inferiority. For instance, one commentator remarked: 'It seems incredible that a team so strong as the Indians undoubtedly were did not try different tactics when they found that the drop shots would not work.'[54] The application of scientific principles and the emphasis on mental tactics can be seen as a means by which the British ideology of 'fair play' could be introduced into matches between Native and white teams; it handicapped the 'innately' better Native players, who did not have direct access to scientific knowledge, thereby giving white teams more of a 'sporting chance'.

The scientific analysis of player positions and strategies provided by Beers resulted in the play of white teams having a different 'look' from that of Native teams, a point which was often commented upon by reporters, and was another means by which the game was claimed by whites. As one reporter explained: 'The "playing together" of the Montreal men is one more indication that science and skill, opposed to strength and endurance without either of the former attributes is, in nine cases out of ten, certain of success.'[55] Playing the game scientifically meant that players were assigned to certain field positions, each of which had its own particular responsibilities. The deployment of white teams on the field could, therefore, look somewhat different from that of Native teams, depending on how well Beers's recommendations for ideal play were followed. There were certainly some perceived differences in the performance of the teams, since newspaper reports frequently remarked that Native players tended to knot or bunch-up at the goals, whereas white players remained spread out, playing their positions in a more disciplined way. The 'Canadian' style of play hence embodied in exercise relationships and values held in other spheres of life; specialization, individual achievement and self-improvement all had to be balanced by the need to work together in harmony for the good of the group.

To aid in training, Beers's book set out explicit, how-to instructions on technique, strategy, training and practice. As an accompaniment to the text, he arranged for a series of instructional photographs to be taken to illustrate correct stance, position, etcetera.[56] These images featured elite white players, thereby proposing them as the authority on lacrosse. White players were substituted for the 'original' experts – Native players, thus claiming the sport as a white 'Canadian' game. Ultimately, therefore, the game was transformed so that it was 'owned' by the white teams, and so that they could be assured of victory.

The emphasis on practising specific skills led white players to 'improve' Native equipment in order to make their play more scientific. The lacrosse stick used by white players from the 1860s on was longer, heavier and had a more triangular shape and more tightly woven netting than that used by local Native players. These changes indicate that emphasis was being placed on the skill and teamwork of passing rather than carrying the ball, and on underhand rather than overhand throwing.[57] Beers frowned on lacrosse sticks with 'bagged netting', namely, loose netting which formed a pocket to aid in catching and retaining the ball. 'To catch and play with the netting flat is the perfection of catching', he claimed, 'because it makes your play scientific.'[58]

At times, though, Beers's arguments became ambiguous, illustrating an ambivalent attitude towards Natives as both noble and barbarous savages. He was not grudging in his admiration of the skills of Native players, yet at the same time he claimed Natives could not play 'as scientifically as the best white players'.[59] For instance, in advocating the use of tightly strung netting, he praised the Natives' skill in catching without bagged nets, which seems to imply that they *were* playing scientifically, but then he added: 'Catching, however, has always been their hereditary accomplishment.'[60] According to this way of thinking, the very fact that whites had to analyse the game intellectually, and had to train and practice to achieve the skills and the physical condition Natives enjoyed innately, made the whites better players than the Natives.

Scientific play was manifested on the playing field by a less brutal, 'more beautiful' game.[61] Beers claimed the Native game was brutal, 'midway between a sport and a deadly combat, because of its serious results to limb and life',[62] as opposed to the regulated game in which 'the worst accident yet known' was a broken arm.[63] He equivocated on this point though, because he also stated that 'you may occasionally see rough play', on the Native reserves, '*since they learned it from us*'.[64] Beers claimed that when Native teams played white teams the level of violence was higher than in Native-only games: 'It is very rare that an Indian is injured or injures ever so slightly when playing with his fellow red-skins; but when red meets white, then comes the tug of war – and we blame the latter for its development.'[65]

Violence was not just a factor in Native–white games, however, since over a quarter of the games played between the senior white clubs had disputes, violence and even rioting.[66] Judging from newspaper reports, it appears this was particularly the case when white teams played the Montreal Shamrocks – an Irish, Catholic, working-class team from Griffintown.[67] In an era when lacrosse was dominated by the Canadian-born middle classes, the Shamrocks team was unique since its identity was fundamentally Irish, and the majority of its players and fans were drawn from the working-class, although the executive was almost exclusively middle-class. This ethnic and class difference led to tremendous inter-team rivalries, which were manifested by violent and acrimonious games.[68] Thus, lacrosse games were cultural performances which conveyed particular meanings for their players and spectators. The games against Native teams and the Shamrocks were more violent than other games because they were sublimations – symbolic battles in which historical race and class antagonisms were fought out or diffused.[69]

While Beers seems to have been extremely successful in proselytizing the cause of lacrosse, he was not entirely without critics. A letter from 'Stumps' to the *Montreal Gazette* in 1867 contested the claim of lacrosse as the national game, arguing instead that cricket be accorded that place.[70] The writer objected to lacrosse on the grounds that it was a young man's game, so a 'game which must necessarily be confined to boys, and those but a few years older, can scarcely deserve to be called a National Game'. He also noted that it was confined mostly to Montreal, whereas cricket was played 'throughout the length and breadth of the British Empire'. The crux of the difference, though, was that the writer conceived of 'us' as British, whereas Beers conceived of 'us' as Canadian. This was precisely the conflict between imperialism and Canadian nationalism which emerged in the political realm in the 1880s.

CONCLUSION

Before 1885, participation in indigenous sports was a vehicle through which a distinct Canadian identity was proposed in Victorian Montreal.

It was a means by which the Anglophone, urban middle-classes of the new Dominion of Canada could define themselves in opposition to their colonial parent and the neighbouring American empire, as well as distinguishing them from the original native-Canadians, namely First Nations peoples and French Canadians. By examining the ways in which Montrealers represented themselves as Canadians through snowshoeing and lacrosse, we can see how national identity is imagined, invented and performed – not in abstract political ideology, but in the daily lives of ordinary citizens. Snowshoeing and lacrosse were initially indigenous activities, exotic enough to provide a distinctive identity when borrowed, yet amenable to the organization and regulation which would render them sufficiently respectable and 'civilized'. Engaging in these activities was a way to demonstrate the civility, autonomy and distinctiveness of the nation's subjects, and a practice which might develop a popular consensus regarding national identity.

Canadian identity had two poles: on the one hand, what was distinctively Canadian was actually Native, whether indigenous or French-Canadian, and on the other, British values and the ideology of order, discipline and fair play were crucial in counteracting the negative connotations of emulating 'primitive' and 'barbaric' indigenous cultural activities. The British pole of Canadian identity provided British immigrants with a sense of continuity with the Imperial past, continued social status, commercial contacts, and so on, but the indigenous pole allowed colonists to connect with the North American landscape and its past, and by its difference distinguished Canadians from the British and the Americans, leaving Canadians somewhere in-between.[71] In playing these games, white colonists took on some of the visual attributes of the original natives so that they looked familiar and respectable, yet exotic enough to be distinctively different from any other nation; and engaging in these sports was a symbolic performance which confirmed the colonists' right to possess the land, as well as a way in which they could link themselves to the history of the continent and its landscape.

After 1885, a growing divergence of Canadian and British political and commercial interests meant that this dual national identity became increasingly untenable. The decline of amateur lacrosse has been attributed to internal causes, including the struggle over professionalism and the narrow player base resulting from an inadequate minor programme.[72] Continuing squabbles over professionalism and violent play detracted from the game's prestige, and mitigated against the church and state support necessary to make it a national game played throughout the nation rather than in a few major centres. However, since the initial popularity of lacrosse has not been attributed to the fact that it was a means by which Canadian national identity could be embodied and displayed, it has also not been considered that the loss of interest in lacrosse as a popular sport may also have been a result of its diminishing value as a national signifier. Lacrosse retained its popularity as a spectator sport until 1914, but after 1885 it was increasingly difficult to hold it up as a 'gentlemanly' and 'civilized' game. The game's growing reputation for violence and contention envisioned and enacted an image of Canadians which lacked the qualities desired for respectable and civilized nations. Furthermore, the image of the barbarous savage was reinvoked by stories of marauding Natives during the 1885 North West Rebellion, as well as by reports of captured and degraded Natives languishing on inadequate reserves because of the subsequent repressive government policy. In an atmosphere of hostile racism, this made the 'primitive' associations of the game unpalatable.[73]

Snowshoeing continued to be popular until the turn of the century, but by that time it was seen as somewhat anachronistic in a modern age. The experience of the First World War had a profound effect on the Canadian self-image; a new sense of Canadian identity emerged and indigenous sports and the Native 'other' lost their potency and relevance as national signifiers. Ice hockey was, however, the modern indigenous sport. Its organized form was the invention of Canadian-born colonists – the new native-Canadians. After the first recorded 'modern' game played in Montreal in 1875, it quickly found the church and school support which eluded lacrosse.[74] Similar to lacrosse and old-world ball and stick games, yet played on the natural ice abundantly available in the Canadian climate, ice hockey was a perfect expression of Canadian identity. By 1886, an organizing body had been formed – the Amateur Hockey Association of Canada – and ice hockey began its phenomenal rise to prominence in Canadian sport and the Canadian popular imagination.

NOTES

1. The distinction between play, games and sports is discussed at length by A. Guttmann, *From Ritual to Record: The Nature of Modern Sports* (New York: Columbia University Press, 1978). In accordance with nineteenth-century usage, I use the terms 'game' and 'sport' interchangeably when referring to lacrosse and snowshoeing. Until the formation of a league system in 1885, lacrosse was strictly speaking a game rather than a modern, organized sport. Except for the

annual club races, snowshoeing was neither a game nor a modern sport, but contemporaries invariably referred to it as 'a winter sport'.

2. W. G. Beers, 'Canada in Winter', *British American Magazine*, 2 (Dec. 1863), 168.

3. W.G. Beers, 'Canadian Sports', *The Century Magazine*, 14 (May–Oct. 1877), 506–27; and 'Canada as a Winter Resort', *Century Illustrated Monthly Magazine*, 29, 50 (Feb. 1885), 514–29. Others included an article by J.C. Martin on the snowshoeing experience in Canada in *Outing*, Feb. 1885. and about winter sports in G.A. Buffum, 'Ralph's Winter Carnival', *St. Nicholas*, Feb. 1885 – both cited in *Week*, 29 Jan. 1885, 146.

4. For example: F.G. Mather, 'Winter Sports in Canada', *Harper's New Monthly Magazine* 68 (Feb. 1879), 391–400, notes the 'peculiarly Canadian' pastimes of tobogganing, sleighing and snowshoeing. A similar comment is made in *Illustrated London News*, 11 Sept 1886, 289–90. Charles Dudley Warner recognized 'a Canadian type which is neither English nor American' in 'Comments on Canada', *Harper's New Monthly Magazine*, 78 (March 1889), 520–48. All cited in D. Brown, 'The Northern Character Theme and Sport in Nineteenth Century Canada', *Canadian Journal of the History of Sport (CJHS)*, 10, 1 (1989), 49–51. See also D. Brown, 'Prevailing Attitudes Towards Sport, Physical Exercise and Society in the 1870s: Impressions from Canadian Periodicals', *CJHS*, 17, 2 (Dec. 1986), 58–70. I have used the term 'British' throughout, but the English-speaking professional and commercial middle classes of Montreal were from all parts of the British Isles, especially Scotland. However, there is some justification for using this covering term since Colley argues that by the early decades of the nineteenth century the idea of being British had been popularized quite successfully. L. Colley, *Britons: Forging the Nation, 1701–1837* (New Haven: Yale University Press, 1992).

5. R.G. Haliburton, *The Men of the North and their Place in History: A Lecture Delivered before the Montreal Literary Club, March 31st 1869* (Montreal: J. Lovell, 1869). For a discussion of the significance of this address and of the Canada First group see C. Berger, *The Sense of Power: Studies in the Ideas of Canadian Imperialism, 1867–1914* (Toronto: University of Toronto Press, 1970).

6. National Archives of Canada (NAC), Montreal Amateur Athletic Association (MAAA) Scrapbook 1 (1873), p.7.

7. NAC, MAAA Scrapbook 3, p.83.

8. W.G. Beers, *Lacrosse: The National Game of Canada* (Montreal: Dawson Brothers, 1869), p.35.

9. D. Morrow, 'The Canadian Image Abroad: The Great Lacrosse Tours of 1876 and 1883', in *Proceedings of the Fifth Canadian Symposium on the History of Sport and Physical Education*, University of Toronto, Aug. 1982, pp.11–23. Contemporary scholars have failed to find any evidence that it was discussed in Parliament: see K.G. Jones and T.G. Vellathottam, 'The Myth of Canada's National Sport', *CAHPER Journal*, (Sept.–Oct. 1974), 33–6.

10. E. Hobsbawm and T. Ranger (eds), *The Invention of Tradition* (Cambridge: Cambridge University Press, 1983), pp.298, 300.

11. S.W. Pope, *Patriotic Games: Sporting Traditions in the American Imagination, 1876–1926* (New York: Oxford University Press, 1997), pp.3–4.

12. D. Brown, 'Canadian Imperialism and Sporting Exchanges: The Nineteenth Century Cultural Experience of Cricket and Lacrosse', *CJHS*, 18, 1 (1987), 60. Other examples where sport is shown to be at the service of nationalism are: D.L. Andrews, 'Welsh Indigenous! and British Imperial? – Welsh Rugby, Culture, and Society 1890–1914', *Journal of Sport History (JSH)*, 18, 3 (1991), 335–64; A. Bairner, 'Sportive Nationalism and Nationalist Politics: A Comparative Analysis of Scotland, The Republic of Ireland, and Sweden', *Journal of Sport and Social Issues*, 23 (Aug. 1996), 314–34; G. Pfister, 'Physical Activity in the Name of the Fatherland: Turner and the National Movement (1819–1820)', *Sporting Heritage*, 1, 1 (1996), 14–35; M. Cronin and D. Mayall (eds), *Sporting Nationalisms: Identity, Ethnicity, Immigration and Assimilation* (London: Frank Cass, 1998). Articles published in *The Sports Historian*, 18, 2 (Nov. 1988) on the connection between sport and nationalism in Cornwall, Scotland and Ireland are available online from http://www.umist.ac.uk/UMIST_Sport.

13. *Souvenir of the Montreal Winter Carnival of 1884* (Montreal: Canada Railway News, 1884), p.14. The anonymous author was heavily reliant on Beers' souvenir programme from the previous year: *Over the Snow or The Montreal Carnival* (Montreal: W. Drysdale & Co. and J. Tho. Robinson, 1883).

14. Homi Bhabha argues that the nation is imagined through the construction of 'myths of origin', which legitimize nationhood by claiming historical roots and continuity. H.K. Bhabha (ed.), *Nation and Narration* (London: Routledge, 1990), p.1.

15. This was graphically demonstrated in a much-discussed television advertising campaign for beer which ran in 2000. It featured a 'rant' by an average 'Joe' Canadian on the difference between Canadians and Americans. This advertisement was subsequently appropriated for political use by the Minister of Canadian Heritage, Sheila Copps, who showed it to an international conference as a demonstration of Canadian identity. Apart from stimulating debate about Canadian identity *vis-à-vis* Americans, this beer advertisement inspired 'hyphenated-Canadians' (Italian-Canadians, French-Canadians, etcetera) to produce their own versions of the 'I am Canadian' rant, and provoked discussions in the media of how ethnic groups retain their distinctiveness in a multi-cultural society. The point is that this was a productive (if at times anti-American) discussion which took place in the cultural rather than the political sphere.

16. These other components of identity – gender, race and class – are discussed much more comprehensively in my 'Becoming Native in a Foreign Land: Visual Culture, Sport, and Spectacle in the Construction of National Identity in Montreal, 1840–1885' (unpublished Ph.D. dissertation, York University, Toronto, 2000).

17. As, for instance, when newspaper reports censured 'unsportsmanlike' players or 'rowdy' crowds.

18. R.S. Gruneau, 'Power and Play in Canadian Society', in R.J. Ossenberg (ed.), *Power and Change in Canada* (Toronto: University of Toronto Press, 1980), p.158.

19. The figure of the *habitant* was an historical stereotype of the French-Canadian peasant or *censitaire* from the French Regime, but French-Canadian farmers and rural dwellers were still frequently referred to as *habitants* or *habitans* by English colonists in this period. *Voyageurs* were contract workers who transported goods and furs by foot and canoe in the fur brigades, while *coureurs de bois* were unlicenced fur traders who sold pelts at the English forts in contravention of the French mercantilist laws.

20. For instance, Beers claimed Americans thought 'The hardy Canadian was supposed to be a cross between an Indian and a *Habitant*', Beers, *Over the Snow*, p.5.

21. Although there are no records for the early years of the MSSC, Hugh W. Becket reported in his 1882 history of the Club that it began in the early 1840s and was formally organized in 1843. H.W. Becket, *The Montreal Snow Shoe Club. Its History and Record with a Synopsis of the Racing Events of other Clubs throughout the Dominion, from 1840 to the Present Time* (Montreal: Becket Bros., 1882), pp.4–6. Nor'Westers was the nickname of members of the North West Company established in 1776 as an umbrella group of predominantly Scots Montreal traders. The last two surviving partners of the Company, Simon Fraser and John McDonald of Garth, were still alive in August 1859: C. Podruchny, 'Festivals, Fortitude and Fraternalism: Fur Trade Masculinity and the Beaver Club, 1785–1827', in J. Fiske, S. Sleeper-Smith and W.C. Wicken (eds), *New Faces of the Fur Trade: Selected Papers of the Seventh North American Fur Trade Conference, Halifax, Nova Scotia, 1995* (East Lansing, MI: Michigan State University Press, 1998), pp.31, 42.

22. P. Carpentier, *La Raquette à neige* (Sillery: Boréal, 1976), p.96.

23. D. Morrow, 'The Knights of the Snowshoe: A Study of the Evolution of Sport in Nineteenth Century Montreal', *JSH*, 15, 1 (1988), 5, 37; and A. Metcalfe, 'The Evolution of Organized Physical Recreation in Montreal, 1840–1895', in M. Mott (ed.), *Sport in Canada: Historical Readings* (Toronto: University of Toronto Press, 1989), p.149.

24. W.G. Beers, 'Canadian Winter Sports', *Bishop's Carnival Illustrated* (Montreal: George Bishop & Co., Feb. 1884), n.p.

25. Sport club membership in Montreal during the period 1840–85 was almost exclusively drawn from the Anglophone professional and commercial middle classes. The only two French-Canadian snowshoe clubs with any permanence were *Le Canadien* (founded 1878) and *Le Trappeur* (founded 1884). It was not until after 1890 that the French-Canadian community participated in sports in a large way. Metcalfe, 'The Evolution of Organized Physical Recreation in Montreal', pp.152, 159. See also, G. Janson, *Emparons-nous du sport: les Canadiens français et le sport au XIXe siècle* (Montreal: Guérin, 1995). Women were marginalized to the status of spectators at lacrosse games and the annual snowshoe club races. They were able to participate more actively in snowshoeing tramps and tobogganing, especially by the 1880s. In the twentieth

century, lacrosse was commonly played in private girls' schools in England.

26. The blanket coat was a version of the French *capote*, a mid-length, hooded coat made from wool blanket cloth. F. Back, 'The Canadian Capot (*Capote*)', *The Museum of the Fur Trade Quarterly*, 27 (1991), 4–15. The blanket coat is the subject of an M.A. thesis by Eileen Stack, University of Rhode Island, 2000. For a detailed discussion of clothing as a form of communication, and of the role of uniforms as a means of legitimating membership and 'maintaining rigorous adherence to norms' even in leisure time, see N. Joseph, *Uniforms and Nonuniforms: Communication Through Clothing* (New York: Greenwood Press, 1986), p.3.

27. This statement is not, of course, true of paintings produced in the West to document the last remnants of a dying race. The expectation for these paintings was that Native people would appear in paint and feathers. It was also not true of images produced by French-Canadian artists. The difference between French Canadian and British artists' representations is examined in G. Poulter, 'Representation as Colonial Rhetoric. The Image of "the Native" and "the habitant" in the Formation of Colonial Identities in Early Nineteenth-Century Lower Canada', *Journal of Canadian Art History*, 16, 1 (1994), 11–29.

28. Carpentier agrees that snowshoe club uniforms referred to rustic and romanticized figures: 'L'image type de l'habitant canadien fut reprise et ranimée par les fondateurs des clubs de raquettes...certains d'entre eux prétendaient être les derniers de la race des voyageurs'. Carpentier, *La Raquette à neige*, p.102. The history of 'Old Quebec' was also a popular literary subject at this time, see: E. Hedler, 'A romance of French Canada: The Creation of a Canadian Heritage in English-Canadian Historical Novels, 1867–1907', paper presented at the Canadian Historical Association annual conference, May 2001, University of Laval, Quebec City.

29. Newspaper reports of the torchlight snowshoe parade held for Lord and Lady Dufferin in 1873, and of the various concerts given by snowshoe clubs in the 1870s are speckled with comments about the 'extremely picturesque' appearance and 'strikingly unique' spectacle created by the members in their snowshoe uniforms. An American reporter called the sight of snowshoers 'eminently Canadian', *Journal* (Boston), 22 Jan. 1873.

30. The Notman studio, for example, produced at least 450 photographs of sitters wearing blanket coats between 1860 and 1900: E. Stack, 'The significance of the blanket-coat to Anglo-Canadian Identity', paper presented to the 25th Annual Symposium, The Costume Society of America, Sante Fe, NM, May 22–5, 1999, p.5.

31. Lansdowne's appointment to Canada was considered political exile because he had broken with Gladstone over Irish policy: R.H. Hubbard, *Rideau Hall: An Illustrated History of Government House, Ottawa, from Victorian Times to the Present Day* (Ottawa: Queen's Printer, 1967), p.72.

32. As a further step in this discursive process, this visual image of Canadians was reinforced by, and may well have been an influence on, the 'happy *habitant*' images produced by illustrators for the popular press, and painters such as Robert Todd, Cornelius Krieghoff and William Raphael. It was not until 1880 or later that the 'empty' landscape itself was employed to signify the nation in painting and photography.

33. The significance of snowshoeing as a colonizing activity and cultural performance is considered in greater depth in G. Poulter, 'Colonizing the Landscape: Snowshoeing in the Environs of Nineteenth-Century Montreal', paper presented at the NASSH Annual Conference, May 25–8 2001, University of Western Ontario, London, Ontario. As a result of the Hind and Palliser expeditions, for example, the North West began to be viewed as habitable, agricultural land, and 'inventory science' gave birth to the vision of Canada as a transcontinental nation. S. Zeller, *Inventing Canada: Early Victorian Science and the Idea of a Transcontinental Nation* (Toronto: University of Toronto Press, 1987), p.257. See also D. Owram, *Promise of Eden: The Canadian Expansionist Movement and the Idea of the West* (Toronto: University of Toronto Press, 1980).

34. See also N.B. Bouchier, 'Idealized Middle-Class Sport for a Young Nation: Lacrosse in Nineteenth-Century Ontario Towns, 1871–1891', *Journal of Canadian Studies*, 29, 2 (1994), 89–109.

35. The rules adopted by the NLA in 1869 excluded Natives from club play, and in 1880 the NLA ruled that only amateurs could play, thus disqualifying Native players and teams. The deleterious effects of the modernization and secularization of *baggataway* are considered by M.A. Salter, 'The Effect of Acculturation on the Game of Lacrosse and on its Role as an Agent of Indian Survival', *CJHS*, 3, 1 (1972), 28–43 and 'Baggataway to Lacrosse: A Case Study in

Acculturation', *CJHS*,Vol.26, No.2 (Dec. 1995), 49–64. A Native history of the game is given by North American Indian Travelling College, *Tewaarathon (Lacrosse)* (Akwesasne, 1978).

36. T.G. Vellathottam and K.G. Jones, 'Highlights in the Development of Canadian Lacrosse to 1931', *Canadian Journal of Sport and Physical Education*, 5, 2 (1974), 40. The development of the modern game in Victorian Montreal is traced by A. Metcalfe, *Canada Learns to Play: The Emergence of Organized Sport, 1807–1914* (Toronto: McClelland & Stewart, 1987), Ch. 6.

37. The best and most complete history of the Native game is provided by T. Vennum, Jr., *American Indian Lacrosse: Little Brother of War* (Washington: Smithsonian Institute Press, 1994).

38. Pre-game delays of two hours were not unusual while these negotiations went on. The necessity to be aware of the time was driven home by the need for visiting teams to catch the 5 o'clock train. Many lacrosse games had to be stopped because of this.

39. Beers, *Lacrosse*, p.54.

40. Ibid., p.59.

41. Beers was, in fact, called 'the father of lacrosse', in complete disregard of (and thereby erasing) the aboriginal origins of the game.

42. This was true also in snowshoeing where in the early years Native competitors attracted spectators to the annual club race days.

43. The frequency of games between the MLC teams and Native teams noted in the Minute Books of the club diminished over time. A graphic example of the waning importance of Native teams is recorded in May of 1887 when the Caughnawaga team was asked to play a MLC team at the Dominion Day celebrations for a fee of $50. The Native team asked for $60 instead, apparently to cover increased train fares. The MLC refused to pay extra and called the game off. The Caughnawaga team capitulated, but the MLC arranged 'a friendly match' with the Shamrocks instead. By 1887 the pleasurable excitement of the game, and a class, rather than racial, confrontation would apparently draw in the crowds. NAC, MLC Minute Book, 1887, pp.53–60.

44. For example, the Prescott Dominion Day celebrations for 1875 included a lacrosse match between the Prescott Club and a team from St Regis, played for a prize of $100. NAC, MAAA Scrapbook 1 (1873), p.340.

45. Indian = Canada = Lacrosse. 'Indians' signified Canada initially, but lacrosse was promoted so successfully as a Canadian sport that the game itself became a signifier of Canada.

46. Native peoples continue to play a role today as signifiers of Canada; along with RCMP in dress uniform, they are a ubiquitous presence at any important ceremony staged by the federal government. Recent examples are the opening of the newly refurbished Canada House in London, England in 1998; and the opening ceremonies for the Pan-Am Games in Winnipeg in 1999.

47. Sawatis Aiontonnis (Big John Canadian), the captain, is shown wearing the headdress, belt and sash in Figure 12.5, and Wishe Tasennontie (Michael Dellebault) is shown with the sash or belt over his shoulder in Figure 12.6.

48. D. Morrow, 'Lacrosse as the National Game', in D. Morrow *et al.* (eds), *A Concise History of Sport in Canada* (Toronto: Oxford University Press, 1989), p.60.

49. Between games the Native team was 'urged to hold snowshoe races on the grass, to dance "war dances" or the "green corn dance", or to hold mock "pow-wows"'. As Morrow adds, 'James Fenimore Cooper could not have contrived a more colourful image of stereotypical Indianness for these early "Harlem Globetrotters" of lacrosse'. Morrow, 'Lacrosse as the National Game', p.61.

50. Morrow, 'Lacrosse as the National Game', p.60.

51. Beers, *Lacrosse*, pp.51, 52.

52. This can also be understood as a middle-class argument against the inherited advantages of the aristocratic elite.

53. It was also a convenient excuse for frequent losses against Native teams! Elias considers this shift as a highly significant point in the transformation of pastimes into sport, and as an indicator of a 'civilizing spurt' in the state-formation process. N. Elias, 'An Essay on Sport and Violence', in Norbert Elias and Eric Dunning (eds), *Quest for Excitement: Sport and Leisure in the Civilizing Process*, (Oxford: Basil Blackwell, 1986), p.174.

54. Report of game between Shamrocks and Caughnawaga, 1878. NAC, MAAA Scrapbook 2, p.177.

55. NAC, MAAA Scrapbook 1 (1873), p. 116.
56. These 12 photographs and accompanying legend formed the frontispiece of Beers' *Lacrosse*. They featured well-known players from the top clubs.
57. Vennum, *American Indian Lacrosse*, p.258. They also illustrate non-Native attempts to take control of the commercial manufacture of equipment in order to capture the opportunity for profit. By 1910 the Montreal Joe Lally Company had gained a stick-making monopoly: North American Indian Travelling College, *Tewaarathon*, p.106. For a discussion of sport as a business opportunity (manufacturing, investment and publishing) see J. Lowerson, *Sport and the English Middle Classes 1870–1914* (Manchester: Manchester University Press, 1993), Ch. 8.
58. Beers, *Lacrosse*, p.134.
59. Ibid., p. vii.
60. Ibid., p.155.
61. Ibid., p.183.
62. Ibid., p.7.
63. Ibid., p.45.
64. Ibid., p.177 (his emphasis). The message was that white players should emulate or take over the skills of the noble savage, but must seek to banish the violence of the barbarous savage.
65. Ibid., p. 205.
66. An estimated 28 per cent of these games manifested violence. Metcalfe, *Canada Learns to Play*, p. 193.
67. For discussions of the Shamrock Lacrosse team, see Metcalfe, *Canada Learns to Play*, pp.181–218; and B.S. Pinto, 'Ain't Misbehavin': The Montreal Shamrock Lacrosse Club Fans 1868–1884', *Proceedings of the North American Society for Sport History*, Banff, Alberta (1990), p.92.
68. Metcalfe, *Canada Learns*, Ch. 6.
69. Historians have differed in their interpretations. Bruce Kidd suggests that the political struggles over the 'manhood' franchise and the right to form trade unions 'inflated the representational coin of competition' between middle-class and working-class teams: B. Kidd, *The Struggle for Canadian Sport* (Toronto: University of Toronto Press, 1996), p.18. Metcalfe's conclusion is that the prevalence of violence in the 1870s and 1880s was not instigated by the Native teams and Shamrocks, but was due to 'the change in focus in lacrosse brought on by the creation of a league and a national championship' which valued winning over playing: quoted by R.W. Simpson, 'Elite and Sport Club Membership in Toronto 1827–1881' (unpublished Ph.D. dissertation, University of Alberta, Edmonton, 1987), p.9. Vennum argues that *baggataway* strengthened group identity and diffused potential hostilities; and, as surrogates for war, matches between white and Native teams channeled aggression into peaceable rivalry: Vennum, *American Indian Lacrosse*, pp.180, 234.
70. *Gazette*, 7 Aug. 1867, cited in Peter L. Lindsay, 'George Beers and the National Game Concept: A Behavioural Approach,' *Proceedings of the Second Canadian Symposium on the History of Sport and Physical Education*, University of Windsor, May 1972 (Ottawa: Sport Canada Directorate, 1972), 27–44.
71. Plamenatz notes the two contradictory rejections: of the Mother country, which must 'nevertheless be imitated', and of native culture, which is an obstacle to progress, 'yet cherished as a mark of identity'. J. Plamenatz, 'Two Types of Nationalism', in E. Kamenka (ed.) *Nationalism: The Nature and Evolution of an Idea*, (London, 1976), pp.23–36, cited in P. Chatterjee, *Nationalist Thought and the Colonial World – A Derivative Discourse* (London: Zed Books, 1986), p.2. Gellner also agrees a choice has to be made between imitation (of the western culture) and identity (indigenous tradition): 'Ultimately the movements invariably contain both elements, a genuine modernism and a more spurious concern for local culture', E. Gellner, *Thought and Change* (London: Weidenfeld & Nicolson, 1964), p.147–8, cited in Chatterjee, *Nationalist Thought and the Colonial World*, p.4.
72. See Metcalfe, *Canada Learns to Play*, Ch.6.
73. I am grateful to Bruce Kidd for his helpful suggestion regarding this point in response to an earlier version of this paper.
74. For the rise of hockey, see R. Gruneau and D. Whitson, *Hockey Night in Canada: Sport, Identities and Cultural Politics* (Toronto: Garamond Press, 1993).

Epilogue

ANDREW RITCHIE and J.A. MANGAN

It might be argued that today in global sport many of the historic battles for inclusion, such as those which are explored here, have now been won. There may still be residual prejudice directed at certain ethnic or racial groups, excluding them from full participation; there may be a generalized exclusion from international competition of some athletes from under-developed Third World countries due to lack of general resources, specific facilities and relative poverty and an inadequate diet, but in the Developed World, extraordinary gains have been made in sport by previously excluded or under-represented minorities. Indeed, to an extent discussion has now shifted from the struggle for inclusion to exploration (again) of the comparative and contrasting nature of the athletic and physiological abilities and merits of the various racial and ethnic groups. This has now become one of the most prominent and controversial issues in contemporary athletic performance.[1]

Major issues concerning race and ethnicity, therefore, are still being debated. Are some racial or ethnic groups intrinsically superior in particular physical activities and do they have greater 'natural' ability and thus inherently superior potential in various sports or are socio-cultural factors of more significance in establishing superiority? What cultural and historical patterns in sport can be demonstrated to have been influential in the performance of particular ethnic groups? What role is sport still playing in the cultural construction and identity formation of minority groups? What is the role of the media in maintaining a small, super-privileged class of black super-heroes such as Muhamed Ali, Mike Tyson, Magic Johnson, Carl Lewis or Michael Jordan (to name just a few)? Does media adulation of athletes from specific minority backgrounds stimulate further successes from the group they represent, or in fact encourage unrealistic expectations? How has the global commercial expansion of international sport impacted on those less affluent ethnic communities which do not have adequate resources?

And, with regards to minorities, to what extent are women, particularly in the under-developed world, still denied full participation in modern sport because of repressive religious, cultural and political policies? In the case of such under-developed groups, do attempts to succeed in international sport advance or retard overall social, cultural and political progress? AIDS in Southern Africa, for example, demands and will demand a considerable proportion of the financial resources of nations. Does AIDS now, and will it in the future, influence adversely the growth of sport in these nations?

The essays in this volume have described some of the difficulties and barriers put in the way of minorities and classes in the history of sport. With regard to the patterns of prejudice and discrimination covered, it is interesting to note the particular sports and the periods involved:

- United States, cycling, 1890s;
- South Africa, soccer and various other sports, 1920–50;
- South Africa, soccer, cricket and rugby, 1950–90;
- United States, basketball, football and baseball, 1900–50;
- India and the West Indies, cricket, 1890 – present day;
- Japan, various sports, 1945 – present day;
- Canada, lacrosse and snowshoeing, late 19th century;
- United States, media representation of black sport stars, 1910–50;

In each case and in each country it has been argued that ruling elites – both political elites and the governing elites of sports bodies – clearly understood the organizing power of sport and attempted to repress and control ethnic group assertion through sport, but that in spite of this repression, the disadvantaged groups succeeded in using sport to assert and reinforce their identity and further their political, cultural and social ends.

The essays published here also demonstrate, of course, that notable individual successes have been won in the United States. Jack Johnson, Jesse Owens, Jackie Robinson, Joe Louis among many others won respect for their excellence in their sports, broke down doors for ethnic minorities, and changed some sports for ever. Many other pioneers elsewhere, of course, have left accounts – indeed these autobiographies in themselves collectively form an exhaustive narrative of the pushing aside of racial and ethnic barriers.[2] The evidence is compelling: much has been achieved; obstacles have been overcome; perspectives have been changed for the better; inclusion has resulted. It can be argued with justification that sport has been a positive agent of change for oppressed ethnic groups, a means by which they have been able to demonstrate their common humanity, express their social and political identity, and achieve their political rights.

The gains have been undeniable. Consider merely the following statistics in Jon Entine's controversial book *Taboo*:

- The Dutch national soccer team is about one third black; France has a large contingent of African players; in England 20 per cent of first division teams is black.
- Forty per cent of American professional baseball players are of primarily West African ancestry.
- In 1960, the racial breakdown in American basketball was 80 per cent white, while today it is 85 per cent black; women's professional basketball is 75 per cent black; the National Football League is 70 per cent black.
- All of the 40 finalists in the last five Olympic men's 100 metre races are of West African descent.
- Runners from East Africa (40 per cent are from Kenya) make up 50 per cent of top times in middle and long distance races.
- Every men's world record at every track distance belongs to a runner of African descent.[2]

As mentioned above, with the increased inclusion of various minorities has come a renewed examination of the nature of an undeniable ethnic dominance in certain sports. Does this dominance indicate simply a 'natural', physiological superiority, now finally being allowed to express itself, or should socio-cultural explanations still be sought to explain it? What exactly is *proved* when black athletes consistently outsprint, out-play and out-marathon their previously dominant white rivals? What social, cultural and political consequences follow on from their ability to command high fees and become media superstars? Is this a superior ability which manifests itself only in certain sports, where certain kinds of specific physiological skills are needed? It is noteworthy, for instance, that among the approximately 200 riders selected annually to ride the Tour de France (cycling's most important event and arguably the world's most demanding endurance sports event) *there has not yet been a successful African or African American competitor*. Why not? Because, notwithstanding what has been suggested earlier, cycling is a sport in which various forms of discrimination are still extant? Because cycling's cultural base has traditionally been European? Because the cost of equipment and lack of good roads has kept East Africans out of the sport? Because there have been no high school or university programmes in the United States to encourage the participation of African Americans in cycling, and therefore bicycle racing has never been an 'in' sport? Various possible answers can thus be offered. Which are correct? Definitive answers are still awaited.

CONCLUSION

Of all the high profile issues which dominate current discussion within sport – for example, doping, commercialism, the influence of sport in world politics, corruption within the International Olympic Committee – perhaps none are so significant as the questions concerning performance, race and ethnicity. Does the global domination of the affluent United States, Europe and Australasia help to promote or prevent a true democracy of participation in modern sport? Development and affluence give an overall advantage in terms of leisure, education, facilities and equipment. Is twenty-first century sport the location of a new kind of global racial and ethnic discrimination involving the 'haves' and the 'have-nots' throughout the world as much as within nations. Should world sports organizations like the IOC and FIFA, with their bulging bank accounts, be doing more at this level? Should this be a major challenge for the twenty-first century?

A final reflection: when African American cyclist Major Taylor (world champion, 1899) wrote his autobiographical memoir in 1928, he looked back on his own elemental struggle against racism for the right in the 1890s to be allowed to participate in his chosen sport, and he was also aware of the more recent successes of African Americans in sport in the period from 1900 to 1925.[4] He had gone where few in sport had gone before him and had succeeded spectacularly, in his own words, 'notwithstanding the tremendous odds and almost tragic hardships that I was forced to do extra battle against owing to color prejudice and jealousy of the bitterest form'. The conclusion he drew from his own career was that, 'there are positively no mental, physical, moral or other attainments too lofty for a Negro to accomplish if granted a fair and equal opportunity...Judging by the manner in which colored athletes have repeatedly demonstrated their skill and prowess in the athletic world, it is quite obvious what might well be accomplished on a whole as a race in other pursuits of life if granted a square deal and a fair field.'[3] The right to inclusion and the possibility of achieving success in sport was thus, for Major Taylor, symbolic of the struggle for democracy and justice in all aspects of life. In the new global and internationalized sport of the twenty-first century, where the privileged and well-equipped athletes of the developed world have so many advantages over the poor and under-privileged athletes of the Third World, let us hope that similar ideals of participatory democracy and justice prevail.

NOTES

1. See especially John Hoberman, *Darwin's Athletes: How Sport has Damaaged Black America and Preserved the Myth of Race* (New York: Houghton Mifflin, 1997) and Jon Entine, *Taboo: Why Black Athletes Dominate Sports and Why We're Afraid to Talk about it* (New York: Public Affairs, 2000).
2. Entine, *Taboo*, pp.19, 20, 21, 22, 31, 34.
3. Marshall W. 'Major' Taylor, *The Fastest Bicycle Rider in the World: The Story of a Colored Boy's Indomitable Courage and Success Against Great Odds* (Worcester, Mass.: Wormley Publishing, 1928), Foreword.

Select Bibliography

THE LEAGUE OF AMERICAN WHEELMEN, MAJOR TAYLOR
AND THE 'COLOR QUESTION' IN THE UNITED STATES IN
THE 1890s *BY ANDREW RITCHIE*

Franklin, J.H., *From Slavery to Freedom: A History of Negro Americans* (New York: Vintage Books, 1969).

Kron, K., *Ten Thousand Miles on a Bicycle* (New York: Karl Kron, 1887).

Pratt, C.E., *The American Bicycler: A Manual for the Observer, the Learner, and the Expert* (Boston: Private Printing, 2nd edn, 1880).

Ritchie, A., *Major Taylor: The Extraordinary Career of a Champion Bicycle Racer* (Baltimore: Johns Hopkins University Press, 1996).

Taylor, Marshall 'Mayr', *The Fastest Bicycle Rider in the World* (Worcester, MA: Wormley Publishing Company, 1928).

'CURT FLOOD STOOD UP FOR US': THE QUEST TO BREAK
DOWN RACIAL BARRIERS AND STRUCTURAL INEQUALITY IN
MAJOR LEAGUE BASEBALL *BY MICHAEL E. LOMAX*

Alexander, C.C., *Our Game: An American Baseball History* (New York: Henry Holt and Co., 1991).

Dworkin, J.B., *Owners versus Players: Baseball and Collective Bargaining* (Boston: Auburn House Pub. Co., 1981).

Lowenfish, L., *The Imperfect Diamond: A History of Baseball's Labor Wars*, rev. edn (New York: Da Capo Press, 1991).

Miller, J.E., *The Baseball Business: Pursuing Pennants and Profits in Baltimore* (Chapel Hill: University of North Carolina Press, 1990).

Scully, G.W., *The Business Of Major League Baseball* (Chicago: University of Chicago Press, 1989).

Voigt, D.Q., *American Baseball Volume III: From Postwar Expansion to the Electronic Age* (University Park, PA: Pennsylvania State University Press, 1983).

JIM CROW STRIKES OUT: BRANCH RICKEY AND THE
STRUGGLE FOR INTEGRATION IN AMERICAN BASEBALL
BY STUART KNEE

'Baseball's Color Bar Broken', *Christian Century*, 44 (23 April 1947), 517.

'Branch Rickey Discusses the Negro in Baseball Today', *Baseball Digest*, 16 (July 1957), 61–3.

'Brooklyn Dodgers Sign First Negro to Play in Organized Baseball', *Life*, 19 (26 Nov. 1945), 133–4.

Chalberg, J.C., *Rickey and Robinson* (Wheeling, IL: Harlan Davidson, Inc., 2000).

Falkner, D., *Great Time Coming: The Life of Jackie Robinson from Baseball to Birmingham* (New York: Simon and Schuster, 1995).

Fitzgerald, E., 'Branch Rickey, Dodger Deacon', *Sport*, 3 (Nov. 1947), 61–8.

Franklin, J.H. and I. Starr (eds), *The Negro in Twentieth-Century America: A Reader on the Struggle for Human Rights* (New York: Random House, 1967).

Frommer, H., *Rickey and Robinson: The Men Who Broke Baseball's Color Barrier* (New York: Macmillan Publishing Co., Inc., 1982).

Henderson, E.B., *The Negro in Sports* (Washington: Associated Publishers Inc., 1939).

Levine, P., *Ellis Island to Ebbets Field: Sport and the American Jewish Experience* (New York: Oxford University Press, 1992).

Mann, A., *Branch Rickey: American in Action* (Boston, Houghton Mifflin, 1957).

Polner, M., *Branch Rickey: A Biography* (New York: Atheneum, 1982).

Rampersad, A., *Jackie Robinson: A Biography* (New York: Alfred A. Knopf, 1997).

Rickey, B., (with R. Rigor), *The American Diamond* (New York: Simon and Schuster, 1965).

Robinson, J., *Baseball Has Done It*, C. Dexter (ed.) (Philadelphia: J. B. Lippincott Co., 1964).

Robinson, J., *My Own Story* (as told by Jackie Robinson to Wendell Smith) (New York: Greenberg, 1948).

Roeder, B., *Jackie Robinson* (New York: A.S. Barnes, 1950).

Rowan, C.T., *Wait Till Next Year: The Life Story of Jackie Robinson*

(New York: Random House, 1960).

Tygiel, J., *Baseball's Great Experiment: Jackie Robinson and His Legacy* (New York: Oxford University Press, 1983).

Woodward, C.V., *The Strange Career of Jim Crow*, 2nd rev. edn (New York: Oxford University Press, 1966).

Young, A.S., *Great Negro Baseball Stars* (New York: A.S. Barnes and Co., 1953).

PERSONAL CALVARIES: SPORTS IN PHILADELPHIA'S
AFRICAN-AMERICAN COMMUNITIES, 1920–60
BY ROBERT GREGG

Edmonds, A., *Joe Louis* (Grand Rapids, MI: Eerdmans, 1973).

Gregg, R., *Sparks from the Anvil of Oppression: Philadelphia's African Methodists and Southern Migrants, 1890–1940* (Philadelphia: Temple University Press, 1993).

James, C.L.R., *Beyond a Boundary* (New York: Pantheon, 1983).

Kusmer, K., *A Ghetto Takes Shape: Black Cleveland, 1870–1930* (Urbana: University of Illinois, 1976).

Levine, P., *The Promise of American Sport: A.G. Spalding and the Rise of Baseball* (New York: Oxford University Press, 1985).

Roberts, R., *Papa Jack: Jack Johnson and the Era of White Hopes* (New York: Free Press, 1983).

Tygiel, J., *Baseball's Great Experiment: Jackie Robinson and His Legacy* (New York: Oxford University Press, 1983).

NEW TRADITIONS, OLD STRUGGLES: ORGANIZED SPORT
FOR JOHANNESBURG'S AFRICANS, 1920–50
BY CECILE BADENHORST

Archer, R. and A. Bouillon, *The South African Game* (London: Zed Press, 1982).

Badenhorst, C.M. and C.T. Mather, 'Tribal Recreation and Recreating Tribalism: Recreation on the Gold Mines, 1920–1950', *Journal of Southern African Studies*, 23, 3 (1997), 473–89.

Couzens, T., 'Moralizing Leisure Time: The Transatlantic Connection and Black Johannesburg, 1918–36', in S. Marks and R. Rathbone (eds), *Industrialisation and Social Change in South Africa* (London: Longman, 1982), pp. 315–37.

Phillips, R.E., *The Bantu in the City: A Study of Cultural Adjustment in the Witwatersrand*, (Cape Town: Lovedale Press, 1938).

DECONSTRUCTING 'INDIANNESS': CRICKET AND THE
ARTICULATION OF INDIAN IDENTITIES IN DURBAN,1900–32 *BY*
GOOLAM VAHED

Aiyar, P.S., *The Indian Problem in South Africa* (Durban: African Chronicle Printing Works, 1925).

Allie, M., *More Than A Game: History of the Western Province Cricket Board 1959–1991* (Cape Town: Cape Argus, 2001).

Bhana, S., *Indentured Emigrants to Natal 1860–1910: A Study Based on Ships' Lists* (New Delhi: Promilla & Co., 1991).

Booth, D., *The Race Game: Sport and Politics in South Africa* (London: Frank Cass, 1998).

Calpin, G.H., *Indians in South Africa* (Pietermaritzburg: Shuter and Shuter, 1949).

Dhupelia-Mesthrie, U., *From Cane Fields to Freedom: A Chronicle of Indian South African Life* (Cape Town: Kwela Books, 2000).

Ebr.-Vally, R., *kala pani: Caste and Colour in South Africa* (Cape Town: Kwela Books, 2001).

Nauright, J., *Sport, Cultures and Identities in South Africa* (Johannesburg: David Philip, 1997).

Odendaal, A. (ed.), *Cricket in Isolation: The Politics of Race and Cricket in South Africa* (Cape Town: C. Blackshaw and Sons, 1977).

Reddy, K., *The Other Side: A Miscellany of Cricket in Natal* (Durban: KwaZulu-Natal Cricket Union, 2000).

CRICKET IN INDIA: REPRESENTATIVE PLAYING FIELD TO
RESTRICTIVE PRESERVE *BY BORIA MAJUMDAR*

Bamzai, S., *Guts and Glory: The Bombay Cricket Story* (New Delhi: Rupa, 2002).

Bose, M., *History of Indian Cricket* (London: Andre Deutsch, 1990).

Cashman, R., *Patrons, Players and the Crowd* (Calcutta: Orient Longman, 1979).

Docker, E., *History of Indian Cricket* (Delhi: Macmillan, 1976).

Mukherjee, S.N., *Calcutta: Essays in Urban History* (Calcutta: Subarnarekha, 1993).

Sorabjee, S., *A Chronicle of Cricket amongst Parsees and the Struggle: Polo Versus Cricket* (Bombay, 1897).

'PHYSICAL BEINGS': STEREOTYPES, SPORT AND THE 'PHYSICAL EDUCATION' OF NEW ZEALAND MĀORI
BY BRENDAN HOKOWHITU

Bederman, G., *Manliness and Civilization. A Cultural History of Gender and Race in the United States, 1880–1917* (Chicago: University of Chicago Press, 1995).
Cornwall, A., and N. Lindisfarne (eds), *Dislocating Masculinity: Comparative Ethnographies* (New York: Routledge, 1994).
Foucault, M., *Discipline and Punish: The Birth of the Prison*, A. Sheridan (trans.) (London: Tavistock, 1977).
Law, R., H. Campbell and J. Dolan (eds), *Masculinities in Aotearoa/New Zealand* (Palmerston North: Dunmore Press, 1999).
Mangan, J.A. (ed.), *The Imperial Curriculum: Racial Images and Education in the British Colonial Experience* (London: Routledge, 1993).
Nandy, A., *The Intimate Enemy* (Oxford: Oxford University Press, 1983).

INSTITUTIONALIZED DISCRIMINATION AGAINST JAPAN-BORN KOREAN ATHLETES: FROM OVERT TO COVERT DISCRIMINATION
BY HARUO NOGAWA

Fukuoka, A., *Koreans in Japan* (in Japanese) (Tokyo: Chuko Shinsho, 1993).
Kan, H., *Why Japan-born Koreans are Superior in Sports* (in Japanese) (Tokyo: KK Best Sellers, 2001).
Kan, J. and D. Kim, *Koreans in Japan: Their History and Future Implications* (in Japanese) (Tokyo: Rodo Keizaisha, 1989).
Kim, C., *Centennial History of Permanent Korean Residents in Japan* (in Japanese) (Tokyo: Sangokan Publishing, 1997).
Kobayashi, Y., *Korean Japanese Power* (in Japanese) (Tokyo: Soyosha, 1988).
Lee, C., and G. De Vos, *Koreans in Japan: Ethnic Conflict and Accommodation* (Berkeley: University of California Press, 1984).
Min, P.G., 'A Comparison of the Korean Minorities in China and

Japan', *International Migration Review*, 12, 1 (1992), 4–21.

Nogawa, H., 'A Study of a Japanese-American Basketball League and the Assimilation of its Members into the Mainstream of United States Society' (unpublished Ph.D. dissertation, Oregon State University, 1983).

Redmond, G., *Sport and Ethnic Groups in Canada, CAHPER Sociology of Sport Monograph Series* (Calgary: The University of Calgary, 1979).

Whiting, R., *Jesse and Sale: A Story of Foreign Sumo Wrestlers* (translated into Japanese by Midori Matsui) (Tokyo: Chikuma Publishing, 1989).

CRICKET AND CALYPSO: CULTURAL REPRESENTATION AND SOCIAL
HISTORY IN THE WEST INDIES
BY DOUGLAS MIDGETT

Beckles, H. and B. Stoddart (eds), *Liberation Cricket: West Indies Cricket Culture* (Manchester: Manchester University Press, 1995).

James, C.L.R., *Beyond a Boundary* (London: Hutchinson, 1962).

Lazarus, N., 'Cricket and National Culture in the Writings of C.L.R. James', in P. Henry and P. Buhle (eds), *C.L.R. James's Caribbean*, (Durham: Duke University Press, 1992).

Malec, M. (ed.), *The Social Roles of Sport in Caribbean Societies* (Amsterdam: Gordon and Breach, 1992).

Manley, M., *A History of West Indian Cricket* (London: Andre Deutsch, 1988).

Manning, F., 'Celebrating Cricket: The Symbolic Construction of Caribbean Politics', *American Ethnologist*, 8 (1981), 616–32.

FROM THE GRIDIRON AND THE BOXING RING TO THE CINEMA
SCREEN: THE AFRICAN-AMERICAN ATHLETE IN PRE-1950 CINEMA *BY*
CHARLENE REGESTER

Baker A. and T. Boyd (eds), *Out of Bounds: Sports, Media, and the Politics of Identity* (Bloomington: Indiana University Press, 1997).

Cohan S. and I.R. Hark (eds), *Screening the Male: Exploring Masculinities in Hollywood Cinema* (New York: Routledge, 1993).

Cripps, T., *Slow Fade to Black: The Negro in American Film, 1900–1942* (New York: Oxford University Press, [1977] 1993).

Dyer, R., *Heavenly Bodies: Film Stars and Society* (New York: St Martin's Press, 1986).

Evans, A., 'Joe Louis As a Key Functionary: White Reactions Toward a Black Champion', *Journal of Black Studies*, 16, 1 (Sept. 1985), 95–111.

Gill, G., 'Canada Lee: Black Actor in Non-Traditional Roles', *Journal of Popular Culture*, 25, 3 (1991), 79–89.

Grindon, L., 'Body and Soul: The Structure of Meaning in the Boxing Film Genre', *Cinema Journal*, 35, 4 (1996), 54–69.

Manchel, F., 'The Man Who Made the Stars Shine Brighter: An Interview with Woody Strode', *Black Scholar*, 25, 2 (1995), 37–46.

Streible, D., 'A History of the Boxing Film, 1894–1915: Social Control and Social Reform in the Progressive Era', *Film History*, 3, 3 (1989), 235–57.

Tasker, Y., *Spectacular Bodies: Gender, Genre and the Action Cinema* (New York: Routledge, 1993).

SNOWSHOEING AND LACROSSE: CANADA'S NINETEENTH-CENTURY 'NATIONAL GAMES' *BY GILLIAN POULTER*

Beers, W.G., *Lacrosse: The National Game of Canada* (Montreal: Dawson Brothers, 1869).

Bhabha, H.K. (ed.), *Nation and Narration* (London: Routledge, 1990).

Gruneau, R.S., 'Power and Play in Canadian Society', in Richard J. Ossenberg (ed.), *Power and Change in Canada* (Toronto: University of Toronto Press, 1980), pp.146–94.

Metcalfe, A., 'The Evolution of Organized Physical Recreation in Montreal, 1840–1895' *Histoire Social/Social History*, 11, 21 (1978), 144–66.

Metcalfe, A., *Canada Learns to Play: The Emergence of Organized Sport, 1807–1914* (Toronto: McClelland & Stewart, 1987).

Morrow, D., 'The Canadian Image Abroad: The Great Lacrosse Tours of 1876 and 1883', *Proceedings of the Fifth Canadian Symposium on the History of Sport and Physical Education*, University of Toronto, Aug. 1982, pp.11–23.

Morrow, D., 'The Knights of the Snowshoe: A Study of the Evolution of Sport in Nineteenth-Century Montreal', *Journal of Sport History*, 15, 1 (1988), pp.5–40.

Morrow, D., 'Lacrosse as the National Game', in D. Morrow *et al.* (eds), *A Concise History of Sport in Canada* (Toronto: Oxford University Press, 1989), pp.45–68.

North American Indian Travelling College, *Tewaarathon (Lacrosse)*, (Akwesasne: 1978).

Vennum, T. Jr., *American Indian Lacrosse: Little Brother of War* (Washington: Smithsonian Institute Press, 1994).

Index